# CAMP AND PRISON JOURNAL

Captain Griffin Frost
(Courtesy of Dan Gobis)

# Camp and Prison JOURNAL

by
Griffin Frost

CAMP POPE BOOKSHOP
1994.

Camp Pope Bookshop Edition

Reprinted 1994 by
Press of the Camp Pope Bookshop

New Materials Copyright © 1994 by
Press of the Camp Pope Bookshop

Paperback Edition Printed 2006

ISBN 1-929919-09-3

Printed and Bound in the United States of America

Press of the Camp Pope Bookshop
PO Box 2232
Iowa City, Iowa 52244
www.camppope.com

# INTRODUCTION.

Griffin Frost, author of *Camp and Prison Journal,* was born March 14, 1834, in St. Clairsville, Belmont County, Ohio. He was the son of William P., a farmer, and Rebecca (Wetzell) Frost. His family moved to Jackson County in what is now West Virginia when Griffin was a boy. At the age of sixteen, he went to Wheeling to learn the printing trade.[1] Thereafter, Griffin, as well as his two older brothers Daniel and William Jr. and younger brother John, were all closely involved with the printing and newspaper business. In 1853, William P. Frost, Jr. started the first regularly published newspaper in Jackson County, *The Virginia Chronicle,* which he sold to his older brother Daniel in 1858.[2] Griffin briefly worked at this paper also.

After his apprenticeship in West Virginia, Frost worked his way west, "holding cases" at papers in Pittsburgh, Pennsylvania, Mount Pleasant, Ohio, and Keokuk, Iowa. In 1854, he came to Missouri and started at the *Sentinel,* a newspaper in Palmyra.[3] He married Elizabeth R. Johnson September 10, 1857, in Houston (today Emerson), Marion County,[4] and in January 1859, their only child Annie was born. Frost moved to the town of Mexico in Audrain County around 1858 to run the *Mexico Ledger,* where he was subsequently joined by brothers William and John.[5] Griffin, with the assistance of John, founded the *Shelby County Weekly* in Shelbyville on March 7, 1861. He gave his paper the masthead motto "Free as the wind, pure and firm as the voice of nature, the press should be." Frost tended to favor the idea of secession, and after the firing on Fort Sumter, his paper came out foursquare for the South. In June of 1861, some irregulars of the local pro-Union Home Guard paid Frost a visit and ordered him to cease publication of what they considered a "treasonable sheet." He submitted, closing down the paper and moving back to Marion County. Sometime thereafter the shop was broken into and the printing equipment destroyed or stolen, presumably by the same Home Guardsmen.[6]

INTRODUCTION.

This incident was most likely the catalyst that led Frost to lay down the pen and take up the sword of the Confederate cause, for in August of 1861, he joined Company A of Martin Green's Cavalry Regiment of the Missouri State Guard (MSG) in Marion County. The regiment fought and lost its first engagement with a group of Home Guards at Athens on August 5, 1861, then joined the main body of the Second Division, MSG, under Brigadier General Thomas A. Harris the following month near Glasgow. After a notable victory at the Siege of Lexington (September 12-20, 1861), the MSG, commanded by Major General Sterling Price, wintered in Springfield in southwest Missouri before being driven out of the state by the advance of a new Union army under Brigadier General Samuel R. Curtis. This movement culminated at the Battle of Pea Ridge in northwest Arkansas (March 7-8, 1862), where Frost's Second Division, now commanded by Martin Green, played a minimal role. In January 1862, Frost reenlisted in the MSG for another six months and was elected Captain of Company A, 1st Battalion, 2nd Division.[7]

Immediately following Pea Ridge, the Missouri State Guard was ordered east of the Mississippi River to aid in repelling an invasion of Tennessee by forces under U. S. Grant. Frost missed the Battle of Shiloh (April 6-7, 1862), but experienced a few tense weeks south of Corinth, Mississippi, awaiting the slow advance of the Union army, now under Major General Henry W. Halleck. After the resultant Southern evacuation of Corinth, at a time when most MSG units were formally transferring to the Confederate service, Frost's company, now in Mosby M. Parsons's Brigade, was sent back to Arkansas to join a new army gathering under Major General Thomas A. Hindman.[8] Frost traveled slowly across Arkansas, repeatedly falling ill and becoming separated from his command. He and a few companions followed the brigade as best they could, recruiting new troops wherever possible, and nightly seeking lodging among the local citizenry. On November 8, 1862, Frost was captured in Carroll County by a Unionist Arkansas cavalry regiment and brought to Springfield, Missouri. He was in a group of about 100 Confederate prisoners transported to Gratiot Street Prison in St. Louis on December 31.

Frost was paroled on April 22, 1863, and taken to City Point, Virginia, for exchange. In mid-May, he was sent west to a parole camp in Demopolis, Alabama. A month later he reported to General Joseph E.

INTRODUCTION. *vii*

Johnston in Jackson, Mississippi, who ordered him back to his original command in the Trans-Mississippi. He journeyed up the Mississippi River, crossing over to Arkansas above Helena, which at the time was under attack by Frost's old commander Sterling Price (July 4, 1863). Frost and a companion borrowed some horses and plunged in, fighting alongside the men of Brigadier General John S. Marmaduke's division. Later he found his way to his old outfit under Parsons, which had also been engaged at Helena.

Fearing another Union invasion of Arkansas, Sterling Price retreated to Little Rock. In the wake of the army went Captain Frost, replicating his meandering march of the previous summer. He fell ill again, this time with smallpox, and was left behind to recuperate. When he finally arrived in Little Rock, Frost met with General Price, who informed him that his company had been reorganized and new officers elected, that therefore he was relieved of further duty.

Frost connected with several fellow officers who were in the same predicament as he: newly exchanged from prison, with no troops to command, and far from home. They determined to embark upon a recruiting expedition and marched into the hill country around Batesville. They found few candidates for military service among the backwoods Arkansans, however. Frost's group continued north to solicit volunteers in Missouri, but wherever they went they were mistaken for guerrillas or jayhawkers, and military-aged men fled before them. In October 1863, the group reached the Missouri River and built a raft on which to cross. Once on the northern side, they were promptly captured by the Unionist Missouri State Militia and taken to Richmond, Missouri. Held next briefly at a prison in Macon, which he described as "certainly the filthiest place I ever saw" (p. 75), Frost soon found himself back in Gratiot Street Prison.

Frost's family and friends wrote to him in prison, pledging to help secure his freedom. They urged him to "take the oath," a means of obtaining release often extended by the Union authorities to captured members of the MSG and to those civilian political prisoners not charged with serious crimes. Frost had resisted such advice the first time he was in Gratiot. He considered himself a soldier and expected to be exchanged. But as the fall turned to winter 1863, he came to realize that he would not be released any time soon. Frost was formally charged with being in Missouri without having enrolled in the militia (which at the time was required of all able-bodied men, regardless of their sympathies), and was transferred to Alton Prison on January 30, 1864. On February 1, he was informed that he had been tried and found guilty, and was sentenced to "confinement during the war."

Efforts continued to get Frost out of prison. Even his brother Daniel, now a colonel in the 11th West Virginia Infantry, sought to intercede on Griffin's behalf with Major General William S. Rosecrans, commander of the Department of the Missouri. In March, Frost was taken back to Gratiot, probably in anticipation of a parole. A month later he learned that Rosecrans had signed an order for his release, but that this had been countermanded and that he was to be returned to Alton to serve out his sentence.[9] He remained at Gratiot for the summer and early fall of 1864, awaiting a response to yet another petition for release. In September, he was informed that his appeal had been rejected by the Secretary of War.

Aside from the personal tragedy of the news that his brother Daniel had died of wounds received at Snicker's Gap, Virginia, on July 18, and the effects of increased tension among the prison guards due to the rumored proximity of Sterling Price, who had begun his famous 1864 raid on September 19, Frost bore his confinement at Gratiot in relative peace and comfort. On October 3, 1864, he was returned to Alton Prison, where he remained until the end of the war.

On April 12, 1865, Frost was released by the Union authorities, and he went home to his wife and child, who had been living in Palmyra. Very soon thereafter, the family moved to Quincy, Illinois, where Frost resumed his pre-war profession, beginning as a typesetter for the *Quincy Herald*. In 1867, he published *Camp and Prison Journal*, his memoir of the war. He started a newspaper in Quincy known as the *Evening Call*, then founded another called the *Morning News*, which he ran until the end of 1873. In January 1874, Frost moved to Edina, Missouri, where he would spend most of the rest of his life. He took over the *Knox County Democrat* and turned it into one of the most influential newspapers in northeast Missouri. Over the years, Frost became the proverbial pillar of his community. He was a Master Mason, a member of the Ancient Order of United Workmen, a member of the Methodist Episcopal Church South, and he served on the Board of Curators of the Knox Collegiate Institute in Edina.[10]

In 1884, Frost returned to his childhood home in West Virginia for

INTRODUCTION.                    ix

the first time since leaving there in 1853. He visited Daniel's grave in Wheeling and renewed his acquaintance with family members still living in the area.[11]

On December 19, 1878, Frost's daughter Annie married William R. Ringer, a lawyer. The couple joined the Frost household and were still living there at the time of William's death at the age of 32 in December 1884.[12] They had one child, a son named Earle, born March 19, 1880, who was in poor health most of his life. In late summer 1905, after Frost had decided to retire from the newspaper for reasons of his own health, the entire family moved to Siloam Springs, Arkansas. Earle died there on June 20, 1906.[13] Griffin Frost followed the only son of his only daughter three years later, dying of heart failure at Siloam Springs on April 4, 1909.[14] His body was returned to Edina and buried at Linville Cemetery, next to his wife Elizabeth, who had passed away on November 28, 1907.[15]

In the preface of *Camp and Prison Journal*, author Griffin Frost states that it is his hope that the terrible experiences of imprisonment in Gratiot, Alton, Camp Douglas and Camp Morton Prisons (the latter two of which are described in two appended accounts by friends of the author) as set forth in his book will silence those who condemn the treatment of Northern prisoners at Andersonville, Libby, and Belle Isle Prisons during the late Civil War. Also, that he is certain that the atrocities reported from Southern prisons cannot exceed those committed by the authorities at such places as Gratiot. Frost was very likely responding to the flurry of negative prison accounts that followed in the wake of the trial of Major Henry Wirz, the commandant of Andersonville, at which the allegation was made that Confederate officials conspired to torture and kill their Union prisoners.[16] The immediate response from the South to accusations of maltreatment was that circumstances of war left the Confederacy destitute of the means of providing better food, shelter, and medical care to its prisoners, and that the North condemned its own with General Grant's refusal to proceed with prisoner exchanges in the spring of 1864. After the war, a committee was formed in the U.S. House of Representatives to hear testimony on and preserve a record of the experiences of Union prisoners in Southern prisons. The committee's findings were published in 1869 as *Treatment of Prisoners of War by the Rebel Authorities*.[17]

INTRODUCTION.

Frost makes reference to this committee in his conclusion, and, in uncharacteristically angry and bitter language, challenges it to investigate the equally brutal treatment of Confederates in Northern prisons. The bitterness of Frost's concluding challenge is uncharacteristic when compared to the overall tone of his journal that went before it. For, aside from two brief reports in the conclusion, the appended testimony of G. M. Brosheer concerning Camp Morton and that of M. J. Bradley on Camp Douglas, and the outrages recounted in the appendices that deal with the Palmyra Massacre and the persecution of Col. Jeff Jones, et al., *Camp and Prison Journal* does not dwell on the subject of Rebels suffering at the hands of the Yankees. Indeed, it must be said that, where his own experiences are concerned, Frost fails in his promise to answer atrocity for atrocity the horrors of Andersonville, Libby, and Belle Isle. Conditions and treatment of prisoners at Gratiot and Alton simply did not compare to the worst of Southern prisons or, for that matter, to Camp Douglas or Camp Morton, as they are represented in Frost's book.

Gratiot (pronounced *grass*-shut) Street Prison, where Captain Frost spent 14 of his 24 months in the custody of the Federals, was the central prison, clearing house, and transfer point for all war prisoners, civilian and military, arrested or captured by Union authorities in Missouri during the Civil War. It was also a place of execution for condemned Confederate spies.[18] It was established on the premises of the McDowell Medical College in December 1861.[19] Joseph Nash McDowell, a physician known both for his brilliance as a teacher and an "erratic temperament that at times approached insanity," had come to St. Louis from a teaching position in Cincinnati, Ohio, in 1838 or 1839.[20] In 1840, he founded the Medical Department of Kemper College and laid the cornerstone of his first college building, which was located at Ninth and Cerre Streets.[21] The building that was to become Gratiot Street Prison was constructed in the following two years 300 yards to the southeast.[22] When, in 1845, indebtedness forced the closing of Kemper College, McDowell continued his medical school in conjunction with the University of Missouri until 1857, when the University began to require all faculty to devote their full time to education, i.e., no private practice. Thereafter McDowell conducted his school as a separate institution, known officially as the Missouri Medical College.[23]

INTRODUCTION. xi

Dr. McDowell was staunchly pro-slavery and a vocal secessionist. On May 30, 1861, after the Home Guard regiments of Brigadier General Nathaniel Lyon had captured the secessionist Missouri militia training at Camp Jackson in St. Louis, McDowell's College was searched for munitions that had been taken from the Baton Rouge arsenal and sent to St. Louis for the use of pro-Confederate forces. It was at this point that Dr. McDowell decided to flee the area.[24] He went south, where he served as medical director of the Trans-Mississippi Department of the Confederate Army. Later he left the country to lecture in Europe, returning to St. Louis after the war.[25]

The first contingent of Union troops assigned to guard duty at McDowell's Medical College was the 2nd Iowa Infantry Regiment, and an unfortunate incident there played a significant role in the unit's first famous battlefield victory, which is worth recounting here. In February 1862, just as the 2nd Iowa was preparing to depart St. Louis to join Grant's army before Fort Donelson, Tennessee, it was discovered that some unknown person or persons among the guard had broken into the college museum on the top floor of the northern wing and damaged some stuffed animal specimens. This was brought to the attention of General Halleck, then commander of the Department of the Missouri, who determined, since the culprit or culprits would not come forward, to reprimand the regiment as a whole. Therefore, as the 2nd Iowa marched to the Mississippi levee on February 10, 1862, they were commanded to do so with their colors furled and drums silent, which was considered a stinging punishment by the men. Colonel James M. Tuttle, commander of the regiment, flew into a rage over the humiliation of his outfit and protested heatedly to Halleck, who refused to rescind the order. Five days later, the 2nd Iowa, still smarting from this treatment and determined to redeem its honor, led the left flank assault on Fort Donelson and carried the Confederate works, for which they were accorded the privilege of leading the Union army into the fort after the official surrender and for which they were praised by an appreciative General Halleck as "the bravest of the brave."[26]

The McDowell College building was a very large, imposing brick structure which stood at the corner of Eighth and Gratiot Streets in St. Louis, hence the name by which it came to be known, Gratiot Street Prison. It consisted of a three-story octagonal tower and two wings stretching north and south parallel to Eighth Street. At its northern

INTRODUCTION.

GRATIOT STREET PRISON
Photo by Emil Boehl, ca. 1875
(*Courtesy of Missouri Historical Society*)

end, the building abutted the Academy of the Christian Brothers, and prisoners occasionally escaped over the roof or through the adjoining basements of the two buildings.[27] Those who succeeded in getting into the Christian Brothers building were routinely allowed to make good their escape by the people there.[28]

The smaller southern wing of the prison, which had been the McDowell family residence, was occupied by prison officials; the upper story was used to confine Confederate officers and, early in the war,

INTRODUCTION.                                                                 xiii

female prisoners.²⁹ The larger northern wing housed the majority of the prisoners, who were confined to common-rooms or dormitories. The basement of this wing contained the cookhouse, laundry rooms, baths, and a dormitory. The first floor comprised a large common-room and the dining room, the second story was the hospital, and the loft was used as a dead room. The prominent octagonal building in the center of Gratiot Street Prison contained more common-rooms; and what had been the college amphitheater here was converted into two stories, one becoming a convalescent hospital and the other divided into lock-up cells or strong rooms for the secure confinement of certain prisoners.³⁰ There were four such cells, each holding up to ten men, divided by a cross hall that was constantly patrolled by a guard. The lock-ups were accessible only by a long exterior stairway.³¹

The common-rooms in the main octagonal building and the northern wing were fitted up with three-tier double bunks and had one or two storerooms each.³² There was a water closet in the hospital in the northern wing and sinks in the prison yard, which drained into the St. Louis sewer system. Gratiot's exercise yard was located on the west side of the northern wing, ran the length of the building, about 70 by 20 feet, and was surrounded by a 15-foot-high fence.³³ The yard was separated into two parts by a guarded passageway for the purpose of exercising the lock-up prisoners in an area segregated from the common prison population.³⁴ The Federal troops that guarded Gratiot were housed across Eighth Street in a row of three-story brick buildings known as Johnson Barracks.³⁵

Gratiot Street Prison was unique among Northern military prisons of the Civil War in that it developed into a repository for all manner of detainees: Confederate prisoners of war and civilian political prisoners were locked up with Federal deserters and other Union soldiers awaiting trial for criminal violations. The population of political prisoners was large and changeable, as anyone suspected of secessionist sympathies, let alone actually guilty of espionage, sabotage, or otherwise aiding the Rebel enemy, could find him or herself hauled into prison. The majority of these individuals were either released on oath and bond or exiled from Missouri. Most political prisoners and prisoners of war sentenced to prolonged confinement were transferred to Alton Prison, about 25 miles upriver from St. Louis on the Illinois side.³⁶

The state of Illinois had maintained a penitentiary at the northern

ALTON PRISON, FOREGROUND (*Courtesy of Missouri Historical Society*)

INTRODUCTION.                                                        xv

edge of the city of Alton since 1831. However, by the late 1850s, the place had grown decrepit, the inmate population exceeded capacity, and the townspeople were no longer amenable to having a prison in their midst. The state determined to build a larger facility near Joliet, and this penitentiary was put into operation in 1858. By the middle of July 1860, all prisoners had been sent to Joliet, and the Alton Penitentiary was sold to private interests.[37] General Halleck first struck upon the idea of using the old penitentiary at Alton in late 1861, when he wrote to the U.S. Adjutant General that he had between 2000 and 3000 prisoners of war and no place to put them.[38] On January 20, 1862, a lease was negotiated with the owners of the property, and Halleck ordered that it be prepared to take in Confederate prisoners.[39] The first contingent was ferried from St. Louis to Alton in early February 1862, despite the fact that the place was not entirely ready to receive it.[40]

While Gratiot Street Prison consisted of one large building with, by 1864, three smaller houses in the area used as annexes,[41] Alton Prison comprised a complex of structures, which, though in disrepair, had been designed specifically for the confinement of prisoners. Gratiot was considered overcrowded when its population rose above 500, as it often did, but Alton could accommodate more and held as many as 1891 at one time.[42] There was a large cellblock building, where inmates were quartered in passageways that ran around the three tiers of cells (the cells themselves were used for disciplinary purposes and to confine those prisoners charged with serious crimes), and a few outbuildings, formerly prison workshops, which contained the hospital, dining hall and more prisoner quarters.[43] The whole complex was surrounded by a high stone wall.[44]

A serious smallpox epidemic broke out at Alton Prison in December 1862. Guards as well as inmates were affected, and by the spring of 1863, the disease had spread to the city of Alton.[45] Prison officials looked for a suitable building outside the prison to isolate smallpox cases, but met with resistance from the townspeople.[46] Eventually, a shanty was constructed on an island in the Mississippi to be used as a smallpox ward.[47] By February 1864, the smallpox epidemic at Alton had been brought under control.[48]

An inspection of Alton Prison in April 1864 revealed that one of the buildings used as a hospital had to be closed because of a backup of sewage. The other hospital ward had a roof so leaky that the patients' beds had to be covered with rubber blankets. Despite this, the hospital and dining hall were considered the cleanest and best policed areas of the prison.[49] In July 1864, a new hospital, 200 by 40 feet in size and capable of holding 200 patients, was constructed, and the old wards, presumably cleaned up and repaired, were converted to prisoners' quarters.[50]

What in fact were conditions like at Gratiot Street and Alton Prisons? It depends upon who is consulted and at what point during the war or after. Loyal Unionists in St. Louis generally believed the local military prisons (Gratiot and Myrtle) to be clean and well-maintained and the prisoners well-treated.[51] To those who leaned more to the Southern side, Gratiot was gloomy and unsanitary, its inmates deliberately starved, allowed to freeze in winter, and otherwise abused.[52] An examination of the various official inspections made of Gratiot and Alton contained in the *Official Records* reveals that at times conditions were good or at least satisfactory, at times they were not.[53] A major factor was the competence and attitude of the officers in charge at any given time. Historian William Hesseltine, in a study of the military prisons of St. Louis, concluded that these places were no better or worse than could be expected of makeshift prisons.[54]

What did diarist Griffin Frost have to say about Gratiot and Alton? When he first arrived at the former on December 31, 1862, he found his initial lodgings dismal, foreboding, and very filthy (p. 27). Gratiot was "a very hard place . . . fare so rough it seems an excellent place to starve" (p. 28). Soon he was moved to the officers' quarters, which were "cleaner and not so crowded," with "bunks instead of that horrid floor to sleep on, and our fare is better and more plentiful" (pp. 28–29). Hereafter, Frost had little occasion to witness and report on conditions among the common prison population, which were probably worse than those he knew in the Confederate officers' mess. In late 1863, he did happen to visit the prison hospital, which struck him as surprisingly neat and orderly (p. 84).

During Frost's first stay at Gratiot, the prison was guarded by the 37th Iowa Infantry, the "Graybeard Regiment," members of which ranged in age from 45 to 80. He called them "nice old fellows, kind and fatherly"; their officers, on the other hand, were "perfect devils – there is nothing too low, mean, or insulting for them to say or do" (p. 32). Upon his second internment at Gratiot, beginning in October 1863,

INTRODUCTION.                                                                    xvii

Frost found the 37th Iowa had been replaced by troops who had "seen some active service and know how to treat a prisoner" with respect (p. 80). He disliked the prison commandant Captain Masterson, who was actually a civilian, calling him "cruel, ungentlemanly, and insulting in a purely personal manner" (p. 119); other prison officals were more agreeable, such as Captain Sullivan (p. 121) and Captain Burns (Byrne), commander of the prison guard (p. 88).

After returning to Gratiot from his sojourn at Alton in March 1864, Frost had this to say: "This morning I was placed back in my old quarters, with the windows on the gallery opened. It is most refreshingly pleasant. I find myself for once with no reasonable cause of complaint. ... My room is comfortable; we are allowed to buy provisions, and newspapers are not prohibited" (p. 122). In June, he reports worsening conditions (sort of): "Our lives are becoming more and more miserable every day, and our fare is growing less. Coffee, tea, and sugar have been cut off from our rations and hereafter we will have to content ourselves with dry bread and meat with sometimes a few potatoes, beans or a little rice" (pp. 134–135). Such a menu would not have been dismaying to the inmates of Andersonville, one may assume.

In addition to the rations that the prison authorities provided, Frost and his fellow officers were supplied by packages from home, gifts from the charitable women of St. Louis, and baskets of food and other necessities sent in by newly made friends – those well-to-do persons arrested for disloyalty and eventually released on oath and bond (see pp. 33, 80, 132–133, 142, 146, 148). This last source of provender was an ingredient of life at Gratiot that shows most glaringly its dissimilarity with Andersonville or Libby Prisons. The fact that Gratiot was located in a prosperous city, under Union control but filled with giving people, many with Southern sympathies, and that the state of martial law and the perceived evil of disloyalty caused even wealthy citizens to circulate routinely in and out of prison[55] brought many comforts of life within reach of the members of Frost's mess, comforts that would have been unimaginable in Andersonville or Libby.

Of Alton Prison, Frost's impressions from his first experience there were quite negative. He found it to be a much worse place than Gratiot, with rats, overcrowding, smallpox, bad food, and 200 unfriendly Federal prisoners who preyed on the Confederates (p. 109). Frost spent two weeks in the hospital there in February 1864, and described the

xviii                          INTRODUCTION.

accommodations as "very poor; but little attention is paid to the sick, and the fare is exceedingly rough" (p. 116). However, by the time he returned to Alton in October 1864, things had changed: "Everything is much cleaner; a large hospital has been built, lathed and plastered and lit with gas.... So far it is decidedly preferable to Gratiot. The fare is much better and we are permitted to correspond with our friends" (pp. 184-185). The prison officials and guards were of a different sort than at Gratiot also: "The persons here in charge of the prison are very sociable. Hardly an evening passes without some of them paying us a visit, and we have very lively times; some fine music, both vocal and instrumental" (p. 186). Frost and fellow officers were frequently permitted to visit the women prisoners at Alton and found that their quarters are "good and comfortable, the floors nicely painted and everything exhibited such perfect order that we were forcibly reminded of home" (p. 200). At Christmastime, the men were allowed to receive packages of food from home, which the ladies used to prepare for them a grand Christmas dinner, to which they were formally invited by prison official Major James M. Morgan (pp. 206-207).

Frost notes more than once that the regulations at Alton were stricter, the slightest offense being punished with great severity: "But those who write the laws legibly in their memories, and are careful to observe and obey them, are treated decidedly better than the same class were in St. Louis. The guard and petty officers manifest no disposition to indulge in disgusting insolence; on the contrary, they are respectful and gentlemanly in their deportment" (p. 214). Toward the end of his imprisonment Frost was even released for a few hours at a time to visit the city of Alton, sometimes without a guard, which was a privilege extended to many of the Confederate officers at Alton Prison.

Let it not be supposed that Frost saw no suffering or cruelty at Gratiot and Alton. Gratiot Street prisoners, Frost included, were often burdened with ball and chain or thrown into a lock-up cell for petty offenses or on the whim of some guard. Daring to look out of a window could result in a bullet in the head from a guard posted on the street (p. 141). Once six members of Frost's mess were handcuffed to posts in the prison yard for hours in subzero weather for attempting to escape (p. 101). Prison officials often arbitrarily suspended privileges such as visits or packages from family and friends. And then there were the

## INTRODUCTION.

not infrequent executions, pending which the condemned suffered not only the anticipation of their fates, but also from the spectacle of parents, wives, and children pleading pitifully without effect for clemency. Despite the social amenities, life at Alton Prison in late 1864 was not perfect. Prisoners were brought in in such large numbers that some occasionally went hungry for a while (p. 199). There was considerable sickness (p. 198), and inmates suffered greatly from the cold (p. 202). For all the accessibility of good things from home, packages were often pilfered before they reached their intended recipients (p. 206). However, without going into a discussion of the conditions at Andersonville, Libby, and Belle Isle Prisons, which we may accept from common historical knowledge, as Frost does from the reports to which his book is a response, were horrific, it is obvious, by the evidence of Frost's experiences at least, that Gratiot and Alton Prisons were near paradises by comparison.

Griffin Frost had every opportunity to twist the facts as he prepared his journal for publication after the war, although he seems not to have done so to any great extent. We have already noted the angrier tone of his preface and conclusion. It would appear that some of the occasional bitter commentaries on Yankees and blacks within the text were added later as well.

The earliest part of Frost's journal, from August 1, 1861, to May 3, 1862, seems either to be a composite of very brief diary entries, or reconstructed from memory. Regular daily entries do not begin until the time that Frost's battalion arrives at Corinth. The fact that these notations get longer and more elaborate as the days pass is not suspicious. Once he had been taken to prison, Frost had plenty of time to write long descriptive entries, as he repeatedly complains that his worst enemy is boredom. Prison authorities who would allow packages from home and from strangers, sales by sutlers, and even letters and the occasional newspaper probably had no objection to Frost keeping a diary.

But, on February 29, 1864, when he had just returned from two weeks in the hospital at Alton, Frost supposedly writes: "I wish some of the sentimentalists of the North who are shedding such bitter tears over Andersonville, Libby and Belle Isle would walk through Alton prison . . ." In reality, the first prisoners were only just arriving at Andersonville at this time. Frost continues his diatribe against the

Yankees: "they indulge no charity, countenance no sympathy, permit no spread of a truth that will not work in and amalgamate with their plans; their peculiar ideas must be developed if the car of Juggernaut rolls over and crushes every bleeding heart in the land" (p. 117). One senses here an element of fatalism in the mix with the writer's scorn; it is as though he were decrying Reconstruction and the postwar rule of the Radicals in the South, rather than analyzing the behavior of his wartime adversary.

The strengths of *Camp and Prison Journal* more than make up for a little padding, however. Although Frost's experiences in the field were limited, he gives the reader a rare perspective on the Civil War as fought by the Missouri State Guard. More importantly, the book is one of very few published accounts of life in the small but significant military prisons of St. Louis and Alton.[56] And the wit and humor of *Camp and Prison Journal* bring to mind and rival those of another Confederate memoir, the famous *"Co. Aytch"* by Sam Watkins.

Frost manifests a keen, self-deprecating sense of humor throughout the book, but especially when recounting his experiences in Arkansas. His recruiting party of 1863 bore a comical look: "Our prospects here are good for recruiting a regiment in about two hundred years. . . . The fact is we are a lot of dead heads, and a dead expense to the Government. . . . Wouldn't the Yanks use it though, if they could take a peep at us on some occasions. Ten officers to three privates and nobody knows who is in command" (p. 59). His observations of the backwoods people of Arkansas are hilarious, as on his first experience there in 1862, when he noted that the women "go barefooted, rub snuff and chew tobacco. I am glad they are confined to small, out of the way, backwood sections. If there were too many I fear they would sicken out the heart of chivalry" (p. 17).

Frost met more examples to deflate the image of Southern womanhood while recruiting in Arkansas the following summer: "Her feet were flat, bare, and very black with dirt, toe nails all split; she was lank, lean, red headed and freckled; eyes crossed, red, and sore; had a long hook-billed nose, which she was continually picking when not stirring the tobacco in her mouth with her fingers" (p. 61). These women of Arkansas taxed the modesty of the young soldiers from Missouri: "God! the women . . . [have] nothing on but their dresses and some of them open in front. As we came along, when we passed a house, all the

INTRODUCTION.  xxi

*wimmen*kind would run to the fence, prop one foot on the third or fourth rail, and stand thus and gaze at us until we were out of sight, however, *we* always turned our heads in another direction" (p. 58). Sometimes, Frost found the hospitality of the people of Arkansas hard to take, as when he and a companion were offered some fruit by an old lady: "We . . . commenced eating, when 'mam' remarked: 'We all been nocerlated, and our arms are jist about rotten, keeps us scratchin' all the time.' I looked at my 'peeled' peach, and thought about the *scratchin',* glanced at Capt. C, saw his peach falling, coughed and let my own drop, and got up to go" (p. 54). On another occasion Frost spent the night with the family of a sick farmer, who for some reason thought Frost was a doctor. The "doctor" nearly killed his patient by giving him opium pills, turpentine, and red pepper. But in the morning, the old man had so improved that he praised Frost as "the only doctor who has done him any good during the last three months" (p. 68).

Frost's sense of humor was not blunted by the experience of being thrown into a Yankee prison. In his journal he plays on Gratiot's earlier history as a medical college, referring to inmates as students (p. 38) and to parolees as graduates (p. 33), who go on to practice their profession in the state militia (p. 38). During his second term at Gratiot, the wit turns a little more bitter as Frost refers to the prison as the "Hotel de Gratiot" and describes in cynical detail the care that Uncle Sam takes in protecting his "guests" (pp. 163-164).

Captain Frost, an educated man and a fairly elegant stylist, is at his best when describing the places he travels through north and south, as soldier and POW, and when portraying the many different people he encounters on the march and in prison. The most unique character in the entire book has to be "Feminine Joe" Elliot, a messmate at Gratiot: "He is quite good looking, medium size, has blue eyes and glossy black hair – which he curls; embroiders like a lady, and has a great fondness for teasing his fellow prisoners by catching them and hugging and kissing them, one in particular, whom he calls 'my Joe' and declares himself in love with; he torments him almost to death – if 'my Joe' starts for a drink of water, the 'feminine' is sure to follow; if he lies down, he is clasped in the loving arms; at table the 'feminine' refuses to eat unless 'my Joe' helps his plate. . . . 'My Joe' gets exasperated occasionally, and deals out a severe tongue lashing, which the 'feminine' accepts in a regular lover like pouting manner, they won't speak for several days and won't sleep together. . . . We are all fond of him, and he is a noble generous fellow; but his feminine airs are often very provoking" (pp. 145–146).

For a contrast, there is Mollie Hays, a female prisoner at Alton, who is quite unlike the many other women of Frost's acquaintance: "Last Saturday I saw the *female man* (Mollie Hays) for the first time, as she was on her way to dinner. She was still arrayed in masculine attire. Her features are coarse, face round and full, a turn up nose, hands and feet small. She has a rather masculine appearance, and is by no means a pleasing object to look upon" (p. 195).

As a final point of interest, Frost's journal provides a touching illustration of the idea of the American Civil War as a struggle of brother against brother. It was while in Gratiot for the first time that Frost learned that his brother Daniel had become Colonel of the 11th West Virginia Infantry, a Union regiment. Of Daniel, Griffin's senior by 13 years, the latter writes "he is a noble man, I love him like a father, but I fear he is fighting against his principles" (p. 33) He wonders how his brother and nephew (Bushrod Taylor Frost, a 2nd Lieutenant in the 11th WV) like fighting to free the slaves (p. 85), indicating that Griffin assumes the other two share his low opinion of blacks. In August 1864, Griffin received word from his sister in West Virginia that Daniel had died July 20 of wounds suffered in battle at Snicker's Gap on July 18 (pp. 154–155). A few days later Griffin notes that younger brother John (who had also joined the Missouri State Guard, was captured at Helena in 1863, and was now imprisoned at Fort Delaware) has also heard the sad news: "[John] feels as nature dictates over the loss of so kind and generous a relative; our difference in politics has made no change in our brotherly love" (p. 158).

Prior to the Civil War, Daniel Frost was a merchant in Ravenswood, (West) Virginia, operating a wharfboat at Ripley Landing.[57] In 1858, he took over *The Virginia Chronicle* from his brother William and ran it until the beginning of the war.[58] In 1861, Daniel was elected to the lower house of the Legislature of the Reorganized Government of Virginia, where he served as speaker in the first and extra sessions.[59] He resigned this post on May 24, 1862, to become Lieutenant Colonel of the 11th West Virginia Infantry and advanced to Colonel on February 6, 1863. Daniel was said to have been "the most hated Union man in [Jackson County] by those having Confederate leanings."[60] His news-

INTRODUCTION.  xxiii

paper was considered "a virulent Union-leaning publication," and the building it occupied in Ravenswood was burned September 4, 1862, by the Confederate cavalry of Brigadier General Albert Jenkins.[61] We know nothing specific of Daniel's feelings for Griffin, although he cared enough to write to General Rosecrans in a bid to have Griffin released from prison (p. 121). Several weeks after Daniel's death, his widow wrote Griffin that she regretted that the brothers had been separated, for she felt that Daniel's influence would have kept Griffin loyal to the Union. We may assume that, despite the wedge of political differences and the distance that divided them, the brothers Daniel and Griffin never lost their love and respect for one another.

Of all the sons of William and Rebecca Frost living at the beginning of the Civil War, only Griffin and John threw in their lot with the South. William Jr., who worked for the *Mexico Ledger* during the war, remained neutral. And of course, Daniel fought for the North. It is obvious, from their letters to Griffin, that his mother and younger sister Rebecca, who had followed him to Missouri, but who had both returned north after the war began, and his older sisters in West Virginia and Ohio were all pro-Union. Why did two brothers in this basically loyalist family fight for the South? Was it a reaction to the fact that certain members of the family were so strongly pro-Union? Griffin's conversion may have begun when he moved to Palmyra, Missouri, and married the daughter of a slaveholder (see p. 218). As early as 1857, he publicly identified himself as being in favor of slavery.[62] His book bears evidence of a genuine love for the people and the places of his adopted region. But it also shows a darker motivation, a deep-seated fear and loathing of Yankees, tinged with an unfortunate racism. He refers to his enemies as "tyrannical, infuriated, fanatical mobs" (p. 61). He believes that, though there may be good people in the North, they are nevertheless "blinded by an arrogant prejudice and led by unscrupulous political fanatics" (p. 116), one goal of whom is to liberate and raise to the white man's cultural level "the jay-heeled, wooly headed improved monkey from Africa" (pp. 115). The blacks Frost sees in Federal uniform on the streets of St. Louis are "like young jay birds [who] open their mouths and gulp down everything the Yankees see fit to stuff them with. [They step along] quite briskly, as though they thought it something grand to be food for powder, and save Yankee hides" (pp. 102–103).

INTRODUCTION.

The most telling statement of Frost's love for the South and his hatred for his Northern enemy is filled with a despair that again seems to be voiced from a post-war, lost-cause perspective: "Yankees and ruin toss about over the country with the desolating freedom of flood waters in a deluge. There is an antagonism between Yankee nature and Southern soil, and according as one or the other predominates, evil or good is the result. New England puritanism is rank poison in the South ... turned loose in all the wild ferocity of their savage nature, [Yankees] assimilate with the negroes, and the barbarous mixture is at once destructive of all the landmarks of civilization. If our forces should be finally vanquished, and crazy fanatics have free course to mix and mingle with the half tamed negroes in all the South, the beautiful garden spots of that heaven favored land will become as dens and lairs for a new breed of worse creatures than the wild beasts of the forest" (pp. 143-144). One hopes that, with the passage of time, Frost was able to face the South's future with a little more forbearance and optimism.

As noted earlier, Griffin Frost wrote *Camp and Prison Journal* while working for a newspaper in Quincy, Illinois, after the Civil War. The book was published by the Quincy Herald Book and Job Service in 1867. On May 6, 1870, the Herald building, along with several others, was completely leveled in a fire.[63] Along with stock, fixtures, and machinery valued at $40,000, most of the copies of *Camp and Prison Journal* were destroyed. Some years later, Frost wrote in a letter that of 700 copies printed, all but 50 had been lost in that fire.[64] Why is it that this book, an at times bitter, but still very rich and full memoir of Confederate service and life in Northern prisons, was never republished in the author's lifetime? He certainly did not want for access to the means of republishing it. Perhaps he considered it best not to. Perhaps one day Griffin Frost finally came to terms with the outcome of the Civil War.

W. CLARK KENYON
*August 1994*

NOTES.

1 *History of Lewis, Clark, Knox and Scotland Counties, Missouri* (St. Louis and Chicago: The Goodspeed Publishing Co., 1887), p. 1039. Hereafter cited as *History of Lewis*.

INTRODUCTION.  xxv

2 *Jackson County West Virginia Past and Present* (Ripley, WV: Jackson County Historical Society, Inc., 1990), p. 71. Hereafter cited as *Jackson County*.

3 *Knox County* (Missouri) *Democrat*, August 25, 1905. *History of Lewis*, p. 1039.

4 *Hannibal Messenger*, September 12, 1857.

5 According to the 1860 Audrain County Census, Frost's mother, sister Rebecca, brother William and family, and John were all living in Mexico. Father William had died in 1854, and Daniel and two older sisters remained in the East.

6 *History of Monroe and Shelby Counties, Missouri* (St. Louis: National Historical Company, 1884), pp. 811-812.

7 Information on Frost's military career is taken from his book.

8 *The War of the Rebellion: A Compilation of the Official Records of the Union and Confederate Armies* (Washington, DC: Government Printing Office, 1880-1901), Series I, 13:855. Hereafter cited as *OR*.

9 In a March 9, 1864, letter to Col. William Weer, the commandant of Alton Prison, U.S. Commissary-General of Prisoners William Hoffman wrote that since Captain Griffin Frost was a prisoner of war, the department commander did not have the power to remit his sentence. *OR*, Series II, 6:1027.

10 *History of Lewis*, pp. 671-672, 746, 1040.

11 *Knox County Democrat*, October 16, 1884.

12 *Knox County Democrat*, December 18, 1884.

13 *Edina Sentinel*, June 28, 1906.

14 *Edina Sentinel*, April 8, 1909.

15 *Edina Sentinel*, December 5, 1907.

16 William B. Hesseltine, *Civil War Prisons: A Study in War Psychology*, Ohio State University Contributions in History and Political Science, no. 12 (Columbus: The Ohio State University Press, 1930), p. 240. Hereafter cited as Hesseltine, *Civil War Prisons*.

17 Ibid., p. 252.

18 Bernard J. Reilly, "Reminiscences of the Old McDowell Medical College, Afterward a Federal Prison at Eighth and Gratiot Streets, St. Louis," *Reminiscences of the Women of Missouri in the Sixties* (Np: Missouri Division, United Daughters of the Confederacy, nd [1913]), p. 71. Hereafter cited as Reilly. See also Frost pp. 175, 225.

19 William B. Hesseltine, "Military Prisons of St. Louis, 1861-1865," *Missouri Historical Review* 23 (April 1929) : 382. Hereafter cited as Hesseltine, "Military Prisons."

20 Marjorie E. Fox Grisham, "Joseph Nash McDowell and the Medical Department of Kemper College, 1840-1845," *Bulletin of the Missouri Historical Society* 12 (July 1956) : 359-360, 361. Hereafter cited as Grisham.

21 Ibid., pp. 358, 364.

22 Ibid., p. 369.

INTRODUCTION.

23 Ibid., p. 370.
24 Hesseltine, "Military Prisons," p. 382.
25 Grisham, p. 370. Dr. McDowell attempted to reopen his college, but years of abuse as a prison at times overcrowded with more than 1000 men and women had taken their toll. The building was found to be so run-down as to be beyond repair, and it was abandoned (Reilly, pp. 71–72). The old college/prison stood for years as a grim reminder of the Civil War. Absalom Grimes, the famed Confederate mail carrier and a former inmate, revisited Gratiot in 1878, and found that most of the flooring had been removed to be reused elsewhere, and that generally the place resembled "the abandoned ruins of old castles which writers of fiction describe" (*Absalom Grimes: Confederate Mail Runner*, edited by M. M. Quaife [New Haven, CT: Yale University Press, 1926] p. 216). The southern wing of the building was demolished soon thereafter, and the rest was brought down in the summer of 1882 (*St. Louis Republican*, August 8, 1882).
26 S. H. M. Byers, *Iowa in War Times* (Des Moines: W. D. Condit & Co., 1888), pp. 95–102; Lurton Dunham Ingersoll, *Iowa and the Rebellion* (Philadelphia: J. B. Lippencott & Co., 1866), pp. 36–45. The 2nd Iowa was the victim of the peculiar circumstances of a time early in the Civil War when it was acceptable for private property to be appropriated for military use, but not permissible for that same property to be stolen or vandalized by individuals. As for the stuffed animals, Frost notes that they were all eventually destroyed by the prisoners (p. 32). See also Reilly, p. 70.
27 Hesseltine, "Military Prisons," p. 389.
28 *Absalom Grimes*, p. 216.
29 Ibid., pp. 86–89. James E. Moss, ed. "A Missouri Confederate in the Civil War: The Journal of Henry Martyn Cheavens, 1862–1863," *Missouri Historical Review* 57 (October 1962) : 29. Hereafter cited as Cheavens. Women prisoners, arrested for spying, sabotage, or general disloyalty, were a problem for Federal authorities in St. Louis as to where best to hold them. In 1863, a Mrs. Margaret A. E. McLure was arrested and confined to her own house, which, when other women prisoners were brought there, was turned into a sort of female prison. Frost reports that these women were later transferred to the "round building" (the octagonal tower) at Gratiot (p. 40). In the summer of 1864, women detainees were held for a time at Myrtle Street Prison (a converted slave pen), then housed in the residence of Gratiot Prison turnkey Sgt. Mike Welch, which was found to be too small (pp. 167, 172). Finally, a building across Eighth Street from Gratiot was fitted up as a prison for women (p. 172; *Absalom Grimes*, p. 197). The preferred method of dealing with female prisoners was banishment to the south or sometimes to the north, however. The Union authorities found that it was counterproductive to have "disloyal" women congregated anywhere near male Confederate prisoners, as they sought "every opportunity to keep disloyalty alive" amongst their male counterparts (*OR*, II, 5:320). Indeed, the presence of Southern women, either in prison or free on the streets of St. Louis where Frost and his compatriots could admire them, was one of the few bright spots of Frost's existence at Gratiot.
30 Cheavens, pp. 29–30.
31 *Absalom Grimes*, p. 181.

INTRODUCTION.  xxvii

32 Cheavens, p. 30.
33 *OR*, II, 6:981-983.
34 *Absalom Grimes*, p. 181.
35 Ibid., p. 94. Chaplain Patterson, who drew the illustration of Gratiot Prison that appears on the jacket of this edition, identifies these as Jackson Barracks.
36 Hesseltine, "Military Prisons," pp. 383-384. Hesseltine's statement that there was "a new penitentiary being constructed at Alton" is incorrect.
37 William Robert Greene, "Early Development of the Illinois State Penitentiary System," *Journal of the Illinois State Historical Society* 70 (April 1977), 188-192. The state transferred ownership of the penitentiary and grounds to Lorenzo P. Sanger and Samuel K. Casey in 1857, as partial payment for their work in the construction of the new prison at Joliet; Jann Cox, *Alton Military Penitentiary in the Civil War: Smallpox and Burial on the Alton Harbor Islands*, St. Louis District Historic Properties Management Report, No. 36 (St. Louis: U.S. Army Corps of Engineers, 1988), p. 48. Hereafter cited as Cox.
38 *OR*, II, 3:169.
39 Ibid., p. 216. Cox, p. 73.
40 *OR*, II, 3:245-246, 257-258.
41 *OR*, II, 7:533.
42 *OR*, II, 8:1000. Alton's capacity was set at 1200 by Union inspectors, *OR*, II, 7:535.
43 *OR*, II, 3:421-422.
44 *OR*, II, 6:663. Absalom Grimes recalled that in 1863 he was taken to Alton's old, original cellblock, which was in ruins and unoccupied, and kept there for a few days before being returned to St. Louis and a specially constructed, secure cell beneath Myrtle Street Prison (*Absalom Grimes*, pp. 156-159). Frost was held briefly in this original cellblock when he first returned to Alton, October 3, 1864 (p. 184).
45 *OR*, II, 5:150; 6:96.
46 *OR*, II, 6:160, 179, 191-192.
47 Ibid., p. 392.
48 Ibid., p. 969.
49 *OR*, II, 7:84-85.
50 Ibid., pp. 535-536. After the war, attempts were made to reestablish an Illinois State Penitentiary at Alton, but the movement was thwarted by industrial interests of the city, who feared the competition of convict labor. The penitentiary reverted to its private owners, who salvaged the stone blocks for lime and building material. Later, a children's playground known as Uncle Remus Park was established on the site (W. T. Norton, *Centennial History of Madison County, Illinois* [Chicago: The Lewis Publishing Co., 1912], I:244). A portion of the original stone wall of the prison near the corner of Broadway and William Streets was restored in 1973, and it remains to this day as a reminder of Alton Penitentiary.

xxviii                    INTRODUCTION.

51 Hesseltine, "Military Prisons," pp. 386-387; Galusha Anderson, *The Story of a Border City During the Civil War* (Boston: Little, Brown, and Co., 1908), p. 189.

52 Reilly, p. 70; Elizabeth Ustick McKinney, "A Reminiscence of the War Between the States,"*Reminiscences of the Women of Missouri During the Sixties,* p. 145. On the other hand, Henry M. Cheavens, a Confederate soldier who came to Gratiot from Springfield in the same group as Frost in December 1862, worked in the hospital and found the place quite clean and orderly. He also noted that the commandant Captain Masterson "tried to do all he could for the comfort and health of the prisoners" Cheavens, pp. 30-31. Concerning Alton, Confederate Captain J. F. Melton complained in a March 30, 1863, letter to a member of the Confederate Congress that he had been "kicked, cuffed, taunted, jeered and maltreated in every conceivable form" when brought to Alton Prison. Melton continued: "Oh! the horrors of this place, the cruelty of my persecutors, tongue cannot tell, neither hath it entered into the heart of man to conceive. I have seen thousands of my companions in arms consigned to a premature and untimely grave here by the cruelty and injustice of my enemies, murdered in cold blood in this lazar house of disease and death." *OR,* II, 5:859.

53 One Federal inspector said of Gratiot's hospital in September 1864: "I do not think that there is a military hospital in this country that exceeds this one in accuracy, cleanliness, and system" (*OR,* II, 7:772). Earlier that year, another inspector reported that the conditions of hospital patients were "not at all satisfactory; bedding, clothing and persons, foul; wards in bad police . . . it is only to be wondered at that the sick list and mortality is not much greater than it is" (*OR,* II, 6:981-982).

54 Hesseltine, "Military Prisons," p. 399.

55 Grimes recalled that "in those stirring war days no man was of importance or standing until he had been locked up in Gratiot Street Prison at least a few days. . . . The citizens referred to would be rounded up about town and locked up without charges, apology, or explanation and after being boarded for from one week to two months they would be called before the provost marshall and presented with the oath of allegiance to the United States, which they had to sign without question, no matter how great the effort" *Absalom Grimes,* pp. 164-165.

56 The only other work of comparable size is *Absalom Grimes: Confederate Mail Runner,* a heavily edited account in which the author's experiences were recalled nearly 50 years after they occurred. Grimes's descriptions of Gratiot are detailed and interesting, but are subordinated to the topic of his many attempts to escape.

57 *Jackson County,* p. 9.

58 Ibid., p. 71.

59 Ibid., p. 7.

60 Delmer R. Hite, comp. "Roster of Jackson County Union Soldiers in the Civil War," in *Jackson Countains* [sic] *in America's Wars, 1775-1918* (Ripley, WV: Jackson County Historical Society, nd), p. 18.

61 *Jackson County,* p. 62.

INTRODUCTION.                                                  xxix

62  Frost's name appears in a list of pro-slavery men published in the January 14, 1857, issue of the Palmyra *Southern Sentinel. Marion Co Mo Palmyra Newspaper Abstracts 1856-1858* (Shelbyville, MO: K. Wilham Genealogical Research and Publishing, 1990), p. 6.

63  *Quincy Whig and Republican,* May 7, 1870.

64  Colton Storm, comp. *A Catalog of the Everett D. Graff Collection of Western Americana* (Chicago: University of Chicago Press, 1968), p. 221.

## ACKNOWLEDGMENTS.

I would like to thank Kathleen Wilham of Shelbyville, Missouri, and Lynn Pauley of the Jackson County Public Library, Ripley, West Virginia, for their help in gathering information on Griffin Frost and family. Thanks also to Jeff Rombauer of Maple Valley, Washington, for his assistance and for his original suggestion that this book be reprinted.

**GRATIOT STREET MILITARY PRISON.**
(ST. LOUIS, MO.)

# CAMP

### AND

# Prison Journal,

EMBRACING

SCENES IN CAMP, ON THE MARCH, AND IN PRISONS: SPRINGFIELD, GRATIOT STREET, ST. LOUIS, AND MACON CITY, MO. FORT DELAWARE. ALTON AND CAMP DOUGLAS, ILL. CAMP MORTON, IND., AND CAMP CHASE, OHIO.

ALSO,

SCENES AND INCIDENTS DURING A TRIP FOR EXCHANGE, FROM ST. LOUIS, MO., VIA. PHILADELPHIA, PA., TO CITY POINT, VA.

BY

GRIFFIN FROST.

---

QUINCY, ILLINOIS:
1867.

Entered, according to Act of Congress, in the year 1867, by
GRIFFIN FROST,
in the Clerk's Office of the District Court of the United States, in and for the Southern District of Illinois.

Printed at the
QUINCY HERALD BOOK AND JOB OFFICE,
Southwest Cor. Maine and Fourth Sts.,
Quincy, Ill.

# INDEX.

## CHAPTER I.
Introductory; Organization of Company "A;" March to Glasgow; Capture of Steamer Sunshine; Battle of Lexington, Mo,; March Southward; Wilson Creek Battle Ground; Battle of Pea Ridge, &c., &c.................................................... 1

## CHAPTER II.
Cheering News from Virginia; Rumored Capture of Gen. Curtis and Seven Thousand Men, in Arkansas; Southern Plantations; Crossing the Mississippi River; Drowning of Luther Marks, &c., &c ................................................................ 13

## CHAPTER III.
Arrival at St. Louis; Gratiot St. Prison; Manner of Eating; what we Eat; Rumors of an Exchange; An Ungentlemanly Officer; Arrest of Ladies; Escape of Prisoners; Arrival of Female Prisoners; Exchange; Trip to Fort Delaware, &c., &c..... 27

## CHAPTER IV.
Great Excitement at Petersburg, Va.; Gen. Whitfield's Residence at Demopolis, Ala.; Capture of Jackson, Miss.; Battle of Helena, Ark.; "Mam and her Gals;" Arrival at Little Rock; Exiles from St. Louis; High Living, &c., &c.................... 46

## CHAPTER V.
Trip Northward; Excitement in Camp; Scarcity of Provision; Crossing the Missouri River; Taken Prisoners; Examination of Papers, &c.; Ladies of Richmond, Ray County, Mo.; Treatment while at Macon City; Gratiot St., Prison; Meeting of Old Friends; Affecting Scene, Capt. J. C. Hill, &c., &c........................................ 70

## CHAPTER VI.
General Order No. 86; A Night with the Condemned; Lecture from Old Masterson; Prisoners Leaving without Permission; The way they Leave; Locked up Night and Day; Removal of Col. Priest to the Strong Room; Accounts from Camp Chase Ohio; How Prisoners are treated there, &c., &c.......................................... 91

## CHAPTER VII.
Arrival at Alton, Ill.; Alton Military Prison; My Sentence; The way we Live at the Old Penitentiary; Extract from the Richmond Dispatch; Singular Attempt to Escape; A Search for Knives, &c.; Col. Weir and the Private; Gratiot Street Prison again, &c., &c...................................................................e............ 108

## CHAPTER VIII.
PAGE.

Sentence of Col. Winston; In the Dungeon; Our Mess; Arrival of Charles Hunt; Release of Dr. Jourdon; Amusing Incident; Reduction of Rations; Arrival of Citizen Prisoners; Removal of Joseph Lanier, for Execution; Struggle for Liberty; Escape of Capt. John Thrailkill, from Alton Military Prison; The Arkansas Lady, &c, &c............................................................................................................ 128

## CHAPTER IX.

A True Southern Lady; Arrival of a Box of Provision; Sentence of Capt. J. W. Livingston; White Men Guarded by Negroes; More Prisoners from the South; Departure of Capt. Sam. Winston and Eleven others, for Alton Prison; Visit to the Hospital; Stealing Money from Prisoners' Letters; Reprieve of Capt. Livingston after his Execution; Stonewall Jackson's Way, &c., &c.................................. 151

## CHAPTER X.

Arrival at the Old Bastile; Improvements since my last Visit; Bucking and Gagging Prisoners; Newspapers Prohibited; Retaliatory Proceedings; More Rumors of Gen. Price's Movements; Removal of a Man named Abshire, for Execution; Regulations of Room No. 1; A Prisoner's Appetite, &c., &c.............................. 184

## CHAPTER XI.

Another Attempt of Prisoners to Escape; "Cook's Pills;" Stealing Prisoners' Provision; The Old Tract Man; The Navy Mess; More Rumors of an Exchange; A Singular Mode of Punishment; Arrival of United States "Gutta Percha" Soldiers; Nailing Down the Windows in the Ladies' Quarters; Arrival of more Female Prisoners; Departure of Col. Winston, for St. Louis; Stringent Orders with Regard to Letter Writing, &c., &c........................................................................... 202

## CHAPTER XII.

Arrival of More Prisoners; Brutality of a Sergeant; Return of Capt. Dawson, from the Hospital; Visit out in town; Federal Prisoners Burning their Beds; Fight Between a "Galvanized Reb." and a Federal Sergeant; A Negro Shot and Killed for Crossing the Dead Line; Death of Mrs. Reynolds; Her Burial by the Catholic Church; Letter from Mrs. Martin; Miss Lundy Released; Letter from Another True Prisoner's Friend, &c., &c................................................................ 231

### APPENDIX.

Particulars of Nine Months' Imprisonment, at Camp Morton, Indiana.................. 246

Horrors of Camp Douglas, Illinois, as Related by a Prisoner................................. 265

The McNeil Massacre of Ten Rebel Prisoners, at Palmyra, Marion County, Mo., in the Fall of 1862............................................................................................... 281

Arrest, Imprisonment and Treatment of Col. Jeff. Jones, of Callaway County, Mo., as Related by Himself............................................................................. 289

Horrible Atrocities—Embracing the Murder of Maj. Owen, of Marion county, Gabriel Close and Black Triplett, of Platte county, and also Lasley, Price and Ridgeway, of Monroe county, Missouri .............................................................. 293

Conclusion.................................................................................................................. 298

# PREFACE.

Whenever we permit our thoughts to dwell upon the "Land we Love" we feel that she has a peculiar claim upon us—we have loved her from manhood, firm and true—and feel anxious to contribute our mite to succor and comfort her in her sad and desolated condition. Rivers of tears have been shed by her dear ones, excited by the fierce and cruel treatment of her foes! War has spread over her fair bosom, its desolation and carnage, and the eyes of her widows and orphans have been bathed in tears. In placing this Journal before the public we claim for it no merit save strict regard for truth; it is embellished by no brilliant scintillations of wit—no towering flights of fancy and imagination, but it tells the plain unvarnished truth—represents facts as they actually existed. And if this poor tribute, will be instrumental in silencing those who are ever and anon invoking imprecations upon the officers having charge of Andersonville, Libby and Belle Isle prisons, neither of which, we are sure, can exceed in atrocities those of Gratiot, Alton, Camp Douglas and Morton, as a careful perusal of this work will convince any right thinking individual, then will we feel compensated for all our perplexity in concealing our notes while languishing in Northern prisons, and for our trouble in gathering together the remaining facts preparatory to publication.

THE AUTHOR.

## CHAPTER I.

INTRODUCTORY, ORGANIZATION OF COMPANY "A," MARCH TO GLASGOW, CAPTURE OF STEAMER SUNSHINE, BATTLE OF LEXINGTON, MARCH SOUTHWARD, WILSON CREEK BATTLE GROUND, BATTLE OF PEA RIDGE, &C., &C.

AUGUST 1, 1861.—Believing the people of the South to be engaged in a just cause, defending the inalienable rights of American freemen, and that principle in the Declaration of Independence which asserts that "all governments derive their just powers from the consent of the governed," and that the States are acting by the authority and in the strength of their reserved rights, I am with them. Their principles are mine; I endorse their course, and engage my life and sacred honor to sustain their action. "Live or die, sink or swim," I am with them—willing to test my faith on the march, the battle field, or in the gloomy prison. If we fail, we will at least have made a stand for the rights and liberties transmitted by our fathers; if we succeed, those who fall will not have shed their blood in vain.

In the month of August 1861, I enlisted in the Missouri State Guards, Company "A," organized in July, near Emerson, Marion county, Mo., John W. Priest, Capt., John Hicks, First Lieut. Our regiment was commanded by Col. Martin E. Green, Joseph Porter, Lieut. Col., and Wm. Davis, Adjt.

We were at the battle of Athens, after which we remained some two or three weeks in the North-Eastern counties of the State, when we received orders to march toward the Missouri river. We broke up camp, which was near Marshall's mill, on the Fabius river, in Marion county, on the morning of September 2nd, and camped same night near Florida, Monroe county. From that point we commenced our march to Glasgow, where we joined the main body of Second Div. M. S. G., under command of Brig. General Thos. A. Harris, member of the State Legislature and author of the "Military Bill."

Here we captured the steamer Sunshine, on which we crossed the river, going into camp on the southern bank. On the 14th we fired into the steamer Sioux City, but did not succeed in taking her. Broke up camp on the 15th and proceeded by forced marches toward Lexington, camping two and a-half miles South of that place, which was then occupied by United States troops, strongly entrenched. Our forces then moved upon the enemies works and commenced an attack about 12 o'clock on the 18th. Col. Mulligan, commanding the federal troops, surrendered about 3 o'clock P. M., on the 20th. Besides arms and military stores captured, we recovered and returned near a million of dollars belonging to the Farmers' Bank at Lexington. Our loss was 70, that of the enemy, killed and wounded, 270. Our boys behaved well.

On Monday 30th, we took up the line of march and proceeded southward; on the 21st of October we halted at Neosho, Newton county, Mo., where we had several interesting sermons, one from Rev. Wm. G. Caples, and one or two from Elders Fink and Roe.

On Sunday night a member of our Company, Thomas Banks, of Marion county, died. We buried him next evening in a beautiful place, and the litle pine board which marks the spot, bears this inscription:

"T. Banks, died Oct. 27, 1861, aged 20 years."

On the 28th the Legislature in session at this place, passed the ordinance of secession. The act was received by our troops and citizens with deafening applause and firing of cannon. We left Neosho on the next day, and continued southward, passing through the towns of Newtonia and Gadfly, and also through the lead mines, on our way to Cassville, County Seat of Barry, which we reached about sunset on the 30th of Oct. It is a pretty little place about 16 miles from the Arkansas line. Here the Legislature convened, John McAfee, of Shelby county, Speaker.

On the night of the 3rd of November, our guards killed a prisoner in the act of escaping. The second command to halt being unheeded, the guard fired, and next morning the body was found a hundred yards from the spot. We left Cassville on the 7th, passing through the roughest country we have seen, large mountains on each side of the road. Reached Pineville, County Seat of McDonald county, on the 8th. Mr. Tucker, of the St. Louis "State Journal," spoke in front of Gen. Harris' head-quarters last night, and was enthusiastically applauded throughout the entire speech.

We left Pineville on Nov 16th, moving northward. Reached Sarcoxie on the 19th, went into camp about a mile and a half from town. Traveled 12 miles on the 20th, stopping near Oregon; next day went 20 miles further, passing through Greenfield, County Seat of Dade.

Commenced our march again on the 23rd, after traveling 15 miles were ordered to camp. The news was received with joy, the day being extremely cold, we were anxious to get near a fire. Dec. 4th found us still in camp near Osceola. Country pretty well cleard of forage for 10 or 15 miles around us. Capt. Priest's Company was this day detached from the regiment and placed in charge of the Ordnance Department, we being appointed Assistant Ordnance master. Waller Boulware, of Palmyra, Marion county, was taken prisoner on Dec. 5th, said he came into camp to see some friends, and the first thing he knew he was arrested, and was, we suppose, compelled to tarry longer than he expected.

Struck camp on the 19th and started back toward Springfield. When our destination was known much disappointment was manifested. We had hoped and expected that our route lay toward the Missouri river, but our forces were too weak, and we were compelled to move southward. O Missourians, if every man were at his post, this need not be! A fatal accident occurred in Gen. Rains' Division on the 21st. The caison to one of the cannons exploded, killing three men and wounding several.

Reached Springfield on the 23rd, and went into camp one and a half miles south-west of the town. Had a very hard march and were anxious to get some rest. Springfield is a beautiful place, and contains about 3000 inhabitants.

DECEMBER, 25, 1861.—To-day is what we used to call Christmas at home, sweet home, where my wife and baby are. "Do they miss me at home, do they miss me?" God bless them and give them "Merry Christmas." They little imagine how we pass our holiday Christmas! Such a Christmas, nothing to do but lie in camp—the dryest place in the world. Did get a chance to go to Springfield, and when we got there found nothing but mud and dirt, could not even buy a little thread to mend our ragged clothes. Hope this is not the sunny side of a soldier's life, but—"Cheer up boys, there's a good time coming."

Visited the city again on the 27th to get some stationery, unsuccessful—officers all busy distributing clothing. Our Division received five wagon loads, not yet given out to the men. Hundreds are leaving the army daily, say they must go home before they enlist again. They probably mean well, but if they are in earnest, it should be the other way. If Missourians would throw off the yoke they must all sacrifice home and home comforts for awhile. They leave us fewer and weaker, but we "wont give up the ship."

On the 29th visited the battle ground, could see bones of every description scattered here and there. Found part of the skull, thigh bone and ribs of a man. Saw the sink hole where some 60 or 70 German soldiers were buried; ribs, leg bones, and arm bones, were sticking above the earth. We took out several bones, also the hand of a man, took up the thumb on a stick and examined it, found nothing left but the skin and nail. A hot stench was continually escaping from the sink which was sickening and almost suffocating. We also found large bunches of human hair in several places scattered over the ground, where we suppose men had fallen and laid several days before burial, the hair falling off in removal. Viewed the place where General Lyon fell, looked at the remains of his horse and secured a piece of his hide. A great many have gotten strips for shoe and hame strings. We have little cause to love Gen. Lyon, but he was a brave soldier. Peace to his ashes. The battle field was literally covered with the remains of horses and fallen timber. There were trees larger than a man's body cut down by cannon balls, and the smaller trees were filled with balls of every description. Observed a large tree where a cannon ball had passed through leaving it still standing.

To-day, Jan. 4th, 1862, Thirty-eight of the old members of Co. "A" were again sworn into the State service for six months longer. John W Priest re-elected Capt, John Hicks 1st Lieut., David Willis, 2nd, and H. C. Newman, 3rd Lieut.

January 13th was a miserable day, snowing very hard. Some of the men were in their tents wrapped in blankets, others hovering round the fire trying to keep warm. On the 25th a member of our Company, Wm. Jeffries, died at the hospital in Springfield. He was a good soldier, and the members of Company "A" will miss him very much. His parents reside in Marion county.

About this time ten dead men were found within a mile and a half of our camp. Supposed to have been jayhawkers—probably killed by some of our men. The enemy is now within 50 miles of us; our scouts brought in 25 of their pickets, who are held as prisoners of war. Had an election for Lieut. Col. 1st Bat., 2nd Div. M. S. G. Capt. Priest was chosen. Company "A" being ordered to supply the vacancy of captain, your humble servant was elected to fill that office.

On the 12th of February, some 80 or 90 wagons, loaded with clothing, arrived from the South, but before they could be distributed we heard that the enemy were advancing upon us. They were accordingly reloaded, and placed in advance of the train, and we commenced our march for Fayetteville, Ark. The first night we camped on the old battle ground—the Feds occupying Springfield. We marched 12 miles and camped the night of the 13th on a high prairie. We were near freezing—wood being very scarce. On the 14th went into camp on Crane creek, tents all pitched, supper just ready, when we heard firing of cannon and saw bombs bursting in the air! We formed in line of battle on the hills, keeping our position until the baggage was out of the way, when we mounted, traveling all night and next day, without food for ourselves or horses. During three days march we had only two meals. Our horses were nearly dead with fatigue; the enemy following and constantly harrassing our rear. At Cross Hollows we took a position; cold, wet, hungry, worn out with loss of sleep and fatigue— still we rejoice at the prospect of a fight.

The enemy did not advance and we continued our march. When we reached Fayetteville, the citizens threw open their doors and pork houses, and bade us help ourselves, which we did—living well for a time. We soon resumed our march, passing through towns and villages deserted, the inhabitants having moved South. The men of Arkansas flock to us by the hundreds, saying that Missourians have stood picket for Arkansas long enough. A large number of Texans are on the way to join us. We hope that General Price will return to Missouri with an army of from 40,000 to 60,000 men. Feb. 22nd, traveled up one of the peaks of Boston mountains, the road very rough, broke four or five wagons before reaching the top, mud in some places over a foot deep. Explored some caves on the 24th, went into four and were well paid for our trouble. Chambers here and there all through them. Went in some two or three hundred yards where we found several springs of very clear water.

Received a reinforcement of Indians, fine warlike looking fellows, well armed. Five thousand more from the Nation, are under way, commanded by General Pike, Indian Agent for the C. S. A. We welcome them all, every new face gives us fresh hopes of an early return to, and a speedy deliverance of our beloved Missouri.

"We love Missouri for herself,
The best of all the earth,
And passing well, we love her as
The land that gave us birth.
But ah, far more than words can tell,
We love her, for the trust
She holds within her sacred breast,
Our urns of kindred dust.

"The meanest slave will sally forth
When tyrants bid him go,
And often bravely shed his blood,
To crush a tyrant's foe.
Then why should we a moment wait
To join Missouri's braves,
And fence if need be with our blood,
The homestead of our graves."

FEBRUARY 16, 1862.—To-day we buried our friend and fellow soldier John E. Mathews. He was taken sick on the retreat from Springfield, and had to ride in a wagon over the rough roads. We left him with a Mr. Russell, near Newburg, Washington county, Ark., where he died suddenly of inflammation of the bowels. John was a good fellow, kind and generous to all, and none knew him but to love and respect. We buried him on the farm of Mr. McClelland, in a private burying ground. Mrs. M. and two other ladies were present; she said she would take good care of the grave and have shrubbery planted around it so that it would be easily found if his mother, who resides in Marion county, Mo., should ever wish to have his remains removed.

Mrs. McClelland informed us that she had 64 blood relations in one company and over 40 in others, making more than a hundred relatives fighting for the rights and liberties of the States of the South. Her heart is with us without a doubt.

We commenced an advance upon the enemy March 4, 1862. Army in fine spirits; traveled all day through a heavy snow storm; stopped half a mile from Fayetteville; reached Elm Spring on the 5th, and next day came in sight of the Feds. We attacked and drove them before us two days—the dead scattered all along the road. Surrounded them and had a bloody fight, with heavy losses on both sides. Gen. Green's position was on a hill to guard the mouth of a hollow. We had been there two days when our scouts came in and reported the enemy coming down the hollow. We drew up in line of battle and awaited their appearance. When they came in sight we let "loose" the "Old Black Battery," under charge of Capt. Jim Kneisley, and it was fun to see them wheel and *skedaddle*. Next morning the fight ended, our brave leaders McCullough and McIntosh, having fallen, cast a gloom over the whole army. Our splendid victory was abandoned much against the will of General Price, who felt confident of his ability to maintain the position. He begged for three hours longer—with his own Missourians he could have finished the fight with complete success, but his noble voice was unheeded, a *smaller* man was higher than he. We then commenced a retrograde movement toward Van Buren. Have not been able to ascertain the number killed and wounded in the fight, but the federal loss must have been greater than ours. The Indians fought nobly, and we believe captured one piece of artillery, (gun wagon they call it,) and not knowing what to do with it turned it over and left it.

Van Buren is a beautiful place, situated on the Arkansas river, five miles below Fort Smith. We laid in camp there some two or three weeks when we left for Des Arc, on White river, which was the hardest trip we have had since the beginning of the campaign. Had to wade through swamps in water up to our necks, from morning till night, drawing the wagons after us, the horses not being able to pull them through, and to add to the pleasure of the trip it was raining constantly. At night we would pitch our tents, spread our blankets in the mud, lie down and sleep soundly till next morning, when, after eating our regular ration of bread and meat, would strike tents and again resume our tedious march, encountering about the same hardships as on the day previous. Oh, it was miserable, miserable.

Reached Des Arc about the 13th of April, and after remaining some two or three days, left for Memphis on the steamer "Sovereign," Col. Priest in command. Had a pleasant trip down White river; arrived at Memphis on the 18th, and went into camp one mile south of the city, where we rested and had a good time, enjoyed especially, the table comforts. Here the Missouri troops were paid off in Missouri script (Jackson money.) After receiving their money they visited the city where they rigged themselves out in new suits from head to foot. After a week or ten days we were ordered to Corinth. There we saw soldiers for certain, camps strung along the railroad for over 20 miles. The enemy within five miles, advancing slowly. Pickets have a skirmish every day; cannon and small arms been heard once or twice. Expect soon to be ordered to our breastworks.

MAY 3, 1862.—Drawn up in line of battle waiting for the opening of the ball.

MAY 10.—In line of battle again waiting orders. Yesterday a portion of Gen. Price's command had a fight at a small place called Farmington. Engaged 20,000 of the enemy, under command of Maj. Gen. Pope, and repulsed them with heavy loss on their side, and considerable on ours. Captured 6000 blankets, 5000 guns, and three or four hundred prisoners. Drove them three miles, and burnt the bridge to prevent their reinforcing and following.

MAY 11.—Still in the same position, enemy not yet made his appearance. Weather extremely warm.

MAY 12.—Still occupying the same place. Had drill this morning on double quick, which we consider rather hard on us this warm weather.

MAY 13.—Making preparations to move, probably toward the enemy. Ordered to cook up three days rations, and be ready to march in two hours. Evening—Now on the move.

MAY 14.—Guarding a bridge on the railroad, 10 miles south of Corinth. Our route lay through swamps the whole distance, and had to cross several streams. While part of Co's "B" and "C" were on a bridge the timbers gave way, throwing several into the deep cold water; one man slightly injured. Half the bridge fell down and we had to cross on a single plank—a pretty ticklish undertaking, especially on a dark night. We reached this place about 12 o'clock at night, spread our blankets and laid down to rest, but not so decided the mosquitoes and buffalo gnats, which kept up a pretty brisk fight all night. We hear constant cannonading this morning—expect a general engagement to-day. Do not know how long we will have to remain here, probably until the fight is over.

MAY 15.—No fighting as yet. Captured some 50 or 60 head of fine beef cattle from the Feds yesterday. Weather very warm, causing a great deal of sickness.

MAY 16.—Still waiting for orders. Probably receive them to-morrow. Hope so, as we are quite anxious to get out of this low marshy bottom. Enemy advancing slowly.

MAY 17.—Col. Priest ordered to report himself and men, minus 160, at headquarters immediately; Cos "A" "B" and "C" left to guard the bridge.

MAY 18.—Heavy cannonading all day in the direction of Corinth, and the men all in line of battle.

MAY 21.—Nothing of interest has transpired during the last two days. A portion of our men left their entrenchments yesterday, and started for Farmington, expecting to attack the enemy. It was supposed the fight would come off to-day, but not certain, as a heavy rain fell last night, giving everything a complete drenching. We will have to make the attack or there will never be a battle, they are afraid to bring it on. We have skirmishes every day with them, killing several on both sides. We are still at the bridge on the Mobile & Ohio Railroad. Do not know whether we will be in the fight or not, put here to guard the bridge, and dare not leave without orders. The place is not a very desirable one, as the mosquitos and gnats are very troublesome, making it almost impossible for us to sleep, besides we have no tents, and only one blanket apiece, so we catch a fresh cold every night. We are all sighing for our old Missouri home.

We have flour which we send to the country and get made into biscuits; have sugar, coffee, rice, molasses and pickled beef, the latter we do not eat. We raised $34.00 among us and sent out and bought some bacon, paying 40 cents per lb. It does not cost our State much to keep us as we buy our own meat, and in fact nearly everything we eat. Butter is worth from 50 to 75 cts. per lb; tough chickens 50 cts apiece; coffee 75 cts. per lb.; soda $1.50 per lb.; pepper $1.00 per lb., and other things in proportion. Citizens are complaining of great scarcity. Some have desired to enchange meal for flour with us, having had no flour for months; others say they have forgotten all about coffee.

MAY 23d.—No particulars from the main army. Still hear heavy firing—probably have news to-morrow.

MAY 24.—Been raining hard ever since yesterday. Visited Rienza about four miles below the bridge; pretty little place, buildings neat and clean; stores all empty. Evening—Heavy firing on our right wing, suppose it is the pickets. However, situated as we are, it is impossible to tell. Every train brings more or less prisoners on their way South. All waiting patiently for the big fight, but suppose we will have to wait in vain.

MAY 25.—Everything quiet, no firing heard in any direction. Yesterday the enemy attempted to plant one of their heavy siege guns, but were attacked and driven back, our forces afterwards resuming their former position.

MAY 26.—General Parsons came down to-day with his entire command. We were glad to see them. After mutual exchange of army gossip, hearing the news and speculations about the big fight, grumbling over its long delay &c., we retired to rest, but were hardly well settled, when we received orders to get up, cook three days rations and be ready to march in the morning. Something in the wind—we "snuff the battle."

MAY 28.—Drawn up in line, full of expectation; heavy cannonading in the direction of Corinth. Our wagons, tents, baggage, &c., all sent off this morning to a place of safety.

MAY 29.—No fight yet. We cooked up three days rations and started, we supposed for Corinth, but within four miles of there we took a road leading South, and after marching three miles went into camp for the night.

MAY 30.—Things look strange. Still moving southward; can it be that we are evacuating Corinth? Troops have been passing all night, and the air is full of rumors.

MAY 31.—It is settled; we *are evacuating Corinth.* Missourians cover the retreat, blockading the road. We passed the place where a portion of our [army had a fight with the enemy cavalry. Saw the effect all along the road, trees barked by balls of every description. Five Federals were found dead lying exposed to the hot sun. The engagement occurred yesterday. Nine hundred of our men were almost prisoners at one time, but a gallant charge from their friends, drove back the enemy and released them from their perilous situation. The Feds succeeded in burning the depot at Boonville, and destroying three car loads of our ammunition. The weather is extremely warm, roads dusty, and water very scarce. Harvesting has commenced—rather early to us Missourians. Provisions are very scarce, have had no meat for over three days, and now the bread is out; will have to march to-morrow without either bread or meat. Don't relish a retreat on an empty stomach.

JUNE 1.—Gone into camp, Had a hard march, sore feet, nothing to eat, and water scarce. We hear it reported that the depot at Boonville contained several dead bodies, which were burned, and the sick not being able to get far enough away, were, many of them, suffocated from the heat; others crawling off would faint on the railroad and be run over by the cars.*

JUNE 4.—We are sending off our sick to the hospital; enemy slowly advancing. It is supposed we will fight them here, as we seem to be awaiting their approach.

---

* This sounds like an Andersonville story, but was no doubt believed to be true, and possibly may have been. Capt. Frost gives it as reported to him two days after it transpired, while still in the vicinity of Boonville. He has not heard it contradicted.—ED.

JUNE 7.—On the march again; started this morning at half-past two, halted at 12. Will resume our march at 3 A. M.

JUNE 8.—Camped in an open field near Tupelo--no shade except our tents. Sun disagreeably hot, but still we are rejoicing; we are going back to Missouri—the garden spot of the Confederacy. Gen. Price has gone to Richmond, will return in eight or ten days, when he will carry us back. God bless "Old Pap," we all love him like a father, and we don't allow any but Missourians to claim him either. Some Arkansas boys tried calling him "Old Pap" but they were soon "dried up." We are elated too, over the victories of Stonewall Jackson. We are full of hope--confident of gaining our independence.

## CHAPTER II.

CHEERING NEWS FROM VIRGINIA, RUMORED CAPTURE OF GEN. CURTISS AND SEVEN THOUSAND MEN, IN ARKANSAS; SOUTHERN PLANTATIONS; CROSSING THE MISSISSIPPI; DROWNING OF LUTHUR MARKS, &C., &C.

JUNE 19.—Struck tents this morning and marched about 10 miles toward the Mississippi river. We believe we have started to Missouri.

JUNE 20.—Passed through Pontotoc, small place, male inhabitants all in the army.

JUNE 21.—Camped at Fayette Springs—a watering place, and is beautifully located. Can accommodate about 400 visitors.

JUNE 23.—Our march to-day was the hardest we have had since we left Tupelo, dust three inches thick, throats dry, water scarce; now camped near a small place called Eddyville.

JUNE 24.—Ordered to cook three days rations, and be ready to march at a moments warning. It is now rumored that we are going to Vicksburg to cross the river.

JUNE 25.—Not off yet; Waiting patiently for orders. Had a fight in Company "B" to-day, small arms engaged, both parties defeated and taken prisoners. Quite a panic ensued among the two gents when they realized their situation. We are now living very well; have plenty of blackberries, and find we have less sickness since we have been using them.

June 27.—Yesterday and to-day still waiting orders; expected a big fight at Vicksburg. The report has reached camp of another battle at Richmond, and that we repulsed the enemy and took 15,000 prisoners.

June 29.—Moved to another camping ground, where we have plenty of good water. Report still current of a great victory at Richmond—grows better as we hear more.

July 1.—More news from Virginia; captured forty thousand prisoners, nearly all their ordnance and quarter master's stores, and a large portion of their artillery. It fills every one with renewed hope. The fire of "76" is not quite burnt out; the same old war is waging over again—British tyrrany in the North, American patriotism with us. Our fathers gained their independence, and *our* cause is more just than theirs. We must succeed.

July 6.—News from Virginia confirmed; have taken 75 pieces of cannon and 15,000 stand of small arms. Men in best of spirits; hope ere long to drive the last invader from Southern soil. May the time come speedily. We would have been on the west side of the Mississippi if some soldiers discharged at Tupelo, had not gone on to Helena and circulated all along the road that Gen. Parsons, with seven hundred men, was going to cross the river at that point. Federal spies there sent word to Memphis, and a strong force was dispatched to destroy the flat boats and carry off the ferry boat, thus cutting off for the present, our means of crossing.

July 14.—Everything quiet; weather very warm. A report is floating round that Gen. Hindman has captured Gen. Curtiss with seven thousand men, in Arkansas. Good news if true; but true or not true, its good while it lasts. We are all in fine spirits; expect to move to-morrow—have sent for our sick, and will have everything ready this evening.

July 18.—Marching toward the Mississippi river. Left Abbeville at 4 o'clock A. M., and marched 14 miles. In camp one-half mile from Oxford, the prettiest place we have yet seen in the State of Mississippi. Large frame houses and plenty of pretty women.

July 19.—Took the cars at eight o'clock, and rode 50 miles to Grenada—a town of about two thousand inhabitants. Reached here at two o'clock this morning; spread our blankets on the sand

and slept soundly till day, when we marched through the town toward the Yallabusha river, where we are now camped. Will remain here until our wagons come up, and then resume our march. Everything grows scarce and high; paid 50 cents for a spool of thread, and other things cost in proportion.

JULY 20, 1862.—Had the pleasure to-day of meeting with and forming the acquaintance of a gentleman, from Canton, by the name of Freeman. He represented himself as being a brother-in-law to a man by the name of Frost, living in Marion county, Mo., and not having seen him for several years, and seeing my name registered at the hotel—having gone there for the purpose of enjoying a Sunday dinner, supposed me to be the person; however he soon became convinced to the contrary, but on further conversation, discovered it was a brother of mine to whom he had reference. At that we became better acquainted, and my brother John and I received a very pressing invitation to accompany him to his home, which we will do if we can get permission from Headquarters.

JULY 24.—Arrived at Canton on the 21st; found Mrs. Freeman a most excellent woman, and Miss Sallie a charming young lady. We had some splendid music on the guitar, violin and flute, Miss Sallie accompanying with her voice, in several beautiful pieces. Formed the acquaintance of several very agreeable persons: Mr. Conn and lady, Mr. and Mrs. Folger, and Messrs. Fleshhart and Mantanin—all full of sociability; and last, but if least, not small, to a hungry soldier, we come to the table which offered a variety of excellent well cooked food. We appreciate their efforts in that line as only hungry soldiers can.

JULY 25.—We left Canton on the evening of the 23rd, and reached Grenada yesterday morning at two; waited there until day when we started after the command; took breakfast at a farm house; stopped at noon by a cool spring, and dined from our havresack, which Mrs. Freeman had filled with nice baked chicken, steak, splendid biscuits, &c. Stayed all night with an old gentleman, who seemed to take pleasure in accommodating a weary soldier. This morning we bought a mule and saddle, which enabled us to get along faster. Caught up with the command this evening, and are now camped by a beautiful lake, near a small town called M'Nutt. Peaches and apples plenty.

July 26, 1862.—Only 35 miles from the Mississippi river; are now crossing Sunflower river in small flat boats.

July 28.—Rested yesterday; started this morning at daylight; marched 22 miles and camped on Bogue Filia, 12 miles from the Mississippi. Water has been very scarce, had none for over 12 miles; the first we found was in wagon tracks, and the men would swarm around it as though it was the last they expected to see. We have been travelling through swamp land nearly ever since we left Greanada. Houses are very scarce, saw only four in a march of 20 miles; but this land was overflowed last spring to a depth of ten feet, so there is not much encouragement to build and make improvements.

July 29.—Resting, after a march of 12 miles, near lake Bolivar, and within a mile of the river. Expect to cross to-night, but anticipate trouble. We have learned that five gun-boats and four transports are within six miles of us. Our first camping ground this evening was about six hundred yards from the river, but just as we had everything ready to get supper, Gen. Parsons rode hastily through camp, ordering us to get ready and leave there immediately, or we would be *shelled out*. We got out and double quicked it for two or three miles to this place, where we are now resting. Have seen some beautiful plantations to-day; the negro cabins, all whitewashed, numbering some twenty or thirty, situated in two rows, the overseer's house in front on the bank of the river, and everything around had a neat and cleanly appearance. On one plantation we counted over a hundred and ten negroes, women and children, and was informed that all the work hands were in the field, numbering in all some five or six hundred, which, we were told, is quite a small number to what some plantations have. It would break us up in Missouri to have to support so many, but the further South you go the less it takes to keep a negro, and the better the work is adapted to his capacity, he comes nearer paying for himself there than any where else. Just been informed that we will not move to-night. Several gun-boats have been heard passing during the evening.

July 31.—Moved to the river to-day and commenced loading on the wagons and baggage; think we will get across safe.

AUGUST 1, 1862.—Worked till 12 o'clock last night, and had nearly all the wagons on board, when a storm of thunder and lightning came up, accompanied with rain, which continued till morning. We sat on the ground with only a blanket thrown over us, and this morning were as wet and muddy as mud and water could make us. The report has just reached us that the coast is clear, both up and down the river, and that being the case we will proceed to cross the river. Now in the middle of the Mississippi; all on the lookout for gun-boats, but thank fortune there are none to be seen; there, we have landed safely on the Arkansas shore, and I will now have to stop writing and go to work.

We are now up Cypress creek, out of the way of gun-boats, (should any happen along,) busy unloading the boats and making preparations to camp about a mile distant.

AUG. 5.—Nothing of interest has transpired since we crossed the river. We are now camped in Desha county, in a cane brake, one half mile from water. I think without exception this State contains some of the roughest people I ever saw, especially women, a great many of whom go bare-footed, rub snuff and chew tobacco. I am glad they are confined to small, out of the way, backwood sections. If there were too many I fear they would sicken out the heart of chivalry; their's is not the style of beauty to inspire one to shed his blood. To-day we all received new suits; clothing plenty on this side except boots and shoes.

AUG. 7.—Marched twenty miles yesterday, and camped on Red Fork Bayou. Resumed our march at four o'clock this morning, and are now in camp on the Arkansas river, fifty miles from Little Rock.

AUG. 9.—Waiting for a boat to take us to Little Rock. We have passed through some splendid country—largest plantations we have seen. One widow lady in Arkansas county, is cultivating 2,400 acres in corn, over 500 in cotton, and owns over four hundred negroes. Rich widows are quite plentiful in this section—fine opening for enterprising young gents who would like to marry big estates with wives thrown in. The only trouble would be to get the widows enlisted in the speculation, but no doubt there will be an assortment of well kept moustaches, that will be willing to venture the undertaking.

AUG. 11.—Among the general orders read yesterday morning while on dress parade, was one commanding us to be ready to march at sun down. Accordingly we set forth at that hour retracing our steps for the distance of fifteen miles, halting at midnight, tired and sleepy, on the bank of lake Lenick. There are several small lakes on our route, the largest of which is called Massachupo. They diversify the scenery, presenting a more pleasing prospect to the eye of the traveler. It is said that we are going back to oppose the enemy at Napoleon who, it is reported, intends making a raid into the interior for the purpose of destroying the crops.

AUG. 12.—Struck tents again last night, marched five miles and camped on the Arkansas river. This morning we moved two miles further down, opposite Arkansas Post. Sundown—Now crossing the river.

AUG. 13.—Worked hard all night--got through about day. Arkansas Post was laid out for a town the same year with Philadelphia, Pa; was an old United States military post for a long time, and was once the Capitol of the State, and County Seat of Arkansas county. It is a beautiful location, but its glory has departed, a few old tottering buildings are all that is now left to show where once the proud city stood—in imagination. The few inhabitants are French, and this much good can be said of them: they are all true Southerners, their patriotism deserves the splendor of Philadelphia, rather than the dilapidation of this deserted Post.

AUG. 16.—Night before last while some of the boys were in bathing, one of our fellow soldiers, Luther Marks, undertook to swim across the river, but became exhausted, and before help could reach him, was drowned. Twenty-five men were detailed from the regiment to search for the body, which they discovered lying on a sand bar, so much swollen that it was almost impossible to recognize him. The accident has cast quite a gloom over camp. The deceased was a most excellent, moral, upright young man, highly esteemed by all who knew him.

AUG. 24th.—Been on the sick list; command moved on, left about 76 at the hospital. Am now conducting the *corps of invalids* in search of headquarters, and being a *weak* force move slow. Some of us instead of resembling "Death on a pale horse," look like pale death on foot.  The principal complaint is "Arkansas chills," and they are hard enough to shake money out of a miser, or charity out of a Yankee.

AUG. 25.—Marched 17 miles by eleven o'clock; camping on the farm of a man named Young, who furnished us with plenty of honey, butter and milk, which we are in a condition to appreciate.

AUG. 26.—Found the command encamped on the plantation of Gen. Mitchell, where they have good water. Hear that we are to move back to the Arkansas river, which causes much dissatisfaction in camp, the men being anxious to proceed to Missouri.

SEPTEMBER 1, 1862.—Still at Gen. Mitchell's; been reorganizing the troops; many have sworn in for the war. We have a great many sick, and our fare is bad. What little flour we get is full of worms, and we often pick them out of our bread after it is baked, although the boys have done their best to clean them out of the flour before mixing it. Our usual diet is corn bread, tough beef and corn meal coffee. Companies "A" and "B" not having men enough to organize a full company, a "skeleton" was formed, of which Col. Moore takes command until we reach the border, where we will fill up and have a new organization. There is quite a stir in camp over hearing that the Feds are crossing White river, and we are making bustling preparations to receive them; will "welcome them with bloody hands to hospitable graves."

SEPT. 4.—Have been quite sick again, and am now comfortably quartered, in company with S. W. Mason, at the farm house of Mr. Belcher, where we are tenderly nursed and provided for by the ladies of his excellent family, and as we sit under this hospitable roof, within the charmed circle of family influence, we are naturally transported to other days and other scenes. Our wayward minds will wander home, and hover with fond imagination over the loved ones there. Twelve long weary months have passed, and not a line has reached us, telling of their welfare. A beloved wife and precious babe; how is it with them to-day? They may be sick, writhing and gasping in pain; or dead! Great God, that cannot be! I left them in blooming health; I almost see the chubby cheeks and sparkling eyes of my darling little daughter, and feel her fat arms round my neck, and her red lips pressed to mine. O, if I could only press her for one moment to my heart. And my wife, I know the tear swims in her eye, when her mind traverses the South seeking in the tent, the field, or may be the hospital, for the "one loved" form. When, O when, shall I clasp my treasures once more?

"It may be for years, and it may be for ever."

Our excitement the other day over the Feds crossing White river was all a hoax; it resulted from a mere trifle. Some men in bathing were fired upon, and of course, very much frightened. They posted off a messenger to Gen. Parsons, with news that the enemy were crossing at that point. However, it does no harm, a fluster breaks the monotony, like a good laugh clearing out the cobwebs.

SEPT. 9.—Still at Mr. Belcher's kindly cared for, and rapidly improving. General Parsons moved his command last night, but we have not learned in what direction. We will start out after him as soon as Mason is able to travel.

SEPT. 11.—We had a big rain and wind storm last night, setting in about dark; at eight o'clock when the storm was raging in all its fury, some men "bellowed" at the fence. They had come for the magistrate, (Mr. Belcher) to go and marry a runaway couple about three miles distant, the accommodating official started off, but in a half hour the whole party returned thoroughly drenched, they had lost their way and had to give it up for the night; but this morning, bright and early, the sympathising magistrate announced his readiness to set forth and relieve the expectant couple. So mounting his mule, he blew his cow-horn, when six lusty hounds answered with a howl, and the party again proceeded on their journey. About noon the Squire and his canine escort returned. The young fugitives were made happy, and sent on their way rejoicing.

SEPT. 12.—We left Mr. Belcher's this morning and traveled twelve miles; are stopping with a widow lady named Walters, living on the old military road leading from Clarendon to Little Rock. Have heard that our command is encamped near Des Arc.

SEPT. 14th.—Have reached Des Arc, but are completely broken down, when we stopped last night we could not have walked twenty steps further. We staid with Squire M'Keevers. General

Parsons had crossed the river when we arrived, expecting to have an engagement with the enemy, but after an absence of three days he came back. They got in a few hours after us. Des Arc is much changed since we passed through here last spring on our way to Memphis. It has a dreary, desolate look; many of the houses have been destroyed, and the citizens moved southward. As soon as we can get our horses shod, they say we will start North. Hope so, truly.

Sept. 24.—Have been down with the fever; Doctor sent Jarred, Kelly and myself to this place, Mr. Ivans', about six miles from Des Arc, where we are ordered to remain and recruit. We will get well as fast as we can, for it is thought we will start in a few days for Missouri. We are all anxious to get back. Our whole command, except Col. Winston's regiment, has sworn into the Confederate service for three years, or during the war. As soon as they have sworn in we will be ready to march. When we get to the border, we can fill up our skeleton companies from men there waiting for us. James Magee, a member of Co. "B" from Lewis county, was buried yesterday, aged about fifty years.

October 7.—We have been at Mr. Evans' over two weeks. Gen. Parsons moved on the 24th of last month; we were very anxious to follow at once, but were not able. To-day we have ventured on making a start; the command is at Yellville, Ark., 175 miles from Des Arc; a pretty good walk ahead of us; have made 15 miles to-day; stopping at the house of a Mr. Stewart.

Oct. 8.—On our weary tramp again; passed through a small town called Searcy, found most of the inhabitants engaged in horse racing; we are near the mountains, and will rest a day or two, before we attempt to climb them. Mr. Creary is our gentlemanly host. Many of the people in some parts of Arkansas are rough and uncouth, but still we find them willing to give the "cup of cold water," and often more too, to the sick and weary soldier. It is not always the learned and polished that have the kindest hearts.

Oct. 13.—At the foot of the mountain, 12 miles from Burrowville. We have been traveling in Van Buren county, over the roughest road I ever saw, and it appeared worse to me from the fact that I have been suffering with severe headache; fear I shall not be able to travel to-morrow; but will keep the road if possible, as we are anxious to reach the command.

OCT. 14.—Within three miles of Burrowville, and near the foot of Backbone mountain, which is the divide between the waters of Little Red and White rivers. In the course of our journey we have met with all grades and descriptions of people. Their mode of life, surroundings and obscure location, necessarily render them rough in their manners and appearance, but still we find the usual diversity in human nature; the back woods as well as New England, has its misers, its egotists and its independent thinkers, defying God or man if he contradicts their notions. On a different scale it is true, and with a change of scenery, but in the same spirit. We see women barefooted, sore eyed, squirting tobacco juice, belching out a miserable jargon for "the right, law or no law," as a more enlightened circle would express it; but if a soldier sick and hungry, wishes to rest his weary bones under their roof for a night, they are quick and sharp for a trade, ready to bleed him to the last cent. I am sorry to record it, but such people are here, whether they sprung from any of the May Flower seed, I am unable to say. But one curious circumstance is, we find these cases among those who have no friends in the army.

OCT. 20.—We are in Searcy county, 16 miles from Yellville, at the house of a Mr. McBride. Kelley and Logie, quite sick, myself improving, all under the treatment of a lady Doctor; she is dosing us with pills and tonic, and I must acknowledge it is doing us a great deal of good. I am not much of an admirer of "old women's remedies," except for themselves and children; but it is a principle with me to "render honor, where honor is due," and this female Æsculapius seems to be a public benefit in this section; she practices for 20 or 30 miles around.

OCT. 30.—Still at McBride's, and still improving—thanks to the female doctress, hope to be able to travel by Monday, but the Lord only knows where we will find the command, they left Yellville last Sunday, and no one knew where they were going.

NOVEMBER 3.—Kelley and I have bought us a horse a piece, and will start to-morrow; we have heard that Gen. Parsons is at Cross Hollows.

We are within one mile of Pilot Knob, stopping with Mr. Pass, until my spell of chills is passed. I am sure Job was never put to such a test as these abominable "Arkansaw shakes," or he never would have stood fire as long as he did. Well, Pilot Knob is as much of a mountain as any we have seen, with a very large rock on top, looking like a solitary house; not a very inviting place to live this cold weather.

Nov. 6.—Enjoyed the felicity of a fine shake, followed by a beautiful fever, have no idea how often the pleasure may be repeated, but as we are within 36 miles of our camp, and a large number of new recruits have arrived from North Missouri, and as they may be able to give us some news of our friends from whom we have not heard for 16 months, we could be induced to sacrifice the enjoyment of a repetition for the sake of expediting a coveted interview with the new arrivals, and on the day after to-morrow we will endeavor to reach the command.

Nov. 30, 1862.—A prisoner at Springfield, Mo; was captured on the 8th inst., at the house of Mr. Pass, Carroll county, Ark., by a squad of Capt. Youngblood's company, 1st Arkansas cavalry. I was taken to their camp, some 12 miles distant, and after remaining there a few days was sent, with five or six others to this place. Kelley made a narrow escape, he had gone after our horses, which he had taken to a place of safety, and was just returning with them when they saw him and gave him chase, but he succeeded in eluding their pursuit, saving both horses. We are now confined in the college which has been used as a military prison ever since the beginning of the war, with about one hundred and fifty other prisoners. The first night of our arrival three prisoners made their escape through the guards, and when about 50 yards from the prison some women discovered them and commenced yelling with all their might and main, "Prisoners getting out," when chase was given and two of them recaptured and brought back. The poor fellows were then taken up stairs, made lie down on their backs, and gagged with a bayonet. They were kept in that position some time, and in the mean time, the officer in command held a lighted candle over the prostrate bodies in order that the other prisoners could get a good look at them, and remarked "that they would be treated in like manner if they attempted to get away." One of the unfortunate ones is named Smith, the name of the other I have not learned. I regarded the above as rather a rough introduction to college life. Four or five have made good their escape since my arrival. The officer in command of the prison is named Waterson, and I believe ranks as lieutenant. An officer was down from headquarters yesterday taking the names of all the prisoners of war. We judge from that that we are to be sent away in a short time.

DECMBER 7, 1862.—It is midnight, the hour when everything should be quiet, no sound heard except the tread of the sentinel as he walks his beat from post to post. All should be locked in the embrace of Morpheus partaking of "tired nature's sweet restorer, balmy sleep;" but this is a military prison, over a hundred and fifty persons are crowded together. Hell let loose could not be worse. Some are dying, others praying, some singing, others swearing, some dancing and some playing cards, while others are engaging all their powers to make a noise generally. How can a man think, or write, or hope to sleep. There have been several deaths since I have been here; two were buried yesterday. One of them died in the night and no one knew anything of it till morning. The dead are put into a rough box, and shoved into the ground without any ceremony whatever. Some of the prisoners have been here over nine months; one young man was married about a week before he was arrested, and after he had been here some five months, his wife came and was permitted to see him. It was too much for the poor creature to see her husband confined in such a miserable place; she went back home, and died in a few days, the husband still in prison.

DEC. 9.—To-day another victim was taken to his long home. An old man, aged 63 years. His daughter came to see him and it was a sad sight indeed, to witness her bending over his dead body, lamenting the loss of her dearest friend on earth—and that too in military prison.

DEC. 16.—Last night an old man named Couch, fell dead in the prison hall; he had been sick for some time, and getting up about 12 o'clock, walked out in the hall, where he fell dead. His family arrived here to-day from Arkansas. When they were informed of his death, I never saw persons take anything so hard, the poor desolate creatures seemed heart-broken. One of the women was barefooted and driving an ox team, and the weather very cold. While I write, 10 o'clock at night, the corps still lies in the hall with no covering but the ragged shirt and pants he had on when he died.

The windows of our prison are strongly barred with iron, and 20 yards from the building, on all sides, is a picket fence made of timbers cut 22 feet in length and set five feet into the ground, leaving us a wall 17 feet high. In one corner is a small room where eight men perform the cooking. Our fare is nothing to complain of. If we only had vessels to cook in we would do well enough in that line, but messing up everything in one camp kettle, the food is not very tempting. It is said, however, that every one has to "eat a peck of dirt", and I think we have a fair prospect for a half bushel, if we continue here many days. When we go for water a guard always attends us, with musket and bayonet at our back.

DEC. 19.—Forty-seven more prisoners were brought in to-day. They were captured at the salt-petre works in Marion county, Ark. We have now some 200 in this prison, and it is almost an impossibility for all to get places to sleep. The room in which I am confined is 18 feet square, I occupy it with 28 others. It is my good fortune to have a bunk to sleep on, but most of my comrades take the floor, which is certainly the filthiest place I ever saw, a hog pen were preferable. The *night buckets* are kept in one corner of the room, and persons are up and down all through the night answering the calls of nature, which renders our quarters very unpleasant indeed. The weather is very cold, and many of the prisoners are thinly clad; their old clothes are worn out, almost rotted off them, and they have no chance to get better. Occasionally a Southern lady manages to send in a few articles, which are distributed to the most needy. God knows there are enough of them, poor suffering wretches; would to Heaven we could be exchanged. I would rather march in July on an empty stomach, without water, through dust six inches deep, in Mississippi, than to lay rotting in this filthy hole.

Three or four ladies from Arkansas came to the prison to-day, to see their friends. One fine looking lady had a beautiful blue eyed babe with her, which looked as though it was nearly frozen. She asked the guard to allow her to approach the fire and warm her child. He told her to stay where she was. The poor mother was dumb with grief and astonishment, and could only draw her little darling closer to her own warm heart. I could not have believed such things as I now see, if my own eyes had not witnessed the scenes.

DEC. 20.—Very cold and disagreeable; several ladies called at the gate, requesting to see two or three of the prisoners, myself among the number. They had permission to supply us with some clothing, which was thankfully received. There are several ladies here who seem to take great interest in the unfortunate prisoners; supplying them with clothing, sending delicacies to the sick, and in fact doing all in their power to relieve them of their sufferings. May God bless them for their kindnes; "Sick and in prison and ye visited me."

Got permission to go out in the city, accompanied by a guard. Visited the family of Mr. Logan, found *them very kind, and before I left they gave me a large bundle of clothing to distribute among the prisoners. One hundred and four of us have been notified to hold ourselves in readiness to leave for St. Louis in a few days. All are in fine spirits over the good news, and hope the day will soon arrive when we are to leave this miserable place.

## CHAPTER III.

ARRIVAL AT ST. LOUIS; GRATIOT STREET PRISON; MANNER OF EATING; WHAT WE EAT; RUMORS OF AN EXCHANGE; AN UNGENTLEMANLY OFFICER; ARREST OF LADIES; ESCAPE OF PRISONERS; ARRIVAL OF FEMALE PRISONERS; EXCHANGE; TRIP TO FORT DELAWARE, &c., &c.

JANUARY 1, 1863.—Arrived, last night, in company with one hundred and four other prisoners, at St. Louis; confined same night in Gratiot street prison. The weather being extremely cold we had a very disagreeable trip indeed, nothing to eat for twenty-four hours, and when we reached St. Louis we were as hungry as wolves. We had to stand in the street for over an hour before we could be admitted to the prison, during which time one poor fellow took a congestive chill and died. Before our admission we were searched, and deprived of our money, knives, papers, and in fact everything we had about us, (except my journal, which they were unable to find.) We were then shown to our quarters, the upper room in the round building—a very dark, gloomy place, and very filthy besides. From Springfield to Rolla we were made to walk most of the way. We had no tents and were compelled to lie out every night without shelter; sometimes it would rain, and in the morning we would find ourselves wet, muddy and nearly frozen, the roads were also very rough, and by the time we reached St. Louis we were nearly worn out with fatigue, and were glad to get to a place where we could rest even though it were a prison. Can't say much about our new hotel as yet, as we have not seen enough to justify us in doing so.

JAN. 2.—Discover this morning that Gratiot is a very hard place, much worse than Springfield; fare so rough, it seems an excellent place to starve. Am not particularly fond of any prison, but must say that I give Springfield the preference over this.

JAN. 3.—Have found several acquaintances since my arrival— a brother-in-law, and one John Miller, a member of company "A," and several others who used to belong to Price's army. They have been here for some time, and as yet see no prospect of getting out.

JAN. 4.—This morning our quarters were changed to the lower room of the square building; it is in many respects a better place, but very cold, almost impossible to keep warm. We have only two stoves to over a hundred men.

JAN. 5.—There are now about eight hundred prisoners in Gratiot, and more coming in every day from all parts of the country. We are allowed only two meals a day, and it keeps the cooks busy to get through with them by dark. Some two or three hundred eat at a time, and the tin plates and cups are never washed from the first to the last table. For breakfast we have one-fifth of a loaf of baker's bread, a small portion of bacon, and a tin cup of stuff they call coffee. For dinner the same amount of bread, a hunk of beef, and a pint of the water the beef was boiled in, which is called soup, and sometimes a couple of boiled potatoes—all dished up and portioned out with the hands; knives, forks and spoons not being allowed. Many leave the table as hungry as they went to it.

JAN. 6.—The hospital, which is the highest room in the prison, contains a great many sick at this time. The Sisters of Charity visit them daily, ministering to them, and supplying them with such delicacies as their poor appetites can receive, and their weak conditions require.

JAN. 7.—Received orders to-day to move ourselves and baggage to the officers' quarters—find it a great improvement on the old position, much cleaner, and not so crowded. There are eight of us in a room sixteen feet square, Lieut. Edmonds, of Shelbina, and Rev. Mc. Bounds, of Shelbyville, among the number. We have bunks instead of that horrid floor, to sleep on, and our fare is better and more plentiful, and brought on the table in better style. We have the privilege of using knives, forks and spoons, which we prefer to the *finger plan* in vogue below.

JAN. 8.—We have the privilege of promenading in a large hall, which we avail ourselves of for exercise. We have a good view from the windows, where we stand and watch for the Southern ladies to pass. God bless them, they always give us a pleasant smile; it is like a glimpse of Heaven to look in their dear sympathizing faces.

JAN. 9, 1863.—For the first time since I left home, on the 2nd of September, 1861, I received a letter; all well and doing well. Hope I shall hear from them every week while I am here, and enjoy the pleasure of talking to them, a few words at a time, with my pen. We are allowed to write but one page only, and our letters are all inspected, and if not gotten up according to the taste of the 'exquisite' who examines them, they are thrown into the litter basket and the envelope returned.

JAN. 12.—Yesterday—Sunday, was a very lonesome day, nothing to do or read, and had it not been for Father Ryan coming in, and preaching us a good sermon, I scarcely know how we could have gotten through the day. We have two or three Methodist divines in prison, who are permitted to preach occasionally.

The ladies of St. Louis are very kind, they are constantly relieving our necessities, and seem thankful that it is in their power to do so. I hope the poor fellows below are not forgotten; their case amounts to actual suffering, while we are comparatively comfortable.

JAN. 14.—Heard some talk yesterday of an exchange of prisoners; hope it will soon come round, God knows we all long to breathe the pure air of Dixie once more, free from the tyrant rule we are now under. To-day we are cooped up in our den, not allowed even to put our heads out of the windows, if we do the guards are ordered to shoot us. One of their own men was put in here for some offence, and probably without knowing of the order, looked out at the window, when the guard fired, and the poor wretch fell dead. Our consolation was, that it was not one of us, but it looked hard to see even an enemy killed in that way.

JAN. 16.—Nothing of interest transpiring in the prison; we go over the same old round of dull monotony, hear nothing from the outside except when a new victim is brought in. If we could have some papers or books we could do very well, but it will do no good to grumble.

JAN. 19.—Yesterday was another long dull Sunday. Time in a prison passes slowly. The officer of the day comes in on a tour of inspection; if he is a gentleman his visit is an agreeable episode, if otherwise, which is most frequently the case, he adds insult to injury, and his presence is a nuisance. That over, and our two meals swallowed, the leaden hours drop on to us again and drag heavily along until nine o'clock, P. M., when the lights are extinguished, then our misery becomes invisible. We and darkness keep the secret between us, and many is the hour we pass in silent sad communion. We hear numerous reports from the lower quarters: prisoners complaining of insufficient food. God help them if it is any worse than when I was there. I wonder if it can be true that the prisoners' rations are sold, and the money pocketed, while the poor fellows are left to starve on less than half of prison allowance. The matter ought to be looked into by those in higher authority.

JAN. 20, 1863.—Still heavy complaints from below about not getting enough to eat, and if this thing continues they will all be in the hospital or grave yard in a very short time. All through the night may be heard coughing, swearing, singing and praying, sometimes drowned by almost unearthly noises, issuing from uproarous gangs, laughing, shouting, stamping and howling, making night hideous with their unnatural clang. It is surely a hell on earth.

JAN. 22.—A very notable day for me, the grand epoch in my prison life. I have enjoyed 30 minutes conversation with my dear wife—*a whole half hour ! !*

> If measured by its length of bliss
> I surely lived an age in this,
> For in a moment's rapturous thrill
> Was joy enough a life to fill.

I could rhyme along *ad infinitum*, but the thirty minutes came to an end. The time was up, she had to go. If possible she will see me again, though I scarce dare hope it. It was with great difficulty she succeeded to-day; the Provost Marshal told her it was against the rules, but she plead so hard that he granted her a permit.

JAN. 23.—Did not get to see my wife to-day. She went to the Provost's office and tried again to obtain a permit, but was denied; the best thing she could do was to write me a note, informing me of her unsuccessful efforts, and that she would leave St. Louis to-night on the one o'clock train. May God protect her in her midnight journey.

JAN. 25.—We hear nothing of an exchange, fear it will be some time before one takes place. Prison life grows duller, wish they would hurry up and get the thing over, it is not very entertaining to sit here and wait the result. Why don't they clear out the prisons and let us fight it out?

JAN. 28.—Some of the Federal officers now guarding us are a disgrace to the military service. They do not understand the first principles of gentlemanly courtesy, and as for bravery, who ever heard of a brave man insulting a woman or a helpless prisoner. An ignorant ruffian might, and the source would be considered, but an officer in the army of a country, making the boasts and pretensions which the United States do, is expected to possess some refinement. Hence I assert that *Col. Kinkaid* is a disgrace to the stars and stripes. He told some five or six Confederate officers that he would not believe one of them on oath, and that their wives, and indeed all the Southern women, were prostitutes of the very lowest class. Such language coming from an object occupying a position which a gentleman ought to fill, needs no comment. Did it ever occur to the *uniform* that the tables might be turned? He would whine a different tune if he were in a Confederate prison, however he will never be so fortunate, for a person of his *stripe* never goes where there is any danger of being captured.

The officers of the prison, Capt. Masterson, sergeants Kyser and Glenn, we find no fault with at present. They extend us all the kindness and courtesy which the nature of the case requires and permits, especially Kyser, who has the respect of every officer in prison; but the officers of the regiment now guarding us, are perfect devils—there is nothing too low, mean or insulting, for them to say or do.

JAN. 31, 1863.—Was introduced to McDowel's College just one month ago to-night. Have learned but little in the way of dissecting the human body, not for the want of subjects however, as there are three or four deaths every day. Received a present yesterday from Mrs. Meredith, the prisoner's friend, consisting of a pair of drawers, pair of socks, and a shirt; articles of which I stood in great need. God bless the aged Dorcas.

FEB. 2.—An old woman has for some time been allowed to visit our prison door, and peddle out such little articles as we have need of, and are able to buy, such as edibles, paper, pens and ink. She was a great *institution;* indeed, we regarded her as a necessity. They tell us she is to come no more—prohibited because she is a Southern sympathizer. Poor old woman, wish she had had Union notions, it was the contents of her basket that we appreciated.

FEB. 3.—We are now guarded by the 37th Iowa, called the "Silver Greys," composed mostly of old gentlemen—nice old fellows, kind and fatherly—wish I could say as much for some of their officers, especially Kinkaid and one Malcolm.

FEB. 5.—Were informed to-day that no exchange of officers will take place until President Davis recalls that "blood-thirsty proclamation" relative to retaining Federal officers. Have seen some fine specimens of birds, which formerly belonged to McDowel's museum, but all in a ruined condition, the prisoners crowding round in their dirt and despair have wrought a great deal of destruction on the Doctor's premises. The walls are literally covered with names and scribble. Many a poor fellow has written here the only epitaph he will ever have. We often hear of prison walls having ears; old Gratiot will have a "tongue to tell a tale," which, if it were told, would "curdle the blood in the veins of youth."

FEB. 7.—Learned to-day that several of the "Grey Beards" or Silver Greys, have deserted, and gone, nobody knows where, probably to Dixie to see Uncle Jeff, as it is said that some of them liked him a great deal better than Old Abe. So much for the wisdom of age. Time may bring all the Yankees to their senses; though I must confess, the old Father will have a pretty heavy undertaking, for they are "joined to their idols."

FEB. 10, 1863,—The Southern ladies of St. Louis by their untiring kindness, make us forget as far as possible, that we are strangers as well as prisoners. Our own families could do no more for us. We are continually receiving from their hands, contributions of clothing, to be distributed among the most needy. The only return the helpless captive can make is fervently to pray, "God bless them."

We are divided into messes, six or seven together, and take it by turns cooking. It looks odd to see a man round with an apron on, cooking and washing dishes. Since they have let our "Old Woman" come back and sell to us, we get along pretty well—fix up a bread pudding occasionally, probably not in the style our lady wives would order, but we enjoy it hugely.

FEB. 12.—I learned to-day that my brother Dan. Frost is a Colonel in the Federal army, and his son a Major. Strange position for them to occupy. With Dan's opportunities he ought to have known better; he is a noble man, I love him like a father, but I fear he is fighting against his principles.

Graduates have been rather scarce this winter, but once in a while we send out a hopeful to take the oath, give bond and security, and join the militia. I won't take my diploma just yet, don't feel prepared to *pay* for it.

FEB. 16.—In the lower quarters are four very old men, who all have a ball and chain, weighing from 50 to 60 pounds, attached to their legs. These implements of torture they drag round whenever they wish to move. Grey hairs and chains did not use to match well in America, they were only found as rare specimens, in the dungeons of the old world, but we are progressive; we manufacture our own curiosities.

Our *gentlemanly* officers in command, have issued instructions to the guard to "run his boyonet through the d—d rebels" if they crowd round the door when the old peddling woman comes.

FEB. 24.—Have just returned from the hospital, was there just one week. The Doctor pronounced my case bronchites; suffered very much with my throat and breast, and a distressing cough. For the first three days I grew no better, the medicine seemed to have no effect, but on the fourth my cough loosened, and I improved rapidly. I was placed in a comfortable room with three others, and we were visited daily by the Sisters of Charity, who administered our medicine, brought us our food, &c. I attribute my speedy recovery to their kind attentions, and womanly nursing.

FEB. 25.—Eighty-five prisoners were sent off to-day—some say for exchange, others for Alton, I lean to the latter opinion. Among them was one man, very feeble, who was kept up with the rest by being pushed along with the bayonet. A pretty sharp argument and strong stimulus.

FEB. 26.—Some 70 or 80 prisoners were brought down from Alton to-day, for trial. Col. Ben. Hawkins, of Marion county, Mo., made his escape from prison last night. May success attend him.

FEB. 27.—Sixty more prisoners left here to-day for Alton. It is said, whether truly or not, time must determine, that they are taken there for the purpose of being sent off on exchange. The weather is miserably gloomy, and the sickness in the hospital is proving very fatal in the last few days.

MARCH 1, 1863.—Some four or five prisoners made an attempt to escape last night and all succeeded but one unlucky dog, who was recaptured. They brought him in and hung him up by the neck until he was nearly dead, when the Captain came in, and interfered, and had him taken down. The bloody villians would have murdered him outright. They tried to make him tell who were concerned in the plot; but he was true to the last, they could not torture him into turning traitor. That's the stuff the martyrs are made of.

MARCH 2.—Yesterday evening the Feds arrested three "Secesh" ladies for waving their handkerchiefs at the prisoners as they passed up the street. They were taken to Col. Kinkaid's quarters and kept an hour or so and then released. It was arranged in going to the Col's quarters that they would either have to pass under the Federal flag or walk out into the street, the tantalizing creatures preferred the latter course; left the guard and took the street, returning to his protection as soon as the obstacle was passed. As they were going home they had to pass us again, and woman like, they gave us another wave, and went off laughing.

> O woman, woman, light of life,
> But cause of so much fuss and strife,
> If I could half your foibles tell
> You'd laugh at me—I know it well.

MARCH 3.—The small-pox has broken out among the prisoners, two cases to-day, taken to the small-pox hospital. One hundred and forty prisoners were notified to leave to-morrow; destination unknown. Several prisoners have been released within the last few days. Andrew W. Lydick, of Marion county, has also been released on oath and bond. He was arrested several months ago and brought to this place, where he has remained ever since. Have never learned the cause which led to his arrest, but suppose it was because he is a rebel.

MARCH 6.—Rumors the last two days of Federal reverses at Vicksburg—large numbers reported drowned. We cannot know anything certainly, as we are not permitted to see the newspapers.

MARCH 8.—This has been another long and tedious Sunday. Over one hundred more prisoners notified to leave to-morrow. Those who went off Wednesday have gone to Washington on exchange

MARCH 9.—Received a box from my wife to-day, containing a lot of butter, some peach, tomato, and blackberry preserves, two bottles of catsup, and a fine large ham. Had to have a fresh introduction; have not seen such delicacies for so long we had become strangers. As none of the mess were better acquainted, we introduced ourselves, and soon enjoyed a sweet familiarity.

MARCH 10.—The prisoners notified on the 8th left to-day for Alton. Old Mrs. Meredith was arrested to-day for distributing clothing to them. A cowardly act, disgraceful to the pantaloons inhabited by the creatures who commited it.

MARCH 11.—Over one hundred prisoners arrived to-day from Alton, and seventy-five or eighty from Tennessee, the latter, after remaining but a short time, were sent up to Alton. Capt. Masterson had the officer who arrested Mrs. Meredith, placed under arrest. Capt M. seems to know the good old lady. Says she has always been known as the friend of the needy and suffering, and since the prisons have been established in St. Louis, she has interested herself particularly in endeavors to alleviate in some degree the miseries within their walls. She is so well known and so thoroughly respected, that she obtained a permanent pass from the Provost to visit the prisoners whenever she saw proper. I hope her works of mercy will not again be disturbed in a similar manner. Capt. Masterson deserves honor for his prompt and manly course.

MARCH 12.—Capt. J. W. Johnson has been sent to the small-pox hospital. The last few days have developed several new cases. The only wonder is, that every disease under heaven does not break out in the lower quarters; half starved and crowded together as they are, in their dirt and rags.

MARCH 13, 1868.—Five Confederate officers made their escape this morning, and because Capt. Barr, Finney, myself and five or six others, *could not* (?) tell how it occurred, we were thrown into the strong room and locked up. It is enough to make the old d—l mad to be confined in such a place. It is dark and gloomy, the weather cold and damp, we have no fire, nothing to sit on, not allowed to have our bed clothes to wrap in, the smoke comes down the chimney, so as to nearly stifle us, and beside, they starved us till after night, when they let us out a little while to *graze*. We have never heard the full particulars as to the manner in which our friends effected their escape, but as near as we have learned is as follows: It seems that the leader got an over coat resembling the kind the Federal officers wear, and yesterday evening went to the guard who stands at the front door, and represented himself as a Federal surgeon, asking the guard at the same time if he had seen anything of the ambulance which was to convey three or four patients to the small-pox island. The guard informed him he had not. The would-be surgeon then remarked that "that was a great way to do business, and if it did not come this evening they would have to walk there in the morning." So this morning, bright and early, the Dr. learning from the same guard that the ambulance had not arrived, made preparations to foot it. He then went up stairs and informed his patients he was ready. They all followed him down stairs, out the front door into the street, which was the last we saw of Major Rucker, Captain Stemmons, Harvey Rucker, and two others unknown to us. As they passed out one of the patients had a bandage around his head, and another his arm in a sling, all of which was well calculated to deceive the most vigilant.

MARCH 14.—To-day I am twenty-nine years old. Its my birth day, and so I must enjoy it. Why not? What's to hinder? No noise and bustle and confusion. Under no obligations to kill myself eating the good things prepared by loving hands. No important business to occupy my time, and interfere with my pleasure. Oh no, on the contrary. I have a retired corner in a military dungeon, in place of shaking hands with congratulating friends, I shake quietly with the cold. I have time and opportunity to reflect, and food for reflection—if not for the stomach. I enjoy myself *exquisitely*, but—I am not selfish—I wouldn't be on my birthday—if I could change places with my enemy I would resign in his favor.

MARCH 16.—Time hangs heavily and drags slowly. They invade the sacred precincts of our solemn dungeon, by placing two mutinous Feds among us to-day which was more than even our pleasure could suffer—if we must take lodgings in the strong room let it at least, be with a select crowd. It ain't so much the way you live as the company you keep. We managed to convey such an intimation to Kyser and he very kindly relieved us of their presence.

MARCH 17, 1863.—Was transferred back to old quarters to-day. Do not know how it happens that *I alone* am sent back, when we were all equally guilty of the same offence—not telling on our friends.

MARCH 18.—Several citzens were brought in while I was in the lock-up. One of them—Dr. Merwin, received the gratifying intelligence that his property had been confiscated, and would be used for the benefit of the United States Government. I thought he would go crazy when he heard it, he was so filled with rage and indignation. They won't allow his wife to come near the prison. I feel sorry for him; his offence, is corresponding with his friends in Dixie. Our institution has *graduated* a few! Suppose they are now practicing their *profession* in the State militia. I had a letter from a brother-in-law in Ohio, advising me to the same course. I don't see it in that light. I replied thanking him for his kind feelings, and good advice; but was not prepared to act upon his suggestions. He seems honestly to love the Union. I wonder if he thinks the North are fighting to restore it? It's my opinion he'll see the negro rise above the Union, if his *patriotic* party have their way.

MARCH 19.—Under a confiscation order issued by Gen. Curtiss, my friend, Capt. Sam. Barr, lost over $500 in gold, his whole wealth inside the prison walls; under other circumstances, the sum would be trifling; but here, five hundred dollars means a good deal. Is the Federal Government bankrupt, that she has to rob her prisoners to raise money for carrying on the war?

MARCH 20.—Last night our College received an addition of 20 new students; among the rest some four or five Yankee deserters.

MARCH 21.—Had the pleasure to-day of looking on two or three familiar faces, Mr. and Mrs. Thompson, and a young lady whose name I do not know, from Palmyra, Mo. They came to see a brother of Mrs. T's—Moses Bates, who was captured at Iuka.

MARCH 25.—Last night about 12 o'clock, two more inmates were added to our room. They are from Columbus, Ky., charged with smuggling goods through to the Confederates, which they deny, and say they are "good Union," and were in the employ of the United States Government. Hope after this when they bring their "Unionites" here, they will quarter them somewhere else, we do not want them with us.

We have heard from some of our friends at Camp Chase, Ohio; they like that prison better than this; they are allowed more privileges, and have plenty of room for exercise.

MARCH 26.—Several prisoners from Alton, arrived here for trial. All the prisoners of war at that point, leave next week for exchange. Wish we could have the pleasure of bearing them company, but I suppose that is impossible, as they say exchanging officers has played out.

MARCH 27.—Learned to-day that Gen. Bragg's wife died on the

23rd inst., at Tullahoma, Miss.; also that Bragg had whipped Rosecrans, and that Gen. Frank Blair and his command had been captured; all of which, however, needs confirmation.

MARCH 28.—Received another letter from my wife, enclosing one from my mother in Ohio, who is very sorry I am not in the Union army. I also am sorry to vex her righteous heart, but I take Davy Crockett's motto, "Be sure you are right, then go ahead."

MARCH 30.—Several prisoners arrived yesterday from the South West. I suppose at last we are going to have an exchange, as rations are now being cooked up for a large number who leave to-morrow. They are in the best of spirits, rejoicing over the prospect of getting back to Dixie once more.

MARCH 31.—Two more prisoners made their escape last night. One had a ball and chain attached to his leg, which he succeeded in getting off before he left; but how it was accomplished, is a fact of which I am not in possession. I only know that I rejoice with them, and send my sincerest congratulations after them; would be pleased to do myself the honor of conveying them in person, for

> "My limbs are bowed, though not with toil,
> But rusted with a vile repose,
> For they have been a dungeon's spoil
> And mine has been the fate of those.
> To whom the goodly earth and air
> Are bound, and barr'd—forbidden fare.
>
> Our bread is such as captives' tears
> Have moistened many a thousand years,
> Since man first pent his fellow men
> Like brutes within an iron den."

APRIL 2, 1863.—Four hundred and eighty-four prisoners left to-day, on exchange, for City point, Va. We understand there is a prospect of an enchange of officers soon. The news is not depressing. Had a letter from a married sister in Ohio, advising me to take the oath and be a good Union man. Will study on it awhile first. Won't join until I am converted.

APRIL 3.—Have not as yet been called on for exchange—hope our time will come soon, as we are all anxious to bid farewell to Gratiot. It is said, however, that we will leave some time next week.

Mrs. Jeff. Thompson, Mrs. Calhoun and a Mr. Bently, were all arrested to-day. The ladies were sent to the female prison, so we are informed by Mr. Bently, who was sent here.

APRIL 5.—Mrs. McLure, a very kind friend of the prisoners, is now under arrest in her own house, which has been converted into a military prison for ladies. Shouldn't wonder if the Yanks succeeded, they are an inventive race. Who but them would ever have thought of making war on women? Wonder if they will hang or burn any of them for witches? Don't blame them for making fun of the word "chivalry;" no doubt it does sound queer to them, they don't understand it.

APRIL 6.—News to-day is: The Feds have taken Charleston— Loss heavy on both sides. Wants confirmation.

APRIL 7.—Witnessed a fight to-day between an officer and a private of the regiment now guarding us. Happy to say the officer came out second best.

APRIL 8.—Twenty-eight prisoners left here to-day for Alton, to remain during the war, but the boat having departed they returned —will go to-morrow. One of them, Lieut. Kennard, from Batesville, Ark., is sentenced to hard labor during the war. Twenty-four new ones have just arrived—captured at Yazoo Pass.

They are now preparing a room in the round building in which to imprison the ladies. I made the acquaintance of the place on my first arrival here, it is admirably adapted, of course, to accommodate the tender natures of the fair sex or it would not have been selected, but I acknowledge my faculties are too obtuse to appreciate the advantages. Our quarters are bad enough for us, but we consider them far preferable to the round building. However, the God-and-humanitarians have too much benevolent intellect to commit a wrong. This is Progress, if we leather-heads could only see it.

APRIL 10.—The capture of Charleston turns out to be a hoax, gotten up for election purposes. Our lady comrades have not, as yet, arrived; their quarters being about ready, we look for them to-morrow. The Yankee plan with regard to the woman part of the war is not fully developed. I don't know how they rank them, or what will be done about an exchange. We have no women prisoners—we have not progressed that far. Do they propose to redeem their men with our ladies? O the wondrous, deep, mysterious depths of Yankee strategy.

APRIL 14.—Been jogging along, for several days, the same old dull rate—nothing of interest transpiring. It seems our side had decidedly the best of the engagement at Charleston; it is also reported that Gen. Foster has surrendered to our forces at Washington, N. C., however, we believe nothing here, either good or bad; any news that falls to us is only waste crumbs any way; if we are ever exchanged we may have an opportunity of ascertaining some facts.

APRIL 15.—Thank God, we have been called for exchange; notified to be ready by to-morrow or next day. Will be sent to City Point, Va.

APRIL 16.—At the writing of this, a large fire can be seen west of the prison; several have occurrred within the last week. It is said one party is trying to burn out the other. The spirit of enlightenment is abroad, it blazes forth in many a burning homestead.

APRIL 18.—Nothing of interest to-day; still making preparations for an exchange.

APRIL 19.—One of the female prisoners arrived to-day, and is now in the lock-up. She is a Mrs. Campbell, from Memphis, Tenn. The male prisoners were locked in their rooms, to prevent them from seeing her as she passed; but it did no good, for we cut a hole through a plank they nailed over our window, and all got a good look at her. She does not appear in the least subjugated.

APRIL 20.—We hear that Gen. Wheeler has been having quite a run of success down in Tennessee. Captured a large number of Federal officers and privates, and $30,000 in money, besides destroying several trains.

APRIL 21.—Will leave to-morrow—at least we have been notified to that effect. We are to be paroled to travel East, which will be much more pleasant than having a guard over us.

APRIL 22, 1863.—Paroled to limits of the city from half-past two until four, when I am to join the rest of the prisoners at the ferry, and all proceed on our way to City Point. Went to Barnum's Hotel, where I met with a lady friend, from Marion Co., who is visiting the city to see her husband, now in Gratiot street prison. We went together to the Provost Marshal's office, where I found my brother and sister-in-law, Mr. and Mrs. Bradley, who were visiting St. Louis on a bridal trip, and were then at the office to procure a permit to visit me in prison. It was a pleasant and delightful surprise. They brought me a letter from my wife, and a bundle, containing among other things, my share of the wedding feast. We returned to the hotel, and remained until four. I insisted on their accompanying me to the river and seeing us off. They kindly consented, and when we reached the ferry the prisoners had gone over; we crossed next trip; how I enjoyed every precious moment. We found the cars just ready to start, bade a hasty "farewell" and I jumped aboard—soon under headway for Indianapolis. We have passed through some beautiful towns, everything is cheering, enjoy ourselves splendidly, plenty to eat of the best quality. The officers in charge, Major White and Capt. Burns, are very kind, showing us every gentlemanly courtesy.

April 23.—Morning—Now traveling in Indiana, changed cars at Indianapolis. Afternoon—In Ohio, changed cars at Crestline for Pittsburgh, Pa. Eight o'clock, evening—Pittsburgh; have had a good supper; been allowed to walk around and see the towns whenever the cars stopped long enough. Could buy a dinner for fifty cents, sometimes for twenty-five. The Yankee officers are quite sociable, they call on us for a song, we give them "Old John Brown;" they reply with "We'll hang Jeff Davis on a sour apple tree," &c. The citizens manifest a good deal of curiosity; ask us many questions, some we answer.

April 24.—Reached Philadelphia to-day. Seem to be regarded as rare and curious specimens; more or less interesting, according to circumstances. We hear such remarks as, "They look something like our men, only not dressed so well." Others approach us and offer to purchase our gum rings, present us with copperhead breast-pins, and tell us that "Old Abe can never enforce the draft, the North will resist it to the last." As we were marching from the depot to the river, we had an exhibition of the milk of human kindness, as given by, and sucked from the breast of some tender fair, of the Quaker City. Women and children called out to us, telling us we were "dirty mean devils," and expressed the opinion, that the best thing to do with us, was to throw us into the Delaware. We listened, hoping to catch some enlightenment, as we passed through the God-favored section. Halting in the street to rest, we were assaulted by a mob, broomsticks were hurled at us, together with every epithet of abuse which adorns the rich language of the eloquent East. We bowed to the storm and acknowledged their superiority; we have seen nothing like it in the South. As we proceeded on our way the crowd followed. We went on board the steamer 'Major Reybold,' laid at the quay about an hour and left for Fort Delaware, situated on an island sixty miles below Philadelphia, which we reached a little after dark, when we were conducted to our quarters, where we met several old Gratiot acquaintances who left St. Louis before us.

APRIL 25.—Discover this morning that Fort Delaware is the hardest prison hotel we have seen. The lower quarters at Gratiot were bad enough, God knows, with disease, starvation and dirt, but this elegant and select little "Island Home" has refined upon the abstemiousness of their habits, the rigorous denial practiced upon our appetites is wonderful, we indulge freely in nothing except the water from the bay, which affects all who use it with diarrhea; many are sick, but our craving stomach must be filled, it cries out continually, "give, give," and the table has almost literally nothing to offer. Five hundred and fifty-three of us starve around the same board.

APRIL 26.—St. Louis and Springfield are paradises compared with this, all are complaining of hunger. Do not know what we would have done if it had not been for a barrel of oysters we were allowed to purchase from an oyster boat. We relished them as only such poor hungry devils could.

APRIL 27.—The boat has at last arrived which is to carry us to City Point. We are anxious for any change from this miserable hell. I am feeling quite miserable in health.

APRIL 28.—Been very sick all night with cholera morbus; bad water and hunger, and then the oysters. We have often wished since we have been here, that we could gather up the crumbs which we have seen our wives shake from their table cloths; we would have a scrabble with the dogs for the best bone. I suppose the Feds think it is all right, and it must be, for they are "honorable gentlemen" and the last best work of Heaven in the way of philanthropy. The self-conceited, cruel, tyranical boasters. How they can stand up in the face of God's daylight, and lay a charge at any man's door, is more than I can see. Let the remnants of their prison wrecks tell the story, and that's only a preface.

APRIL 29.—After signing a parole not to take up arms against the United States until regularly exchanged, we left Fort Delaware on the steamer "State of Maine" for City Point, passed Brandywine lighthouse, and at six o'clock went into break-water and anchored for the night. Break-water is a place constructed by Uncle Sam for the protection of vessels during a storm. The boat is much crowded, and many sick on board; scarcely any room to lie down. It is horrid, but we hope for a change.

APRIL 30.—Weighed anchor this morning, passed Capes Henlopen and Charles, and at six o'clock this evening, cast anchor off Fortress Monroe, and in sight of fort Rip-Raps. We lost sight of land three times; the sea was rough, and a great many were sea sick all the while. The commissary arrangements of the vessel are still worse than those at Fort Delaware. The sour musty bread, chopped into scraps, is in one barrel, and slices of pickle pork—cooked at the fort, in another. A man stands by both, and when rations are to be issued, they plunge their dirty hands into the barrels, and draw out the disgusting morsels and hand them to the prisoners; some swallow them, other stomachs find it impossible. Sick any way, I turned in loathing from the fifthy looking stuff. How I could have relished some of our clean, plain Dixie cornbread. The Federals should never complain of our not feeding their prisoners, whose fare is far preferable to ours; besides being cleaner.

There are a great many vessels of all kinds, lying off Fortress Monroe, some of them mounted with heavy guns, which look as though one broadside would tear a vessel to atoms.

MAY 2, 1863.—Weighed anchor this morning, and arrived at City Point at four o'clock this evening. Have seen the ruins of the first brick church ever built in Virginia. It was erected by John Smith; also the ruins of several fine residences, destroyed by the Federals. The scenery on James river is beautiful, the eye feasts along its banks. We came through from Fort Delaware with Colonel Zarvoni. He had been in confinement over twenty-two months, and twelve of that time in a dungeon; two weeks before he was exchanged the light had to be let in to him gradually. Close confinement has very much effected his sight and hearing. Another vessel also arrived this evening, at the Point, having on board the wife and nieces of Alabama Simms, being sent outside the Federal lines.

MAY 4.—Still on board the transport, will not get off until night. Several ladies came down from Petersburg to-day; they were in fine spirits over Lee's big victory at Chancellorsville, achieved over "fighting Joe Hooker." We gave three rousing cheers for Lee, Jackson, Davis and the Confederacy. It did our lungs good.

MAY 5.—Last night at one o'clock, we reached Petersburg, Va., to-day at ten A. M., in parole camp—find several friends from St. Louis; among the number Capt. Sam. Barr, who came through under a ficticious name.

## CHAPTER IV.

GREAT EXCITEMENT AT PETERSBURG, VA.; GENERAL WHIT-
FIELD'S RESIDENCE, AT DEMOPOLIS, ALA.; CAPTURE OF JACK-
SON, MISS.; BATTLE OF HELENA, ARK.; "MAM AND HER
GALS;" ARRIVAL AT LITTLE ROCK; EXILES FROM ST. LOUIS;
HIGH LIVING, &C., &C.

MAY 6.—There is great excitement prevailing in Petersburg to-day, caused by the success of a body of Federal cavalry in making a raid within three miles of Richmond. The people are wild with the spirit of pursuit; every horse and mule that can be had is pressed into service; ladies visiting the city in their fine carriages, give up their horses leaving themselves no means of getting home. Our people are making a terrible struggle with a cruel, relentless, vindictive foe. Surely God will not curse the land with their ultimate success, for it is beyond the scope of imagination to conceive the length to which their unbridled fanaticism might run. There is nothing, human or divine, too reverend or sacred for the pollution of their unholy touch. We are but a little flock standing in the breach against them, if we are swept away the last vestage of constitutional liberty in America perishes with us, and in place of the old safeguards, and solid substantial law, we will be blown about by every newfangled notion that hitches itself in the crochety brain of the few leading Pharisees of the North. Petersburg is an interesting place, softened here and there with footprints of the olden time. The Old Virginia air seems pregnant with the invisible presence of departed statesmen. Ah, "there were giants in those days." Provisions are scarce and high; the poor suffer. We are ordered to report at the parole camp at Jackson, Miss.

MAY 10.—Thursday, Friday and Saturday were traveling on the cars from Petersburg, Va., to Montgomery, Ala.; passed through portions of North and South Carolina, and Georgia. Augusta, Ga., is one of the prettiest places we have seen. The streets are very wide with a row of trees in the centre, making a cool delightful shade. We arrived to-day per steamer Virginia, at Selma, Ala., where we had the pleasure of listening to an excellent old fashioned Methodist sermon, which reminded us of the fact that there was a high official claiming our loyal allegiance without any regard to the petty chieftians under whose banners we might fight out the ephemeral quarrels of this transitory scene; high above the din, and dust, and smoke of our puny collisions, floats the true flag, the royal banner, the standard of salvation. It is meat and drink for the soul to be thus lifted above itself. If our ministers would all soar beyond the trifling concerns of time losing themselves in the radiance of Heaven, and bearing us with them into that pure atmosphere, we would come down into the actual walks of life, better and stronger men, but when they too fight with us in the same arena, we contend with them, man against man, my opinion for your opinion, the cross is so mixed up with the "bars" and "stripes" that we only perceive it when it is carried near our own flag.

MAY 11.—We dined to-day with Mr. Gaius Whitfield, at Demopolis, Ala., on the Tombigbee river, expecting to leave by the train in the afternoon; but the cars being full and running over, we were compelled to wait for the next trip. The Whitfields are a highly refined and elegant family, and blessed with abundant stores of this world's goods. We visited the brother of our host, whom we found living in palatial splendor, his house and grounds were perfectly enchanting; all that taste and comfort could require and wealth procure, we found in magnificent abundance; but among fruits, flowers, and fountains and lakes, grottoes and statuary, books, music and paintings, furniture—modern and antique, mirrors, carpets, and all the costly etceteras of a rich mansion of modern times the rarest gem we found, was Miss Bessie, Gen. Whitfield's daughter, the lovely fairy of the place.

MAY 14.—We are now at Brandon, Miss., stopping with Capt. Sam. Barr, who is very sick. When we reached this place we found an excellent dinner at the depot, prepared by the ladies, who feed from one to six hundred soldiers a day. Capt. Barr is at the house of Mrs. Col. Jaynes, who is giving him every care and attention. At one time to-day while on the train, we thought the Capt. was in great danger. It seems he was taken with cramp in the stomach, and it was some time before we could get anything that would give him relief. The ladies on board were very kind, and did all in their power to relieve him. Some would send us their camphor bottles, and others would suggest this thing and that as an excellent remedy, but one old lady was particularly anxious that we should give him some turpentine, remarking, at the same time, "that whenever any of her mother's children took the colic she would always give them that, and it was certain to carry the misery smack smooth off with it." However the Captain got better before we found it necessary to resort to the above remedy.

We hear constant firing in the direction of Jackson—feel a vague uneasiness. Evening—The Feds have taken Jackson and we have to *skedaddle* on the back track, the way we come.

MAY 15.—Left Brandon this morning at day break, and arrived at Meridian at three o'clock, P. M., where we will remain until further orders. The citizens are much frightened all along the railroad, expecting the Feds every minute.

MAY 17.—Ordered yesterday to report at Demopolis at parole camp, which we did to-day at twelve o'clock. We occupy the Fair ground, which is used as a camp for paroled prisoners.

MAY 18.—Took breakfast this morning with the Hon. Frank Lyons, Congressman from this district; was introduced to his wife and daughters, who are fine specimens of the Southern lady. We were entertained by the family with the most hospitable kindness and courtesy.

MAY 22.—Time passes slowly in camp. Capt C., quite ill, and I not much better. A prison does not turn out very able bodied men. The ladies in this vicinity, especially Mrs. Gaius Whitfield, have been very kind in supplying us with comforts, and even delicacies.

MAY 24.—Growing worse. Yesterday, Capt. Reynolds of Mo.,

made arrangements for sending us into the country. Accordingly we find ourselves at the residence of Mrs. Torbot, in a neat, comfortable room, with a servant at our command, and ourself in charge of that excellent lady, who seems determined to nurse and feed us into health and strength. She is an English lady, and very particular, gives us to understand that she commands this post. We will be most happy to obey orders.

MAY 29.—To-day it is beautiful; bright and clear with a cheerful breeze, the green woods and waving fields, fairly laugh in the sunshine, and the happy little birds twittering and hopping from bough to bough seem to pour out their grateful songs in sweet melodious notes of praise to God. Would we were as happy and cheerful as they.

MAY 31.—Notice no change in cough; thought the palate of my throat too long, and had about a fourth of an inch of it cut off this morning. The doctor had to make three attempts before he succeeded, and the operation was somewhat painful.

JUNE 1, 1863.—My throat is very sore to-day, caused by having the palate clipped, it is almost impossible to swallow. If well enough will visit Mrs. Torbot's plantation to-morrow.

JUNE 4.—Visited the plantation Tuesday, had a fine plum hunt; next day visited Mrs. Rebecca Torbot's where we were regaled with splendid refreshments, wine, cake, &c. To-day I feel much better, excellent appetite, and plenty of good things to gratify it. My furlough is extended ten days longer. I believe I prefer this to Gratiot.

JUNE 5.—During "the lone starry hours" of last night, I was awakened from my slumbers by a beautiful serenade. I arose and looked out, six young ladies were beneath my window, making night all melody with their entrancing notes. Of course I would rather have seen a Federal guard with their bayonets glistening. The singing was splendid, and I would have enjoyed it much better had I not, while feeling my way in the dark, toward the window, hit my foot against a rocking chair, and fell sprawling on the floor.

JUNE 15.—My furlough having expired I report to Gen. Johnson, at Jackson, Miss. I shall ever remember with lively gratitude, my pleasant sojourn under the hospitable roof of the kind and excellent Mrs. Torbot. My lot has seldom been cast with a more choice and genial circle, her neighbors partake of her own warm spirit, they are full of love and all good works. It is worth while starving and freezing in a Federal prison, sworn at and kicked round by Yankee officer's, and mobbed by the women, to have it all repaid by such gentle nursing and kind attention. Am now at Demopolis, will leave to-morrow.

JUNE 18.—Staid Monday night with Mr. Whitfield, at Demopolis—his lady being ill we did not see her. On Tuesday we were in Meridian; Wednesday we reached Forest, where the hotels were so crowded we had to sleep in the cars, a prey to the mosquitoes. To-day I am in Canton, stopping with my old friend Mr. Freeman, where, in company with my brother John, I had such a pleasant visit last summer. Miss Sallie is as handsome as ever. At Jackson we reported to Gen. Johnson, who ordered us to our commands, over in the Trans-Mississippi department. We will start in five or six days.

JUNE 21.—Wrote a letter Friday to my wife, will send by Mr. McLure, a conductor on the underground railroad. Have plenty of fine music, keep Miss Sallie busy singing and playing for us. We had a pleasant walk to-day to the graveyard, in the centre is a summer house, where we rested in the cool shade. We found written in pencil mark on the wall, the following lines, which cannot be too well considered and remembered :

"Beneath our feet and o'er our head,
Is equal warning given:
Beneath us lie the countless dead,
Above us is the Heaven."

JUNE 24.—Leave Canton to-day. The people are as full of kindness, and generous hospitality, but have not the same active public spirit, which was manifested here last summer; the streets and buildings show a want of attention, and business is not so flourishing; natural result, no doubt, of the state of the whole country. Afternoon—Arrived at Grenada at four o'clock, P. M. Some ladies took us for Federals, we lost no time in correcting the mistake. Had an opportunity of showing them a genuine article, as eighty-two were brought down from above, poor fellows, I know how to sympathize with them; they are not going to downy beds and fairy banquets ; prison life does not hold out an alluring prospect in any country. If they are from the far North, the change will be prostrating, crowded into prison this hot sultry Southern summer time. Our boys that were taken from Florida to Johnson's Island in the winter, died in great numbers from the cold; and those who survived were nearly all diseased. Prisons kill more than the sword.

JUNE 25.—Left Grenada yesterday for Panola, where we bid farewell to the railroad, and prepared to foot it to the river. The Federal army has been over this country and everywhere left footprints of its ravaging track. It reminds one of the hordes of Northern vandals who swept down over the Italian plains during the dark ages. Nothing is spared or protected in their devastating course. Bridges and houses are burned, and women and children turned out of doors to starve. The land is full of squalor and destitution—God help the poor. They carried off a large number of negroes, fifteen hundred from one county. While the act was one of high-handed robbery, it is probably well enough as it leaves fewer mouths to be fed with the scraps which escaped the ruin. To make the deed more insulting they would take the family carriages and fill them with negroes, and have them driven off; then the soldiers would rob the houses and afterwards burn them. Letters that come through to us tell us that people, who were once considered honest and respectable, receive these stolen goods, and use them. We stop this evening with Mr. Short, who shares his crust with us.

JUNE 29.—Stopping within one mile of the Mississippi river, with a Mrs. Godfrey, have had a weary tramp of it—were directed wrong once by a deserter and had to wade through a cane brake in water up to the knees for over two hours; have managed to pick up a little food on the way, found houses occasionally in out of the way places. We wish to cross the river to-morrow, but have our fears—gunboats and transports are pretty thick.

JULY 1, 1863.—Staid last night with Mr. Harrison, near the river bank, and fifteen or twenty miles above Helena; were too tired to cross last night, but to-day we got over, and struck out for a long march, pushed ahead vigorously until we discovered we were lost, when we hunted quarters; found them with Mr. Robinson, near the St. Francis river. He received us cordially, and is entertaining us first rate, his two daughters sing for us, and make us enjoy ourselves splendidly. We went fishing in the evening, and took a canoe ride on the river.

JULY 4.—Having heard that a fight was expected at Helena to-day, we made all diligence to be present on the occasion. Mr. Weatherby, with whom we were stopping, loaned us horses and came with us. We heard the cannonading at a distance of fifteen miles, reached the battle field at nine o'clock, found the fight raging in all its fury; went in with Gen. Marmaduke's men, shot fell thick and fast, and bombs bursted all around us. Continued till twelve, when we were ordered off the field, having celebrated the glorious fourth with a brilliant defeat. We fell back about six miles and remained till morning, when Capt. C. and myself started on the hunt of Gen. Parson's command, which we met on the retreat, five miles from Helena, on the Little Rock road; found several acquaintances who used to belong to my old company, who informed me that my brother John and fifty-nine of the company to which he belonged, had been taken prisoners. The boys said it was the hardest and bloodiest fight they had been in during the war. Gen. Parson's brigade alone lost over seven hundred men, killed, wounded and captured. They were in good spirits, although defeated, and say they are ready to try them again. The road was lined with citizens who come to see if any of their friends had been hurt, and to assist in taking care of the unfortunate wounded.

JULY 5.—Camped last night 18 miles from Helena, weather hot, water scarce, and dust plenty. Marched twenty miles to-day—infantry almost suffocated for water.

JULY 8.—Yesterday was a hard day on the soldiers, they were not able to travel over ten miles, the roads were horrid—mud knee deep in some places. This is a wild rough country. This morning we got a pass from Col. Standish, Gen. Parson's Adjutant-General, and started ahead of the command, and after traveling twenty miles, halted and waited for them to come up. The men were nearly worn out, had been wading through mud and water waist deep. This Arkansas is a delightful country, always a favorite of mine.

JULY 11.—Now at Mrs. Davis' in Woodrough county. Have

been here ever since the ninth. Heard yesterday that Vicksburg had fallen—don't believe it.

JULY 12.—Started again this morning, got to Cash river where we took a boat for "Surrounded Hill;" did not find the command as we expected—will wait here till to-morrow, and then go on to Des Arc.

JULY 13.—Walked to White river this morning, which we crossed in a canoe, and went on to Des Arc, staid there an hour, and struck for the country; reached the house of my old friend Mr. Ivans, six miles from Des Arc, where we will camp for the present.

JULY 14.—Read a dispatch to-day, stating that Lee has had another battle, and captured forty thousand prisoners. Hear also, that the Vicksburg rumor is false, but that Port Hudson has fallen.

JULY 16.—Had a hard chill yesterday, caused by exposure—wading through these sickly swamps. Learn that our command is crossing at Des Arc.

JULY 22.—Have been quite sick, but now improving. Thanks to Mrs. Ivans for her kind nursing. The news now is that both Vicksburg and Port Hudson have fallen. It is impossible to know the straight of anything out here.

JULY 26.—Continuing to improve. I thought last Friday I could venture to Des Arc, while there learned that the command would start next day for Little Rock, and not feeling able to go with them, we turned back to Mr. Ivans', but before we had gone a mile, I was taken with a severe chill, and had to stop over night with Parson Cox, and did not reach Mr. I's until next day. Am grievously tormented with sores, in addition to my other miseries, to say mothing of the confounded mosquitoes that almost run me mad. We are having a fine rain, guess that will mend matters all around. I am feeling better to-day, and hope I will remain so.

JULY 28.—Lying up now at Mr. Adams' until I get over the *verioloid*. Left Mr. Ivans' yesterday, and traveled twenty-five miles; have come eight to-day. Met Dr. Bell, who explained my case to me, the sores are accounted for now. I little thought I would have to come away down here to have the small-pox, when it was so plenty in St. Louis while I was there, and I had so much leisure to enjoy it.

July 29.—Nothing of interest to-day. The command is camped eighteen miles from us. It is reported that the Feds are marching on us in three different columns. Well, let them come, we are prepared to run again, as we have been doing ever since Gen. Price has had a commander over him; if he had the management of affairs we would soon clear the Yanks out of these swamps. It is very galling to the pride of our troops to submit to such continued defeat, when they believe the man of their choice could lead them on to victory. Whether it is true or not, they have an idea that they are disgraced by the incompetency of their leaders.

July 30.—While Capt. C. and myself were on the way from Des Arc to Austin, we stopped for a drink of water at a house where there was an old lady, a married daughter, and a younger one aged about twelve years. As we entered I asked for a drink. The old lady said:

"Thar it is strangers, jes hep yerselves."

We complied, and helped ourselves to seats also. She then ordered the girl to hand us some peaches which had been prepared for dinner.

"Why mam, them's peeled," said the little one.

"You shet your mouth, it don't make no difference, they can eat them as well as eny."

We partook of the proffered fruit and commenced eating, when "mam" remarked:

"We all been nocerlated, and our arms are jist about rotten, keeps us scratchin' all the time."

I looked at my "peeled" peach, and thought about the *scratchin'*, glanced at Capt. C., saw his peach falling, coughed and let my own drop, and got up to go. Asked "mam" if Hickory Plains, a place six miles off, that we had to pass, was a town. She replied:

"'Deed I don't know stranger, I never was thar, nor none of my gals neither, but I *expose* it is."

We left, and on enquiring at the next house, learned that "mam" and her "gals" had been living there ten or twelve years. I give this as a specimen of the Arkansas Traveler.

July 31.—After a walk of 8 miles, reached camp at 10 o'clock this morning; a great deal of sickness among the troops; found some old Gratiot street friends in camp. We leave for Little

Rock to-morrow, to report to Gen. Price and have him decide what we are and where we belong; for my part I shall not grumble if he lays me on the shelf for a while until I can recruit my health some, in my present state I am more of an incumbrance than a help to the army.

AUG. 1, 1863.—Little Rock—arrived to-day at 2 o'clock—pretty place. It contains a great many lady refugees, driven off from their homes in St. Louis, by the sons of light and liberty, the glorious champions of a higher order of civilization. Dont they "thank God they are not as other men?" I do. The following story I heard on my arrival at this place. Among these exiled ladies is one, the wife of a Confederate General, who was forced to leave an infant behind. She begged with all a woman's and a mother's eloquence, not to be seperated from her babe; but her petitions were unavailing. She then remembering the immense sums stolen in the South, thought to bribe them with their glittering God, and offered a large sum of money for permission to take her little one with her, but cruelty was stronger than greed for gold. She was compelled to leave her nurseling, and forced outside the Federal lines. Another lady was with her, and fortunately for them, they succeeded in bringing through a considerable amount of money, their dresses were heavily trimmed with gold coins, covered as buttons; bank bills were rolled up and quilted in their clothing also, and besides they had a good deal more in their pocket books, than was allowed. Just before the boat on which they were sent reached Memphis, the Captain, a man of some delicacy it seems, informed them that they would have to be searched, and pointed out two Irish girls who were to perform the interesting ceremony. Mrs. ——, the General's lady, handed over her pocket book to the Captain and both ladies submitted to the Irish inspection, that through, the pocket book was gallantly returned; the Captain guilty probably, of not stealing in the name of the best government under the sun, but true and loyal to the instincts of a noble manhood.

AUG. 2.—Passed off the day in walking around and looking at the city. The streets present a filthy, neglected appearance. Showing that the attention of the citizens is directed out of the natural channel; everything bears the impress of the war. Having called on Gen. Price yesterday and found him engaged, I repeated my visit to-day, when on examination of my papers, he decided that my company having been reorganized, and new officers elected during my imprisonment, I was released from further duty. Such being the case we desired to return to the east side of the Mississippi, and requested of him a pass, which he granted for that purpose. So we expect to be off in a few days.

AUG. 3.—Left Little Rock this afternoon at three, crossed the river, went as far as Maj. Duff's and put up for the night. Board in Little Rock is from three to five dollars per day. Chewing tobacco five dollars per plug. Smoking do., eight dollars per lb. Melons from one to two dollars apiece. Whiskey sixty dollars per gallon, everything else in proportion. Met a great many old prison acquaintances, officers like myself, without commands. Hear considerable talk about conscription. In passing the depot, we learned that a young lady from the city had gone down as far as Duvall's Bluff to meet a friend just from the army and while there she stepped out on the cow-catcher—when the cars started and ran over her crushing her leg from her thigh to her foot. It is thought she will not recover.

AUG. 4.—Started for camp at seven and arrived at two o'clock. The weather being very warm, we had to travel slowly. The young lady mentioned yesterday has died, she was amiable, intelligent, and beloved by all who knew her.

AUG. 5.—Met with my old friend Col. Priest to day; he is accompanied by Col. Goode—formerly on Parson's staff; they have a recruiting camp in the mountains, and are in procuring salt and ammunition. They are anxious for Captain C. and I to return with them. We will take the matter into consideration and perhaps comply.

AUG. 6.—Our men are becoming disheartened, say the Feds are bound to whip us, many are deserting—six from one company last night; they will find themselves worse whipped if they are caught before they get into the mountains, they will give up the ghost, as well as the cause. We hear that the enemy is crossing White river near Clarendon, we are fortifying for their approach.

AUG. 7.—Enjoyed the pleasure of meeting with Parson Primrose, who made his escape from McDowel's College, while we were fellow students of that institution. We have concluded to go with Cols. Goode and Priest, and try to recruit a company on the border; if all the loose men could be gathered into the army, we would have sufficient strength to make a respectable stand and our soldiers would have their spirits and courage revived. We will make the attempt, and see what we can do.

AUG. 8.—Had a general review of Parson's Brigade to-day. The soldiers made a splendid appearance, and marched well; but they are still deserting every night. There must be a change, if something is not done they will verify their own prophecy. If every shoulder was at the wheel, how readily we could push the thing right along. There is too much "go boys," and not enough " come." In such a cause as ours there should be no half way friend, all who are for us, should be with us, else they are practically against us. A few in the field cannot do it all, while the majority are at home taking the oath and scrambling to save their property. Who saves our property while we are offering our lives for the liberty of all? But it was thus in the time of Washington; he was once left with no more than three thousand men, and they daily deserting, flocking to British posts and taking the oath.

AUG. 9.—Cols. Goode, Priest and Winston, Capt. Winston, myself, and John Miller, left Camp Bayou Metae this morning, and started for the mountains in Izard county, northern part of this state. We travelled fourteen miles and camped near Austin.

AUG. 13.—Been on the march every day—camped last two nights by fine springs of water. Yesterday we had a refreshing rain, took shelter in an old deserted out house, roads rough and mountainous—stopping this evening at Mr. Allen's, three miles from Batesville. We are dirty tired and hungry, but find a remedy for all while our *paper money* lasts. Mrs. A. did some washing for us and when asked to name her charges drawled out " T-w-e-n-t-y fi-v-e c-e-n-t-s a-p-i-e-c-e i-n p-a-p-e-r m-o-n-e-y, t-e-n c-e-n-t-s i-n s-i-l-v-e-r." We chose to pay in *paper money*, for the very good reason that we had no silver, and have not seen any for eighteen months.

AUG. 16.—Been marching along slow and steadily, through the mud, and up the mountains; doubling teams, exerting ourselves, and sometimes using what might in polite circles, be termed, " too emphatic language." But Arkansas is infected in that manner.—Wandering about through the air, and in the woods, and over bad roads particularly are the disembodied spirits of all the rough old words and ways of the early pioneers; ready to jump into the mouth and express themselves through any weary traveller, who may chance to get excited. Our tender wives may rest assured that it is not we who speak, but " those spirits" speaking in us; for they "Play upon a harp of a thousand strings; spirits of just men made perfect."

Well we have reached our regular camping place at last—two miles from Lunonburg—right in the mountains, and on a stream which is aptly called Rocky Bayou. We are a formidable host, strongly intrenched—mountains our bulwarks are, the stream our fresh supply. We marshall thus—

> Three Colonels, Winston, Priest and Goode,
> One Major also, says he's Goode,
> Five Captains of the bravest mood
> Winston and Cosby, and Mitchell and self,
> And C——, (who ordered his name to the shelf,)
> Then privates; we've three, of the highest degree,
> A Shacklett a Miller and Priest,
> If the Feds should attack, we will hurl ourselves back
> And escape without danger the least.

When we arrived the camp was full of visitors; the roughest looking set I ever saw, men women and children, God! the women are all chewing tobacco; with nothing on but their dresses and some of them open in front. As we came along, when we passed a house, all the *wimmen*kind would run to the fence, prop one foot on the third or fourth rail, and stand thus and gaze at us until we were out of sight, however, *we* always turned our heads in another direction.

AUG. 17.—Went out foraging to-day, brought in some beets and beans. The citizens around are very kind—send us in many articles of food. The children are quite primitive in their mode of dress, wear nothing but long tailed shirts, which would be decidedly picturesque if their legs were painted sky blue, however, they are usually ring, streaked, striped, and speckled, with dirt scratches and bites—the interesting little dears, no doubt they would all be kissed on election days, if the women voted.

AUG. 18.—Col. Priest and myself took a ride to day, passed

through some very rough country; rode under the highest bluff on White river, which is six hundred feet above the water. Soldiers, and citizens, names are written all over the face of the rocks, as high up as they could reach or climb; it was a grand sight. The country is very thinly settled, houses five or six miles apart.

AUG. 19.—The weather is warm, the gnats are bad, the ticks bite, the forces are all out, I am lonesome and out of humor. We have got to leave this *shebang* if we expect to do anything. Our prospects here are good for recruiting a regiment in about two hundred years, if we should be visited with no epidemic to carry off the troops. The fact is we are a lot of dead heads, and a dead expense to the Government, and the sooner we make a change, the sooner we will be in a position to command our self respect, if we have no other command under our orders; as it is we are fit subjects for a splendid burlesque. Would'nt the Yanks use it though, if they could take a peep at us on some occasions. Ten officers to three privates and no body knows who is in command. We have pitched upon the wrong place for recruiting; it is farther west than this that Missourians pass, and where *they* are is the place for *us*. There is nothing here to recruit, unless we drive in some of the wild boys and wait until we raise them.

AUG. 24.—Still at the old *shebang*. Nothing "to do, to be, or to suffer," that is worth taking action on. Sometimes we have a turn at pitching horse shoes, then some one goes fishing, and may be we have a fish fry, occasionally we make a raid on a melon patch, then we set around and watch the gradual sure decay of our shoes and pants, wondering what balmy spring, with fragrant breeze and vernal shower will come to them renewing the strength and beauty of their youth. I got into the writing desk of a comrade to day and discovered an old Album which contained the following rude but expressive lines. They run thus:

"I'd rather be a speckled dog,
And pick a well skinned bone;
Than to live such a life as this,
And never hear from home.
Twelve months or more, I've been away,
And s-o-l-d-i-e-r-i-n-g all the time;
And yet up to this very day,
I've not received a line.
Perhaps my name has been forgot
Save where my note is due,
If that's the case, O, who would not
Have out an I. O. U."

AUG. 28.—Have whiled off a few more tedious days, our force is slightly increased, but we are still not strong enough to be sanguine of success in case we should engage a large body of the enemy, who are advancing upon us, hence we will fall back for a better position.

AUG. 29.—" All quiet on the Potomac." We have crossed White river, travelled ten miles, and are camping near an excellent spring of cool water. As we came over the river, the wagon in which John Miller and myself rode, stalled in the middle of the stream where it was deep and swift, our mules could go no farther. Maj. Goode seeing the situation came to our assistance, bringing two horses which we succeeded in hitching to the wagon without getting out. We drove forward, but had not gone more than twenty feet when the Major's off horse, on which he rode stepped on an old sobby plank and fell. Master and horse plunged around for awhile, creating some excitement, but finally we all got to shore with "nobody hurt," but the clothes, and I don't know that the water was bad for them. We are camped on Little Rocky Bayou, a nice stream full of fish, and eel, neighbors are scarce, mountains too thick and rough for settlement.

SEPTEMBER 1, 1863.—As we marched along Sunday, I was surprised at the immense number of women and children, especially the latter: one would imagine that they sprung up spontaneously. We came on them at times, so suddenly and unexpectedly it reminded me of the whistle of Roderick Dhu, when.

"Instant, through copse and heath, arose
Bonnets and spears and bended bows;
On right, on left, above, below,
Spring up at once the lurking foe.
From shingles gray their lances start,
The bracken bush sends forth the dart,
The rushes and the willow-wand
Are bristling into axe and brand,
And every tuft of broom gives life
To plaided warrior armed for strife.
That whistle garrisoned the glen
At once with full five hundred men,
As if the yawning hill to Heaven
A subterranean host had given."

Yesterday Col. Goode had a severe chill, and we were compelled to go into camp. We heard of a good many of our deserters—lurking in the houses in the day time, in the woods at night, they are not worth recruiting, or we would be after them. Poor devils, let them eke out their little span of life. We have traveled fifteen miles to-day, and are now camping within twenty miles of Clinton, wish to reach there to-morrow.

Had an interview this evening, with an old lady, which I will give, after a short description of her personal appearance: Her feet were flat, bare, and very black with dirt, toe nails all split; she was lank, lean, red headed, and freckled; eyes crossed, red, and sore; had a long hook-billed nose, which she was continually picking when not stirring the tobacco in her mouth with her fingers. When she ejected the juice of the weed, the stained saliva would stream from her mouth corners and settle on her chin. I addressed her from curiosity—enquiring about the country. She answered quite glibly:

"Wall, stranger, this is about the roughest country I ever seed, and has got some of the ignorest people; they don't know nothin' theyselves, and don't give they childern no edication at all, they never seed a town nor a steamboat, nor never was no whar."

"No doubt madam, you have traveled, and seen a great deal, and received a fine education?"

"Wall stranger, I do know sumthin, I've been to Batesville, and nigh as sixty miles to Little Rock. Have you got any good *chawin terbacker*, can't git nothin' but *long green*, and I'm tired o' that."

We gave her some tobacco, and then asked her if she enjoyed good health.

"Lawh no, I've been a cripple for I dunno how many years, jis look at my *sore leg*."

I was in for it, and had to look, in order to satisfy the old lady. After that I beat a retreat.

SEPT. 2.—Two years ago to-day, I left Marion county, Mo., and all the friends most near and dear to me on earth, started out full of hope and vigor, to contend for the rights and liberties of my people. It has been my lot to suffer much, but I do not murmur, the sacrifice is freely made, if our independence is established, but the process is slow and discouraging. I sometimes almost lose hope. The North has every advantage but a righteous cause, and we have more than once in the history of the world, seen the "wicked flourish as the green bay tree." We are prone to think God blesses, or curses, as He grants or denies our wishes; but we must remember the countless numbers of His chosen saints, which He has permitted in all ages of the world, to fall victims to just such tyrannical, infuriated, fanatical mobs as are persecuting us.

Though we believe we are right, that our warfare is self defensive, and a solemn duty. Still, in the fulfillment of some design, working out the inscrutable purposes of Heaven, God may permit our overthrow.

SEPT. 3.—Arrived at Clinton to-day at noon, and went into camp one mile South of town. Col. Wood is here with his recruits. Among them I saw several old prison acquaintances, also met with Capt. Wm. Payne, from Palmyra, Mo. Have not decided on a line of action, will await the course of events, and seize on the first promising opportunity. Jayhawkers are thick and troublesome, sometimes collecting in large numbers, and committing serious depredations. They are a band of Kansas outlaws, hated and despised as much in their own State as they are here— the natural off-shoots of old John Brownism, drank their inspiration from the same polluted *pond*. That was the infernal nest that hatched the egg of all our woes. Talk about Fort Sumter's hearing the first gun fired, they forget the Sharp's rifles which Beecher & Co. sent, and John Brown fired at Harper's Ferry, and the churches draped, and muffled bells tolling, in the North, the day he suffered for his crimes.

SEPT. 4.—We were told to-day that Capt. Payne, with forty men, went out yesterday after jayhawkers, had a little brush, and killed one. The jayhawkers have recruited largely among the lower classes in this State. A community of feeling exists among ruffians of all sections. It should be the common object of the regular armies on both sides, to route out all such bands; they are a disgrace to the country that breeds them. In their raids of destruction they spare neither friend or foe, killing both Northern and Southern men indiscriminately, and burning without mercy nearly every house they come to. They follow in the wake of Col. Wood's command, and will, without doubt, visit Clinton when he leaves, and destroy the place.

We hear that a fight is expected in a few days at Little Rock. If the Feds attack on this side the river, it is thought Gen. Price will whip them; but if they cross below, and flank him, he will have to retreat; he is prepared either way. It is to be hoped we will have a big victory this time. One brilliant affair of that kind would be like an electric shock in this department; it would fill the whole country with new life. The Feds are said to be fifteen or twenty thousand strong.

SEPT. 5.—Did not move to day as was proposed yesterday; on account of having our wagons to repair. Col. Wood left this morning, we find he leaves a bad name behind him, have heard damaging comparisons between his men and the jayhawkers; hope it results from some personal malice and not general misconduct of his command. There are always some to complain no matter who is concerned. Capt. Winston went fishing to day—baited his hook with a minnow and threw it in—received a bite which broke his line—came back to camp for a new hook; baited a second time with a minnow—another bite—drew out carefully a splendid pike, brought it in, and on dressing it, discovered his first hook, with the minnow partly digested. Had an arrival to-day, Judge Price, three days out from Little Rock—full of good news—"Price's army in fine spirits, confident of success." "Old Pap in full command of the Trans-Mississippi Department." "Gen. Holmes removed." "Kirby Smith Secretary of War in the Trans-Mississippi." "Contest nearly at an end." "France has declared war against the U. S." "Landed a fleet at the mouth of the Mississippi." "U. S. called for one hundred thousand men for Mexico," and—all this needs confirmation, but is too good to be lost, true or not true. We will give the Judge the benefit of our doubt, until the contrary is proven, knowing that he would not wilfully spread a false report.

SEPT. 7.—A protracted meeting is being held in Clinton, principally among the women, as most of the men are in the army. Additions are few and far between, but it is not improper for the wives to pray while their husbands go to the battle field. Went last night to preaching and heard a genuine backwoods sermon; after the minister was through, ten men rode up and halted at the church, we were sure they were jayhawkers from the mountains. The women and children were terribly frightened, the few men were preparing for the worst, when we discovered them to be a party of Wood's men; the relief was intense, as no one has any idea what to expect from the jayhawkers.

SEPT. 8.—Stood guard last night, on account of jayhawkers.— Could hear the wolves howling in every direction. Their barking resembles that of a young "purp," only a great deal faster. Started this morning for Lewisburg, on the Arkansas river, about forty miles from Clinton. We are camping for the night with Mr. Ragsdale.

SEPT. 9.—Camped this evening seven miles above Lewisburg, on the Arkansas river, and near a stream called Point Remove. The natives call it "Pinter Move" for short. Lewisburg is on a very high bluff, has a lonely desolate look. I did not see more than four or five persons in the place, except some movers who were waiting to cross the river, on their way South, with their families and servants.

SEPT. 10.—The following story was told me to-day by a gentleman who said he is well acquainted with all the facts, and also the parties concerned in it: "There was a rich man, and highly connected, lived not far from here, who considered a private soldier no better than a dog, and treated him accordingly. While the army was on the march from Fort Smith to Little Rock, last January, a broken down soldier stopped at this man's house, and begged permission to stay all night; he was turned out and ordered off. He dragged himself along nearly two miles further, and laid down in a fence corner and *died*. A short time after the above occcurrence the old scamp was "taken in" rather nicely by a couple of privates while on their way to join their command. They called at his house after dark, and desired to put up for the night—he refused to take them, had no room, &c. One of them said:

"Well Col. it is a pretty hard case for us to have to walk to Lewisburg to-night."

"Yes," replied the Captain, "it is a very hard case, and one that I do not like at all."

With that the old sycophant said:

"Walk in gentleman, walk in, I'll do the best I can for you."

They "walked in" to a good supper, comfortable bed, refreshing breakfast, and then walked off rejoicing. He finally had to go South to save his negroes, thirteen of whom ran off on the way, he left about thirty thousand bushels of corn in the field, with word for the soldiers to use it. When he found the Feds would get it, and he couldn't help himself, he was willing for his own men to have it. They say he had a card on his door with "No admittance for privates." Such a course is very wrong, and justly unpopular. Men who are staying at home, enjoying their ease and comfort should be careful how they treat those who bear the heat and burden of the battle field; they expect them to fight for their rights and liberties and protect their property and should extend to them every "aid and comfort" in their power. Nothing is more disheartening to a soldier than unkindness from his friends, nor more inspiring than generous cordial sympathy; in the one case, he is tempted to give up, and go home, and take care of himself—in the other, he is filled with fresh zeal, and is ready to make any sacrifice or dare any danger for the common cause. I was led to this train of reflection by a little incident which occurred to day. We went to a house to purchase some milk and melons, the latter were a reasonable price, but for a gallon jug of sour milk we were asked "*one dollar.*" I indignantly started off, leaving both milk and jug, but John Miller thought the jug too valuable to lose, and when he took it up to empty, they told him he could take it along for nothing. Arkansians, or "Rackensackers" as some call them, seem to imagine that Missouri soldiers are made of money. However, some of Nature's noblest handiwork, in the way of men and women, are sons and daughters of this State.

SEPT. 11.—Went foraging again to day with much better success, found plenty of good milk and sweet potatoes, &c., which were given to us "without money and without price" by as noble a specimen of a Southern lady as the land produces. Met with a very interesting sad looking young girl, who told me that her father some months ago, had been assassinated in his own door yard, leaving her mother, self, and two little sisters in a lonely, and almost helpless condition—with no one to call on for advice, nor to look to for assistance. Farther on we met with a gay, dashing Miss, tricked out in holiday attire, all of mam's old ribbons and laces on, and the *Sundayest* coat she had, besides gloves on her hands; it was a charming picture—but her feet came too far through, and they were unwashed—which rather spoiled the effect.

SEPT. 13.—Our forces concluded to dissolve partnership, and start out in different directions; we divided into two companies, Col. Goode commanding one, Col. Priest the other; the majority are with the latter. Our object is to go into Missouri, we think there is a good work for us there, but one full of dangers and difficulties; if we succeed, we will accomplish something worth the trial; if we fail—why, nothing can be much worse than the way we are living now. The Feds are nailing things to the wall in this State, and we have not men enough to help ourselves. Old Pap has had to fall back from Little Rock, and no telling where he will fall to next, unless he is reinforced, or some movement made to turn the Yankee's heads in another direction. As long as there was any force here to command, Gen. Price was kept under, but when the Department was ruined, they gave him the fragments, and it will take time for him to patch them up into anything like an effective body.

SEPT. 16.—Camped last night on the Washita river, in Montgomery county. Everybody is leaving northern Arkansas. The roads are lined from one end to the other, so it is sometimes almost impossible to pass with wagons ; horses, mules, cattle, men, women, and children, all enroute for Texas. There are ladies born, and always accustomed to wealth and luxury being hauled along in ox wagons, shaking with the chills as they go, through rain or shine ; they dare not stop, for the enemy is abroad in the land, and the people are filled with terror. If perdition should have the colic, and belch Old Nick with all his swarms into the State, it could not produce a greater consternation. They expect nothing less than murdered men, misused women, burning homes, and plantations destroyed. Their fears of course, exaggerate the evil impending ; but they are not without some foundation, as western Missouri can testify, and Kansas jayhawkers have shown them. We traveled about three miles this morning, when the tongue of Col. Priest's wagon was broken and while a new one was being made, Mat. Priest and I took a ride ; we found an old woman in a cabin, who told us of a tan yard and shoemaker's shop, about five miles off. We started in search ; over high roads, and by roads; through paths, and through bushes, pushing along for a distance of some seven or eight miles, until we became disheartened, gave it up, and retraced our steps—described our wandering to the ancient crone, who informed us that a half mile's perseverence would have brought us to the desired haven, and thus we lost——a chance for a pair of shoes. Saving the old woman, we saw only two live creatures on our trip ; a man and a snake, we made the latter bite itself to death, and hurried up to camp to find we had been left about half an hour, hit the mules a fresh crack, and started in pursuit, rode fifteen miles and overtook the party—all went five miles farther, and camped for the night on a farm, where we found the folks at home. The old gentleman, Mr. Brown, was sufferring with diarrhea. I gave him two opium pills, which greatly pleased him; his daughter sold me jeans for a pair of pants, which in turn pleased me much better.

SEPT. 17.—Had a pretty jolly night of it, taking it altogether, tragic and comic. Mr. Collier being sick, we got permission for him to sleep on the floor at Mr. Brown's house, with me to take care of him. Mr. B's family consists of himself, aged 65; his wife, 21; and daughter, 18. I asked the ladies to make my jeans into pants—they agreed, and went to work. I put my patient to sleep, and drew up my chair to entertain the fair needle women; they were full of life, and kept their tongues as busy as their fingers. Towards midnight I grew drowsy and laid down by Collier, had slept but a short time, when I was shaken violently by the shoulder; looking up I saw the young wife bending over me. She was saying: "Doctor, doctor, get up, that old man has got the cramp." I arose as quickly as possible and went to their assistance. They had the old fellow down on the floor, and were rubbing his hands and chest. "Doctor," said the wife, "What is good for the cramp?" I told her to give him some turpentine and red pepper. She fixed it, and made him drink it, when the old man, thinking he was going to die, commenced: "Oh children, hover around yer old dad—he's got but a few minits longer to stay on this ere yearth—yes, yer ole dad—is—about—gone. Oh God Almighty, send salvation down to my soul—oh—oh—oh!" Wife and daughter were screaming too, and we began to think that our *opium pills* were going to play the dickens. A neighbor man came in, the wife asked him if he could do anything for the old man? He told her to give him some narvine tea, and while she was making it the old fellow gave another yell, declaring he was going to die. I told him there was no danger as long as he was able to make such a noise. We then gave him the tea, after which he vomited freely, and was easier. All becoming quiet I hunted my place on the floor again much amused at having played the doctor; but it occurred to me that it might not be so funny under other circumstances. Suppose a lady was in question, who needed the prompt attendance of medical aid; the complexion of the joke would be considerably changed.

This morning the ladies finished my pants, the legs look like two meal bags; I would be lost in them. A friend comes nearer fitting them, so he has taken them off my hands. Mr. Brown is doing well, and this morning when I asked for the amount of our bill, he replied: "Not a cent, that if we were willing to balance accounts he was, and that I was the only doctor who has done him any good during the last three months."

SEPT. 23.—We are camping in Sevier county, Ark., fifty-five miles from Texas. Our final destination is Missouri; but circumstances force us around in a very circuitous route. The direction from hence is not yet determined—will remain here a few days, collect all the information we can, and then decide according to our judgment. We have learned that Gen. Price is at Arkadelphia, where, it is thought, he will make a stand for the present. It is said that our forces have retaken Fort Smith; also that the port of Charleston is open to the Commerce of the world, and that a fleet of Confederate gun boats are making their way to the mouth of the Mississippi, to give the Feds a trial there. These are rumors, and though of a most pleasing character, are not to be relied upon without further confirmation. Provisions in this section are scarce and very high; dry goods are exorbitant; shoes very difficult to obtain at all. We managed by the hardest, to procure some leather, which we are now having made up. The salt works are not far from here, and doing a flourishing business; some fifteen or twenty furnaces in operation, each furnace boiling twenty or thirty kettles, turning out about thirty-five bushels of salt per day. The woods are full of muscadines, large and sweet, the finest I ever saw. This fruit is one of the principal products of Arkansas, and very justly prized.

John Miller and Jesse Stith are shaking dull care with the chills. Mr. Collier is getting better, and my own health once more appears to be good. The balance, I believe, have nothing to complain of. Weather delightful.

SEPT. 24.—In looking over some old papers I come across the following letter, which speaks for itself, and shows the true position of our Southern ladies:

MOBILE, January 24, 1862.

GEN. STERLING PRICE—*Respected Sir:*—I have this day shipped to you, by Adams' Express, *via* Memphis, care of the Quartermaster at that Post, Maj. W. J. Anderson, a box of clothing, consisting of flannel under clothing, blankets, socks, hats, pants, coats, &c., to be distributed [among the needy soldiers under your command. I should have forwarded them sooner, but the scarcity of woolen goods necessarily delayed the work of making them up. You will please accept them for the noble defenders of our soil, who are under your gallant leadership.

An acknowledgment from you, by letter, of the receipt of the box, would be extremely gratifiying to me. I sincerely hope it will reach you speedily, and now, with my prayers for the success of our cause, I beg to subscribe myself, most respectfully, yours,

MRS. J. R. EDWARDS.

A council of war having been held, Cols. Priest and Winston, Capt. Winston and myself, Mat Priest and John Miller, have determined, if possible, to reach Missouri without delay.

## CHAPTER V.

TRIP NORTHWARD; EXCITEMENT IN CAMP; SCARCITY OF PROVISIONS; CROSSING THE MISSOURI RIVER; TAKEN PRISONERS; EXAMINATION OF PAPERS, &C.; LADIES OF RICHMOND, RAY CO. MO.; TREATMENT WHILE AT MACON CITY; GRATIOT ST. PRISON; MEETING OF OLD FRIENDS; AFFECTING SCENE; CAPT. J. C. HILL, &C., &C.

SEPT. 29.—Since our last writing we have been travelling steadily toward the Missouri river. Heard yesterday that all the late good news is true, with this addition, England and France have recognized the Confederacy—it seems to be reliable—but we never know what to believe down here. It has been raining all day. We camp at Caddo's Gap, an outlet through the mountains. Maj. Wousley with two hundred men are camping at the same place, they are on a trip to catch deserters. Claim to have pretty good luck. Am reaching my old chill region, and begin to feel the effects of it—been sick all day.

OCT. 1, 1863.—We have sold our wagons and tents, and will continue the trip on horseback. We can proceed more rapidly, and with a greater degree of safety; having the mountains to climb and the jayhawkers to elude. In spite of the vast numbers moving southward, we still find a sparse population scattered here and there over the country, mostly the poor and ignorant classes, who manifest a great deal of curiosity with regard to us, asking such questions as these: "Whose Company do you 'uns belong to?" "Whar do you 'uns live?" &c. We tell them that we are Missourians, and belong to "Mr. Price's Co." It is difficult to procure either provisions or accommodations on our route, the land is overrun and destroyed, and the people completely worn out. Sometimes our patience is tried over their want of patriotism, and the selfishness they exhibit, but when we stop to consider, there is no room to blame them. "Self-preservation, is the first law of nature." For the present we take shelter under the wing of Col. Reynolds and his sixty men—if all works well, we will have a wing of our own one of these days.

OCT. 5.—Been pushing right along, almost day and night, for forty-eight hours, *pressed* food for our horses, but observed a *fast* ourselves. We hated to take a grain of corn, or a blade of fodder, it was actually robbing women and children; but necessity knows no law, we made as little do as possible and hurried on. To day we were blessed with a plentiful meal, for both man and beast. Pitched our camp to night about nine o'clock, near where some Missouri ladies are camping, they are from Dade Co., ordered out of the State, and beyond the Federal lines, and to keep going South as the lines advanced, and never to show their heads again where the Old Flag waves. Pretty tough sentence for the feminine gender, but characteristic of its source. Our camp was aroused about midnight by the rushing in of the pickets with the news of the approach of a heavy body of cavalry. We dressed and saddled up, with all speed prepared to give the best fight we could—they advanced—we halted them—they enquired who we were, and what we wanted? We asked who they were, and where they were going? They replied "Missourians, going to Price's Army." A parley ensued, with exchange of men as hostages, in case of foul play. The ladies recognized our man and vouched for him, when the whole party was invited in—Col. Reynolds acting as host. It was an agreeable surprise, and pleasant meeting. The Missouri strangers are fine, healthy looking fellows, able to whip twice their weight in Yankees. They are about six hundred strong, have no tents or cooking utensils, but managed bravely and cheerfully; cook their bread on sticks, and sleep in their blankets, except when it rains, then they fold them up at the foot of a tree and sit on them—it is a good plan—I've tried it—keeps the blanket dry.

OCT. 11.—Been journeying every day—left Brooks and Reynolds on the sixth and started on our own hook—have made it tolerably well—got lost Wednesday, in the mountains, and frightened all the folks that saw us. We were taken for jayhawkers. When we approached a house, the old men and boys would break for the brush, and the women prepare for the attack; hiding everything they considered valuable. We could not get anybody to stand and give us directions. Thursday we rested at Keytsville, and Friday saw a St. Louis Republican, giving the defeat of Rosecrans by Bragg. Saturday we passed over the worst section we have seen—the greatest destruction of property I ever witnessed—hardly a house left standing—the few we found were deserted—citizens all gone, either North or South. We passed to day within six miles of Bower's Mill, which Gen. Price run a short time, on his retreat from Lexington; it is now burned. Will resume our march to night.

OCT. 12.—Halted this morning at two and rested until day, when we again started and traveled until ten, at which time we came in sight of a small cabin, almost hidden from view by the brush. Being very anxious to get some information concerning the route before us, Capt. Winston and myself rode up to the fence, and just as we got there a man was seen to come from the house and make toward the brush. We hailed him and requested him to come to the fence, as we wished to see him on business, but that he would not do, and seemed quite uneasy, and wanted to know who we were, what we wanted, and where we were going? Not being acquainted with the gentleman, we respectfully declined answering him, but told him we wanted him to give us some information as to the road to the Osage river; said he would not give it, but told us there was a lady in the house who would give us all the information we desired. He then went into the brush and the lady came out, and wished to know our business. We told her we were Southern men, and were just from Gen. Price's army. She then remarked that we were traveling through a very dangerous country, and that we would certainly be picked up by one party or the other, before we traveled much farther. Just then we heard the heavy tramp of approaching feet, and followed the fashion, "into the brush;" found our party where we had left them. Had been there but a short time when we saw the lady coming toward us; told us we need not be alarmed as it was only *cattle* we heard. After conversing with her awhile, and getting what information we could, we started on our way rejoicing, and had traveled but a short distance when we came to an apple tree, and while we were engaged in plucking the fruit which lost our grandsire Eden, an armed band sprang from somewhere, with arms at a "ready," and wanted to know who we were. We told them we were from the Southern army, and endeavoring to overtake Gen. Jo. Shelby's command. The leader then remarked that if we were Southern men we were all right, and to come forward and show our papers, and after an examination they seemed satisfied; took us by the hand and wished us a safe trip, and also gave us a very pressing invitation to visit their camp, which we gladly accepted. After our arrival we discovered we were in a camp of new recruits, who were endeavoring to make their way South to join the Southern army. They gave us the use of their cooking utensils and told us to help ourselves to whatever we wished, and cook it to suit ourselves, and after partaking of a hearty meal and enjoying a rest of two or three hours, we procured a guide and again proceeded on our weary trip.

Oct. 17.—After leaving our kind friends, we traveled until twelve o'clock at night; reached the Osage river, rested until morning; rode about twelve miles; stopped and grazed our horses; started again in the evening; got into brush and had to lay up until morning; off again at daylight, only resting when compelled to; rode all Wednesday night with nothing to eat. Thursday and Friday, traveling day and night without food. To day we are on the bank of the Missouri river; will cross as soon as we can, but it is impossible to get a skiff. Will endeavor to night to construct a raft.

Oct. 18.—We built a raft last night, and this morning, after getting ready, discovered it was not large enough to take us all at once, so Col. Priest and myself crossed over on the hunt of a skiff, leaving the rest to await our return. We had not been over more than two hours, when we were captured by a squad of Militia. They took us to Richmond in Ray County, where we were turned over to the Provost Marshal, who took us to the hotel and gave us an excellent supper; after which we were brought to the College, where we were comfortably quartered. We do not know what became of our friends, whether they crossed over or went back. Our horses are with them, which is better than having them confiscated.

as they would have been if they had been with us. We were treated very well by our captors, who were polite and gentlemanly. They took us at first to be jayhawkers, but we soon convinced them that we were Southern soldiers. Being found inside the Federal lines will probably make against us, as *our* business was not their "edification." However, we will make the best of it, and wait the result.

OCT. 19.—The Major and Captain examined our papers, (some of them) and were satisfied of our being Southern soldiers. Our saddle pockets were then searched for contraband articles. Col. Priest's contained some powder and shot, and a small *Confederate flag* was found in mine, one my wife made before I left home. The Maj. tells us we will be sent to Chillicothe as soon as convenient. A couple of "Secesh" ladies passed as we were standing at a window. One of them smiled, and waved a handkerchief. Just the same; we find them wherever we go. We have had a most agreeable walk, accompanied by Lieut. Page, a Federal officer. Went to the hotel; were introduced to Col. Black and lady, found Mrs. B. very pleasant indeed; sang and played for us; gave us several Union songs; then requested the Lieut. to take us to see some Southern ladies; he very kindly called with us at the residence of Mrs. Holmes, where we met Miss Kate Wamsley, Miss Martha Crowly, and two others, whose names have escaped me. They favored us with several Southern songs, the visit was very pleasant. From there we returned to prison; under many obligations to Lieut. Page for his kindness and courtesy. Our new lady friends have sent us a basket of apples, with compliments.

OCT. 20.—The ladies came this morning, before we left for Chillicothe, and bade us farewell, and wished us God speed. Mrs. Holmes told me when we arrived at St. Louis, to tell her husband, who is Assistant Provost Marshal, that she had done all she could for us. Lieut. Page remarked that she ought to be of the same politics with her husband. She replied that she had an opinion of her own, separate from his, a kind of patrimony in her own right. Have a strong guard, and all seem to be gentlemen. We are stopping for the night at a Union man's house.

OCT. 21.—Arrived at Chillicothe to day at ten, were conducted to the Provost office, from thence to prison, where we will remain until to morrow, and then leave for St. Louis. We are treated splendidly, our meals are sent to us from the hotel, and we are allowed to take a guard and go where we please in town. Visited Miss Mattie Page and had a long and pleasant conversation, then promenaded a while longer and went back into quarters; very comfortable ones at that, all things considered.

OCT. 22.—Left Chillicothe at nine o'clock this morning, and at twelve arrived at Macon City, where we will remain for the present. We were taken to Head Quarters, and from thence to prison. I hardly know how to describe the latter place. I thought the lower quarters, at Gratiot, were the ultimatum of human cruelty; Fort Delaware cured that illusion, and the steamer "State of Maine," made even Fort Delaware seem tolerable. Now Macon City "out Herod's" the worst Herod of them all. It is certainly the filthiest place I ever saw; floor covered with dirty, lousy straw, windows all open; one old broken stove, such as they use in stores, with one camp kettle, a little tin bucket and a frying pan, to be used in cooking for forty men, besides having to serve other menial purposes. We are confined with a villainous negro, who is imprisoned for the most brutal outrage in the catalogue of crime, perpetrated on the person, and resulting in the death, of a little white girl. The detestable wretch—his life is an insult to humanity, and yet we have to bear his presence. The cowardly guards cursing and swearing and using the most abusive language to the prisoners Calling them low vulgar names, and using such expressions as "you G——d d——d niggers, we will show you how to work this evening when we take you out to cut wood. You d——d grey canaries. If I had my way, I'd shoot your d——d brains out." Gen. Odin Guitar, commands the troops at this post. One would expect better things, under the jurisdiction of a man of his opportunities, but it is probably the result of bad company.

OCT. 23.—We were notified this morning that we would leave for St. Louis in a few hours, and ordered to hold ourselves in readiness. The news was highly agreeable, and the order gladly obeyed. We were satisfied that *no change could be* for the worse. At two o'clock we were *more* than ready, jumped aboard the cars and were off for St. Louis, where we arrived about two hours ago; found the march from the depot very tiresome, on account of the mud. Vacation having expired, we find ourselves once more ma triculated at McDowel's College, and it may be our lot to become useful members of the society. Our case is not so clear this time; if we had only held out a little longer we would have been in a better fix, or else gone back through the lines; now we must make the best of it and watch the chances.

OCT. 24.—Occupied a portion of my time to-day in writing to my wife, from whom I have not heard for six months; amused myself awhile with watching the Southern ladies who, I am told, are as true and patriotic as ever. Found two or three old acquaintances who were here when I left. Prison life seems more of a tread mill than ever.

OCT. 25.—Nothing of interest to-day—lonesome, very lonesome. Saw my capture, arrival, &c., noticed in the Republican. Wrote to my brother, at Alton, who was captured at Helena during the exercises of our Fourth of July celebration at that place. I don't "take much stock in the Fourth" any more, it "went back on us." Went to lower quarters this evening, to hear a sermon from a Boston man, did not expect any good from that source, but thought we'd try him, any way, for variety. He opened his exercises by reading the parable of the prodigal son. We saw his application, he would make us prodigals, and ask us to return to the bosom of Father Abraham, and not wishing to be recruited for that service, especially on the Sabbath, we sought the retirement of our own quarters. If he had spoken as an ambassador from Heaven leaving it to us, and our own judgments, to regulate our political affairs, respect for the court which he represented would have commanded a hearing, but he must not roll up the cross in the stars and stripes, and expect us to see "the flag" printed on the face of God, before we can worship him. Man can draw no veil between us and our Creator.

OCT. 27.—We had a most affecting scene in prison yesterday. A young man named Nichols, is sentenced to be hung next Friday. His sister came to see him, the interview was heart rending. The poor fellow had ministers with him all the evening, it is to be hoped they were faithful, and fed him with the pure bread of life. There are none so ready but they need the aid of spiritual comfort at such a time, and woe unto the hand that should offer them husks. Nichols no doubt, is a sinner, like the rest of us, but he thought he was right in fighting the enemy in his own way. Bushwhacking is the mode of warfare practiced in Missouri by both parties, but any candid man must acknowledge that the Federals have been the worst and most destructive. Look at the long list of men butchered in cold blood: Jim Lasly and two others, as they were coming home one Sunday, from church—Lasly dying in his wife's arms; Col. Owens, Frisby McCullough, and hundreds of others, shot down like dogs, when they were helpless prisoners, many of them, as Lasly and his fellow victims, having taken no part in the war. These things will come up when we see the hand so red with innocent blood, daring to pretend to lift itself in vengeance.

Some twenty-two officers left here to-day, on parole, for Camp Chase, Ohio. Several ladies were on the street to see them off and wish them well. Saw Mrs. Meredith from the window—she looked as kind as ever, and was still assisting the needy. Angels yet do walk the earth.

OCT. 29.—My room mate came in yesterday evening, and said he had just received cheering news. We asked what it was, when he remarked that he was sentenced to be shot, and the order gone to Washington for the President's approval. He has been removed to the strong room. Jasper Hill, from Chillicothe, is also locked up, and Mr. Gentry, from Shelby county, is ornamented with a ball and chain, for knocking a man down who insulted him.

OCT. 30.—Dull as ever—same thing over and over, Snowing hard all day—no ladies on the street. Ninety-two prisoners left for Camp Morton, Ind., and, bad as the weather was, they went off cheerfully as all Southern soldiers do. Young Nichols, I suppose, is quietly slumbering in his grave, as this was the day for his execution. If all, guilty of the same, or even worse offences, among the ranks of those who tried and punished him, were to share a like fate, there would be weeping and wailing in many a household; but mad party fanaticism was never known to mete out equal justice.

Mr. Waukley, the prison clerk, was arrested to-day on the charge of having carried out a letter to Mrs. Clifford—a prisoner's wife. We have quite a number wearing balls and chains—they are very fashionable this season.

Capt Hill and Lieut. Sebring, of the strong rooms, are making the best of it—are in good spirits. They are not allowed to communicate with any one, but we believe they manage to get all the news. Four Federal deserters arrived to-day.

Nov. 3, 1863.—It is bright to-day, but it rained all day yesterday—the Heavens weeping I suppose, over the way the election was going; the Radical destructives had it nearly all their own way. Missouri is completely subjugated—has no more power than a chained and muzzled dog, while the swine are rooting up everything. It is reported that secret arrangements were being made for the release of Gen. Morgan, from the Ohio penitentiary, when a traitor gave information and defeated the plan. We enjoy two blessings to-day—God's clear sunshine, and a glimpse of the ladies as they pass.

Nov. 4.—Had a letter from my brother at Alton; they are writing and urging him to take the oath, but the boy has not come to that yet. Bravo for John! I like his grit.

Received a note from my friend Capt. Hill, in the lock up, who says he is sentenced to be shot for violating the rules and regulations of war; he remarked that "the jig is nearly up," as the priests visited him this morning, and concludes with,

"Let all things wag as they will,
I'll be gay and happy still."

From Lieut. Sebring, locked up for the same offense, I have not heard; but a young Federal, they say is to be shot next Friday for desertion, and other grave crimes. Twelve o'clock, night—Went to bed four hours ago, but find it impossible to sleep on account of chintz, or what is commonly called *bed bugs*. The night being warm they came out from their holes and opened upon us with their *pikes*. We fell into line as soon as possible, at the same time throwing out skirmishers on the right and left wings, with instructions to return the fire at every opportunity, which was done with a hearty good will. After fighting them some ten or fifteen minutes their line gave way in the centre, and all we did not kill, beat a hasty retreat. Some of them showed themselves several times afterwards, but our sharp shooters were on the look out, and at the sight of every blood-sucker they would commence hurrahing for Jeff Davis, when all who escaped the fire would be off for their holes *instanter*. And now, as everything seems to be quiet once more, we will again seek our couch and try and go to sleep. So good night to all.

Nov. 7.—The young Federal under sentence of death, has been pardoned, as we expected; half his offenses would have shot a whole company of us Rebs, though I judge he is as good as any of his gang. Found an old letter to-day which I received while in the South, from Miss Sallie Freeman. A portion of it reads thus:

"You leave us to return to the tented field. We dislike very much to part with you, but our country's call demands it. It is to preserve unsullied the liberties and institutions of our beloved South that you have left your home. May God bless you—and all the brave sons engaged in this noble and patriotic enterprise. And may peace with wide spreading wings, soon perch upon our banner, when you can return to the home and friends that await you, crowned with victory. Your cause is one of justice and humanity, and in the maintainance of consistent virtue, you will not fail to have, at all times, the sunlight of divine favor upon your deeds of valor. Go then, and remember you have with you our prayers, our sympathies, our confidence—and

"Strike, for your altars and your fires,
Strike, till the last armed foe expires,
Strike, for the green graves of your sires,
God—Missouri—and the sunny South."

Nov 8.—Another long, tedious day has gone; passed the time as usual, looking at the ladies, and promenading the hall. Six more prisoners brought in two Feds and two Rebs—the Feds were put in one of the *lock-up* rooms where Clifford is confined. This Clifford is an awful chap, he escaped from here last summer in open daylight, but was retaken in Illinois and brought back. This evening he got to quarreling with some Feds, and pitched into them and gave them a complete threshing, after which the belligerant individual was invited into the dungeon. I don't know how the poor fellows will fare that are in with him, but perhaps if they give him no offence, he will give them no trouble.

Nov. 9.—Some thirty five more prisoners from the Southwest, among them three officers from Frost's and Shelby's brigade, arrived at Gratiot last night, and after undergoing the pleasing little ceremony of being searched, were sent to quarters. It was amusing to see sergeant Roe, an old Irishman, performing the search, the business was new to him. He would go to the prisoners, and instead of running his hands in their pockets, would stand off and ask them if they had any money or knives, saying that "he niver put his hands into a gintleman's pocket, and did not like to do it *sure*," but Capt. Masterson happened to see him, and went to him and gave him some instructions, after which the old fellow could search a prisoner as well as any of them. When he came to the blankets he was very anxious to know if they had any "Whistling Dick" wrapped in them? I suppose he was thinking of the "Whistling Dick" that gave them so much trouble at Vicksburg.

The men who are guarding us now are more like soldiers than those of last winter; these have seen some active service and know how to treat a prisoner, but the "Silver Greys" had never been in the field, and some of them imagined that prisoners ought to be made to feel the lash on all occasions; and right well they knew how to use it, never letting an opportunity pass without exhibiting their valor in that way. Ladies, on errands of mercy, frequently visit our gloomy abode. Mrs. Shoteau and Miss Rayburn came in to-day, with clothing, to be distributed among the needy. Miss Laura Elder sent me in some stationery of a superior quality. The weather having turned very cold, we shall have a dull time around the stove, as the bright faces of the fair ones, like dancing sunbeams, will not be seen flitting about the streets, the tender flowers will all be sheltered in the warm conservatories of home. We shall watch for their reappearance, as eagerly as children search for the early spring blossoms. Meantime we are all possessed of a literary streak, every one in the room is either reading or writing. Yesterday morning's paper stated that Fort Sumter had fallen, and the old flag was waving where it was first brought down; but this morning they tell us the old Fort is true to her State. The Yankees find it hard to bamboozle her with their thundering arguments. They think their gab and guns ought to turn the world upside down, but Fort Sumter seems to be as impregnable as a nigger's skull, or a Yankee's charity bag. Clifford was released from his dungeon last night. They were afraid he would escape if left there much longer.

Nov. 10.—Three more prisoners from the Southwest were brought in last night. One of them told the prison clerk that he had tried at Rolla to get a parole, but was not successful, and would like to get one here. The clerk replied that paroling such men as him had "played out," and asked him if he did not want to be exchanged, and go back and fight some more? He said no, he was tired of that, and thought the South was about *played*—at least things looked that way to him. He is just the kind of a man the South don't want exchanged, he would do more harm than good; if all such were weeded out of the Confederacy, and stacked away in Northern barns, it would be the best thing that could happen. Seventy six more prisoners left here to-day for Camp Morton; each man drew two rations of bread and meat for the trip. Mr. M. B. Bransford, a gentleman whom we left a prisoner here last April, was released this morning unconditionally. It is the "best Government under the sun" surely, when it takes a man, and boards him that way for nothing. Misses Laura Elder and Dora Harrison, are registered on the prisoners' book of thanks, for a basket of nice fruit, nuts, &c.

"Bright be their dreams, and blest their awaking."

Nov. 11.—Several more unconditional releases to-day. Is Uncle Sam tired of extending his charitable hospitality, or are his household expenses too great to admit of such unnecessary expenditures? Retrenchment, Uncle, that's the remedy, it would save you many millions if you would confine yourself to your own business entirely—many a man has been ruined by undertaking a job too big for his brains. More ladies have visited us bringing clothing for their friends, Our "Mail Boy, *Bottle Neck*," left this evening with a heavy mail.

Nov. 12.—Received a box from home. Every prisoner knows how to interpret that. What a sensation it produces in *our mess*. With what eagerness we watch the opening; how we peep—here they come—pants, drawers, shirts, socks, handkerchiefs, &c.; they are the substantials. Now for the "chicken fixens"—fresh butter, baked chickens, nice biscuits, apples, apple butter, dried peaches, and so on. A letter came with the box, of course, but the Provost ain't done hunting for contraband in that yet. All right—will be good when it comes. The weather is fine once more, and our dear friends are out again, tripping along the side-walks, or riding by in their carriages; occasionally they stop at the door, and sometimes come in with bundles for the prisoners.

Had another letter from John, at Alton; they are still writing him to take the oath. He tells them he'll wait awhile; he is not ready just yet to face a dozen Confederate muskets as a deserter.

Nov. 13.—Good old Mrs. Meredith was in to-day, scattering benefits and receiving blessings. She brought me some stationery, from Miss A. E. Dean, another gentle friend, who pities the sighing of the prisoners. Surely St. Louis must be the treasure house of the Lord's jewels, or at least the headquarters of one of the departments—though the enemy is in pretty heavy force here too. Got my letter from home; wife says the blacks are all with them yet, but the Rads are doing all they can to get them away; thinks by Christmas there will be none left in the county. She speaks highly of Gen. Schofield; also of the Provost Marshal, at Palmyra, but fears they will be removed, as they have too much soul for the Radical programme. We exchange greetings now and then by the "*Bottle Neck* Mail Boy."

Nov. 14.—John C. Carlin, captured somewhere in Illinois, was brought in to-day, with a ball and chain attached to his leg. He was sent to Clifford's *lock-up*; if they should fall out it will be Greek meeting Greek. Carlin is a son of an ex-Governor of Illinois, and as brave a fellow as ever contended for principle against his own interest; if the mass of the Democracy at the North had been possessed of his back bone, the country need not now have been groaning under a despotism; but dear as liberty is said to be, and much as it has been sung about, the almighty dollar can buy up its pretensions in more cases than national honor would like to acknowledge.

Nov. 15.—Another long, lonesome and gloomy day has passed, but not so gloomily to those outside, as to us who are incarcerated within the strong walls of Gratiot. We had preaching in the lower quarters, and all the officers were permitted to attend; most of us went down. A Catholic Priest officiated; he wore a long black robe—a short white one over that, and a scarf around his neck; all gave him a respectful hearing, but being a foreigner, his speech was broken, and we not being edified as we probably would have been if we could have understood all he said, found it impossible to follow the thread of his remarks, and so silently pursued the path of our own cogitations. I wondered if any of the passers by had any idea what was going on in the guarded prison.

Of course not—they did not even turn their heads this way, but walked carelessly along as though all were as free as themselves. Then I thought, it is too true that "one half of the world knows not how the other half lives."

No news of interest, only that the negroes of Missouri have been called on to enlist, and freedom promised to all who do so. Loyal men are to be paid three hundred dollars apiece for theirs; but it is no harm to "covet thy neighbor's man servant" if he differs from *thee* in politics. O the beautiful consistency of the great moral idea "freedom to worship God" as *we* may dictate. If my conscience is to be in leading strings, and the divine right of private interpretation of scripture, usurped by a politial party, give me the black robed priest from the cloister. I either hold my bible myself, or else commit it to worthier hands than those of the blood stained demagogue.

Nov. 16.—We are having a new style of regulations inaugurated on the pretence of retaliation. They say our authorities at Richmond, won't let the Yankee women visit their prisoners, and so our ladies are denied admittance to Gratiot. Not allowed either to come in, or to send anything to their friends.

Nov. 17.—A prisoner escaped from the hospital last night, but before doing so, he played a very shabby trick on our old market woman. It seems his plans were all laid, and money alone was needed to put them into execution, and his only hope for success was to victimize poor old Mrs. Smith. So he asked her if she would not like to change green backs for gold. She was eager for the trade—brought him twenty-five dollars, which he was to take around among the prisoners and exchange for gold; he took the old creature's money and left for parts unknown. It is to be hoped he will repay her with interest, when an opportunity arrives.

Another singular circumstance occurred at the hospital last night. Two men—one a Confederaet, the other a Federal, died, and were laid out side by side. This morning when the dead room was entered, the body of the Fed was found to be terribly mutilated by the rats, while his neighbor was sleeping quietly and undisturbed. What cause could have produced the difference? Most probably the nature of the disease, or medicine employed, but the curious fact has been the occasion of a good many queer remarks by the way of comment.

Nov. 18.—A great many deaths have occurred lately among the prisoners; some were taken off very suddenly. Lieut. Clinton left our quarters yesterday morning for the hospital, and this morning was a corpse. I went with Capt. Burns to see him—the work of death was done. We walked around the hospital, and I was surprised to find as much order and neatness, and as good provision for the comfort of the sick. They have a small library furnished by the ladies of St. Louis—those daughters of mercy—turn where we will, we see the seeds of their good works springing up, and bearing fruit for heaven, and gliding in and out like the pure air of the gentle zephyr, is the professed Sister of Charity, a nameless creature, and yet "a thing of beauty, and a joy forever." How little we appriciate in the daily routine and drudgery of life, the elements of good at work about us. If our senses were not too blunted to perceive it, there is a grand sublimity hedging us in on every side.

Nov. 20.—Eighty-five more prisoners left for Camp Morton. That point is becoming quite a fashionable place of resort for our Southern gentry. I am not posted with regard to the accommodations; but my experience is not favorable in crowded hotels, nor particularly happy in the Northern states any way; the Philadelphia ladies left a serious impression on my mind. We have an addition of four Confederate officers newly arrived; Gratiot is not so popular as formerly. John writes me again from Alton, he is doing finely; a Federal Lieutenant has presented him with an overcoat, which he thinks will ensure his comfort for the winter. John is somewhat of a philosopher; he thinks a man usually has his luck in his own hands, and harsh treatment either North or South, is the result of unruly conduct on the part of the prisoner. A man must not expect the fare of a parlor boarder in a military prison; but if he will observe his duty as a prisoner, submitting to regulations made by others, not trying to dictate, nor caviling or snarling, but cheerfully making the best of everything, his manhood will have but little to complain of. John hates a simpering, whining, would-be sensational *male* prisoner, he leaves pitiful yarns for women to tell. Maj. Brasher, in one of his letters used the word "Hessian" which proving offensive in certain circles, his Majorship was taken down among the privates. Mr. Gentry from

Shelby county, Mo., has been released. Several of the boys in the lower quarters tried to release themselves, but their guardians thought it not advisable, and for a change are allowing them the use of a *lock-up*, with *half rations* of bread and water; their adventurous spirits will no doubt be *weakened* considerably before they get out.

Nov. 21.—Carpenters and blacksmiths have been busy all day, putting iron bars to our windows, and iron gratings to the doors leading into the hall. Guess after this, we will all be in a *lock-up*. Robert Shultz, from Palmyra, Mo., came to see us to day. He is a prisoner, but has the position of Steward in the Branch Hospital, and gets along first rate. Troops are leaving here for Springfield, Ill.; the "Old Harry" is to pay out there somewhere, and I suppose these fellows are due. We can't get the straight of it, but a Fed tells us, the Copperheads are resisting the arrest of some deserters. Some poor dupes I suppose, who went to fight for the Union, but did'nt bargain for the nigger too. My brother Dan. and son are fighting for the Union also, I wonder how the Ethiopian digests on their stomachs. Some of our fellow citizen prisoners, leave for the sunny South to morrow, on *banishment;* several ladies I am told, *leave home* under similar circumstances. How could any one criticise this kind paternal government which condescends even to persecute women? There are not many countries where the governing classes would stoop so low. It must be "higher law," intellect, and great moral ideas, which sway them.

Nov. 23.—Been busy cooking all day, and find it very fatigueing. Our mess consists of twelve, and we cook by turns, we try to imitate what we have seen at home as nearly as our means will allow, and sometimes we get up a really inviting meal. Col. Priest received his charges and specifications to day; he has been called out before the Provost, a number of times, but they are very tedious in conducting the business of trials. I presume my case will be commenced soon; it cannot differ much from Col. P's, as we were taken together. No particulars from the Illinois troubles. Ladies been passing all day; always give us a pleasant smile which seems to say "God bless you, how we sympathize with you in your unfortunate situation." Our iron gratings were completed to day, and I suppose we will be locked up to night.

Nov. 24.—Nothing of interest has transpired in Gratiot to day. Our quarters are unusually dull. The chaps down stairs, however, seem to be pretty gay. Maj. Brasher is stirring things around since he has been down there. He writes as follows:

LOWER QUARTERS, U. S. Prison, Nov. 24, 1863.

Dear FROST:—I am getting along nicely; having a lively time. We have organized a Battallion of five Companies, which I have the honor of representing. We have officers' drill; company drill, and dress parade, every day. Exercising vigorously for the health of the command. You ought to come down and see us, and hear the *very important* General Orders read before the dress parade. We style ourselves the "Enraged Missouri Mules." If you get any news for me let me know immediately and oblige

Your Obedient Servt., E. M. BRASHER.

P. S. The following is one of the *General Orders* read before the Brigade this afternoon, while on dress parade.

HEAD QUARTERS, Enraged Mo., Mules, }
Nov. 24, 1863. }

The Colonel commanding, seizes this opportunity to thank his *veteran* soldiers for the glorious services they have rendered their country in defence of their rights, their liberties and their honors, and takes pleasure in thanking them for the gallantry displayed on the 22d inst., in the charge on the *Under Mining Set;* though the battle raged for some time, and our noble battalion was in the hottest of the contest, not a man wavered, but all stood at their posts like heroes. The casualties of the enemy were two killed and several wounded. Our loss none. By order of

E. M. BRASHER, Col. Commanding.

R. G. ROBERTSON, Adjt. E. M. M.

The above seems to be a complimentary address, instead of a General Order as stated. I am at a loss to understand the nature of the *gallant charge* alluded to, unless they were after *rats.*

Capt. Hill has received a letter from his father, who has prominent men at work in his behalf, and he hopes they will succeed in getting his sentence changed from death to some milder form of punishment. The Captain is in good spirits.

We have an oddity in our room, a prisoner from Cape Girardeau, one of those long drawling fellows, that talk through the nose. He says: "T-h-i-s i-s t-h-e fi-r-s-t t-i-m-e I e-v-e-r w-a-s i-n p-r-i-s-o-n, a-n-d I d-o-n'-t l-i-k-e i-t n-e-i-t-h-e-r, I d-o-n'-t, I h-a-d r-a-t-h-e-r b-e a-t h-o-m-e w-i-t-h t-h-e o-l-d w-o-m-a-n. We dont blame him.

Nov. 25.—The Military Commission is turning off its work pretty rapidly the last few days; quite a number of prisoners were notified this evening to be ready to-morrow to leave for Alton to serve out their sentences. Col. Priest has had his trial, but has not recieved his sentence. Several releases on oath and bond have taken place. We are thinning out, as business is being dispatched, only to make room for others, as they are constantly arriving. The great ball at the Lindell Hotel comes off to-night. *Shoulder straps* and *brass buttons* I suppose will shine in all their splendor.

Nov. 26.—Thanksgiving day. Well let those thank who are prospering; as for me, I have no political occasion at this time, and shall not "bow myself in the house of Rimmon." The papers are out in full blast with a big victory achieved by Grant over Bragg in Tennessee. Whether true or false, the story is valuable, for it will fire up the dead coals of patriotic enthusiasm, and furnish the Yankees with a new theme for self glorification. The Lord will receive a grand report. Alexander, Cæser, Bonaparte, &c., will stand around and scratch their heads when they hear the news. All Heaven will be astonished, unless somebody telegraphs South for the truth. The sentenced men were not removed to Alton; left over out of respect to the day. Inside of Gratiot, where *the day does not dawn*, we are dull, lonesome, and sleepy; moping gloomily away the bitter hours of the Yankee holiday.

Nov. 29.—Was out to day for examination. In the prisoner's room at the Provost's office, I found the following lines penciled upon the wall:

"Oh, for liberty, that my gallant steed
May carry me to the battle field—
There I can fight; I'll never yield!
Then away, away, to the battle field.

Dark and crimson is the tide,
Forms are scattered far and wide,
Death and victory will be won—
I'm a prisoner, I'm undone!"

Maj. Brasher has gotten back to his old quarters, and I presume after this, will be more guarded in wording his letters, having felt the force of their extreme sensibility, he will be particularly careful not to make any allusion to the "Hessians."

Nov. 28.—The weather has turned freezing cold, and many of the prisoners are suffering for want of sufficient clothing. Mrs. Shoteau and Miss Rayburn were allowed to bring in some overcoats, pants, &c., for distribution among the most needy. Capt. Burns, the prison keeper, is a perfect gentleman. An act of his to-day manifested the true spirit of chivalry. Mrs. Soward, wife of Judge Soward, of Canton, Mo., not succeeding in procuring a pass at the Provost's came on to the prison, when Capt. Burns invited her to his house, and sent for the Judge, who was delighted; had quite a pleasant interview, and is full of gratitude toward the gallant Captain. Twelve new arrivals; four officers added to our quarters. The men who have received their sentences have left for Alton to serve out their doom, some at hard labor during the war, others in solitary confinement. Grant's victory is confirmed. Bragg in full retreat. Gen. Morgan, with six officers, has escaped from prison in Ohio. Morgan is a brave, dashing officer, one of the high souled sons of old Kentucky—may success attend him.

Nov. 29.—It has been a cold disagreeable day, and we have kept rather close to the fire. Nothing called for comment, except a lady in passing the prison, threw us a kiss, and was seen by the sergeant, who ordered her to keep her hands to herself; she told him she would use them as she pleased, and throw kisses whenever she passed, if it suited her. He made some reply which we did not hear. Shortly afterward an old Irishman came along and touched his hat to us, the sergeant saw him also and asked, "who he was bowing to?" Paddy said, "he was going down street." Sergeant "did'nt ask where he was going, but who he was bowing to?" "O, my hat was falling off, and I was pulling it on." The petulant official seeing he could make nothing off the son of the Emerald Isle, allowed him to pass on.

Nov. 30.—Had a a letter to day from my sister in Ohio, she tells me that our old mother has had a paralytic stroke and was helpless and unconscious for over two days. She thinks I will never see her again. I fear it will be so, as there is but little hope of her living until the close of the war, and no prospect of my seeing her before. Old Mrs. Meredith has been permitted to visit the prison again. She brought in clothing for the needy. More prisoners constantly arriving. Another letter from John, he is still urged to take the oath, but mantains a stoical indifference; will act on his own judgment. My wife writes insisting on the same course for me. Think I will see my trial out first, any way. Have received my charges and specifications from the Provost Marshal. The following are the charges:

"Entering, on or about the 30th day of September, A. D. 1863, the lines of the regularly authorized military forces of the United States, and within the State of Missouri, and without ever having surrendered himself to the nearest military post, or to any of the military forces of the United States, and did travel and *lurk* about within the State of Missouri, until arrested, on or about the 18th day of October, A. D. 1863, at the county of Ray, and State of Missouri, in violation of the laws of war and General Order, No. 86, of the Department of Missouri."

Dec. 3, 1863.—Judge Sowards of Canton, has been released, but I have not heard on what terms, of course he had to accept such as were offered, whether they were dictated in the spirit of justice, humanity, or spite. He was an agreeable and gentlemanly fellow prisoner, and we would mourn his exit, but we know that our loss is his gain; so with resignation we pronounce, "may the bunk which has known him here, know him no more forever," and so mote it be, with some of the rest of us. I trust we are fully prepared for such a change.

A Federal revenue officer has been put in with us, for stealing. Such arrangements are very distateful to our circle, as almost the the only privilege we try to exercise is that of being select in our associations; and it is exceedingly offensive to have to come in contact with plebeanism of this style. We consider it quite a sufficient condescension to have intercourse with the better class of that party without having their thieves thrust in among us.

Prison life is dull and disagreeable at the best, with all our efforts to keep a stiff upper lip, and looking at the bright side, we will have heavy gloomy days. Maj. Brasher has recieved a lot of novels and magazines, with which we while away some of the tedious hours, and the revenue officer, after all, affords us quite a fund of amusement. He is almost frantic over his imprisonment; thinks he will go crazy if it lasts long. One of the boys remarked he would'nt have far to go. Letters drop in occasionally advising me to "take the oath." My sister at Cairo speaks to day. I would like to say, once for all, and once to all, that first; I don't know that I would be permitted to take the oath, as I was captured this time under peculiar circumstances, and, second, I have no wish to leave prison in that way, if I can escape by a more honorable route. I shall await the result of my trial; if I am booked a prisoner for the war, without hope of exchange, I will begin to consider what is best to be done. Meantime I am truly thankful for the interest manifested by my friends, and grateful for their efforts in my behalf. Brasher, the noisy fellow, is trying to fill our cage with the melody of his song he is rattling off.

> "We met, 'twas in a crowd, I thought he would shun me,
> He came, I could not breathe, for his eyes were upon me,
> He spoke, his words were cold, and his smiles were unaltered.
> But I knew how much he felt, for his deep toned voice faltered.
> I wore my bridal robe; I rivaled its whiteness,
> Bright gems were in my hair, how I hated their brightness;
> He called me by my name, as the bride of another,
> Oh thou hast been the cause of this anguish my mother."

We receive a free lecture every now and then from Capt. Masterson, and it is amusing indeed to hear him; talks as though he was lord and master of all he surveyed. He has such a beautiful way of delivering his remarks; always comes up with one eye closed and a grin on his face, and commences: "Now boys, did'nt I tell yees so, and so, and why in the divil don't yees mind me." After lecturing us some five or ten minutes, he starts off grumbling, saying "its no use talking to rebels—they are a bad set." We think so too.

## CHAPTER VI.

GENERAL ORDER, NO. 86; A NIGHT WITH THE CONDEMNED; LECTURE FROM CAPT. MASTERSON; PRISONERS LEAVING WITHOUT PERMISSION; THE WAY THEY LEAVE; LOCKED UP NIGHT AND DAY; REMOVAL OF COL. PRIEST TO THE STRONG ROOM; ACCOUNTS FROM CAMP CHASE, OHIO; HOW PRISONERS ARE TREATED THERE; &c., &c.

MONDAY, Dec. 7, 1863.—I was notified on Saturday last, to be ready for trial to-day. The following is the General Order, which they say I have violated:

HEAD QUARTERS, DEPT. OF THE MISSOURI.
ST. LOUIS, Aug. 25, 1863.

*General Order, No. 86.*
Large numbers of men are leaving the broken rebel armies in the Mississippi valley, and returning to Missouri—many of them doubtless, with the purpose of following a career of plunder and murder, under the form of guerrilla warfare while others would gladly return to their homes as peaceful citizens, if permitted to do so, and protected from violence. It is the desire of the commanding General, that all those who voluntarily abandon the rebel cause, and desire to return to their allegiance to the United States, shall be permitted to do so under such restrictions as the public peace shall require. All such persons may surrender themselves and their arms at the nearest military post and will be released upon taking the oath and giving bond, &c.

The above order is one of Halleck's, and as I failed to comply with the terms offered, it is presumed that I had other intentions. I made no remark, but this morning obeyed the summons which called me before the Military Commission. That learned and august body soon disposed of my case to suit themselves, but have not, as yet, vouchsafed a knowledge of their conclusion to the humble object of their sage deliberations. I would like to know, but prisoners learn patience. After the trial was over, I asked for a guard and permission to go shopping, which being granted, I started out, went first to a picture gallery and got a glass for my little daughter's picture, then went to a furnishing store for some toweling. While making my purchase, the merchant asked me what regiment I belonged to? I told him I belonged to Gen. Parson's command, of the Confederate army, which seemed to surprise him. Six or eight ladies being present, one of them asked me if I wanted to go back South? I answered in the affirmative. She enquired if I did not think I ought to reform? I replied that when convinced I had done wrong, I should probably think of reformation. "Are you not convinced now?" said she. I confessed that I had not received sufficient light to comprehend my error. She smiled good naturedly, and as I passed out I heard a couple of her companions who had remained silent, saying in a half whisper, "he's all right," "he's O. K." They were rebel ladies. On our way back to the *Hotel de Gratiot* I was pleasantly surprised by meeting in front of the Planter's House, with Samuel Anderson, of Palmyra. I would have enjoyed a good talk with him, but was only allowed a few words, and had to pass on. Dinner was awaiting my arrival; after it was dispatched, we were informed that our friends, would in future, be deprived of the permission which has heretofore been occasionally granted them, of sending in clothing, provision, &c., to relieve our necessities. I made a few remarks in the way of remonstrance which excited the dander of a self important little official, who politely invited me up stairs and locked me in the room where the condemned criminals are kept. Two of them are sentenced to be shot. I managed to communicate with my old quarters through a hole in the partition, learned that quite a little gust of anger had sprung up in consequence of my remarks. How sore they are where the truth hits. The sergeant came up about nine and took me down for my bed clothes. I shouldered and brought them up. So here I am with my tent pitched in the wilderness of sin. One of my room mates is named Fornchell, a young married man, who was in prison with me at Springfield; he also has been exchanged and recaptured, and is now wearing a ball and chain, it is said he is sentenced to be shot, but he denies in toto the charges against him. While he was in Jefferson City he had some photographs taken with his ball and chain on; it is rather a sad looking picture for his young wife to contemplate.

MONDAY, Dec. 14.—They only kept me one night in the condemned cell, but it was a night of horrors. I could hear the rattling of chains, and the thumping of balls, every time the poor fellows would turn over on their pallets of straw. They seemed cheerful enough when awake, but the moaning and groaning in their sleep told a story which their manly spirits could not hide. I was forcibly brought to reflect on the contrast—McNeal murdered ten men in Palmyra, and was promoted; Combs murdered Lasley, Price and Ridgeway, a cold blooded butchery, and is a hero; Haith Jones of Frankfort, Pike county, Mo., was foully assassinated at night by the home guards, and is unavenged; twenty seven prisoners, a surgeon, Dr. Davis, among them, shot down like dogs at Kirksville. was a valorous achievement, and so on, name after name, murder after murder, might be added, committed with every attendant circumstance of savage brutality, endorsed, applauded and rewarded by the same Pharisacal hands that are now stoning to death these poor chained starving wretches. Sinners they may be, probably are, and God help the hypocrite, who pretends to be otherwise. Still death to them and honor to guiltier hands, is a bitter perversion of God's eternal law of justice. Thank Heaven there is a court of appeals where the Chief Justice can neither be blinded, bribed nor brow beaten. My friend Major Brasher, exerted all his ingenuity to divert my mind and scatter its gloomy reflections; saluting me through the "hole in the wall" with questions and comments; before retiring he gave me a parting volley—would have my opinion of my new "posish," &c. I do not know that my answers were particularly amiable, however they were a happy reflection of my mood. In the morning I told the sergeant I wanted my clothes, if I had to stay there. He started off, but soon came back and ordered me to load up my bedding and march for the old quarters. I obeyed without a murmur. Don't know that I shall attempt to reason with these fanatics again, they give me the worst of the argument. Capt. Burns interposed for my release or I might have been there yet. We are not a great deal better off here, as we are not allowed to see friends, receive packages, buy provisions, or anything else. Having no stamps, I waited on Capt. Masterson, made my politest bow, and humbly enquired if I could procure some, as I wished to send a letter to my wife. He answered me, "no, not a d—d thing?" I retired in disgust. Newspapers are also forbidden, and we have to do our own washing. If they come down on the lower quarters in the same proportion they have on us, I don't see what's left for them, as they have never had any surplus in the way of provisions or privileges. We are told that Masterson is the cause of all our troubles; if so, he certainly delights in human suffering. The other morning before I got up, he bolted into our room and turned to me in a sneering manner, saying:

"Well friend Frast, yeer plaasure will now end, you'll not enjoy yeerself any more when the ladies pass, in thrawing kisses, and wavin' yeer handkerchief. I shell put a stop to all sich sports." And sure enough the comical old monster had the windows weather boarded. When he had it all fixed to his notion, he delivered himself of a lecture. Great guns! I wish some of the scolding old women could have heard him, I think it would have shamed them out of the business. I think he must have inherited the virago propensities from forty cracked voiced old grandmothers. How he did come down on "proper places," "looking out of windows," and "other things in general." If he ever lets us buy anything again we must vote him a night cap with a big ruffled border, and a calico recticule, with smoking tobacco and cob pipe. If he was an opium eater, like many old grannies it would enhance our peace and quiet. He has had all the Federal prisoners removed from here to Myrtle, so he could let himself out on us. We jogged along under the thumb screws, giving him as wide a berth as possible and being very circumspect in our words and ways until Saturday night when the storm burst in its fury. About three o'clock in the morning, with great bustle and confusion we were waked and ordered out to answer roll call. Prisoners had escaped! Three or four officers—several from the lock-up, and a number from the lower quarters; fourteen in all. One man, Lieut. Lavalle was recaptured by the guards as he was in the act of climbing a fence. They were so enraged he thought they would shoot him after surrendering, but they brought him in and the officers plied him with many questions concerning the escape. He told a plain straight forward story. Said there were ten or twelve others, who were just ahead of him and who got off. That in the first place they went to the lamp house cellar, where they took underground passage through a hole which they had dug for that purpose, and which extended for forty or fifty yards, terminating in an another cellar, from which they emerged into a yard, climbed the fence and were off; at least those who were quick enough. He was covered with mud and dirt that he had gathered in the hole, which was barely large enough for a man to squeeze himself through. In working the tunnel they hauled the dirt back in a box and packed it down tight in the cellar. It must have taken three or four weeks to complete all their arrangements and they certainly deserve great credit for their skill and management; the only pity is, that more could not have availed themselves of so fine an opportunity, for we will not have such another offered again soon, as old Masterson will be more rigorous than ever. He closes the iron doors now, and locks us in at seven. He is in a regular stew about the digging of the passage, and is making great effort to ascertain who were engaged in it, but his success is not encouraging however. He sends all the officers whom he questions down to lower quarters, whether they know anything or not. The men in the lock-up, up stairs, descended by means of a rope made of blankets—I have the names of four of them—W. Owsley, who had just gotten through his trial, and was charged with murder, robbery, bushwhacking, &c. Thinking it would go hard with him, he took an appeal by way of the blanket ladder. Also — Watkins, who was one of a party that charged upon the guards last spring and escaped, but was recaptured, and has been in the lock-up ever since, concluded to enlarge his quarters; and two Lieutenants, Martin and Stewart, thought they would go down and take a walk. There were others, whose names I have not been able to pick up, but whoever they are, the best wishes of their late prison comrades attend them, notwithstanding we have to suffer for their good luck, our keepers being stricter than ever; I cannot even write to my wife. George Henly and George Phillips, our Confederate roll callers were sent below on suspicion of being implicated in the escape. The Feds are worse beat than they have ever been before, with all their splurge and splutter they cannot get any new light on the subject, for every prisoner is a Know Nothing.

DEC. 21.—The week past has been dull and disagreeable, and I have been quite sick, but have weathered it along without going to the hospital. The boys soon cut through the plank over our windows, making little holes to peep out; if Masterson knows of it he says nothing, and we make no comments; he is showing his spleen by searching prisoners who come in from the Provost's. Two Lieutenants, Brown and Thaxton were overhauled Tuesday, and Brown lost a small knife which he brought with him when he first came to Gratiot.

Col. Priest and another officer have been put in the strong room to remain for the future; they have no idea what led to the movement. Lieut. Gowing visited them to-day, and old Masterson caught him there, when he ordered him to stay, and had him transfer, bag and baggage, saying he supposed the Lieutenant liked their quarters better than his own. On Sunday there was an order recieved from the Secretary of War, permitting us to buy tobacco and stationery, so we will be able to write to our families again. We are allowed to buy tobacco because they fear we will get sick if deprived of it, and they will have to furnish us medicine and medical attendance which will cost them more than the comfort derived from our punishment will come to. We had quite an addition to our number on Friday, about seventy Confederates arrived from Little Rock; men and officers, who were left there sick when our forces evacuated the place. They tell us that Old Pap has taken Washington, Arkansas. One of these men, Capt. Caldwell, had a surgical operation performed on his side yesterday, by Dr. Dudley, who took out a piece of bone from a wound which was recieved last September. Twelve other prisoners have also dropped in, one of Jo. Shelby's Captains among them. New arrivals are gladly welcomed, from the fact of their bringing in something fresh to talk about. When a citizen is thrown to us, we consider we have drawn a great prize, as he brings in all he knows, and takes out all he learns; it is the best show we have to keep the U. G. R. R., in repair. The Feds don't know how they play into our hands in such cases, or they would be a little more careful how they thrust citizens into military prisons. I am indebted to the U. G. Express Co., for postage stamps, which came shortly after Capt. M's, ungentlemanly refusal.

DEC. 28.—Another week of prison life, has dragged its long length slowly by, taking a joyous Christmas in its train. Tuesday was a day of perfect stagnation. The Feds thought of no new method of cruelty, and we submitted to all the plans in operation. Old Gratiot was like a ship becalmed in Southern seas. Wednesday a little breeze sprung up on the admission of a citizen prisoner, a Mr. O'Neal, from Herman, Gasconade county, arrested for speaking disloyally. He seems somewhat uneasy, and well he may if there is any prospect of his being shipped east. We see in an old copy of the Columbus Crisis, which an underground accident threw in our way, that political prisoners at Camp Chase fare even worse than prisoners of war do here. The following is the article in full, which we copy for future reference—it bears date December 24, 1862.

"We speak wholly of the *political* prison, of the State, as we know nothing whatever of what occurs in the prison where "rebels taken in arms" are kept—that is, "the prisoner of war."

It must not be forgotten that there have been from six to seven hundred political prisoners at Camp Chase at a time; and although several hundred have been lately discharged without trial, there are yet there some four hundred—one or two hundred of these have arrived there within a few days past from Kentucky and Western Virginia. These men were taken from their homes, some from their beds at night, some from their homes in daytime, and a great many of them are picked up in their fields at work, and never suffered to see their families before being spirited off to Ohio and incarcerated in the celebrated Bastile, which will soon be as famous as Olmutz itself.

Our Ohioans are put into the same prison with these men from other States, and from them we have learned some facts which the people of Ohio ought to know. Many of these men have been kept in this prison for over one year, a great many for five, six, seven and eight months, without even seeing outside, or being allowed to communicate personally with any one, not even wife, child, father, mother, or stranger.

They are furnished with nothing but a single blanket, even these cold nights, unless they are able to purchase additional comforts with the money they may be able to command. Many are poor men, and unable to purchase; they were not permitted to bring along a change of clothing, and many had on when seized nothing but summer wear, and that has become filthy, worn out, and scarcely hangs upon their backs.

They have no bedding, and are therefore compelled to sleep on bare boards. They have not enough wood furnished to keep fires up all night, and hence the suffering is intensified by the cold weather. If they attempt, after night, to walk out in the yard to take off the chills of the dreary night, they are instantly threatened to be shot by the guards, as ordered by those in command.

Dr. Allen, of Columbia county, Ohio, said he laid on a bare board until his hips were black and blue. The wood furnished them is four feet long, and they are compelled, each mess, to chop it up for themselves. Recollect, always that these are political prisoners, against whom no one appears as accuser, and no trial is permitted.

The prison has become filthy—awfully so—and the rats are in droves. If the prisoners attempt to kill one of these rats, they are forbidden, and threatened with being shot instantly. Recollect, as we have said before, these are political prisoners, against whom some malicious negro-worshipper has created a suspicion of disloyalty, but whose name is kept secret, and hence there can be no trial.

The prison is perfectly alive with lice, and no chance is given to escape the living vermin. A dead man, one of the prisoners, was the other day carried out to the dead-yard, laid there over night, and when visited in the morning by other prisoners, who heard there was a dead man there, they found the hair on his head stiff with lice and nits—the lice creeping into his eyes in great numbers, and, as he lay, they were thick, crawling in and out of his open mouth.

Not long since two of the prisoners got into a scuffle in trying their strength, and finally into a fight, as was supposed, and several other persons rushed to part them, when the guards from the lookout above fired on them, killing an old man by the name of Jones, from Western Virginia, and a ball grazing the skull of another; he fell, and it was supposed at first, he was killed also; another of the balls passed through a board at the head of a sick man in the hospital, and only escaped him by a few inches. The two men in the scuffle were not hurt. We might go further, but God knows this is enough for once. It is enough to make one's blood run cold to think of it.

Now, if any one doubts this—if the authorities at camp or at the State House doubt it—if the Legislature, when it meets, will raise a committee, we promise to name the witnesses who, if sent for, will, under oath, prove all this, and as much more, some of which is too indecent to print in a newspaper for the public eye."

This was their programme a year ago, and as the Yankees are a progressive race, the inference is, that if O'Neal should chance to tarry a few months at Camp Chase he could pick up a world of rich experience which would startle the military outside—that is if he should live to get out with his story; but we have heard it said that "dead men tell no tales." I know that live ones don't dare to tell all they know—even in underground letters much less in those carefully worded concerns which we send through the hands of prison inspectors. For instance, if I should tell my wife, how on Christmas eve, we offered an humble petition for liberty to purchase a Christmas dinner, and how unfeelingly we were denied, my letter would not pass, and I would be sent to the lower quarters or dungeon to learn better manners than to write the truth. Nor would it do to inform her of how I "peeped" out at the window, and saw ladies come to the prison with bundles of clothes for their friends, and after standing at the door for some time, go away, carrying their packages with them, while the men for whom they were intended are actually shivering in rags. One aged mother came with clothing for her "sick boy, who always needed warm clothes in winter." She begged, and cried, but it was no use, the "sick boy" must abide in his tatters. The kind old mother stood on the corner, looking toward the prison, and crying for a long time, then she turned her poor old blinded eyes away and walked off.

Friday was Christmas day—I cannot speak for those jamming and crowding around in their rags in the lower quarters, nor for those in the lock-ups whose heavy balls and chains are eating into their ankles, while the still more deadly iron of despair is cankering in their souls, their Christmas enjoyments are best known to themselves, but as a specimen from our quarters, decidedly the best in Gratiot, I will chronicle the events of my holiday operations, commencing at six o'clock in the morning, when I arose and answered to roll call, then breakfast—pickled pork, bread and coffee; went out in the hall and peeped from the window awhile, then went back to our room and warmed, from thence to the window again— in and warmed, and out again; this time saw some Feds starting off; also saw several lady friends; went in again and watched the boys play cards, which is the only amusement they have; got tired of that and returned to the window; stood there and wished for the privilege of being out where I could enjoy myself with my friends, but wishing was all I could do, so I yawned and sighed and went into the pickled pork dinner. Frank Noel declared he would not insult his stomach with the cod livery stuff, and so confined himself to a limited supply of baker's bread and coffee. Frank has not been here long—he will come to it yet—he ought to sojourn in the lower quarters, if he wants the kinks taken out of his stomach, there is not much turning up of noses down there I guess, no matter what is set before them. After dinner a fellow prisoner sent me a pear, I don't know how he obtained it, but I regarded it as a most acceptable Christmas gift, appreciating it for its own intrinsic sweetness, as well as the generous refinement which actuated the doner. Fine fruits are not so plentiful in Gratiot as to be given away without self sacrifice. We did not tarry unusually long at the festal board, but sought the more inviting precincts of the hall window; saw some ladies pass—did not "throw kisses or wave my handkerchief," but I thought "as long as I have the spirit of a man I will peep." I won't say the ladies didn't peep some too. They looked at our gloomy walls as though they would like to have Alladin's Lamp, and make the Genii spirit us off, prison and all, into some far country where they could have opened our doors, and feasted us in the most royal manner, but their wishes were no more effectual than mine. I gazed for awhile longer at the paving stones, imagined they had a hard hearted appearance, lying there watching us; went back to my room, picked up the romance of "Zaidee," read an hour or two, and—went back to the window for a last look, stood some ten or fifteen minutes, saw nothing of interest and left; went to the lamp room, brought up our lamp, pulled out the table, and played cards till time to go to bed, and thus ended Christmas day 1863, in the officer's quarters, Gratiot street Military Prison, St. Louis, Mo. Not much after the style in vogue in the palmy days of old Dr. McDowel and his Medical College. Wonder how that gentleman would feel to walk around his premises and take a view of the students now gathered in the institution together with the faculty presiding over the establishment. His remarks on such an occasion would be rich beyond a doubt. More

than one Yank would burn beneath the touch of his caustic wit.—
Christmas day passed off dull enough, and we stole to our beds
as quietly as chained dogs to their kennels. Slept till midnight,
when a militia horse thief from the lower quarters, came running
up and informed the prison officers that the lock-up prisoners were
about to make their escape. Of course the whole gang were out in
a minute, they went down and discovered that a hole had been cut
through the floor of Clifford's and Carlin's room, through which
they proposed to let themselves down by blankets, when they would
be joined by a lot from the lower quarters, and all make a rush on
the guards and as many escape as possible. It would have been a
perfect success if it had not been for the coward who reported.
The next day Clifford was thrown into a solitary dungeon, the
darkest pit in the prison; and Carlin, Sebring and one other, were
taken down into the yard, and hand-cuffed and chained to a post—
after they had stood there for several hours, a second squad was
brought down and chained to another post, where they could be
seen from a Southern residence across the street. They were kept
there until late at night, although the weather was extremely cold;
they stamped, shouted, and sung to keep from freezing; we
could hear them after we went to bed, thumping the pavement, and
singing "Hard times." The same thing was repeated yesterday
and to-day, except Carlin had a post to himself, and the weather
much colder; we find it difficult to keep comfortable by the fire,
and yet we hear "Hard times come again no more" pealing out on
the frozen air. They unchain them and take them in to eat their
meals. While passing near the kitchen one of them struck an old
fellow over the head and "made the blood flow" pretty freely, it
was the father of the horse thief who reported on them, and said to
be the cause of his son's doing so. Desperate measures will cook
desperation. I guess they would have killed the old sinner if they
could. While they are chained at the post, old Masterson goes out
and stands and scolds as long as he can endure the cold, then he
comes in and takes an easy chair, smacks his lips, and admires his
own bravery; chuckling over the big things he said to them. Had
another letter from John, and one from home, the latter reads:
 "I have a bid to a Christmas dinner, but do not expect to go, for
I could not enjoy myself and you in prison. All the pleasure I

expect to see is when Annie gets her doll, which I have been dressing to-day. Dear little creature, she is more company for me than all the rest. She talks a great deal about "Old Kris," and what she expects him to bring her. I would like to send you a turkey, but know it would be useless."

We have had a letter also from Johnson's Island, written by Lieut. Coale, who mentions Col. Dawson as being there, and sending his respects to all. Col. Dawson and I went on exchange together last spring, and the same kind of fortune still seems to cling to us both. It appears they are dying off pretty rapidly on the Island, resulting I suppose, from change of climate and want of clothing. I have learned from other sources than through the hands of inspecting officers, that there is great suffering in that prison. The ladies of Hannibal, Mo., have made an effort to relieve them, sending boxes of clothing, &c., but I have not heard as to whether their contributions reached the prison or were refused admittance.*

MONDAY, JANUARY 11, 1864.—Two weeks have elapsed since my last writing, and but little has occurred deserving notice. The chain gang were faithful at their posts, never omitting their duty for any change of wind or weather. On the night of New Year's eve, snow fell to the depth of ten or twelve inches; but the boys tramped round with their "Hard Times" song. I am told that some of them were badly frosted. I have not heard that any whined or begged, on the contrary, they bore themselves as true soldiers, showing their superiority over their persecutors, by the unflinching firmness which they manifested under the torture. All honor to their heroism, and success to their next adventure. A Secesh negro has been confined here for some time, but I learn is now released. I do not know the particulars, but as he is a rare circumstance, I should like to have seen Sambo. He must have a mental developement considerably superior to the generality of his race. Most of them are like young jay birds, open their mouths and gulp down everything the Yankees see fit to stuff them with. Saw some of them a few days since in Federal uniform, they were

---

*I am able to say from personal knowledge, that the boxes were received, and their contents distributed, to the great relief of many—while others suffered and died, who might have been saved if their wants could have been supplied. The ladies of Hannibal did what they could, but those acquainted with the history of that place during the war, will readily comprehend the difficulties under which the citizens labored in all their efforts of that nature.—ED.

stepping along quite briskly, as though they thought it something grand to be food for powder, and save Yankee hides. Several of our citizen prisoners have been released; among them, Messrs. Wilson and O'Neal, the latter on a three thousand dollar bond. A Mr. T. Roberts of Marion county, was released on oath and bond, not to leave the limits of his county. Such terms are very common; usually imposed for what are termed "disloyal speeches." A man is not heard in his own defence, and his word, if anything, is taken against him. I suppose more "false witness" has been borne in such cases than any one person would be able to imagine. Every petty spite seeks that method of gratification; no one being safe. The weather continued intensely cold, up to Thursday the 7th, when a few ladies could be seen on the streets, but only such as were called by business seemed to venture out; it was awfully rigorous on the post gang in the yard and then locked up without fire. I suffered on New Years's day, as near the fire as I could get, wrapped up in my shawl and blanket; had a terrible time, and would have complained of my condition if there had not been hundreds in the house in a worse fix. Prisoners are being brought in all the time; over a hundred on the 6th, about a dozen officers with them. Gratiot occasionally gets very much crowded, and when such is the case there are many and just causes of complaint. The prisoners are poorly fed, worse bedded, and nearly suffocated in the impure air. It is said there has been as many as seventeen hundred men at one time in these lower quarters. That number could scarcely find standing room, sleeping would be out of the question, of course they must suffer, sicken and die. If each individual case, could be recorded, even the hard heart of Northern humanity, blunted as it is to all but the imaginary hardships of the negro's lot, would surely for a moment indulge in the luxury commiserating a fellow creatures woes, but they mantain a persistent deafness and blindness, and most hardened unbelief whenever an incident is mentioned as having occurred outside the pale of their political church, and yet how they gulp down every exaggerated story of so called rebel cruelty, without ever investigating for the truth, or considering any mitigating circumstance. On the night of the 9th, a fresh attempt was made by some of the prisoners to escape from the lower quarters. They were discovered and prevented, and are now wearing a ball and chain as a punishment. The roof of the hospital building caught fire on Saturday, creating quite an excitement among the sick prisoners, but the flames were fortunately extinguished in time to prevent any serious damage, except such as might have occurred to the invalids in consequence of the shock to their nervous system. That interesting and gentlemanly character, Capt. Masterson, is still piping his cracked voice in odious authority, within the classic halls. I presented myself at the office the other day, to obtain an axe for chopping wood, not knowing but it would be thrown at my head, but greatly to my surprise he said :—"Walk in Capt. Frast, and take a seat." I stated my errand—he renewed his invitation, or rather order, at the same time shaking me cordially by the hand. I was completely mystified, and dropped into the proffered seat. "Captain," said he as blandly as it was possible for him to speak, "I would thank ye for the note yees recieved this morning from Clint. Burbrige in the lock-up." I replied that he was mistaken, as I had recieved no such note. He affirmed that I had. I protested I had not. He said, he would be sorry to be under the impression that I had the note notwithstanding my denial. I challenged him to say if he had ever known me to prevaricate—what I did not wish to tell, I refused to, and suffered the penalty, but I was not in the habit of lying. He waved me out of the room, saying, "that will do—this is a matter between you and me." Capt. Beltzhoover was then called down; he acknowledged the receipt of the note, and stated that I knew nothing of it.

JAN. 18.—For the past week all things with us have flown on smoothly. Scarcely a ripple appearing on the calm surface of the bitter waters of prison life; this is true, at least, as regards our immediate quarters. We know nothing of what walls and floors may hide from our view, doubtless there have many painful scenes transpired at the hospital, as numbers are dying daily. Almost every hour witnesses the exit of some freed spirit, which drops its chains and its bondage and under the pale flag of death's unquestioned truce, soars away to that blessed land where "the wicked cease from troubling, and the weary are at rest," and in every instance the haggard corpse, handled roughly by rude strangers and stowed quickly away in its rough pine box, is the dear form of "somebody's darling, God only knows who." There is a man among us who is looked upon as a traitor, and who is naturally regarded with peculiar hostility by his fellow prisoners. Every man's hand is against him, and little things which would pass unnoticed from others are hotly resented from him. He is buffeted on all sides, there being no sympathy or forbearance for a spy in our midst. He came in collision the other day with a young scion of the chivalry, who let him feel the weight of his aristocratic fist, for which act the chivalry pines in a dungeon, and the traitor skulks around dodging everybody's boots for fear of the kick which he deserves.

Several prisoners left here to-day for Rock Island. They went off in fine spirits. Any change is desirable, after long continued confinement in one place. I hope they will write back and let us hear something of their new quarters. We can form some idea of it by their saying it is better or worse than Gratiot. Col. Dawson writes me from Johnson's Island, he is looking anxiously forward to an exchange.

JAN. 29.—On Tuesday the 19th, a man was released on oath and bond, who had been confined in prison for over seventeen months; his dull, joyous apathy on the occasion was like Bonnivard's, who said:

> "At last men came to set me free.
> I asked not why, and recked not where,
> It was at length the same to me,
> Fettered or fetterless to be—
> I learned to love despair."

On Wednesday the tramp of time was noiseless, leaving the clatter of no event to echo down the corridors of coming years. We slept, eat and yawned; yawned, eat and slept, and thus through the heavy hours, until Thursday noon we crept, then the Feds came in and raised a stir shearing off our buttons, it was comical; some made a pretense of resistance, but it was no use. The Government must have "the last button on Gabe's coat." It passed off in pretty jolly style, but I confess it looked like shearing sheep, or picking geese, neither of which comparison is a very sweet unction with which to salve our wounded vanity. One says we slip around in our buttonless coats like peacocks robbed of their gayest feathers," another says "we are Bonapartes stripped of our kingdoms," while another says, "nay, we are suns shorn of our beams." Our keepers were not ungentlemanly in performing the act, which was required by an order from a higher sphere. It took several days to complete the work, and we had a good many laughs while it was going forward. Sources of amusement are so exceedingly scarce, we would fain make the best of whatever is presented even though the joke is enjoyed at a heavy expense. Friday was my day to cook. I flattered myself that I reflected great credit on the old darkies whom I had seen "bile the kittle." I think I can make as big a dinner out of pickled pork, stale bread and a little coffee as any Dinah that ever presided over a kitchen fire. On Saturday I had a letter from Alton, telling me of the unmannerly departure from that prison of two of my old company, W. Parker, and Stephen Kerrick, who left without giving notice, returning thanks, or saying "good-bye." The friends whose hospitality they had been enjoying, were much exasperated at their ungrateful conduct, and would, if they could find them, force them to come back and finish their visit; but the blundering clowns did not even leave word where they were going. So the interesting Alton family will have to pocket their chagrin, and submit as best they may. At our house things work differently. On the same day I heard the news, Clinton Burbrige was taken from his lock-up and transferred to a dungeon. Mr. B. is a citizen of Louisiana, Mo., he is a high toned honorable gentleman, thoroughly imbued with Southern fire, which will flash out in spite of chains and dungeons. He cannot teach his proud spirit to bow and submit tamely to a prisoner's doom, although he bruises his own wings as he beats against the cage. If he would cringe, and flatter, and lick the feet of his oppressors, it would be just to their taste; they would make a prison hero of him, but unfortunately he is made of sterner stuff, and will be true to his manhood though he rot in a dungeon.

I continue to receive letters from home and friends, they do not think I will be exchanged and are anxious that steps should be taken for my release. Any move in that direction will be taken without my approval, until I have satisfactory evidence of the hopelessness of an exchange. When such shall be the case, I am not so in love with prison life, as to prefer it to the society of home. It is no benefit to the South for me to lie in prison unless I am counted against a Yankee, on the other side, if I am not so counted

I am "hors de combat" any way, and my family have claims which demand attention when I can no longer serve my country. Thirty eight officers left here this morning for Camp Chase, but transportation not being provided they were sent back from the Provost's office, and will now, not be off before next week.

They were considerably disappointed, as they all seem anxious for a change of some kind, no matter if it is from one prison to another. However they will have to honor old Gratiot with their presence a few days longer, and listen to the interesting lectures of Capt. Masterson.

One of our Lieutenants fell into the sink to-day, and had to be drawn out with ropes, and several attempts were made before his friends succeeded in extricating him from his miserable situation—having remained in some ten or fifteen minutes, and the filth was between five and six feet deep. Some think he went down on an exploring expedition for the purpose of finding a way by which to escape, but it seems he was unsuccessful—no subterraneous passage being visible, and even if he had, it strikes me the remedy was worse than the disease.

## CHAPTER VII.

ARRIVAL AT ALTON, ILLS.; ALTON MILITARY PRISON; MY SENTENCE; THE WAY WE LIVE AT THE OLD PENITENTIARY; EXTRACT FROM THE RICHMOND DISPATCH; SINGULAR ATTEMPT TO ESCAPE; ANOTHER SEARCH FOR KNIVES, &C.; COLONEL WEIR AND THE PRIVATE; &C, &C.

ALTON, ILLS., Saturday January 30, 1864.—I had little idea when I laid aside my pen last night in Gratiot, that it would be resumed again in Alton, but thus the fates have ordered and prisoners are only footballs for destiny, kicked here, there and everywhere, just as those in authority may decide. Our transfer was unexpected, up to two hours before we moved. Col. Priest, myself and some twenty-six others, were notified in the afternoon to prepare for change, which we did by packing up, and then going round and bidding our friends "good bye." We left old "Alma Mater," who by the way has been something of a step mother, at three, but did not reach our present quarters before dark; immediately on our arrival we were carefully searched, person and baggage, but I was fortunate enough to smuggle my book through wrapped in a shirt, which I honestly exhibited, but which looked too beggarly to invite scrutiny. Thirty-two of us occupy a room eighteen feet square; some have bunks, others take the floor. I have seen my brother and several other acquaintances, all well and doing as well as circumstances will permit. John says they have some pretty tough times, some of the men are treated shockingly, but it is usually the result of a hasty or impudent act, or speech on the part of the prisoner; if a man will strictly obey orders and forbear comment, he is generally safe.

JAN. 31.—Discover that our change is very decidedly for the worse, this is a much harder place than Gratiot—it is almost impossible to sleep on account of the rats, which run over us all through the night; it is hard to tell which are the thickest—rats or men, there are over two thousand of the latter, and many of them entered for the war; in some of the buildings it is difficult to turn around. There is much sickness; the small-pox is prevailing, and many are dying daily. Some are allowed to cook their own rations, but the balance have to eat in the dining room, which is a fair representation of that *hell hole*, Fort Delaware.

MONDAY, February 1, 1864.—Besides the vast number of Confederates, there are about two hundred Federals imprisoned here. The latter are the very dregs of creation; too mean to be at large even among the Yankees—they are a most detestable nuisance with us, nothing is safe that they can get their hands upon. Two young men, one of them named R. G. Robertson, were last night, robbed of all their clothes; the thieves saturated a handkerchief with chloroform and threw it near their heads, and when it had taken effect proceeded to rob them. They are high handed in their daring, knowing that an effort to right ourselves would be apt to result in our greater damage. When a complaint is entered the unlucky individual is told he ought to be able to defend himself, but if he interprets the reply too literally he usually winds up in one of the cells, or if the thing is too outrageous, and the authorities are bound to punish the Fed, the Confed party is almost certain to nearly lose his life soon after. This seems to be the manner in which matters are conducted at Alton Penitentiary. A circumstance from which we derive some pleasure, is the fact of our being near the river and having a fine view; the Mississippi smiles at us with the familiar countenance of an old friend. The ice upon her broad bosom reminds us of the bonds upon our liberty—and so we sympathize—when the early spring casts off her shackles she will tap at our walls every morning bringing fresh water from near our old homes.

"Flow gently sweet Afton."

I asked to-day for an interview with the Provost of the prison, and was permitted to wait upon him in his office, when I desired to be furnished with a copy of my sentence—he handed me the following:

"Tried, and sentenced to confinement during the war, at such time and place as the commanding General may direct. Confirmed, and will be carried into effect at the Alton, Ill., Prison, under the direction of the Provost Marshal General, Special Order, No. 4, Dept of the Mo., of date January 16th, 1864."

Such is my sentence for being inside their lines, as they say, without permission from the United States authorities, it is very light in comparison with some—especially those who are sentenced to hard labor and wearing a ball and chain. Their work consists in breaking rock, filling holes in the yard, sawing wood, &c. Altogether, to be a sentenced prisoner is not a very enviable situation, and now with regard to my release, I say "Lay on McDuff," the time has arrived for work in that direction. My friends, notwithstanding my opposition, have been busy in my behalf, as they have felt from the first, that something of this nature would be the result. I very much fear that we shall not be able to accomplish anything—however, my duty to my family demands that the trial be made.

FEB. 2.—Have been busy to-day fixing up, as the prospect is good for my remaining here some time I want to be as comfortable as possible, accordingly I have bought myself a plate, knife, fork, and a spoon, we being allowed to buy such things from the sutler, who, by the way charges an extravagant price for everything we get. A guard is placed at his door whose duty it is to admit but three Confederates at a time. I also visited the principal kitchen of the prison, where cooking is done for a thousand men. Two hundred and fifty eat at a time. The dishes are not washed from one table to another, consequently those who eat first, are the only ones that get clean plates. It requires an immense amount of food to supply such large numbers, and must be a heavy expense to the government. I noticed the other day an extract from the Richmond Dispatch which I would like for old Masterson to read, as he justifies all his cruel tyranny, by abusing the Southern prison keepers; he was careful to keep such things out of our sight while we were with him. Here, although we fare worse in many respects than at Gratiot, still we are not insulted by false charges against our friends, and are not annoyed by petty contemptable restrictions. In alluding to the large number of Federal prisoners at Richmond and the scarcity of provisions consequent upon supplying their wants, the writer in the Dispatch, illustrates the fact by giving an incident which came under his own observation. It is as follows: "Several persons of respectable standing in this community endeavoring to obtain a small quantity of the beef which has been permitted at the commissary shops to be sold to the general public, were informed that they could not have it, as it would all be required by the Yankee prisoners." The Dispatch goes on to comment after this style: "Here are our people denied provisions for themselves and their children, to feed these Yankees who came here to destroy us. We do not mention this by way of complaint, on the contrary, we give the government credit for its merciful disposition, but this simple fact sufficiently proves the base and malignant falsehoods that we are seeking to starve the Yankees, when in reality it is our own people who are in danger of starving in order that these prisoners may be fed." That's a cud for old Masterson to chew in company with his next mouthful of "retaliation." "Seeing the immense amount consumed here by our prisoners, I can well conceive the great difficulty our government must labor under in feeding and taking care of a like number of men from the North. Our country is everywhere desolated and destroyed by the Northern armies, our territory grows smaller every day, and of course as the people fall back with the lines, more densely populated, making without a possibility of avoiding it, provision high and scarce. Our women and children deny themselves, our sick soldiers poorly fed, our well ones fight almost on empty stomachs, and the enemy, who are prisoners in our midst, taken in the act of murdering us and destroying our homes, should be satisfied if they fare as well as our wives and children. If their friends in the North are disposed to grumble, the remedy is in their own hands. *Let them exchange.* At the door of that government which refuses this call of humanity, more pitiful than any which ever issued from ebon lips, at that door, lies the guilt of all the sufferings and accumulated prison horrors, North as well as South."

FEB. 3.—This morning about one o'clock, some ten or twelve prisoners were detected in trying to make their escape by digging underground from one of the buildings outside the walls, they would have succeeded if they had not been overheard by the sentinel, who, it is thought by many, was warned by a traitor in their midst. There are without doubt, spies posted all through the prison, but it is difficult positively to detect them. The men engaged in the attempt of last night, have been thrown into the cells, where they will be kept an indefinite length of time. Such things are of very frequent occurrence—the men having nothing else to think about naturally fall to planning escapes, and sometimes very strange fancies get tangled in their brains. One of the most singular and painfully interesting of these adventures was attempted to be carried out by two Confeds, one of whom was named Rutherford, the name of the other I did not learn. It was after this wise: Feigning to be dead, they were duly coffined in company with a Federal to whom death was no joke, but a stern reality. The latter, by carelessness or mistake, had been started on his long journey with a pair of hospital socks on his feet; this being considered a breach of etiquette on the part of the corpse the sergeant waited on him to secure the property before his departure. He lifted the lid which he supposed covered the socks in question, when in place of the emaciated form from the hospital, a dead rebel rose up and asked, "What was wanted?"—he had opened the wrong coffin. The poor sergeant was frightened nearly to death, and fled, reporting that a dead man had come to life. The rebel was not much more comfortable over the blunder, for he had taken the sergeant to be a friend into the secret. When the facts were reported at Head Quarters the poor fellow was ordered to be buried alive, and was nailed up in the coffin, and carried out as for burial. After a short time the lid was removed and he was permitted to taste the sweets of a resurrection, threatening him at the same time, to be much more severe if his reckless daring should ever call for a second punishment.

FEB. 5.—This morning we all received orders to fall in line in the yard, which being done we were carefully searched and all the pocket knives which could be found, were taken, with a view, I suppose, to prevent gophering experiments—in other words, any effort at cutting out.

I notice the boys have an amusement which they dub with some

French name, and which is very funny to all except the victim. They pounce suddenly upon a man, hold him, bend him over, like our mothers used to do when they spanked us, and paddle him with a board paddle, most outrageously; all laughing and shouting with great glee, except the unfortunate individual selected to bear the most conspicuous part in the comedy. I have never joined in the sport and have thus far escaped being victimized. I observe that a fellow who has once suffered, is ever afterwards fond of using the paddle.

Regulations are very strict; we must positively retire at nine o'clock, and we are allowed to procure no luxuries, nor any relief from unpleasant tasks. Every man is required to do his own washing, and this of itself is in some instances, a cruel hardship, an ungainly awkward wretch, who hardly ever saw a wash tub, will rub all the skin off his wrists and none of the dirt from his clothes.

FEB. 6.—While sitting in the window this evening, I had the pleasure of seeing the beautiful steamer David Tatum arrive at her landing from St. Louis. Could also see across to the small pox hospital on the Island, opposite the city, where many poor Southern men are lying at the point of death, with this terrible disease, having no one to care for them except the rough soldier nurse detailed from the prisoners. No wife, mother, or sister are there, to give them a kind word, or bid them be of good cheer. No tender hands to smooth the pillow, cool the brow, or sweeten the bitter dose, with the magic touch of woman's loving fingers; but all night long, from morning till night again, they lie and suffer, the mind perhaps rambling in delirium, and the parched lips muttering incoherent sentences, with now and then the word "home" articulated more distinctly. Or, perhaps, in that interval, after fever and before death, the happy home, the family circle, the cheerful fire, the days gone by, will pass in mournful procession before the feeble eyes now moistened with tears which flow down the emaciated cheeks, which soon will be cold and glazed in death. From looking with melancholy interest at that abode of suffering and sorrow I withdrew my glance to the limits of our own prison bounds; here also was added proof that "man was made to mourn." I saw balls and chains fastened on several Federal prisoners which are to be worn during the war. Quite a commotion was excited in that department of the prison to-day, in consequence of a stone being pitched at Weir, the Col. commanding, who seems to be as notoriously unpopular as our quandom host, Capt. Masterson, of Gratiot. Weir, in order to find out the real offender, had the whole lot of that class of prisoners thrown into the cells, one of them, who is sentenced for the war, on his way to the cell, looked at the Colonel in a manner rather significant, and not very pleasant, at which his honor stepped forward, and slapped the silent but expressive countenance, exclaiming with an oath,

"You look at me sir, as though you owned me."

The reply being of a still further provoking character a ball and chain was ordered, and during the process of fastening it on, the prisoner expressed himself quite freely to his official greatness—promising to settle with him as soon as his time was out, which he said would be in a few months; he further declared the opinion, (and some may agree with him) that no gentleman would strike a prisoner, waxing warmer, he told him he might put a ball and chain on him, and he might threaten him as much as he pleased, but he could not frighten him,—he was not the kind to be frightened at *little things.* The Colonel was now pretty furious, and demanded what he was in prison for, and what regiment he belonged to. He replied:

"I belong to an Illinois regiment, and am here for knocking my Captain down and breaking two of his ribs, an act which I still justify, and would repeat under the same circumstances."

The exasperated Colonel belching forth volumes of blasphemy, blurted out:

"I thought so sir, I thought it was something of that kind, and now I suppose, you would like to knock down the Colonel commanding, would you? you ——," winding up with an oath.

"Yes, I would," replied the undaunted prisoner, "and most certainly should, if I were on equal footing."

Col. Weir thinking probably it was useless to say any more, ordered them to put him to work, and the last I saw of him, he was marching off with his ball and chain under charge of a sergeant.

Col. Priest is very sick, caused by exposure and change of prisons.

FEB. 7.—No preaching, or other sign of recognition, marking a knowledge that this is a day claimed by a higher potentate, than even the despotic and all powerful government Abraham Lincoln, who permits the arrest and incarceration of delicate women. Great Heavens, my blood boils—women in this hole of filth and blasphemy! I could scarcely believe it until I saw with my own eyes, Mrs. Mitchell, who is here with a little daughter five or six years old. She is charged with smuggling goods through to the Confederates. The Northern armies move making deserts in their tracks, and a loving woman is imprisoned for stretching out her hand to the needy. Other ladies besides Mrs. M. are confined here, but I have not learned their names. Col. Priest is still very low, suffering from sore throat—almost impossible for him to swallow. Several new cases of small-pox discovered to-day. I have met with an Indian in this prison whom I saw last winter at Springfield, he was an interpreter there for the other Indians, but here it is almost impossible to get him to speak a word of English. His conduct is very strange, and I have no idea what his motive can be.

MONDAY, Feb. 8.—To-day I was detailed for duty—had to perform the following service: 1st.—Clean the spittoons. 2nd.—Carry out the ashes. 3rd.—Empty the buckets which were used last night. 4th, and last.—Guard the water and see that our barrels were filled. When my task was ended, I went to work to wash my dirty clothes, rub, scrub and splatter; the dirt stuck fast as ever; but not so the skin on my knuckles. However, after working an hour or so, I finished—washed and rinsed, and provided I can find an iron, intend ironing them—if I must be a washer-man let me not be a disgrace to the profession. While I was "up to my eyes in the suds" we had a visit from a Catholic Priest. The reverend Father seems to think that even in these sinks of iniquity there may be some jewels which are worth redeeming for their Master's crown. One difference between these priests and most others who come electioneering among us is the service they wish to enlist us in. The Boston man, who preached over in Gratiot, would hardly hint at a Heaven for us unless we "should go up through the tribulation" of fighting under old Abe's proclamation for the liberty of the jay-heeled, woolly headed improved monkey from Africa, which we beg leave most respectfully to decline. The Holy Father, on the contrary, seems to know no party, king or country, except that "better land," and Him who sits upon "the great white throne." "Honor to whom honor is due." Had I never known such men as brothers Caples, Marvin, Spencer, and a host of others of different denominations, I should certainly believe that the Catholic Priest is the only type of the true christian minister. As it is, I reverence him standing in his appointed place and doing his Master's work—while I still remember the soul-stirring words I have heard fall from the lips of his earnest devoted, Protestant brethren.

A man named Bernard, has been released from here and banished to the State of Maine. It is possible he may find clever people, and kind friends even among those cold North-eastern Yankees. I believe there are true hearted men and women all over the North, who, if they were not blinded by an arrogant prejudice, and led by unscrupulous political fanatics, would be fully equal in all the essential characteristics of manly or womanly nobility, to the brave and the fair of our own sunny South.

MONDAY, February 29, 1864.—I have just returned from the hospital whither I was taken on the 12th. My sickness was sore throat and neuralgia, from which I suffered a great deal; throat ulcerated several times over and on being lanced discharged freely. The accommodations at the hospital are very poor; but little attention is paid to the sick, and the fare is exceedingly rough; baker's bread of the poorest quality, or half cooked corn bread, with something resembling coffee, are all that are furnished; except indeed on rare occasions, when a gill of diluted milk is allowed to some sufferer. It not unfrequently happens that a man dies in his solitary bunk and the fact is not discovered for several hours, and when it is found out, no one looks astonished or seems to care. The corpse is carried out like so much rubbish, thrown into a rough box, and literally tossed into a shallow grave.

"Rattle his bones, over the stones—
He's naught but a "rebel," whom nobody owns."

"God pity the hearts
That wait fond and true,—
For some hearts are waiting,
God only knows who."

While at the hospital I recieved a letter from my kind friend, Miss Laura Elder, enquiring if she could send me a basket of delicacies; something suitable for the sick. I was compelled to inform her that the privilege would not be granted. It is almost impossible to get medicine or medical attendance, and the diet is enough to make a well man sick. Miss Laura's basket would have brightened many a face where the death palor was already creeping, if it could have worked its way through the cruel restrictions. It was shockingly heartless not to admit it, even though they had kept it themselves and dealt it out to the most needy. Col. Priest also came back to his quarters to-day, he has been very ill, his case finally terminating in erysipelas. I have a letter from my brother-in-law R. P. Bradley, mailed on the steamer Lucy Bertram, telling me he is on his way to St. Louis with a view of making an effort for my release on oath and bond; if he succeeds I am willing to accept the terms, as I prefer the society of my family and friends to remaining here during the war.

Five hundred prisoners left here this evening for some other Bastile, Olmutz, or Black Hole; destination not known. They were searched four or five times before they got off and many of them had all their Confederate money taken from them. I wish some of the sentimentalists of the North who are shedding such bitter tears over Andersonville, Libby, and Belle Isle, would walk through Alton prison, they might perchance, if they knew the true state of affairs, scrape up some "crumbs from under the children's table" to throw to the rebel "dogs" in their own custody.

But the thought is vainer than vanity—there is a "method in their madness," they indulge no charity, countenance no sympapathy, permit no spread of a truth, that will not work in and amalgamate with their plans; their peculiar ideas must be developed if the car of Juggernaut rolls over, and crushes every bleeding heart in the land. Thousands of prisoners, North and South are languishing in hopeless despair for mere political capital. It is all very well to lean from the pulpit, and wail out an echo of the Andersonville agony, to harrangue mobs, and show pictures of sick men, stirring up the million with a bitter hatred; very well, because it educates the masses, and from the stepping stone of the wrath thus engendered, they can reach farther and make longer strides, which they would not dare attempt in the face of a sober people. If they are not prompted by a motive purely diabolical why do they not speak the word and set the captive free?

MARCH 4, 1864.—On Wednesday I had a letter from Mr. Bradley written in Alton, he has been laboring for my release, and came to the city expecting to see me and take me home with him, but Col. Weir thought best to take the matter under advisement for a few days, and suggested that Mr. B. return to St. Louis where he would communicate with him shortly. On Thursday the authorities were engaged all day taking the names of five hundred prisoners, who are to leave soon. Some say on exchange, but it is impossible to tell. Newspapers are forbidden again, hence we are all in the dark, except as one is smuggled in occasionally. Have heard nothing from Mr. Bradley since Wednesday. In answer to a written request sent in some three weeks ago, I was this morning ushered into the presence of Col. Weir, for the purpose of enjoying the then coveted interview, but the time and circumstances having passed, I had now no special desire to sun myself in his gracious presence, hence I felt something like the boy who forgot his errand, however, I asked him concerning my release, when he informed me he had written to Washington to ascertain if Gen. Rosecrans had the power to release me, and that he would hear from there in a day or two.

A prisoner of war, subject to exchange, finds no difficulty in getting out on oath and bond, and some are availing themselves of the opportunity, their long confinement has made them melancholy and hopeless, besides every leverage is brought to bear upon them for that purpose. Why cannot they send them South for an equal number of their own.

MARCH 5.—Received orders to-day to get ready for St. Louis. Obeyed and started; within a square of the prison met Mr. Bradley who knew of the order, and came to accompany me. When we neared the depot we discovered that we were too late for the cars. Mr. B. requested of Col. W. permission for me to remain with him in the city until Monday, when I am to start again for St. Louis, but was denied. I was ordered into my old quarters. Mr. B. is quite hopeful in my case, and thinks there is no doubt of my being with my family soon. I trust he may be correct, for I am not like the "young man who has long lain in the grave for his own amusement."

MONDAY, March 7.—I hail this morning from the old homestead, the venerable "Mother of learning," (to suffer) the classic shades of Gratiot's walls. How strikingly familiar are the strong locks, the iron bars, the boarded windows, the thumping of balls and clanking of chains, and even the posts in the yard, around which Carlin, Grimes, Sebring and others, froze while they sung, making music with their chains, the mockingly suggestive chorus, "Hard times come again no more." Mr. Bradley has gone home, and I am not released. The whole matter is postponed indefinitely; some little quibble about the papers. So I resign myself once more to the humdrum existence of a prison monotony.

MARCH 9.—Discovered yesterday some changes in our official circles. Masterson and Burns are both removed—the latter, though ever kind to me, and gentlemanly in his conduct, has left I find with some, as bad a name as Masterson. I cannot believe it was in the man's nature to be cruel, except as he was compelled to be in obedience to orders; Masterson was cruel, ungentlemanly, and insulting, in a purely personal manner. New prisoners are constantly coming in from the South. Some ten or twelve officers from near Little Rock were brought in last night, among whom I recognized an old acquaintance, Capt. Hobbs, C. S. A. It is a pity Capt. Masterson was removed quite so soon, as a brick wall is being built between the lamp house and street which will effectually prevent us from catching a glimpse of the dear ladies as they pass. I suppose they think they will spite somebody by building it, and in my case I will admit they succeed.

MARCH 13.—Last Saturday we scrubbed out our quarters and when through, I was so much fatigued as to be compelled to lie down. Suffered all night with neuralgia and next day felt very unwell. Monday I had a letter from my wife. She was so bitterly disappointed when Mr. Bradley arrived without me. She had Annie with her, and was waiting at the depot with a buggy to take me home. She knew I had been sick, and expected to find me feeble, and so was all prepared to take charge of an invalid husband. Tuesday and Wednesday were dull heavy days, and prison life seemed more gloomy than ever before. To-day a new order has been issued changing the aspect of affairs, and making a very material improvement in our condition. A sutler has been appointed for the prison, and we are permitted to buy whatever he chooses to keep, or we to order in the way of provisions; the only difficulty now is, the money to buy with. It can be furnished by our friends on the outside, and will be, in most cases, but such as have no friends to whom they can apply, must suffer on as before, and there are more of this class than one would imagine. We have availed ourselves of the new programme so far as to purchase some apples, which we have enjoyed as those outside can never know anything about.

MARCH 18.—Had last night some fine music on the guitar, by Joe Leddy, who sometime since at Batesville, Ark., was sentenced to be hung, but the sentence being commuted, he was sent from there here, and is now locked up night and day. It was sweet and sad to hear his mellow notes warbling out from his gloomy cage. We listened while song after song poured itself forth, now low and tender, now deep and grand, and anon wild, strong, and thrilling. Music at all times pleasant, is entrancing here.

MARCH 25.—It is useless to repeat that time drags heavily—the old complaint is worn threadbare—yet every day that comes and goes, but adds another link to this chain of incontestable truth, "time drags heavily." A week has elapsed—fourteen of us occupy a room sixteen feet square. It is thick standing up, but when we wish to lie down, it is somewhat crowded. I spread my pallet on the table and thus escape the jam.

On Sunday a lot of Feds from Myrtle prison, were placed in with us having been fighting among themselves. One of them had his nose bitten off. They were as hard a looking set as I have seen; after remaining a short time in our quarters they were taken to a strong room and put under lock and key. Wife writes, they have not despaired of my release and are still working to obtain it. Yesterday morning we had a "dashing" time for a few minutes, hot coffee flew in abundance, it ended by one man getting his head cut with a cup. It was not exactly a "tempest in a tea-pot" but one very much mixed with coffee. Altogether it was a foolish affair; with the common enemy leagued against us, there should be peace among ourselves.

I was surprised to find among a lot of new arrivals my old friends Col. and Sam. Winston, who were captured in Platte county, Mo. They have been imprisoned at St. Joseph, and while there, the Col. got into trouble with some Federal horse thieves, about forty of whom were in the same prison, they handled him pretty roughly, giving him a "black eye" which he brings into Gratiot.

MARCH, 26.—Col. Winston was called before Gen. Rosecrans to-day, who lectured him severely for being inside the Federal lines, asking him if he did not know that he had laid himself liable to be tried and hung as a spy. Witnessed a sad and affecting sight, such as too often occurs in a military prison. Capt. Sullivan carried up the little daughter of Mr. Robert Loudon to see her father. She could not be admitted within his cell, but the kind hearted Captain held her up so she could kiss her father through the iron bars; he put his hands through and touched her soft silken hair, and asked her if she nursed little baby sister. Then he kissed her again, and told her to kiss her ma for him. Capt S. is liked by all the prisoners, but it is feared he will not be permitted to remain long in charge as he has too much soul for the position.

TUESDAY, April 5.—On the night of my last writing, an attempt was made to dig through the wall into the building of the Christian Brothers, but unfortunately it was discovered before the design was completed and no escape was made. Those engaged in the enterprise were promptly locked up. Mr. Bradley wrote me a few days since, informing me that my brother Dan., a Colonel in the Federal army, had written to Gen. Rosecrans concerning my release. My friends are very kind indeed, and I am truly grateful, but it makes me sad every time I see a man go out on oath and bond; every one seems a stroke of the funeral bell for our beloved South: it will be a sorrowful day when I throw my shovel of dirt and march away. It appears however that it is going to be my fate to be reserved for one of the "watchers." The following document was sent me this morning from Head Quarters:

HEAD QUARTERS, DEPT. OF THE MISSOURI,
OFFICE OF THE PROVOST MARSHAL GENERAL,
St. Louis, April 4, 1864.

*Special Order, No. 89.*

The instructions of the Commanding General, directing the release of Capt. Griffin Frost, of the rebel army, having been revoked by Special Order No. 66, par. "G," Head Quarters, Department of the Missouri, of date of March 7, 1864, he will be transferred under guard from Gratiot street prison to the Military prison at Alton, Ill., to serve out his sentence.

J. P. SANDERSON, Provost Marshal Gen.

Capt. GRIFFIN FROST, Gratiot St. Prison.

APRIL, 12.—Heard last week that a number of prisoners had escaped from Alton. My brother John has been sent from there to Fort Delaware, it seems he finds the latter place a little too tough even for his philosophy. Says he very much prefers Alton. He tells as much as he dares, but what John says means a good deal. He is by no means disposed to be a grumbler, and things have to be bad indeed when he complains. Four thousand prisoners are there awaiting exchange. Having been there myself on a similar errand, but when the crowd was not so great, I can form some idea of the situation. May the good Lord put it into the heart of old Stanton to allow an exchange soon. Col. Winston was out before the Provost on Saturday in company with other officers. Sunday they were preparing to send off a number of prisoners, about 140 privates, who left Monday. Forty-one officers left to-day for Johnson's Island, where they go to wait for exchange. Would it could be general, and take us all. If the South could gather up all her waste material, she might be strong enough to make a good rally yet.

A Federal prisoner named Cantrel, disputed the word of Lieut. Sebring this morning, when the latter pitched into him and gave him a genteel pummelling leaving a rather ugly cut near the left eye. Matters rested thus until breakfast, when Cantrel slipped up behind Sebring and with a lick unbottomed a bucket over the latter's head. After which he made all possible speed to the office, on going down stairs he ran against McGinnis and upset a bucket of sugar he was carrying, but nothing stopped Cantrel until he had reported the affair, and was transferred to other quarters, for well he knew that he had best keep out of Sebring's way.

APRIL, 13.—I give this day a special mark, for reasons hereafter explained. This morning I was placed back in my old quarters, with the windows on the gallery opened. It is most refreshingly pleasant I find myself for once, with no reasonable cause of complaint, a circumstance so rare, I think it demands notice. My room is comfortable; we are allowed to buy provisions and newspapers are not prohibited. I have said before that Capt. Sullivan is a gentleman. Well, I was ordered before the Provost. Nobody could inform me what was wanted. Getting ready—a guard with his musket took me in charge and we reported at the Provost's.

At the door I met an old gentleman, Mr. Daniel McLoud, of Marion county, Mo., whom I knew; after shaking hands, I went into the office, and there sat *my wife and child*. The former I saw but a short time fifteen months ago, but the little Annie, not since the war commenced—then she could not talk—now she is equal to an old woman. Our interview lasted nearly three hours. My wife still entertains a hope of my speedy release. When I could stay no longer I bade them an affectionate farewell and reluctantly came back to my prison. My sweet little daughter—she seemed like some bright fairy, or ministering spirit, as she clung round my neck and nestled her head of shining clustering curls so lovingly on my bosom. My noble wife has been a true mother to our darling child. I can write on no other subject—have room for no other thought, so I will close for to-night.

APRIL 17.—Thursday was a cold disagreeable day, no sensation whatever. Nobody had a laugh, none a fuss, and the musical fountains were all frozen. So we sat the day out like a Quaker meeting. Friday some ladies came in. I don't know who they were, or on what errand of mercy they descended, but as we saw them enter and heard the low music of their gentle voices, we felt like that Peri, who,

> "At the gate
> Of Eden stood, disconsolate:
> And as she listened to the springs
> Of life within, like music flowing,
> And caught the light upon her wings
> Through the half open portal glowing,
> She wept, &c."

Saturday some of the occupants of Myrtle street prison, were turned over to the tender care and keeping of the Gratiot authorities. Among the number was a son of Judge Soward, of Canton, Mo., who was assigned to our mess. On that day we scrubbed and whitewashed our quarters. To-day we are very nice and comfortable, enjoying the fruit of yesterday's industry, so we concluded we would celebrate the occasion by having a good dinner, and got one of the sergeants to take a bucket and go out and hail a milk man:

"What's wanted?" asked the vender of food for babes.

"A bucket of milk for the prisoners," was the reply.

Gathering up his lines, and giving his horses a crack, he started off, saying:

"I never have, and never will, sell anything to rebels."

The good natured sergeant had no other alternative but to return with his empty bucket, and thus faded the bright anticipations which clustered around the good dinner "that might have been." More prisoners arrived to-day.

APRIL 26.—On Monday we were fully compensated for the failure of our negotiation with the milk man by Miss Laura Elder's sending us an abundant lot of delicious cake, which we relished as none but prisoners know how. Tuesday a scrap of gossip from Rock Island was handed round; it seems that one of their prisoners, a portly young fellow in Confederate grey, was lately delivered of a fine boy—a new recruit for Uncle Jeff, of course.

Wednesday had a letter from home saying that Gen. Rosecrans had power to release all sentenced prisoners, and as I am in that category hopes are entertained of a favorable action in my case. The monotony of Thursday was broken by Lieut. Sebring's receiving from Miss Lucy Glasscock, of Ralls county, Mo., a choice variety of most tempting edibles. Ab. C. Grimes was also remembered from the same source. The regiment which has been guarding us was removed on Friday and sent South, some cavalry from Michigan taking their place. We were sorry to witness the change, for the officers of the old regiment were gentlemen, and we had some excellent friends among the men. While they were strict in enforcing orders, they harrassed the prisoners with no petty personal malice or contemptible exhibition of ephemeral power. The new authorities are yet to be tried, they appear to have seen service, which is an argument in their favor. We will forbear comment, and watch the course of events. Yesterday it rained hard all day, continuing through the night, and the clouds are not taken in to-day. Some ladies however, ventured through the damp to church; wonder if they will hear any prayers offered up for the "prisoners in our midst." One thing, they'll hear sure, is the President prayed for. An old Baptist preacher at Hannibal, named Cleavland, had a cannon drawn on him to make him pray for Old Abe, but that was early in the war and I guess they are all whipped into the traces by this time. Abraham ought to be a blessed and fortunate individual, when so many prayers are forced to "spurt out" at the point of the bayonet for him. Our room has become much crowded again, which interferes materially with any effort at comfort, we have hardly room to lie down on the floor, and when all are up stirring about it is impossible to read or write with any pleasure; every one following the bent of his peculiar humor converts the place at times into a perfect Bedlam. I manage to write a few letters, and jot a few lines now and then in my journal, but it is toiling against wind and tide.

SUNDAY, May 1.—This is a beautiful May day morning, warm, soft and bright. How delightful it would be to take a good long walk, far away from the sight of guards, prisons, and all the machinery of war, into the grand old solemn woods, those primeval forests, where nature reigns alone in undisputed majesty, but we are of those, "that never pass their brick wall bounds to range the fields and treat their lungs with air."

> It matters little unto us, how softly winds may woo,
> Or birdlings twitter in the woods, or flowerets blink in dew
> There is a bound we may not pass, death stands upon a line;
> And armed men in bristling ranks, hedge in each fond design.

So I withdrew my eager eyes from the inviting scene, and fell to posting up my journal. Monday I received the following note from Judge Dryden, relative to my release:

SUPREME COURT ROOM,
ST. LOUIS, April 23, 1864.

CAPT. FROST—*Dear Sir:*—I have received your note of the 20th, and have gone to Hd. Qtrs. in obedience to your request, where I had the most satisfactory assurance that you will be discharged and permitted to return to your home and family at an early day. You must, in the meantime, in patience possess your soul. In haste yours, &c., JOHN D. S. DRYDEN.

GRIFFIN FROST, Gratiot St., Prison.

On Tuesday Dr. Wright was locked up in close confinement. Sad news of the severe illness of my little daughter reached me on Wednesday. I trust the mother's fears may be exaggerated and ill-founded. God forbid that she may be called upon to bury our only treasure. Thursday John Frost reports from Fort Delaware. They are anxiously awaiting an enchange; the tone of his communication is not quite so hopeful and buoyant as was want at Alton—though he says but little. I would like to talk with him a half hour, and have the whole story. Friday I received an official notice, which seems to postpone the matter of my release, as it says that no action will be taken in the case at present. Yesterday was a blank in the calendar—a damp sultry day. Nothing new to-day.

MAY 5.—On Monday Mrs. Loudon, wife of Robert Loudon, who is sentenced to be hung to-morrow, was admitted to her husband's cell. She was accompanied by the same sweet little girl that we saw kiss her father through the iron bars. After the sorrowful interview was over, and mother and child were in the street, the precious dear stopped, and looking up at her father's window, threw showers of loving kisses from both her soft little hands, the mother waited with her pale sad face turned toward the window. There was not a dry eye among all the rough men who witnessed the scene.

Some thirty prisoners left here yesterday for Alton—most of them sentenced during the war; among the lot were two from our room, Capt. Dawson and Robert Lavalle; the latter being the one who was caught in the act of escaping last December, when the long tunnel was made. Several were also released on oath and bond; one of them, a Mr. Bacon, was a fellow sufferer with me in the lock-up. Amid the other events of yesterday, and not the least important to me personally, was the arrival of a letter announcing the improvement of my little daughter's health.

To-day a great gloom has settled over the prison. One of our number, a beloved fellow prisoner is to be executed to-morrow. This morning's papers speak of it, and say everything is in readiness, and that he will be executed in the jail yard between the hours of ten and twelve. His wife came to see him again, and the poor lady looked as though her heart was almost broken with grief. His friends are making a desperate effort to have him reprieved—it is certainly to be hoped they may succeed. The Priests have visited him several times. He is firm, and will no doubt meet his death as becomes a hero and a brave soldier.

MAY 6.—Friday morning—The papers say that yesterday evening the side-walks from Gratiot to the jail, were thronged with people watching to get a glimpse of Loudon, who, it was supposed, would be taken to the jail at that time.

Noon—The execution has been postponed, and the multitude will be disappointed in the feast of human suffering on which it expected to gloat its human eyes.

When the reprieve was read to him he said he felt as if he had risen from the grave—his wife was the happiest looking woman I ever saw—we were all rejoiced, for Robert Loudon is a man whom we highly esteem, and his interesting family command our warmest sympathy. Bless that loving hearted little girl, how tears and smiles will commingle when she hears the news.

MAY 12.—Frank Noel has left on exchange—if one is ever effected. One old man named Murphy, has been added to our room, imprisoned, he says, for selling miscegenation photographs. Twenty-four prisoners left yesterday for Alton. Dr. Wright, Fornchell and Capt. Phillips, sentenced during the war, were of the number. This evening Sam. Clifford and two or three others, from strong room No. 3, came over with their instruments, banjo, guitar, violin and castinets, and entertained us for some time with both vocal and instrumental music. It was quite a feast of soul and flow of song, with a lively sprinkle of wit. With what infinite gusto, old Masterson would have "come down on us, and cleaned us out." Long life to his absence.

## CHAPTER VIII.

SENTENCE OF COL. WINSTON; IN THE DUNGEON; OUR MESS; ARRIVAL OF CHARLES HUNT; RELEASE OF DR. JOURDAN; AMUSING INCIDENT; REDUCTION OF RATIONS; ARRIVAL OF CITIZEN PRISONERS; REMOVAL OF JOSEPH LANIER, WHO IS SENTENCED TO BE SHOT; STRUGGLE FOR LIBERTY; ESCAPE OF CAPT. JOHN THRAILKILL FROM ALTON PRISON; THE ARKANSAS LADY; &C., &C.

WEDNESDAY, MAY 18, 1864.—Yesterday was the opening day of the great Sanitary Fair. The city is doubtless thronged with visitors, eagerly seeking the excitement of something new, or else fired with a patriotic philanthropy they are devoting their time and means toward the accomplishing of some substantial good for the benefit of their sick and wounded soldiers. The object is truly noble, and I trust the work will prosper, and in the ultimate result reflect credit on the heads and hearts of those engaged. There is no doubt but money will pour into their hands in a perfect stream, and it is to be hoped they will turn it into such channels as will reach the special objects for which it is contributed. The Captain commanding at Gratiot, is from Ravenswood, Va., and is acquainted with my relatives; I have also met with a guard who was raised in Wheeling, Va., where I learned the printing business; although they differ from me so essentially in views of political right and wrong, still they excite a kindly feeling for old association's sake.

Col. Winston left to-day with five or six others, to serve out in Alton the sentence imposed upon him, which is five years confinement in the military prison of that place. Rather a sad conclusion of the bright dreams and glorious anticipations with which we started out on our recruiting expedition; we little imagined when we were pushing day and night on empty stomachs through the devastated regions of northern Arkansas and southern Missouri, that we were running with all speed to slip our heads into the noose, yet such was the fact, for Col. Priest and myself were picked up before we had breathing time. Col. Winston, with the others had an opportunity of looking around, but they found things very different from what we had supposed when we started North. The best that could be done was to effect a secret organization and remain perfectly quiet, awaiting a turn in the course of events. The "turn" came sooner than was anticipated, and of a character not at all in accordance with the nature of the plans proposed. The Winstons were captured. How the fine chivalrous nature of the Colonel will brook the bondage of prison life, remains to be seen. Col. Priest has purchased his liberty with an oath and bond ; I am negotiating a similar arrangement, and others are looking forward to the same mode of exit. The Winston spirit has not yet bowed to sue for pardon where no wrong was done. Whether he will bear his fate with sullen, gloomy pride, or yielding to inevitable destiny, dodge the cataract which will surely drench him, I have no idea. I was interested in observing him a few evenings ago, as he sat gazing pensively from the window. Two young ladies—Miss D—. H—. and her sister—came on some mission of mercy to the prison door, Col. W. watched them as long as they were within sight, then taking out his pencil, he dashed off the following lines :

### TO MISSOURI LADIES.

'Neath Yankee rule, are many gems
In darkness brightly shining,
Which sparkle with the purest beams,
Heaven's choicest rays adorning.

And flowers of beauteous tint I ween,
Their fragrance are exhaling,
As rich and rare as ere have been
When Federal sway's prevailing.

These gems and flower's, more precious far,
Than mines of gold and rubies,
Or finest flights of song—are
Missouri's Southern beauties.

At the conclusion I remarked, "That will do Colonel, I will take that if you please as an item for my Journal."

May 22.—Nothing worthy of note during the last three days. This morning the sergeant came up stairs to call the roll, and as some of our room mates were not up, when a certain gentleman passed our door, he took it upon himself to inform the sergeant that we were in bed, and that we were always late, which is untrue. With that the sergeant came to the door, looked in and counted us, and closed it with the remark that "we could stay in," and went on calling the roll. Some of the boys went out and answered to their names, but three or four staid in. When he was through, Mr. sergeant reappeared and called for Lieut. Carson, who answering, was told to carry down the night buckets. Dr. Hardinge, was then called, and ordered to get the broom and sweep the halls. My turn came next, and I was told to go down and cut wood, which I refused to do. The order was given a second time, accompanied with an oath, and was again refused in corresponding language, when I was threatened with the dungeon. I admitted that he had the power to put me in a dungeon, and could use it, but that I had committed no offense whatever, and would not become a party against myself, merely to gratify his foolish anger. A few more passes were exchanged between us, which only served to widen the breach, when he ordered me to take my coat and follow him. I obeyed. We reached the dungeon, where I was turned in and locked up—found it very dark; a damp unhealthy hole, with a strong offensive smell. I did not think I would stay long, so I took it easy—whistled and wondered if I was going to get any breakfast. I thought of the poor fellows who have to lie in dungeons for months, with their heavy balls and chains, wearing the life out of them—many of them better men than I. I can congratulate myself on the easy time I have had. After remaining a few hours I was released and sent back to quarters.

May 26.—On Tuesday, among a lot of prisoners brought down from Alton was a man named Highly, who has been the subject of a rather curious and interesting mistake. He was arrested, imprisoned, tried and sentenced to be hung on the twentieth of next month, and on being sent down was discovered to be the wrong man. Some one else bearing the same name is the individual sought for. On the same day a theatrical performer named Simpson, was introduced to Gratiot, taken just as he was going on the stage.

Yesterday a couple of gents from the lower quarters were adorned with balls and chains, to prevent a contemplated escape. To-day we have been quiet all day, but crowded as we are the weather begins to be oppressive. The principal amusement in vogue is the jewelry business, which is decidedly flourishing at this time. Rings, breast pins, sleeve buttons, and indeed every thing imaginable in that line, being produced in great abundance; and often in a style highly creditable to the genius and perseverance of the workmen. Gutta percha and pearl buttons comprise the material chiefly used, though it sometimes happens that silver or gold coins are obtained by some enterprising genius, more fortunate than his companions, and when such is the case, we are prepared to say to the world that Gratiot presents attractions which are unequaled in any other prison North or South, and which defy competition in the choice variety, exquisite workmanship and distingue finish of her rare assortment of elegant bijoutry.

MAY 27.—Stealing seemed to be the principal part in the programme of last night, and our guards were the chief actors. Samuel Winston, Dr. Boyed and Capt. Trimble lost their hats, and I was relieved of a ring and a silk handkerchief. Complaint being made to the officers, they ordered a search, and succeeded in finding Capt. Trimble's hat, but the other two and my articles were not discovered. The hats were hung near the windows and stolen through the iron bars, and my vest pocket was robbed in like manner. The guard, on being questioned as to his motive in committing the theft, asserted that it was not want which drove him to do the deed, but simply a desire to "keep his hand in," and he thought as hats had not been issued to his company for a good while, he would draw some and issue them himself. As for the ring and handkerchief, I suppose that was a private affair drawn for his personal use. He made no public explanation concerning them. They are a miserable set, overbearing and brutal in their treatment of prisoners—having no self respect, they do not understand the term as applied to others. One of my room mates, Joseph Elliot, went down stairs this evening and stepped towards the door leading to the office, when the guard presented his bayonet and told him "if he did not stand back he would job it into him." Joe looked at the fellow for a moment, smiled contemptuously, called him some suitable name, and left. Thus at every turn they thrust their disgusting insolence into our faces. It is not the officers, but the low beastly men—in most cases they have been the better part of the regiment; we have found friends among the privates, when their officers have acted the dog, but in this instance quite the contrary was the fact.

Our mess consists of the following gentlemen: Dr. James Hardinge, Samuel Winston, Joseph Soward, W. H. Sebring, Joseph Elliot, James A. Carson, Dr. Victor Jourdan, and myself. Dr. Jourdan received a rich basket to-day, and at supper we enjoyed with infinite zest the trial and discussion of its contents. It is a source of great joy and congratulation to the whole mess, when any of its members receives so substantial a token of remembrance from the outside; and no one dispenses his hospitality with a more royal munificence than Dr. Jourdan. His whole soul delights in the happiness and good cheer of others.

Charles Hunt, the Belgian Consul, was arrested to-day and sent to the Hotel de Gratiot to board at Uncle Sam's expense, and our theatrical friend Simpson, was released.

MAY 28.—Our mess has this day sustained a great loss in the person of that incomparable good fellow, the noble hearted Dr. Victor S. Jourdan, who has been released on oath and bond. His arrest was caused by his selling magnesia to a detective, who expected to catch him indulging in contraband practices with quinine. But Dr. J. being too sharp to be caught in such a trap, succeeded in practicing an admirable "sell" on the detective, which so exasperated the honorable fraternity that they ordered his arrest, and thus conferred upon our mess the pleasure of his most desirable acquaintance. He left us this morning, but after an absence of an hour or two, returned laden with presents, just the things we most needed, and which we will prize the highest, summer shirts to one, photograph album to another, a lot of fine stationery, a gutta percha rule, pearl buttons for jewelry, &c., &c., and lastly, a lot of fine chewing tobacco for us all. Long life and success to Dr. Jourdan. May his shadow never grow less and frequently "darken our door."

The Feds are doing a pretty lively business to-day arresting citizens. Gratiot has received several for her share, one of whom is Capt. McDonald, brother to the Cofederate hero Emmett McDonald. A letter, which has just arrived from my wife, tells me of the death of her cousin, James Johnson, who volunteered in the Confederate service at the commencement of the war, but after remaining two years and discharging his duty as a soldier, his health failed him and he started homeward. He was captured on the way and brought to Gratiot, but on account of his condition was released on oath and bond. When he reached home the malice of personal enemies would not permit him to remain, and he was forced to go North into Iowa, where he has lately died of that long lingering disease consumption.

THURSDAY, June 2, 1864.—We have a large number of citizens lodging in our hotel at this time; thirty-seven new ones were brought in last night; they are a jolly crowd, full of music. Mr. Hunt, the Consul, is very lively—amuses himself and entertains his listeners with singing portions of his favorite opera pieces; he belongs to mess No. 2, but is disposed to cultivate a kindly relationship with his neighbors. Our mess received from him on Monday a splendid treat of strawberries, which were duly appreciated. Such little courtesies are much more highly valued in prison, where they are necessarily rare, and where the great dearth of comfort renders them conspicuous, than they are among friends in the social circle outside. There are many in this prison who are poor—whose friends have been robbed—their houses burned—their stock taken, their all, in fact, destroyed, except the bare land, and themselves dependent on charity for a means of support. Such of course have no remittance, and can procure no change in their prison fare; day after day the same old thing—barely enough, and that of the cheapest commodity, on which soul and body can be induced to continue their copartnership. To these, a handful of fresh strawberries would be a luxury whose worth could scarcely be computed. But their* great number renders it a hopeless task for any fellow prisoner to undertake to supply them all with even a taste. The officers are more fortunate, fewer in number we can easily divide our subsistence, and besides, we are frequently favored with gifts from kind hearted ladies of the city, several of whom were in yesterday, seeing friends, and bestowing bundles and baskets of clothing and food. Their steps were not directed toward our quarters, still we were heartily rejoiced to see them enter the prison gates, for we knew that some poor fellow's eyes were brightened, and their hearts made glad before they left. Messmate Joe Elliot, received a handsome lot of provision to-day, consisting of good things generally.

JUNE 3.—Quite an amusing incident occurred this afternoon between a couple of our room mates and some young ladies across the street. The lady of the house, mother to one of the girls, and aunt to the other, also mother to a sweet little Miss about five years old, had during the day added to her household treasures another infantine member; of which fact of course our friends were ignorant. The little five year old cherub, by her many winning and charming graces, had quite captivated the heart of the inflexible Dr. B —, who when the party accross the street made their appearance at the window, requested his friend J — S —, to enquire of the young ladies, by spelling on his fingers, the name of his little favorite. Joe, to cut the matter short, spelled out, "what's the baby's name?" The question was like a bombshell bursting in their midst—they scattered instanter, but a merry peal of laughter that rang out behind them showed that "somebody was hurt." Doc. and Joe were puzzled to know what was the matter, but when they found out, they wisely concluded not to push their inquiries concerning the "little girl" any farther.

MONDAY, June 6.—A young man named Joseph Green, nephew of Gen. Martin E. Green, was arrested and added to our mess on last Saturday and to-day was called out before the Provost, who offered to relieve him on oath and bond of $3,000; he refused to give the bond and was ordered back to prison; on the way he took his guard into a saloon, got him drunk and left him there, while he walked about the city as long a time as suited him. In the evening he dropped in and reported himself to the prison officers; showing plainly that as a man of honor he did not require the restrictions of a bond. The act was noble and worthy of his glorious uncle, than whom a more gallant officer, and thorough gentleman has never suffered in behalf of right and justice. We admire Joseph Green, but with our experience of prison life, we think the temptation would have been too strong for our resistance. Our lives are becoming more and more miserable every day, and our fare is growing less. Coffee, tea, and sugar have been cut off from our rations, and hereafter we will have to content ourselves with dry bread and meat with sometimes a few potatoes, beans, or a little rice. We were stinted enough before, and had to go to bed many a time with a hungry stomach, and of course will do so often hereafter. John still writes from Fort Delaware, they are very impatient for exchange, but see no prospect as yet, he thinks probably the fight now pending in Virginia may produce something decisive.

JUNE 7.—Our friend Joe Soward, was cook to-day, and great praise is due his laudable effort in that department. Before dinner he called on each member of the mess and took his order for the preparation of the all important potato. Considering the matter a joke we each one gave different directions and dismissed the subject from our minds. But when dinner was announced we were surprised to find every man's potato served up according to the desire expressed, baked, boiled, fried, mashed, &c. We had a hearty laugh, and enjoyed the meal much more than usual. Joe is a splendid fellow, and if there is any kernel of enjoyment in prison life, he will crack the nut and pick it out,

JUNE 9.—Yesterday four citizens were brought in from Callaway county; three were physicians and one a lawyer—Jeff Jones—they are suspicioned of being connected with the Knights of the Golden Circle.

Joseph Lanier was taken from here about midnight last night and sent to Savannah, Andrew county, Mo., where he is to be shot to-morrow. Ten or fifteen minutes later, would have placed him beyond their reach. He and his room mates were working vigorously; had a rope already prepared and a hole cut nearly through the wall. Their effort was a desperate struggle for the life of a fellow prisoner. Lanier knew it was his only hope. They continued work until the tramp of the jail men at the door told them that all was over, and it was too late. The doomed man was taken and loaded with irons and carried off, and his companions are now chained around posts in the yard as a punishment for their assistance. They are to stand from two in the afternoon, until twelve at night, to be continued twenty days. Ab Grimes, Joe Leddy, Thad Ripley, a man named Shultz, and two others, constitute the unfortunate chain gang crowd. It is brutally shocking to see men suffer thus for obeying the greatest impulse of the human heart. What a sensation is sometimes produced, and how men will rush on to deeds of daring, when some noble animal of the brute creation is standing at bay and waiting with a quiet majesty the approach of a devouring element. What shouts applaud its rescue! But here how different. These men with the sublime energy of despair labored almost into the jaws of death to release a beloved comrade from an unjust and ignominious death. They failed, and their reward is to be chained up like dogs to a post.

A number of prisoners were notified this evening to be ready by six in the morning to start for Jefferson City where they are to serve out a term of years in the Penitentiary. Col. Hunt was called out before the Provost to-day, and had the pleasure of an hour or two's conversation with his wife; on his return he brought in some elegant pearl for the jewelry department.

JUNE 12.—Among the prisoners sent off Friday to Jefferson City were two of my acquaintances—Taylor and McGinnis. Yesterday I had several letters—one accompanied a package of newspapers from my brother William who is foreman in the Audrain County Ledger office. Dr. George Hardinge and Robert McDonald were released yesterday, and to-day the Doctor made us a call. He is a gay widower, and dashed up to old Gratiot in grand style, with a handsome lady and child in the buggy with him. We were glad to see him faring so well although our own comforts are "growing small by degrees, and beautifully less." I cooked to-day and with my best efforts, we have been on the borders of hunger all day, I hope some of us will get a present soon.

MONDAY, June 13.—We have a gentleman in our quarters known among us as Capt. C—, from Illinois, who says he is a married man, has a pretty wife and three interesting children, but a stranger would certainly take him to be a single gentleman endeavoring to get a wife; as he is constantly bowing and throwing kisses to a certain young lady who sends him handsome boquets accompanied with notes filled with pretty talk, &c. But during the last few days the Captain has met with a rival who also receives boquets, &c., and it puzzles the former to keep up with the new aspirant. They have taken to poetry, which they send by one of the sergeants, and in that channel the rival is a little ahead, besides having rather the advantage in personal appearance. They have been carrying on this amusement for several days, sending out poetry and receiving flowers, which one of our room mates thinks not sufficient to keep soul and body together, and desiring to see something coming in more substantial than bouquets and billet-doux, has dedicated the following lines to the young lady in question, which he unbeknown to the infatuated rivals, has posted off to the fair Dulcina.

### A NODE TO ——.

Oh ! loveliest of thy sex,
Beauteous art thou as an angel's smile,
I love to contemplate thy fairy form,
Thou art so gentle and so free from guile.

Oft at midnight's hushed still hour,
When Luna, gentle queen of night,
Surrounded by obsequious stars,
Softly o'er us, sheds her light :

'Tis then, in dreams angelic,
Thy image comes in all its splendor,
Wreathing bright hopes for me, dear one,
Which none save thee canst ere engender.

Thy glance is bliss, thy smile is heaven,
In adoration to thee I kneel,
Then listen to my prayer, fair —,
In pity for the love I feel.

The Vernal flowers are appreciated,
Also your dear kind notes and letters;
But send us something more substantial,
As a "brandy cock-tail," or a "mess of taters."

"Feminine Joe" being in the secret, lets off the following "bust" on the occasion. "This is the best hit of the season. We, the initiated, can alone see the jibe or feel it. I am expiring to witness the denouement. What will Mrs. Grundy of Gratiot say when it comes? What a wonderful place this is for unearthing talents. Poets take the lead, and foremost in the ranks comes Jones, the Gratiot poet, par excellence; then Capt. C., J. L., S. C., and last, but by no means least—stalks forth "my Joe," whose muse assumes the comic mask ; sarcasm and irony too, form part of the ingredients which he works up to so much advantage. "With him I am well pleased." The artists and artizans are innumerable. Such sculptured forms were never created under the chisel and mallet of Cannova, Angelo, Thorwaldson, "or any other man," as are brought forth from the stores of Gratiot—forms divine—from the Medusa of E —, to the chained figures, and pipes covered with strange hieroglyphics of C —, Geo. S., Billy the "lamp boy," and others."

A fellow prisoner named John Monroe, for attempting to whip an Irish Federal detective, was honored with a ball and chain, and while it was being fastened on, Dr. Flore stood by quietly watching the operation, when a corporal of the guard drew his revolver and threatened to blow his brains out if he did not go up stairs immediat'ly. The Doctor was taken by surprise, for there was nothing unusual in his conduct in any way, and he did not know how to interpret the corporal's anger. His whole object was evidently to be insulting—things are becoming very disagreeable indeed.

JUNE 15.—John Monroe is relieved of his ball and chain, but he and all in the lock-ups are under more restrictions than they have been since Capt. Harvey has had command. Seventy-eight men were sent off to-day to some other prison to await an exchange. Lieuts. Ponder and Turner were with them; after they started the latter had to come back, being a cripple with a wooden leg, he was unable to keep up. Capt. Trimble was notified the other day, but this evening his name was not called; being a regular prisoner of war he is unable to account for it, and is much disappointed.

While the lock-up prisoners were hanging out their blankets to sun this morning, the porch on which they stood gave way, and came down with a tremendous crash, injuring one of the prisoners badly and several others slightly. Ab. Grimes caught the iron bars of a window, and saved himself from falling with the rest. It is remarkable that they escaped as well as they did, for they were all wearing heavy balls and chains. Fate and the Federals seem disposed to play sad pranks with this devoted band, but with all and through all, they maintain an undaunted front; their courage never quails, whether *freezing* or *baking* around their posts, or dangling from grated windows with chains rattling and balls bobbing, or going down with the crash of a building, they are the same indomitable set—they never grumble, make no complaints, submit to all orders, and work steadily at their own plans. Prison walls have never held Ab. Grimes very long yet, and the worse they treat him, and closer they watch him, the sooner he snaps his fingers at them and leaves for parts unknown. Ab. is a whole souled, good natured fellow, with a host of warm and true friends wherever he is known.

JUNE 17.—Had a letter from Alton prison to-day, telling of the escape of Capt. John Thrailkill, who was sentenced there during the war. We have had a queer customer in to-day—one of those wild Arkansas women, whose husband is a prisoner here and who once belonged to the Southern army, but is now a vile exterminating radical. The woman went to the Provost Marshal and said, "Mr. Provost Marshal, you'ns have got my man a prisoner, and I want to see him."

The Provost sent and had a guard bring her "man" to the office. How they behaved there I am unable to say, but I happened to be in the Captain's office when they returned to the prison. The Captain invited her into the office. After she got in, she turned to see if her husband was coming and finding he did not advance, she made a whirl which threw her clothes in most ungainly manner, and springing at the Captain, said, "I say—Lieutenant, Colonel, Major, or Captain, or whatever you are, can't he come in too." The Captain told her he could, and they both took a seat near the window and commenced with their pretty talk, and continued for some time until two or three ladies came in desiring to see their friends, when lady No. 1, raised up and seated herself in her husband's lap, and commenced hugging and kissing him at a great rate before all present. At dark, she was still there, and said she was going to stay all night, or have a fight. One of the sergeants said he expected they would have to let her stay. She had a little daughter with her about ten years old. I think if the Yanks had not stolen that family from us, we could have pitted her against the Philadelphia mob women, with this difference, that she shows her spirit in love, theirs in hate. Col. Hunt was out for examination before the Provost to-day. Mr. Ray, a citizen, was also released, but do not know the terms.

JUNE 18.—This has been another day of excitement and sorrow to the inmates of Gratiot, caused by a number of prisoners attempting to make their escape. The particulars as near as can be had are as follows: It seems there was an understanding between a large number of the prisoners to make their escape by rushing on and overpowering the guard. Men from our quarters, the lock-up and the lower rooms were engaged in it, and this morning about eleven o'clock they made the attempt. Procuring an axe, they rushed on the guards, took their guns, and made for the yard in which the lock-up prisoners were permitted to exercise, and from which there is a gate leading into an alley outside. They succeeded in knocking off the lock, and opening the gate, and then started on the run. Some four or five were successful in making their escape—Col. John Carlin, Capt. J. C. Hill, Lieut. Sebring, and two privates, named Yates and Douglas. One Shultz—a U. States detective, who used to be in the Southern army, and was at the battle of Helena, and a man named Colclazier, were killed—the former shot through the right side, the latter through the head. Ab Grimes was wounded in the ankle, and another man in the thigh. Grimes received his shot while in the act of opening the gate, after which he ran a short distance, but was compelled to give up, on account of the pain from his wound, and the heavy ball and chain which impeded his progress. I never witnessed such excitement in all my life. Mike, the sergeant, was the only one to give the alarm, and he ran from place to place, yelling at the top of his voice, "Shoot! shoot!! shoot!!!" when some of the others took up the cry of alarm, and rushed into the street, crying out, "Call out the guard! call out the guard! ! the prisoners are making their escape," and it was not long until the soldiers were running in every direction. In about ten minutes we saw a squad returning with the body of Shultz. We were all ordered to stand back from the windows, and if we did not, the guards were ordered to fire on us; but we took the hint and kept away. When the excitement was somewhat subsided, the sergeant came up and called the roll, when two were found missing from our quarters—Capt. Hill and Lieut. Sebring, after which we were ordered to our rooms, and the gate leading to the hall was closed. We hear many reports as to the mode of punishment we are to receive hereafter. Some have one story, and some another, but the last report says, we are to be locked in and kept on bread and water. However, late this evening we were allowed to go down for the purpose of cooking some dinner, but "our mess, No. 3," bought a bucket of milk, and we dined on milk and crackers. The residence of Mr.

Harrison, opposite the prison, was searched on suspicion of some of the prisoners taking refuge there, but I am happy to say they were not paid for their trouble. The weather is excessively warm, and since we have been deprived of the privilege of the hall, which is the only pleasant place in the prison, we find it almost impossible to get air sufficient to keep us from suffocating.

JUNE 19.—We are still locked up—do not know how much longer it will continue, nor do I care. The citizens seem to think it rather hard, but soldiers who have seen all sorts of hardships, take it very easy. During roll call this evening we heard the report of a gun, and on making inquiry, learned that one of the guard had fired into the lock-up, but fortunately did no damage. We are leading a *very pleasant* life at this particular time, but we must "grin and bear it," for it is the best that we can do. There seems to be no remedy at present, though it is said there will be a general investigation to-morrow. We have learned that the sentence of Capt. Hill was received at the office last evening, and that it was imprisonment in the Missouri Penitentiary during the war. Luckily however, Capt. H. is now in a position to live without it.

JUNE 20.—Locked up again to-day as usual, and expect a continuation. A guard fired again this evening, at one of the prisoners in the hospital, but missed his mark. Joe Soward was in the yard at the time, and a piece of the bullet glanced and struck him on the neck causing the skin to change color, which was fortunately all the damage done. There appears to be some misunderstanding in relation to the orders given to the guards, as the Captain and one of the sergeants disclaim all knowledge of any order authorizing them to shoot the prisoners. I hope the matter will be looked into and remedied, as it places us in a very critical situation. Joe Elliot was called out and had another examination before the Provost to-day; he hopes soon to be discharged.

JUNE 22.—I was cook yesterday, and in going from the kitchen to the hydrant, one of the guard, a thick headed Dutchman, would not allow me to walk, except in a certain place. They have been mad ever since Saturday, and only wish us to give them the slightest cover, when they would take delight in firing on us. For my part, I did, and walked just as he said. Ab. Grimes is suffering very much; it is thought he will die of his wound—it is excessively warm and the inflamation is very great. We are still locked up; think we can extend a measure of sympathy to the occupants of the Black Hole of Calcutta.

MONDAY, June 27.—We are allowed the privilege of the hall once more, and it is one we prize very highly. Our mess also received some provision from Dr. Hardinge, of Boone county, Mo., which was a very timely reinforcement. Col. Jeff. Jones and Dr. Boyd were out before the Provost—the latter was offered his liberty on oath and bond, which he refused to accept, a parole bond was then proposed; but the Doctor told them he would neither give nor accept any other kind of a parole than that of a Confederate officer, which he claimed to be, and if his word was not sufficient he would remain in prison until exchanged.

JULY 3.—Last Tuesday, a citizen named May, was arrested and added to our mess, but after remaining a few hours, was released. In the meantime, however, his daughter called and brought him a basket of nice edibles, which he left with us, besides giving us all the small change he had about him, to purchase more when that is gone. We have the name of "Poor Mess," and we consider it very justly applied, as most of us are soldiers from a distance, whose friends cannot well keep us supplied with money, or send us things as we need them—hence a liberal well endowed citizen is always most heartily welcome to a portion of our quarters.

Nineteen prisoners left on Wednesday for Alton—some of them hand-cuffed together in pairs; noticed Thad. Ripley locked on to another gent—suppose it is feared they might make an attempt to escape. Lieut. Carson, from our mess, went with them. Thursday and Friday were so distressingly warm that other items were of minor interest; no one thought of being comfortable, we only sought a measure of relief, but the hall, our universal remedy, proved ineffectual. No place seemed any cooler than the rest; the air was hot and almost stifling as it boilded up from below, and our rooms were like bake ovens—we really suffered—but a merciful Providence sent down "showers of blessings" on Saturday. Cool, delightful, life-inspiring showers. We quietly luxuriated on the rainy day, which was succeeded this morning by most delicious weather, and in the course of the day an Episcopal clergyman (McKinnon) came in the prison and set up an altar, around which could gather those who desired to make an offering of prayer or praises to the great Author of every good and perfect gift. The sacred service was conducted with all due solemnity. Cannon bristling on every side, pointing into the prison, offered no obstruction to the incense which was wafted upward to a throne of grace; that is a line of communication which no "military necessity," usurping proclamations, or perfidious strategy can interrupt. The cannons with which we are surrounded were placed here in consequence of an alarm which has taken hold of the authorities; their brain seems to be infected with strange phantoms tricked out in all imaginable ways, but each one bearing conspicuously the ominous letters "K. G. C." Astounding rumors are afloat, about a rising of the citizens of Illinois and St. Louis, for the purpose of releasing the prisoners here and at Alton. Our keepers, if their fears can create the danger they apprehend, are prepared to slaughter as many of us as possible at the outset. We give no credence whatever to any part of the story. Consider it an old woman's night mare, and fancy that when their blood gets to circulating the crisis will be over.

MONDAY, July 4, 1864.—-This day one year ago, occurred the battle of Helena, which I heard and partly witnessed, and in which John Frost and a number of his comrades were taken prisoners. It was a day of sad disaster to the Confederate arms; besides our humiliating defeat, considering we made the attack, and proposed to celebrate the day. The fall of Vicksburg was the darkest scene in the drama of the war; the crash of that event shattered the whole Trans-Mississippi Department, and it has been impossible ever since to "solder" together anything like an organization. Yankees and ruin toss about over the country with the desolating freedom of flood waters in a deluge. There is an antagonism between Yankee nature and Southern soil, and according as one or the other predominates, evil or good is the result. New England puritanism is rank poison in the South, unless its fangs are drawn. When this is effected they can be tamed and afterwards taught a great deal; but turned loose in all the wild ferocity of their savage nature, they assimilate with the negroes, and the barbarous mixture is at once destructive of all the landmarks of civilization. If our forces should be finally vanquished, and crazy fanatics have free course to mix and mingle with the half tamed negroes in all the South, the beautiful garden spots of that heaven favored land will become as dens and lairs for a new breed of worse creatures than the wild beasts of the forest. If our civilization could be undisturbed and the strong intellect of well balanced Southern minds predominate, both classes could be made useful; we have in the South some Yankees who have been drawn away from Northern influences that make a portion of our best and most respectable citizens, as soon as they have been for a sufficient time removed from the infected atmosphere; the scales, as it were, drop from their eyes, and being prepared then to see things in a true light, they at once become rational beings, useful, and often ornamental members of society. But thus looking beyond the bounds of our prison house does not in the least, mitigate the horrors that are within.

We are surrounded by bayonets and artillery, guarded by soldiers who curse, swear and fire among us when they please, and resort to balls, chains, and dungeons for the slightest offense. Our fare is rough and course, and we never have of prison furnishing, sufficient for a full hearty meal—I speak for the officers—and it is not reasonable to suppose that privates are better treated. This day has been peculiarly irksome, as we are not at all in sympathy with the celebration outside; the national salute is a burlesque and while its echoes rumble around old Gratiot, her inmates are whiling away the dull hours as best they may. No business at the Provost's to-day, and only one prisoner added up to dark.

JULY 7.—Would to God we were out of this miserable place, the weather is so warm it is impossible to be comfortable; we go almost naked—wear nothing but pants and shirts, and then nearly suffocate; to make it worse, we are locked up in the evening—the coolest part of the day. Some take off all but their pants, and go in that garb until nine o'clock, when we are ordered to bed, where we find a new enemy co-operating with the heat; the lamp which is kept burning all night, shows them by hundreds, nay thousands, getting ready to make a charge, and when they come, we alone know what we have to suffer. We brush them off our pillows by dozens—it would be labor lost to try to kill them—and all night long groaning and swearing may be heard from persons suffering under their attack. They are everywhere—bed bugs in the walls, in our blankets, our boots, and even sometimes in our bread. This morning one of my mess mates found a big fat fellow in the bottom of his cup after he had sipped his coffee. They are on our clothes all day—go where we will we are sure to find them; and in addition to bed bugs, we are overstocked with rats, thirty or forty are often found helping themselves in our cupboard at one time, they rob us of nearly all we have to eat—prison rations we don't regret so much, but when we lose our "good things" which have been sent to us, and which we are saving up to make them last, the loss is as distressing as a fire with no insurance.

July 8.—Mess No. three is now composed of seven persons, and being called the "poor mess" do not dispute the title; we acknowledge the poverty, and are bound to admit the hunger. Joe Elliot is the only one who has been fortunate enough lately, to receive any presents; he has a basket sent in once in awhile, from which we appease our hunger while it lasts. But, though bound to admit the justice of our sobriquet, we do not allow our wants to interfere with our regulations, and we think we have as good claim to be styled the "neat and orderly" as the "poor mess." The following rules have been adopted and posted up for the government of our little society:

### RULES AND REGULATIONS OF MESS NO. 3.

1st.—It shall be the duty of the cook to wash all dishes and culinary articles, and leave them in good order and condition for his successor.

2nd.—He shall sweep and clean up the room at least twice during the day—especially the cupboard and mantlepiece.

3rd.—Each member shall carry down "Sumter" in his regular turn as per list.

4th.—Two members shall sweep the halls every fourth day.

5th.—Substitutes positively not accepted unless in case of sickness.

We have one eccentric genius in our number who I think deserves a sketch. We style him "Feminine Joe;" he is quite good looking, medium size, has blue eyes, and glossy black hair—which he curls; embroiders like a lady, and has a great fondness for teasing his fellow prisoners by catching them and hugging and kissing them, one in particular, whom he calls "my Joe," and declares himself in love with; he torments him almost to death—if "my Joe" starts for a drink of water, the "feminine" is sure to follow; if he lies down, he is clasped in the loving arms; at table the "feminine" refuses to eat unless "my Joe" helps his plate. We all get provoked sometimes, and read the offender a genuine scolding lecture, but it is merely a waste of words. "My Joe" gets exasperated occasionally, and deals out a severe tongue lashing, which the "feminine" accepts in a regular lover like pouting manner, they won't speak for several days, and won't sleep together—and all the time "feminine Joe" pretends to be in great trouble over the little "family jar." We are all fond of him, and he is a noble generous fellow; but his feminine airs are often very provoking.

JULY 9.—Had the pleasure to-day, of receiving a box of provision from my home friends in Marion county, Mo. On opening it we found two nice large hams, a lot of biscuit and light bread, maple molasses, peach jam, ground coffee, spiced cherries, jelly, sugar, rice, tea, dried apples and peaches; some clothes, needle book, &c. They were sent by wife, her father, mother, and sisters, and they together with a similar lot which Joe Elliot received yesterday, make the prospects of the "poor mess" quite as flattering as that of our neighbors as long as the supply holds out, or we can succeed in fighting off the rats. Our cook is instructed to practice a rigid economy in using from the store of delicacies; it being the wish of all to have them "string out," and a little kept as long as possible.

JULY 10.—Witnessed a love scene while sitting near the window this afternoon. A very pretty young lady came to the street corner, near by, and commenced looking round seemingly for some friend; she was soon attracted to the guard house window, where a Federal soldier was confined for some misconduct. She made signs to him which soon brought him down into the street, when he was greeted with a squeezing hug, and smacking kiss. During the conversation the lady drew closer and closer, while the soldier backed off, until a brick wall fetched him up standing—after which he stood still, while she played with his suspenders or held his hands—talking all the time, and both appearing very happy.

Presently he made a motion to leave, but she caught him around the neck and kissed him again, held on to his hand—then she took something from her pocket, which we supposed was a ring, and handed to him, and after about five minutes, she hugged and kissed him again and then left. Very affectionate truly.

JULY 14.—On Monday there was nothing new; some of the boys, we thought, were too much fascinated over their game of cards, as they allowed their interest to betray them into bad temper and high words, but they were "O. K." in a short time with "nobody hurt."

Thursday there was exciting talk about a "so called" rebel raid near Washington—presume it did not amount to much, as it soon died out. Wednesday Joseph H. Green, of our mess, was released; also two others named Atkins and Armstrong. To-day we hear that Yates, who escaped with Capt. Hill and Lieut Sebring last month, was recaptured in the southern part of this State, and taken to Potosi, where he again attempted an escape and was shot dead.

We concluded to-day, to change the name of our mess; so hereafter we will be known as the "Poor and Hungry Mess" instead of "Poor Mess," as heretofore. There is a foolish rumor in the city about a band of guerrillas coming in and attacking the place, and the consequence is, we are deprived of the front gallery, which is no small inconvenience this hot weather. My friend Capt. Winston, has this day stood his trial before the Military Commission. We had a ham boiled whole to-day, and after it was cooked done in this way: We had it covered with sugar and baked—it was very fine indeed.

Another letter from John, reports only the firing of a few cannon at Fort Delaware on the Fourth. A fine rain this morning has left it very pleasant this afternoon,

JULY 16.—We were agreeably surprised to see our old friend and messmate Dr. Hardinge, to-day. He came into the prison but we were not permitted to speak to him, however, it was a pleasure to look at him without "cracking a smile, or showing our teeth," and he sent us a note wishing to know if we needed anything. We sent him word with thanks and compliments, accompanied by a ring made by Joe S., a picture of the round building, drawn by

Joe E., and a breastpin made by myself, that some stationery would be very acceptable, and this evening he came with a basket of new potatoes, tomatoes, onions, and apples, also a large ham, a lot of rice, coffee and pickles, and last but not least in the way of edibles, some cocoa nuts, with a fine assortment of stationery and newspapers, and some material for the jewelry shops—for all of which, he has the lasting thanks, and warmest wishes of the "Poor and Hungry Mess."

JULY 17.—Dr. Hardinge visited Gratiot again to-day and brought our mess a fine lot of lemons, plums, and tobacco. He appears to be enjoying himself in the city, as he came in a fine carriage, and when he left, took two of the officers with him—they will probably go to some hotel and have a grand time. Dr. is a widower, and a decided votary of pleasure. He would have made a fine epicurean in the sunny days of ancient Greece. Some of our citizen prisoners are very uneasy over a report that five thousand guerrillas are near St. Louis, and that all the prisoners are to be sent to Fort Delaware, for fear of their being released. Such sensational rumors are too frequent for much reliance to be placed in them.

JULY 18.—A man named Sherin, from Audrain county, was added to Gratiot last Saturday, and since his arrival the boys have had a great deal of sport at his expense. At one time they frightened him nearly to death by telling him that every few days, two or three rebels were taken out and shot, and that his time would come ere long; I never saw a fellow so uneasy in my life. They told him if he had any friends, he had better get them to attend to his case immediately—he stated he had a brother-in-law a Colonel in the Federal army, who would go to Washington for him if necessary, and I believe the poor fellow has written to him to that effect. To-night the boys were all singing songs, and requested him to give us his favorite, when to our surprise, he struck up,

"Am I a soldier of the cross, &c."

The scene that followed may be better imagined than described. He was arrested, he tells us, for not enrolling in the militia.

Our old friend and mess mate, Dr. Hardinge, is again a boarder at Gratiot, but for what offense I am not able to say. We were all glad to take him by the hand and welcome him back to his old mess, although we are sorry to see him in prison. It seems to be the settled policy that we shall be deprived of the hall in the hottest weather.

JULY 23.—Col. Hunt was called out before the Provost to-day, and not having returned, it is supposed he has been released. The iron doors leading to the gallery are locked again. We learn from the papers, that Capt. John Thrailkill, who was sentenced to Alton during the war, but made his escape some time since, is now in Northwest Missouri, at the head of several hundred men, endeavoring to join Thornton, who is engaged in fighting the Militia in that part of the State. The citizens are suffering very much from the presence of the two contending parties. The Militia revenge upon private families, the deeds committed by Southern soldiers in arms—and thus men are murdered in cold blood, and women and children turned out of doors—their houses being destroyed by fire.

MONDAY, July 25.—Benj. Dobyns, an old acquaintance from Mexico, Audrain county, Mo., is now a fellow boarder at this hotel, lodging in the lower quarters. At the beginning of the war he enlisted in the Old State Guard, served out his time, and went home, where he has remained unmolested until the present time. The charges against him now I have not heard. Col. Hunt called this evening for his clothing; has been released on oath and bond of ten thousand dollars—so we learn. Some five or six prisoners left here this evening, under guard, for Jefferson City, where they are to serve out their sentences from five to ten years, or during the war. Three new ones were brought in hand cuffed, charged with fighting the Militia, which is a gross violation of the rules of war, only equaled in atrocity by the daring boy who cut the cake that was baked for company. The Militia are not intended to be fought, their occupation is to roam round the country, frighten women and children, burn houses, shoot old men; and any one who opposes them, is a "bushwhacker," and ought to be shot as soon as taken, without judge or jury; if a true history of the Missouri Militia could be written, it would present as foul a record as ever disgraced a printed page.

Dr. Flore was called out for examination to-day. Feminine Joe is very busy knitting a tidy; he has finished one which is quite handsome. He can do nearly everything that ladies claim as their work.

A negro regiment passed the prison to-day and presented a very warlike appearance, it is said they will be guarding us in a few days. Capt. Carter has been sentenced to Alton at hard labor during the war. Pretty rough treatment for a man of his bringing up—but they will fail to crush his spirit with the worst they can do, or I am mistaken in the ring of his metal.

JULY 29.—On Tuesday I had a letter from my brother William, of Mexico, Audrain county, who tells me that there are serious troubles in his section arising from the presence and collision of the Militia and the opposing Southern force. Such warfare is almost to be deprecated, it will have no bearing on the final result of the main contest, and produces only present confusion and calamity; both parties are highly culpable, and neither to be excused. Capt. Carter and Lieut. Scott have been sent to Alton, and Dr. Hardinge released unconditionally; he says he will make it his duty to keep out of such places in the future, as he finds no attraction in prison life. Capt. Winston has seen his sentence in a city paper, which is ten years at Alton at hard labor. Benj. Dobyns has been transferred from below to the officers quarters, and is now one of Mess No. 3.

## CHAPTER IX.

A True Southern Lady; Arrival of a Box of Provision; Sentence of Capt. W. J. Livingston; White Men Guarded by Negroes; More Prisoners from the South; Departure of Capt. Sam. Winston and eleven others for Alton Prison; Visit to the Hospital; Stealing Money from Prisoners' Letters; Reprieve of Capt. Livingston after his Execution; Stonewall Jackson's Way, &c., &c.

Saturday, July 30, 1864.—I dedicate the note of to-day to Miss Bessie Bury—a true Southern lady, both in heart and action. Although we have never seen her, yet her name is well known, and she has many warm friends in Gratiot. I say we have never seen her, I mean we have never met, or held social converse, but the North Star is not more familiar to the eye of the mariner, than her form to us, as we catch a glimpse of her tripping along the streets. The mention of her name will bring our whole mess to the window, and we never withdraw our eyes until she is lost to our sight; for in looking at her we behold the special benefactress of mess No. 3. Whenever the prison regulations are such as to permit it, we are constantly receiving evidences of her kindness. Among the last, was a blank book, in which I sketch these prison notes, and on the first page of which I leave this poor tribute to her abundant worth. In laying this thank offering at the feet of Miss Bessie, we by no means forget the many other ministering spirits, who come down on missions of mercy to the gloomy haunts of our wretched abode. Kind old Mrs. Meredith—her name will be a familiar word in our households after the war. Miss Laura Elder, the two Misses Harrisons, and Miss Sallie Linton, will be spoken of around many a far distant fireside; and others too will be called forth by a grateful memory, and their kind deeds discussed and handed down.

JULY 31.—Another long and lonesome Sunday has passed and gone. We had preaching in the hall this evening, or rather a minister read a sermon to such as chose to listen, but his reading being rather dull, he had a slim congregation, and part of them went to sleep. Gratiot has changed a great deal since last winter. The rooms we now occupy, were then filled with regular Confederate officers, whose only pretended crime was belonging to the Southern army. But now every class is represented. We have prisoners charged with all varieties and grades of crime thrown in together, without any respect being paid to their political sympathies or former social position; preachers, lawyers, doctors, printers, farmers, merchants, engineers, pilots, &c., mixed up with a heterogeneous mass of gentlemen without any visible means of support. We have a number suspected of belonging to that mysterious organization known as the "Knights of the Golden Circle," whose weird and elfin exploits are fast approaching the awful notoriety of the ancient witches of New England. God grant they do not poison the minds of the West, as those withered crones did the intellect of the land where they were burned and hung, for at this late day it is easy to discern that the spell is still over these people. They are as much bewitched now, as when with false oaths, they swore feeble old women to the gallows.

Then we have "bushwhackers," those unnameable demons, who, when part of their families are shot in their door yards, their houses burned, their women insulted and imprisoned, their children turned, in worse than orphanage, upon the cold charity of the world, with the last expiring embers of manhood kindled into a despairing blaze, dare to stand forth against the Militia and dispute their right to desolate the land—these men are consigned to the darkest niche in the catalogue of crime; an ignominious death is hungry for their blood.

Next, the "Rebel Mail Carrier," lifts his head, bathed, unabashed in God's free sunshine, after the shocking and unscrupulous deed of conveying a "line from home" to the exile, whom an adverse fate has banished for years from his native soil. The monster deserves no mercy—give Shylock "his pound of flesh." A multitude of minor offenders throng around, conspicuous among whom are a factious crew, that refused to join in the laudable amusements of the Militia's innocent pastime. Stiff-necked rebels—if they won't help murder and plunder their friends let them pant this hot weather in Gratiot, they may get melted down into a smaller compass and the dregs done over into loyalty.

We cross the line, and find Uncle Sam's boys with various charges locking them in; mutiny, desertion, stealing, counterfeiting, &c., with occasionally a turn coat "Johnny Reb" in their ranks. With this motley mixture we have all sorts of characters and dispositions, and a great deal to try the patience of all. Card playing is almost universally practiced, and though innocent of itself, it frequently leads to most disgusting scenes of altercation.

Ben. Dobyns "of ours" had a box of provision yesterday, and a letter from his sister, which said that his father and twenty others were arrested and held by the Militia as hostages for five prisoners taken by the "bushwhackers." The "noble daring" and thrilling heroism of the chivalrous Militia would have appeared in more dazzling splendor if they had captured their prisoners from their armed opponents. However they need not publish that they took grey-headed old men from their beds, and if any of the twenty are women, it need not be mentioned.

MONDAY, August 1, 1864.—I had a letter to-day, from a sister, saying that my brother Dan's wife had received a letter from Gen. Rosecrans stating that I was to be shot. She is naturally very much concerned—wants to know if it is true, and if she would be permitted to see me if she came to St. Louis. I think there must be some mistake, as I have had no intimation of such a doom hanging over my head. Sister writes that she has kept the news from our mother, which was very thoughtful and prudent. Also received an envelope containing six photographs of Dr. Hardinge, which I distributed among the members of his old mess. We are under obligations through Joe Elliot, to Miss Bessie Bury, for a fine assortment of reading matter. A number of prisoners have been sent off again from Myrtle and Gratiot to serve out their sentences in the Alton Penitentiary.

A prisoner captured at the fall of Vicksburg was brought to Gratiot where he was taken sick. He had a congestive chill, which was so severe that he lost his sight. When they took him out to the Provost, the guard had to lead him along. He took the oath and has been released.

The general Inspector of Prisons from Washington, visited Gratiot to-day, in company with Drs. Youngblood and Dudley. After going the rounds on our floor, they pronounced No. 3 the best kept room in the officers' quarters, giving special praise to our cupboard, which was equal they said, in neatness and order, to the housekeeping of ladies. We were highly gratified with their flattering commendations and they seemed equally well pleased to be able to bestow them. The report about a negro guard being placed over us, I am told is untrue.

A touching circumstance occurred to-day in connection with a released prisoner, who having no money, home or friends, and darkness approaching, came back to the prison and begged a night's lodging, which was granted him. The bed-bugs and rats have been reinforced by that species of "flying artillery" known as mosquitoes. Our troops are greatly annoyed by them, and often completely routed under a charge of their combined forces. Last Saturday we poured a scalding volley into the ranks of the bed-bugs, which served to cripple their movements for several nights, but they appear at this time to be thoroughly reorganized and in good fighting condition. About dark a husband and wife were added to the guests boarding at this hotel, and were provided with separate rooms. I have just heard through a letter from home, of the death of one of the friends of my youth, Miss Kate Asay, a very noble and pure minded young lady.

"Green be the turf above thee,
Friend of my better days;
None knew thee, but to love thee,
Or named thee but in praise."

AUG. 4.—Capt. W. J. Livingston this day received his sentence, to be hung on the 2d of next month. He was tried and condemned as a spy, and is now in close confinement awaiting his fate. A letter from a sister living in Wheeling, Va., brings me very sad intelligence; the nature of which, the following extract will announce. "You wanted to know where brother Dan. is. He is lying in Mount Wood Cemetery. He was shot in the bowels at Snicker's Gap on the 18th of July, and died on the 20th. His remains were brought here on the 26th and were laid in the vault the same evening. His funeral was very large—the papers state the largest ever known in Wheeling. Uncle John is also dead, he died the same day Dan. was buried."

AUG. 6.—Robert Loudon's wife and daughter were in yesterday, and brought him a basket of nice refreshments. A basket also came in to our mess from Miss Bessie. Capt. Livingston is now confined with a Federal soldier who is condemned to be shot on the 19th of this month, and Capt. L. has been notified that he would be executed on the same day, instead of the 2d of September as was first appointed. We thought yesterday that our female prisoner was released, as she was out before the Provost and came back, and then left again, but we are informed to-day that she is still a prisoner. Her name is Wilson and her *situation* evidently demands other accommodations than Gratiot can afford. They have the appearance of being a very respectable couple, and it must be very harrowing to the husband's feelings to have his wife dragged round and exposed as she is. I copy the following from a number of the Mexico (Mo.) Ledger, which I received to-day.

### FUNERAL OF COL. DANIEL FROST.

"The funeral of Col. Daniel Frost, who was killed during the late engagement at Snicker's Gap, took place yesterday afternoon from his late residence on Centre street. Notwithstanding there was no announcement of the arrival of his remains in the morning, the funeral was one of the largest which has taken place in the city for some time. The remains were interred in Mount Wood Cemetery. Capt. Over, in command of what force he could muster at this post, turned out to do the military honors. The coffin was wrapped in the American flag and the large procession was preceded by a brass band which discoursed music appropriate to the occasion. It was a most solemn and impressive scene, and there was many a full heart, and many a moistened eye as the procession moved slowly through the streets, bearing the mortal remains of a gallant soldier to his last resting place. At the Cemetery the usual ceremonies were observed and the farewell volleys were fired over the grave. The bereaved family in this their irreparable loss, have the warmest sympathy of the community."

"The above we clip from the Wheeling (Va.) Intelligencer, of July 27th. Col. Frost was a brother of Mr. W. P. Frost of this office, and early in the war, took a prominent position in favor of the government. He was at one time editor of the Parkersburg (Va.) Gazette, and also the Ravenswood (Va.) Chronicle. He represented Jackson county in the Virginia Legislature, and was speaker of the House of Representatives in West Virginia."

AUG. 7.—Four white men were conducted past the prison this evening by a squad of negroes, who looked as if they felt the dignity of their new position. We have often seen negro men, women, and children walking the streets and when opposite the prison they would turn toward us, make all manner of faces, roll their eyes, stick out their tongues, dance, and appear perfectly delighted at seeing us in prison. We observed it a curious illustration of what that species of monkey can be taught. Therein consists their great value as slaves, they can be made to reflect the views and desires of their masters, and if the Yankees only manage them well, it was a "big haul" when they were stolen.

Wm. Conklin is to be released on oath and bond of one thousand dollars, as soon as he can get the bond filled; he has been a prisoner eleven months, and fully appreciates the prospect of regaining his liberty.

This Sabbath day has been passed off by some in reading and sleeping, by others in playing checkers, or sitting at the windows looking at the citizens passing and repassing. At the time of this writing, the occupants of No. 1 are busily engaged in singing hymns. Those of No. 2 are discussing different subjects, while a member not interested in the talk, is quietly picking his banjo. In No. 3, we are mostly writing to friends, which is our chief enjoyment. In No. 4, they have gone to bed but with a very poor prospect of sleep, both bugs and mosquitoes are combining to make that impossible.

TUESDAY, Aug. 9.—Mr. Wilson and lady were removed to lower quarters yesterday, as their room was required by one Boebush, a famous counterfeiter who was ordered to solitary confinement. I have had an explanation to-day in regard to my being shot. Gen. Rosecrans, it seems, wrote to my brother Dan., in answer to one he had written in behalf of my release, advising my brother how to proceed, and remarking that he "had saved me from being shot," at least so I was informed. From this originated the rumor so distressing to my sisters. The letter from Gen. R. reached my sister-in-law, while my brother was on the march, and before she had an opportunity of sending it she received the intelligence of his death. This afternoon an Irish woman came to the prison and stopped on the sentinel's beat, when he came to a "charge bayonet" and made her get off, at which she became very angry and yelled out at the top of her voice, "I don't care if the secesh do win the day, and I hope to God they will," after which she went off in an excellent humor.

AUG. 10.—Messmate Felix Myers received his charges and specifications to-day, which are somewhat as follows: "Assault and battery, with intent to kill one — Martin, on board the Silver Wave, between the ports of Helena, Arkansas, and Memphis, Tennessee, on or about the 25th day of June, 1864." An opportunity was offered yesterday, to all who were so disposed, to procure their liberty on the following terms: Take the oath, and enlist for six months or one year in the U. S. service; those enlisting one year to receive two hundred dollars bounty, as soon as mustered in. From fifty to sixty recruits were found willing to close in with the terms, three of whom were from our mess. A prisoner named Dick Lloyd was brought in to-day, who lost both his arms at the battle of Lexington. They are afraid to allow him to run at large for fear he might go to "bushwhacking." A Federal detective was also added to mess No. 2, who says he was arrested for allowing Miss Emma Weaver, from Batesville, Arkansas, too many privileges.

AUG. 11.—We are guarded by a regiment of hundred day men, the 10th Kansas having been mustered out of service, their term of enlistment having expired. It appears that Mr. Swain, the gentleman who examines the prisoner's letters is getting very particular, finds it tedious we suppose to get through with them, and so determined to have them cut short, sent Joe Soward a small portion of one and instructed him to warn his correspondents not to write so much. Ben. Dobyns got an envelope containing a slip which informed him that a letter had been received which was written to him, but was too lengthy to pass. The boys are vexed and very much tantalized and think that after Swain had read their letters, he might have the courtesy to let them have a look. It is much better for persons writing to prisoners to comply with prison regulations and thereby save them from mortifying annoyances.

Aug. 12.—Thirty-seven prisoners arrived from Arkansas, with two commissioned officers among them, and were introduced to Gratiot this afternoon. W. Conklin, a Confederate soldier took it upon himself to lecture one Carney, a detective, for his filthy habits and declared he was the dirtiest man in prison, which Carney denied, giving Conk. the "lie," when the latter struck him several blows about the face, cutting his lower lip through to the teeth Carney was taken to the hospital and Conklin was ornamented with a ball and chain, which possibly may cool down his missionary ardor, and teach him to be a little careful how he "casts his pearls before swine."

Capt. Harvey, the commander of Gratiot, leaves to-morrow, and this evening he brought up his successor, Capt. McLure, and gave some four or five of us an introduction to him. The new Captain is rather a large man, with a gentlemanly pleasing countenance, or, as we expressed it after he was gone, "looks as though he might be good natured," which is with us, an item of extreme importance.

While looking from the window to-day, we witnessed a most disgusting sight, a drunken woman in the hands of soldiers. They brought her to the prison, but finding she could not be admitted they took her to the calaboose. We never heard such vile abusive language as rolled from her vulgar tongue, and our cheeks burned with shame as the blistering epithets which she heaped on President Lincoln, showed that the degraded creature classed herself with Southern women.

Aug. 13.—A letter from Fort Delaware, tells me that John and all of Co. "A" were well, he had heard of our brother's death, and feels as nature dictates over the loss ot so kind and generous a relative ; our difference in politics has made no change in our brotherly love. My wife writés that two men, Mr. William Flanigan and Mr. Mallory, citizens of Marion county, were a short time ago, shot near her father's house, by a party of Militia. The bodies had lain in the woods some four or five days before they were discovered. After they were murdered the Militia rode up to a house and informed the occupants that there were two dead rebels down in the woods, and that they had better go and bury them; but thinking such thing an impossibility, paid no attention to what was told them. When the bodies were found it was discovered they had been partly eaten by the hogs—one of them having an arm torn from the body; and that they had been dragged some distance from the place where they were shot.

The new Captain has had Conklin relieved of his ball and chain.

AUG. 14.—Had a splendid dinner to-day, served up by Messrs. Elliot and Winston, from provision sent in by our friends. The first course was gumbo soup, then mutton chops, beef steak, boiled potatoes; and for desert, a couple of excellent pies, sent in by Felix Myers' mother.

AUG. 15.—Seventeen prisoners were called for Alton to-day, but owing to some misunderstanding in relation to the guard, their trip was postponed until to-morrow. Our mess mate, Charley Green, desiring to visit the hospital, requested of Davis, the clerk, permission to do so, and on being refused went, contrary to the rules and regulations of the prison, to one of the new corporals who passed him in, for which offense, Mike was sent up to take him bag and baggage into a lock-up. We were sorry to lose Charley as he is a clever fellow; but when after an hour's absence he returned all right, we were prepared to greet him with hearty congratulations. Barns, the prison keeper, considering no harm was done concluded to let him off with a slight punishment.

Mrs. K—g, our elegant quondam friend from Arkansas, called again to-day to see "her man," but was not allowed the pleasure of passing the night with him in prison—don't know that she engaged in any "fight" in consequence of the refusal.

AUG. 16.—The prisoners called for Alton yesterday, left to-day; went off in the best of spirits. Capt. Livingston's wife came in to see him to-day; and the poor woman shows by her appearance, that she is full—full—of trouble, it is enough to make one's heart ache to look at her; she was allowed to stay with him about two hours. Our mess received a new member this morning in the person of Mr. Newland Holmes, of Louisiana, who had not been initiated more than an hour, before he was called out before the Provost, where he had the pleasure of meeting his wife and child, and although he was not allowed over ten minutes conversation with them, the meeting afforded him a great deal of satisfaction.

AUG. 17.—Conklin has succeeded at last in getting his bond filled, and this evening bade farewell to Gratiot. Through Felix Myers, our mess received some sugar and coffee to-day, which was very acceptable. We were disturbed this morning by an unpleasant and very unnecessary row, which occurred as follows: Charles Green and Sherin (the man the boys scared so about rebels being shot) got to cutting up, pulling and hauling each other about, until they became angry, and G. pushed S. against the wall, when S. in return threw G. on the bed and tore his shirt. The romp stopped here, and all was quiet, until Sam. Clifford came into the room, and seeming to have a spite at S., told G. to "pitch into him," himself leading off by shoving S. up against the cupboard, and striking him a tremendous blow under the left eye, from which the blood flowed in a stream. The sergeant came up at this juncture, and after investigating the matter took Clifford off to the lock-up, and put the other two boys in a dungeon for two hours. Clifford is a meddlesome, overbearing fellow, and though brave as a lion, his valor is of no benefit to himself or his country, from being squandered in foolish and misdirected channels; he is continually violating the rules of the prison, and bringing trouble on himself and others.

AUG. 18.—Capt. Sam. Winston with eleven other sentenced prisoners, left to-day for Alton, where they are to serve out the doom pronounced by a Military Commission. My friend Winston is sentenced for ten years.

This is the last night in Gratiot for Capt. Livingston, who is sentenced to be hung some time to-morrow. The priests have visited him frequently since he received his sentence, and have no doubt assisted him greatly in composing his mind and preparing his soul for the awful change. His wife was with him again to-day for a short time. I am told that last Tuesday was the first time she has seen him since the beginning of the war. They only meet to say—farewell. Capt. Livingston operated with his company during the early part of the war in Ralls and Marion counties, where he has many warm friends who will regret his untimely fate. Our "poor and hungry mess" is getting ahead in the world, as we have employed a "hired girl" in the shape of a big Dutchman to do our cooking. We will now have ample leisure for all the calls and duties of the social circle. The "lady of the house," our incomparable pet, "feminine Joe," will have nothing to obstruct the free course of his embroidery and crocheting, while his "lovyer" will receive more devoted attention than ever. Our two Joe's, with their odd conceits and witty sallies are the life of our mess. Sam. Clifford has been pleading with the Captain to be restored to his old quarters, but his eloquence is so far unavailing.

A red headed six-footer was brought in and added to mess No. 2, this evening. He was rather full of "red eye" and like every person else who is brought here, says he will be released in the morning. We have our doubts, but the morning will show.

Aug. 19.—Last night at nine o'clock, Capt. Livingston was taken, handcuffed, and under a guard of 25 soldiers, from Gratiot to the jail, where he was kept until ten o'clock this morning, when he was taken out and hanged by the neck until he was dead—dead. I was told that he met his fate bravely, and declared to the last, his innocence of the charges brought against him.

While sitting at the window to-day, I noticed in a building opposite the prison, where a Federal officer has taken up his abode; the said officer, sitting in an arm chair, by an open window, with his wife standing near him. He threw his arms around her, drew her down on his lap and nearly smothered her with kisses, repeating the experiment several times; after which they went to the piano where the lady played several pieces very nicely—and then both disappeared; all of which was very appropriate and interesting, except the open window part; it hardly agrees with the highest degree of refinement, for a married couple to make so public an exhibition of their affection.

Aug. 20.—Visited the hospital this evening, where I saw my old friend Col. Jeff. Jones, whom I found rapidly convalescing; also saw a prisoner who is sentenced to be hung some time next month at Pilot Knob, but who is very sick, and it is thought will not live to meet his horrible doom. He converses freely with all, and seems to be awaiting his fate with patience. Two prisoners, named Smith and Moore, were transferred from lower quarters to a strong room last night, to remain there, and await their execution next month. They are both sentenced to be hung by the neck until they are dead—dead. Smith is an old grey headed preacher. Moore is young. Our female prisoner is very sick, and considering her delicate situation, it is extremely hard to be confined in such a place as this.

Dick Lloyd, the man with no arms, was moved around in the prison to-day, but it was hard to get him quartered, as no one volunteered to wait upon him, and he is quite helpless, requiring constant attention, which either his friends, or those who keep him from them, ought to give him. It is sheer nonsense to keep such a creature as he is in prison. He ought to have been sent out with the blind man the other day. An order from the Secretary of War prohibits us receiving any more provision from our friends.

AUG. 21.—As I sit with my book open, and pen suspended in the air the hum of voices on all sides arrests my attention, and diverts my mind from its proper business. I will jot down a few expressions as they greet my ear. "Old Burns is going down the street." "Checked." "I love old Burns." "Play." "What's trumps?" "Clubs." "Checked." "You are not going to sleep, and keep me awake all night."
"Soft o'er the fountain."
"Or any other man."
"Have they settled the bed question?" "Have you ever had your trial?" "Thought you were dying." "Ca'nt see it." "There comes my sweetheart." "Is she cooked?" "Has she red hair?" "How are you Jake?" "None of your business."
"And spring would be but gloomy weather,
If we had nothing else but—"
"Jump." "Checked." "Oh, pshaw! that beats me." "Wake up, I tell you, I am not going to let you—" "Give me a match."
"Do they set me a chair at the—"
"There are a very few persons in the army who know any thing about me." "Is this all they sent?" "Mike, is he waiting for an answer?" "Don't do any business at all to-day."
Oh, the flowers I saw in the wild wood."
"We had nothing but bread for dinner to-day." "Elliot, that hair oil of yours is ruining my moustache."
"I soon got here, 'twas about New Year."
And so on, and so on; it is impossible for me to write, so I will close for to day.

MONDAY, August 22.—Had a letter to-day from my wife—the first for over three weeks. She had written before enclosing money, but neither letters nor change have reached my quarters. The money I suppose impeded the progress of the letter, and the hand of some Fed proved too tight a place for them to get through. The rascal ought to have had more soul than to steal a little remittance to a prisoner, especially since the new order cuts off all hope of provision from friends, and prison fare is reduced to almost nothing. We need money for milk which we are still permitted to buy. Sam.Clifford has gotten back to his old quarters, and though he made some fair promises with regard to his future conduct, I notice he is as noisy as ever, but it seems of a pacific character.

Myers was out at the Provost's this morning, where he had an interview with the lawyer who is defending him in his cutting scrape on the steamboat. Mr. Holmes' wife came to see him to-day, bringing her babe, about three months old with her. The little fellow went the rounds in the prison, calling at the different rooms and was everywhere greeted with a hearty welcome; such visitors are very rare in Gratiot, and consequently were highly appreciated. The innocent little face was a gentle reminder to us of other and brighter days; speaking to some, of the babes we had left in the arms of weeping wives, and to others, of the brother or sister which clung to its mother's neck as she gave her blessing to her eldest born, and sent him forth to battle for the common heritage and right of all. "Little children, blessings on them."

AUG. 23.—It is just ten months since I was introduced as a boarder, at the Hotel de Gratiot, and whilst I do not like to utter complaints against a house in which I am making my home, still candor compels me to say, and I think the peculiar circumstances of the case will justify the utterance, that I have met with more desirable places of entertainment. The fare is decidedly inferior to that furnished at the Lindel, and other accommodations are subject to the same criticism, while the servants are by no means such as we would employ if we were called upon to make a selection; and yet strict justice will require us to admit that there are some considerations which are highly creditable to our hotel, and one of very special importance to us in the present straightened condition of our finances. We refer of course, to the great interest and blinded partiality manifested by our aged and doating "Uncle Samuel" toward this house and others of a similar character; his insisting on defraying the expenses of all his nephews who are boarded and lodged therein, and at the same time giving such explicit directions with regard to our care and keeping; having us watched and guarded with more precaution and solicitude, than is bestowed by a loving mother upon the children of her household. We cannot leave the hotel for a moment without the servile attendance of one of our Uncle's servants, who go forth armed to the teeth for our defence and protection. In the morning we are carefully called by name, and if one of the flock so vigilently "watched and tended" should have strayed from the fold, the rest are carefully locked in to shield them from harm. While the whole force of our domestics, (landlord and all) exert themselves to bring the missing one back to his accustomed place, and if they fail in their laudable efforts, the rest experience in a still greater degree than before the watchful devotion of their protecting care. Our landlord, Capt. McLure, is one of the younger sons of our Uncle, and while he manifests a great affection for his father, and a firm determination to enforce all his wishes, still he is by no means disrespectful or overbearing in his intercourse with his dependant relatives, but affords us all the privileges he possibly can, consistent with the regulations established by his whimsical but beloved parent. But still,

"As the little girl sang on the summer day—
There will be briars where berries grow."

And the "thorn in our flesh" is the fact, that while it is so easy to get into one of Uncle Sam's boarding houses, it is exceedingly difficult to get away, the old gentleman holds on with the grip of a maniac whenever he gets a nephew in his clutches, and he has been known to squeeze some of them to death rather than let them go, and this consideration detracts very much from the pleasure of our visit and hinders our proper appreciation of his munificent hospitality. So taking it all in all, as I said above, I think I have met with more desirable places of entertainment.

Aug. 24.—We have a rumor floating through the prison, which if true, is of a most painful character, to the bereaved family. It is said that on the night before the execution of Capt. Livingston, a reprieve reached the hand of some one, and was withheld from the proper authorities until after his death. It is impossible for us to ascertain the truth or falsity of any such reports, but we cannot regard, except with horror, the men, or set of men, who would perpetrate or encourage, so cruel and heartless a crime.

David French was notified through the papers this morning, that he is sentenced to two years imprisonment, at hard labor in the State Penitentiary. Miss Cassell, of Marion county has received the same sentence, though probably without the labor; and Felix Myers, of our mess, has been paroled on oath and bond, to appear for trial when called for.

Two of our friends, Col. Jeff Jones, and Maj. Rucker, called on us from the hospital, but ere our greetings and congratulations were over, sergeant Raglan appeared and ordered the gentlemen back, stating that they were not allowed to visit this part of the prison until discharged from the hospital. We were sorry to have them disappointed, and can see no possible harm that could originate from their sitting and chatting an hour or so in our quarters. We hear a talk of preparation being made for a general exchange, but we have learned to wait, and prove all things and hold fast only to what is true. News items blow through the prison on the wings of the breeze that brought them, and are often as little heeded, and as soon forgotten.

We are having a spicy discussion at the present time as to what is the best material the Yankees have, of which to make a President. Sketches of leading notables are being struck off with quite a lively effect, and if the individuals whose names are handled, could stand quietly by a few minutes, I imagine they would utterly discard the homely wish of Burns, in which he exclaims,

"O wad some Power the giftie gie us,
To see oursels as others see us."

The polls close, I believe, with a majority for Fremont.

AUG. 26.—Robert Graham, and two others, in attempting an escape, succeeded in sawing one of the window bars, and had another nearly in two, when a fellow named Rollins, went to the office and informed on them. So in place of the liberty they expected last night, they were balled and chained and thrown into a dungeon. Graham is from Audrain county. They are no doubt very amiably inclined toward Mr. Rollins, as they lug their chains and revel in the dark, and will probably show the kindly effects of their gratitude when the war is over—unless indeed they can be noble enough to forgive an injury.

A letter from Ben Dobyns' sister, Julia, tells him of the arrest of Mr. and Mrs. Ringo, the latter guarded at her residence on account of ill health until sufficiently recovered to be taken to St. Joseph. A note of a later date, informs him that the couple were immediately released on their arrival at St. Joseph. Our little baby visitor called on us again yesterday; it laughed and looked around as pleasantly as though it was visiting in a parlor instead of a prison.

"Where ignorance is bliss, 'tis folly to be wise."

Felix Myers also called to get his clothes, he was in fine spirits over his release. Joe Soward received our congratulations on the occasion of his final success in a protracted effort to make a pair of sleeve buttons. They are highly creditable to the ingenuity and perseverance of the indefatigable workman. We were amused on reading in yesterday evening's paper an announcement of the sentence of Capt. W. G. Watkins and two others, to be shot on the 23d day of next month. Capt. Watkins having made his escape last winter, with the company which took their exit through the hole dug from the lamp house cellar, and not having been heard from since, it is the supposition that he will fail to report himself in time for the occasion, so as to be "in at the death." As for the other two I know nothing concerning them—but would rejoice to hear that they were as "uncomatable" as Capt. W. The cruelest death which can befall a man, is to be immolated on the altar of political hatred. The father of our friend Ben. Dobyns, called at Gratiot to-day, and sent his son word that he entertained a hope of his speedy deliverance. The old gentleman looked well and hearty. We notice in the same paper that we were looking over this morning that Col. Weir, of the 10th Kansas, who was in command of the prison at Alton while I was there, has been cashiered for conduct unbecoming an officer. He bore a better reputation at Alton than Lieut. Markham of the "Grey Beards." In speaking of the latter, John once said to me, "he was a devil incarnate—never hesitated to shoot down a prisoner for the slightest offence. A poor, emacaited ragged prisoner once asked this *brave officer* for a pair of pants and was told to "be gone," as though he were a dog. The prisoner said something saucy, when this Markham drew his revolver and fired at him. The fellow ran into the large stone quarters, followed by Markham, who penned him up between two bunks, and then deliberately fired at him, until he wounded him in the leg, and all the while Markham was smoking his cigar."

MONDAY, Aug. 29.—Saturday passed off with nothing worthy of note—Sunday but little better—it is always a dull heavy day, and various are the expedients which are resorted to to hurry up the hours, all kind of games are practiced, intermingled with songs, hymns, and noisy debates. We had a little excitement over a report that Joe Shelby, with six thousand men, was within seventy-five miles of the city; but the Feds seem to take it harder than we. In the afternoon, Rev. Mr. McKim came in and read a sermon, but religious services are not in as great demand in Gratiot as could be wished; somehow, the robes of the holy office do not inspire that respect which they commanded in other days. Where rests the fault? Are the people hardened, or the ministry degenerated? The matter is worth being looked into, the cause determined and a remedy applied. If we have souls, and they need saving, and the christian religion is the only chance, it is certainly a better work to remove obstructions in the way of that salvation, than to—to—build a railroad.

A notice was posted up yesterday, saying that if any of us wrote more than one page a day, our letters would not be mailed; we must learn the art of writing *a la* "multum in parvo;" it is sometimes tantalizing to have to quit right in the middle of what you want to say—however, some of them write "to be continued" and take it up where they left off next day, which does very well unless postage stamps are scarce. Learned to-day, that all the female prisoners are to be removed from Myrtle street prison to a small building in the rear of Gratiot, in which Mike, the seageant lived. They were expected to-day, but Mike did not move out in time. Mrs. Wilson, our female prisoner, will be removed to the same building, but we have decided that her little "coming event" should be called "Gratiot" in honor of our institution and in commemoration of her first experience in prison life; her health has been very poor since she has been confined in Gratiot, and it is to be hoped the change may prove beneficial. We hear a great many complain of feeling badly, and the hospital contains a large number of patients—mostly dysentery, with some cases very low indeed. While sitting at the window to-day, I saw a big doublefisted negro man walking down street with a white woman, who was tolerably good looking. No doubt it looked all right and proper to those whose sentimentality is spun out into so fine a thread, that common sense has been discarded long ago. How extremes do meet. Our great intellects have towered so high, they have become dizzy, and fallen, from the highest hight, to the lowest depth, and yet a "lower deep still opening wide, seems threatening to devour them."

The Joe Shelby scare yesterday turns out to be a hoax—the fluttering of feathers was all over a false alarm. Hope the St. Louis Democrat will get its nerves composed in due time.

Aug. 31, 1864.—Yesterday was one of our blank days, no life or activity in any department, except among the jewelers, that industrious and energetic class of our citizens, who may be appropriately styled the "irrepressible." To-day I received a letter from the widow of my brother, Col. Daniel Frost, with whom I used to live when a boy. She referred to the time when I was a member of her family, and regretted that I had been separated so far from my brother, whose influence, she is confident would have held me on the side of the Union. She finds it hard to understand or excuse the position I have taken. A person born and living all his life in the extreme South she can imagine would be influenced by the popular Southern errors, but with my opportunities she finds it hard to conceive how I could be so mislead. Like all persons siding with the North, she speaks of Southern citizens and soldiers, as "rebels" and seems to feel very bitterly toward them, which is easily accounted for since the death of her husband, as few ladies reason beyond the precincts of their own affection.

One of my fellow prisoners, Capt. Robt. Trimble, whose name was placed on the exchange list, but was not called when the others left, has had the mystery explained by a string of charges long enough to hang a half dozen men. Such as murder, robbing, guerrillaing, all preferred by a fellow named C. Y. Mason, who was confined in Gratiot two or three months, and left with money that did not belong to him.

As usual the evening's performance is about to commence, and I'm necessarially compelled to stop till to-morrow. However, before I close, I will give one of the "Stonewall Jackson" songs which is regarded with especial favor, and sometimes sung with a great deal of spirit and feeling, by the inmates of Gratiot, and is called

STONEWALL JACKSON'S WAY.

Come, stack arms, men! pile on the rails—
  Stir up the camp fire bright,
No matter if the canteen fails,
  We'll make a roaring night!
Here Shenandoah brawls along,
There burly Blue Ridge echoes strong,
To swell the brigade's rousing song,
  Of "Stonewall Jackson's way."

We see him now—the old slouched hat
  Cocked o'er his eyes askew,—
The shrewd dry smile—the speech so pat,
  So calm, so blunt, so true.
The "Blue Light Elder" knows 'em well,
Says he "that's Banks,—he's fond of shell,
Lord save his soul!—we'll give him"—well,
  That's "Stonewall Jackson's way."

Silence! ground arms! kneel all! caps off!
  Old Blue Light's going to pray:
Strangle the fool that dares to scoff!
  Attention! it's his way!
Appealing from his native sod,
In *forma pauperis* to God,—
"Lay bare thine arm, stretch forth thy rod,
  Amen!" That's "Stonewall's way!"

He's in the saddle now! Fall in!
  Steady! The whole brigade!
Hill's at the ford, cut off; we'll win
  His way out, ball and blade.
What matter if our shoes are worn!
What matter if our feet are torn!
"Quick step! wer'e with him before morn,"
  That's "Stonewall Jackson's way!"

The sun's bright lances rout the mists
  Of morning—and by George!
Here's Longstreet, struggling in the lists,
  Hemmed in an ugly gorge.
Pope and his Yankees, whipped before,
"Bay'nets and grape!" hear Stonewall roar,
"Charge, Stuart! pay off Ashby's score,"
  Is "Stonewall Jackson's way."

Ah! maiden, wait, and watch, and yearn,
  For news of Stonewall's band!
Ah! widow, read with eyes that burn,
  That ring upon thy hand.
Ah! wife, sew on, pray on, hope on!
Thy life shall not be all forlorn!
The foe had better ne'er been born,
  That gets in "Stonewall's way."

SEPTEMBER 1, 1864.—Capt. McLure, our new commander, appears to be a very kind and accommodating gentleman, he is very popular with all the prisoners—has a rough bluff hearty kind of way, does not care what he says or does, and is always in a good humor. Comes to our quarters once in awhile, and enquires what we "d—d rebels are doing—and how we are getting along?" Says we "are pretty good fellows, but all wrong, and fighting on the wrong side of the question." We are always glad to see him, and no matter where we meet him, he has something cheerful to say. The other day he came along where I was at work, and called out, "Well Griffin, you d—d old rebel, what are you doing?" and yesterday evening he was standing at the foot of the stairs when Baker called me to come get the clean clothes, when I got to the steps he told me to be in a hurry—they had come to the conclusion to take me out and hang me; I asked him if he would'nt give me time to eat my supper, said he would—but I must make haste, as he could not wait long on me, and went off laughing. We are afraid he will not remain long in the position he now occupies, he has a soul too big for the place, and it will run over. The orders are not to allow us to buy anything to eat, but when he sees us getting a bucket of milk, or some crackers, or a watermelon, he does not interfere; we appreciate his generosity and only fear that it may be the cause of his removal. Another female prisoner from Mississippi county, Mo., was added to Gratiot this evening; she is rather good looking, and seems to be intelligent. Suppose she will be consigned to quarters with Mrs. Wilson. The negro who cooks for the prison officers, says he "thinks when they get to putting such pretty young ladies as she in prison, they must be nearly played out."

Heard from Ab. Grimes to-day, he is nearly well of his wound. Ab's life ought to be witten, it is a perfect romance, splendid love story, all founded on fact. Miss Augusta J. Evans ought to have a few notes.

SEPT. 2.—Our new lady prisoner, of last evening, is a Miss Jane Hancock, arrested for smuggling ammunition through the lines. Eleven of the Myrtle street ladies were brought over this evening and all except two are young ladies, one of the two is a very old lady, seemed quite feeble, scarcely able to walk; the other had a little child with her. Nearly all of them were dressed in black.

On their arrival at Gratiot, supper was prepared for them in the officer's dining room, after which they were conducted to their quarters. Mrs. Wilson and Miss Hancock were taken from the round room and placed with them, making thirteen in all, in the feminine mess.

The only return which it is in our power to make for the many kindnesses shown us by ladies and other friends outside, is prison jewelry. I had the pleasure of seeing our two excellent friends, the Misses Harrison, wearing sets of sleeve buttons which I had made and offered for their acceptance, and it was a source of great gratification to think that our little mite was received in the spirit in which it was contributed, and appreciated, it may be, like the widow's offering in the ancient days. Mrs. Youngblood was also kind enough to receive a set of our manufacture. It occasionally occurs, that an order is sent in which we fill, and for which we receive money—which also in its turn, is very useful, especially when we are permitted to purchase anything additional to the rations issued. It is now five days since our "Uncle" furnished us any meat, and trimmed down as we were before, we have come to the point at last, of appriciating, and missing our allowance of pickle pork. I bade adieu to home and friends and buckled on the armor of a soldier starting out full of life and vigor, and sanguine hopes of ultimate and early success. I made up my mind to obey orders, to suffer hardships, to die, if death met me in the path of duty, and I thought I was prepared for prison also; but alas, how little can we judge of solemn facts by the fitful flights of a heated fancy. Slow tedious hours lengthening into days—days adding up weeks—weeks multiplying into months, while the months stretch away into years, with still a dark and indefinable future surging and lashing its gloomy waters at our feet. Strain our eyes which way we will, no white sail of a happy peace specks, even in the dim distance against the far horizon, the wild waste of desolating waves—seventeen months of days and nights have stalked slowly by through our prison walls, slipping across our path, emerging from the infinite future, and disappearing amid the wrecks of the eternal past, and yet no sign or token has appeared, telling even in a whisper, of an approaching end, but comrade after comrade is called forth to stand before a Military Commission, an engine of despotism more cruel and vindictive than the secret "council of ten" which sat as a canker in the heart of Venice, and receive a sentence which consigns him to a still longer and more loathsome period of incarceration, two, or five, or ten years of labor in a penitentiary, often clogged with a ball and chain, or else, as is now becoming more frequent, the gallows is chosen as the surest and safest remedy for his political ills. We are forced to cry out "How long? How long ?" and look eagerly round for a door of egress, or some method of escape. The siren song of release sometimes sends an echo to my cell, but hopes based on military clemency or justice, are as deceptive as the mirage which misleads the traveler on the sandy plain. Men have lain within these walls for twelve or fifteen months, without a trial or examination.

SEPT. 3.—We learn that Capt. J.C. Hill, and Lieut W. Sebring, who made their escape from here on the eighteenth of June last, have arrived in Canada, where they will no doubt meet with a number of fellow refugees, and find friends who will extend to them a hand of helping kindness. There are some noble hearts in Canada that may truly be said to be enlisted in the cause of "God and humanity," not going out of their way to meddle with the concerns of their neighbors, but sending in their lot and doing the work which the Lord places in their hands, being "careful to entertain strangers," &c.

Another female prisoner was introduced to Gratiot to-day. She is a large fine looking lady, reported to be from Kentucky, her name I have not heard. The following is a list of the shipment of ladies consigned to our house from the firm on Myrtle street: Miss Jane Ward, Mrs. Eliza Spencer, Mary Spencer, Mrs. Harriet Spencer, Mrs. Welthy Robinson, and Miss Fannie Little, of Johnson county; Miss Sue Bryant, of Cooper county; Miss. Mary Call, of Henry county, and Mrs. Mary A Harlow, of Lafayette county. All the above ladies are from Missouri, and are quartered in a building opposite Gratiot, as the house in the rear was found to be too small to accommodate them, and old Mike, the sergeant, has them in charge. He is an accommodating old fellow, and is probably the best selection that could be made about the prison for such a purpose. Ben. Dobyns and myself were allowed the privilege of visiting the hospital to day, where we remained two or three hours, talking to our friends Col. Jones, Dr. Shore, Ab. Grimes, and others. While there, two ladies came in to see some sick relatives, one of them was a very old lady, whose son is at the point of death. She trembled with age and grief as she sat by his bed vainly endeavoring to fan into strengh, the flickering flame of life's expiring lamp. The hospital nurses are called upon to witness so many sad and harrassing sights, it is a merciful arrrangement of Providence that their feelings become somewhat hardened; if they were affected like casual observers they would be unnerved, and become unfit for the performance of their duties.

SEPT. 8.—Last Sunday evening (the 4th) we were visited by a tremendous storm of wind, rain, lightning and thunder. It was grand and terrific—a splendid battle of the elements. When the engagement was over, and the forces had retired, the field was left in a decidedly improved condition, the atmosphere was cool and pleasant, insuring a better night's rest than we had enjoyed for some time. Also on the same day, Dr. Hardinge and Joseph Green paid us a most welcome visit. It seemed quite natural to have them around.

Next day, Mrs. Sarah T. Waitman and Miss C. J. Mayfield were added to the list of Gratiot female prisoners, which gives us seventeen. Myrtle has but ten at this time—including both sexes. We had four hundred and thirty boarders on the morning of the 6th, but during that day, a man we called Giles, made his escape from the guard while on his way to the office of the Provost Marshal.

On yesterday the following document from Head Quarters was placed in my hands.

HEAD QUARTERS DEPT. OF THE MISSOURI,
OFFICE OF PROVOST MARSHAL GENERAL,
St Louis, Mo., September 6th, 1864.

OFFICE COMMANDING GENERAL OF PRISONERS,
Washington, D. C. Aug. 31, 1864.

COL. J. P. SANDERSON, Prov. Mar. Gen., St. Louis, Mo.

COL:—I have the honor to request by direction of the Commanding General of Prisoners, that Capt. Griffin Frost, a prisoner of war, at Gratiot street prison, may be informed in reply to his petition for release, that previous papers in his case were submitted to the Secretary of War, by whom they were not favorably considered, and that no further action can be taken at present.

Very Respectfully, Your Obt. Servant,
(Signed)   G. BLOGDEN,
Maj. 2d Mass. Cav.; Asst. to Com'g. Gen'l. of Prisoners.
To Capt. Griffin Frost, Gratiot street Prison.

Ben. Dobyns was called out yesterday before an examining committee, who seemed very anxious to discover if he belonged to, or knew of a secret organization known as the O. A. K's. A man by the name of Grider, of mess No. 2, was transferred to the lock-up, and some two or three more female prisoners were brought in; orders came with them for seperate quarters, as they were not of a character suitable to be mixed with the respectable ladies now residing at Gratiot, consequently they are confined in the lower round rooms. This place is becoming very disagreeable indeed, owing in a great degree to the throwing together of prisoners of such various characters and dispositions. The Feds and Confeds are very sensensitive in their intercourse with each other, and the slightest difference is often sufficient to lead to brawls; especially at the card table, where they are almost sure to become excited. We had a "flare up" of the kind to-day, between Clint. Burbrage and a Federal Lieutenant. Harsh words were used first, then the Lieutenant got a club, and Clint. resorted to his knife, but a collision was staved off by the intervention of friends who carried Burbrage off to his room, while the difficulty was settled by one of the sergeants, but they were unable to save him from the lock-up, to which he has been transferred.

Mr. Durdy, and our messmate J. B. Jones, were also sent to a lock-up in accordance with an order from Head Quarters. Sometime to night, our fellow prisoners, Smith and Moore, will be conveyed from here to the jail, and to-morrow they are to be hanged by the neck until they are dead! dead!! dead!!! Mr. Smith is an old man and a minister of the gospel. Moore is quite young. Dr. Baker has been busily engaged for several days past in writing for them to their friends, directing them how to act in the future and what disposition to make of their property. Mr. Smith is very calm—says he is ready to die. Moore, declaring his innocence, finds it hard to resign himself to death—has written to Gen. Rosecrans, and though he has had no word of encouragement, he still seems to think something must happen to save him from what he considers so unjust a doom. The poor old preacher will not be robbed of many days, and seems to feel that for him "to die is gain."

We have heard from Col. John Carlin, who escaped from here

on the 18th of last June, and was afterwards recaptured in Illinois, during a fight, in which he was severely wounded. Our intelligence assures us that he is again in the enjoyment of his liberty, procured by his own wit and daring in effecting an escape.

SEPT. 9.—This afternoon between the hours of one and two, our unfortunate fellow prisoners, Smith and Moore, were taken from Gratiot to the gallows. During the time of their removal we were all locked in our rooms, but from the rear windows we saw them passing from the back yard; they had their arms tied, and looked very sad. Moore bowed to every one he saw. They were taken to the place of execution in a wagon surrounded by a strong guard. A great crowd was assembled, and among them a number of females. The gallows was erected about two blocks from the prison where the execution would be public. On the falling of the trap, Smith went down with such force that the rope broke, but the cruel work was done—he breathed his last in about five minutes. Moore hung seventeen minutes and was cut down, and so ended the lives of two more Confederate soldiers.

While on the street procuring milk, Parson Patterson had the misfortune to receive the point of a bayonet in his face, about one inch below the left eye, the weapon piercing to the bone, it was thought to be an accident resulting from carelessness.

SEPT. 16.—Am sorry to hear to-day that Capt. McLure is to leave us. He is to be superseded by Capt. Allen, of whom we know nothing, but we do not expect in any man to find a more gentlemanly officer than Capt. McLure. We are now guarded by the 41st Missouri, one of the new regiments raised according to Gen. Rosecrans' order, the hundred day men having been mustered out of service. The room formerly occupied by Smith and Moore, is now appropriated to the use of two of the women from the lower room of the round house. They are very hard cases. News from Alton tells us that some 41 prisoners at that place, made a rush on the guard, on the morning of the 18th, and fifteen of them succeeded in making their escape; five were killed, and the rest recaptured. A Miss Sallie Byrne has been enrolled on our calendar as one of the prisoner's friends. We are indebted to her kindness for a most welcome and opportune donation. Col. Jones and Ab. Grimes also from the hospital, sent us tokens of their remembrance. These little courtesies are the more valued within our prison bounds from a knowledge of the sacrifice which must be made to extend them; no prisoner is so blessed with superfluous luxuries that he need give any away "to keep them from spoiling." James Keelan of "our mess" is medicating at the hospital.

Capt. Charles Bowen, a Confederate officer tried before a Military Commission for recruiting inside the Federal lines, has been released. This case is not altogether clear if there is any uniform standard of action in such matters, as several guilty of the same offense have been sentenced to Alton. Had two letters from home friends yesterday, containing money, which I was beginning to need very much, my last remittance being lost. I have however earned a little at my new trade of jeweller; but our accommodating sergeant Jack Norman, was kind enough to invest that sum in a pair of slippers for my benefit. Jack is a clever fellow, always ready to do an errand, or confer a favor, whenever he is called upon. Our nocturnal enemies are still vigorous in their attacks; the allied forces of bed bugs, rats and mosquitoes are a formidable host. The rats are organized into a corps of "sappers and miners;" the bedbugs are squadrons of infantry, while the mosquitoes have charge of the artillery. When the whole army is moved forward for an assault, our fortifications are completely demolished, we are surrounded, taken prisoners, and given over to be sacked and plundered until morning. Sleep flies before the invading cohorts, until day comes to our relief.

MONDAY, Sept. 19.—Friday and Saturday, quite a number of releases were extended; two of our friends, W. Sherin, who was so teased when he first came in, but who silenced us all when he sang,

"Am I a soldier of the Cross,"

and Newland Holmes the father of our baby visitor, were among the lucky individuals who drew tickets to "get out," but our Federal friend, sergeant Barnes, drew a ticket, it seems to "get in," he is charged with drawing money out of the prisoner's letters. The last order posted declares that all prisoner's not up for roll call, are to be severely punished. I think its issue might have been postponed a week or two, until the mosquitoes have finished their carnival; it is often nearly day before we can get to sleep, and then it is worse than thinking of a dentist to have to break up our nap and answer roll call.

Several more females were added to Gratiot yesterday; it is a nice little Sunday amusement to run around and gather up ladies and throw them into prison. Men are so used to it, they take it as a matter of course when they are arrested, and march right along, so it has gotten to be an old thing to pen them up, and there is no sport about it, but the ladies still "revel in their right divine," will talk and storm in their feminine way, and it is a spicy treat to the lucky squad which is ordered off to fetch them in, and then the elevating and refining influence which such proceedings have on society should be well weighed and duly considered, for, "verily, we are the people, and wisdom will die with us."

Fourteen prisoners started this morning for Alton—one lady among them. She was separated from the male prisoners and had a guard to herself, thus they marched off—but like the king of France, who with

"forty thousand men,
Marched up a hill, and then marched down again."

They returned to their quarters in the evening, having missed the train we presume—nice little excursion for the lady. Who bids for the situation for his wife, mother or sister? The present incumbent would doubtless resign in favor of any ambitious aspirant. We have had some releases also. Among a lot of nine, two from our quarters drew prizes—Graham and Byggart. Our new guard are very zealous in the performance of the important duty intrusted to their hands, and it is interesting to listen to the course of instruction which they mutually volunteer to each other. It runs after this fashion: "You must shust valk up and down der hall, past der vindows, unt see dat der rebels do not cut or saw der bars, unt shust not allow tem to make too much noise; unt vens tey do it you must shust tells dem ter stop it, or you will shust shoot dem, by tam."

SEPT. 22.—It is plainly evident that with Capt. McLure old things have passed away, and under Capt. Allen all things become new. Our knives and forks have been taken from us, and also our tools, and we are notified that none but *Union prisoners* will be permitted to purchase bread and milk. *Rebels* will have to be content with such rations as they draw. We have still a little

(12)

coffee that was furnished us by our friends, but when that is gone we will have to resort to water. Joe Soward is disposed to be comical over our new style of eating, he says, "carving a piece of tough beef with a spoon, is like eating soup with a fork, and both are very pretty operations to—a man up a tree." But my greatest grievance, as my old favorite, Capt. Masterson, could testify, is the stopping up the little "peep hole" through which we used to watch the ladies passing. Ben. Dobyns was told by his lawyer that he was looked upon at Head Quarters as one of the most active rebels in Audrain county.

SEPT. 24.—We have in Gratiot a prisoner named Davis, who is a great McClellan man, and awful hard on old Abe's sympathisers. One Harris who came west to procure negroes to take east for substitutes, is an especial victim to his love of tantalizing. He says everything that could be imagined belittleing of the white man that would put himself on a level with a negro. We hear his voice early and late, on all occasions, and his speeches and spats are often quite amusing, though we sometimes tire of his uselessly throwing words away. Our friend Keelan, lately released, sent us in a fine selection of reading matter, and tried to pass some tobacco in, but it was "no go." Feminine Joe received to-day from Miss Bessie Bury, the following articles viz: Four cans of oysters, five cans of peaches, two cans of pine apples, one can of strawberries, two large jars of pickles, one bottle of tomato catsup, six mince pies, five pounds of cheese, two pound cakes, two bottles of Worcester sauce, six boxes of sardines, and a lot of crackers. It causes a great deal of hard feeling among some of the prisoners, because Elliot is allowed to receive such things while they have been refused; other prisoner's friends have brought things to them and have not been permitted to pass them in; and such are at a loss to perceive a just cause for the difference. I have no complaints to utter, as Joe belongs to "our mess," and is as liberal hearted a comrade as one could wish. Had an order to-day from a lady in the city, for two sets of sleeve buttons and would be happy to accommodate her if I had any tools, but it don't matter so much since we are not allowed to buy any thing.

SEPT. 26.—The father and uncle of Miss Emma Weaver who escaped from the former residence of Mrs. McLure, on Chestnut St., which is now used as a military prison for ladies, were brought in to Gratiot yesterday, to be held until she either gives herself up or is recaptured. To-day, although we are still in our old quarters, the Lord only knows how much longer we well remain, we are expecting every moment to be ordered off to Alton. Everything is full of excitement, both in and out of prison. General Price is invading (?) the State at the head of a large body of men. Dr. Boyd was out in town, and reports a dispatch received at Head Quarters, stating that Gen. Price had crossed the Arkansas river on last Thursday, with 1,200 wagons, and between 25,000 and 30,000 men, and is now marching into Missouri in three columns; he says the streets are crowded with drafted soldiers and Militia, and Federal officers can be seen riding at full speed in every direction. The greatest excitement seems to prevail throughout the entire city. This evening the news boys could be heard crying out, "All about the capture of New Madrid!" when some one went down to buy a paper, but was informed that newspapers are contraband. We seem to be looked upon with a very jealous eye, and find it necessary to be uncommonly circumspect in our movements. However, we can sing with the Yankee prisoners on a like occasion,

"Tramp, tramp, tramp, the boys are marching, &c."

Joe Shelby is said to be in the vicinity of New Madrid with 8,000 men; but as near as we can "pick up" by looking and listening, he does not appear to have taken the place. It seems also, from what we can gather, that a train has been fired into within twenty-five miles of this city. Our writing and receiving letters have been suspended for the present and we are strictly confined to the prison allowance of food; nothing is permitted to be passed in. Capt. Robt. Trimble was called out to-day for the fourth time, and remanded back to prison without a trial; his case will not be disposed of until further orders. Father Wilby came in and held confession in room No. 2, where from fifteen to twenty, called on him and unbosomed themselves to his holy ear. Suppose they made a clean breast of it, and received full absolution; it is a nice little arrangement if one can have faith in it; but we Protestants prefer to whisper our secrets into the ear of Deity alone; not choosing to confer with an agent when we can obtain an audience with the principal. And yet, as these "Holy fathers" glide in and out among us, there is a sanctity which hedges in their office, extending to their person, which does not fail to command our reverence. The news concerning "Old Pap" produces an uneasy restlessness among the prisoners; and our tools having been taken from us, we have nothing to engage our attention. All through the night, there was passing to and fro in the prison, there seemed to be a difficulty in keeping the sentinels awake; we could hear them frequently shaking them, and calling them—one fellow, they awoke four times, and had finally to take his gun and put on a fresh man.

SEPT. 27.—The excitement over Old Pap's visit, seems to be raging as high as ever. We are not allowed to see papers and get the news from them, but we have a way of finding out things which answers as a tolerable substitute. We learned this morning that heavy firing was going on in the neighborhood of Pilot Knob; Feds having fallen back about twelve miles; also that the telegraph wires had been cut in several places on the H. & St. Jo. R. R. Among some rubbish the other day, a rope was discovered, made of blankets, and this morning that rope was made the pretense for locking us up, however the thing was thought better of in the course of the day, and we were unlocked. This afternoon a couple of ladies came to the prison with refreshments for some friends; among other things they had a teapot of very nice tea—and on being refused admittance, and not allowed to send their provision in, one of the ladies became very angry, and I suppose for the want of something else to do, she vented her spite in emptying the teapot in the street. No doubt it was a sad disappointment, and a heavy cross, after all the pains they had taken, to meet with such a refusal, but we did not feel particularly proud of the Southern dignity displayed in scattering the tea leaves in front of Gratiot. We do not like to see our Southern ladies intruding upon the domain which we have set apart as the exclusive patrimony of a certain portion of their gentle cousins.

SEPT. 28.—Have had a great many rumors to-day, concerning the movements of Gen. Price. Some say he has had an engagement with Smith, driven him back twelve miles, and captured a large number of prisoners, but it is impossible to get the straight of anything. We hear too, that Bill Anderson has captured a train on the North Missouri Railroad—that he robbed the passengers, and killed about twenty Federal soldiers, then set fire to the train and started it off down the road; and afterwards had a fight at Mexico, in which he was repulsed, with a loss of from five to ten killed and wounded, and about the same on the Federal side. The citizens here, we are told, are leaving for Illinois by the hundreds. We were locked up again to-day, and the guard were very insulting and tantalizing over it; continually calling to us in abusive language, and uttering all kinds of threats, one or two of the sergeants lead off, and are disposed to make merry over our misfortunes—declaring that we are to be kept on bread and water.

SEPT. 30.—Locked up again all day as usual. Yesterday a lot of us were notified to get ready for Alton, which we did, packed up everything and waited patiently until three o'clock, when we were notified that we would not go to-day. About a hundred privates, however, were sent off—and their places pretty well filled with citizens brought in for refusing to enroll in the Militia. The naughty boys could not be induced to take up arms against their friends. To-day we were offered the privilege of promenading in the hall and yard, if we would give a parole not to attempt an escape, and to report on all who did. Only one or two have signed it, but several are willing to obligate themselves to observe the first clause, while the latter is looked upon as a very degrading proposition. The result of the negotiation was reported to the Captain, but we have not heard what he intends doing; the supposition is, we will be locked up as usual—for my part, I expect to leave for Alton to-morrow, and am not by any means low spirited, over the prospect of a change.

OCTOBER 1, 1864.—Some fifteen or twenty women and children were brought in this afternoon, and are now quartered in a building opposite Gratiot. I do not know whether they are prisoners or refugees, but one thing I am certain of—they are the raggedest and dirtiest set I ever saw; some of them have not sufficient clothing to hide their nakedness. They were picked up out in the Southwest. Some of the women would be really good looking if they were properly dressed, but they are a pitiful looking crowd in their present condition. I presume they are fair samples of the wretchedness and squalor of those destitute regions.

All through last night, troops could be plainly heard marching in every direction—officers giving commands, such as "Halt," "Shoulder arms," "Forward march," &c. We were at a loss to comprehend the nature of the commotion. All we could do was to keep quiet, listen, and wait for morning, when we learned that the whole stir was caused by troops being shipped on the Pacific Railroad for Jefferson City and elsewhere.

OCT. 2.—It is rumored this morning, that all the sentenced prisoners, and prisoners of war, will leave for Alton to-morrow on the packet. We cannot tell how true it is, but presume that none will offer an objection, as Gratiot becomes every day a less desirable place of residence.

The cars have been running constantly to-day, conveying troops to some point on the Pacific road. Some thirty or forty of our citizen prisoners have been released; they claimed British protection, which was found sufficiently strong to open their prison doors, and ensure their freedom without enlisting in the United States army. Mr. Burr, uncle of Miss Emma Weaver, who made her escape from the female prison a short time since, received a letter from the Provost Marshal, informing him that as soon as he made known who the person or persons were, that aided in her escape, or gave information concerning her whereabouts, he would be released and not before. If such is the case, I fear the old gentleman will remain a prisoner for some time, as he knows nothing concerning her. Ben. Dobyns' father, from Mexico visited him to-day and informed him that he thought he would be able to have him released in a few days.

OCT. 3.—About two o'clock this afternoon, I was notified to get ready for Alton which I did as soon as possible—was then called down to the office, where I received a *beautiful bracelet* in the shape of a handcuff. John A. Bayse being ornamented in the same way, we were chained together. About a dozen others were adorned and paired off in a similar manner. Jack Norman, the officiating sergeant expressed a very great regret at having to perform the operation of handcuffing us, but he was forced to do so in compliance with a special order from Col. Darr, who, it seems, is very much frightened over the reports concerning Gen. Price and his soldier boys. He is also the person who ordered our knives, forks and tools taken from us, for fear another rush would be made on the guard, and some of the prisoners make their escape.

Robt. Loudon, who was sentenced to be hung, but afterwards reprieved, was chained to a companion also, and we were marched out; a number of ladies were waiting to see us off; among them I recognized two friends. The streets were very muddy—making the walk quite disagreeable. The Lieutenant in charge was a gentlemanly and accommodating officer. On the boat he allowed us all the privileges it was in his power to grant—permitted us to purchase apples, nuts, &c. The trip was very pleasant indeed, but when we arrived at Alton considerable surprise was manifested at finding Loudon's partner left alone. "The last link was severed, which bound him to"—Bob; but how did it happen, that was the question? A file had been used, it was very evident—but the heart of the mystery was, "Who used it?" and "What had become of Loudon?" There was no one found to give the desired information, and we were ordered to "move forward."

## CHAPTER X.

ARRIVAL AT THE OLD BASTILE; IMPROVEMENTS SINCE MY LAST VISIT; MEET OLD FRIENDS; BUCK AND GAGGING PRISONERS; "THE PROCLAMATION;" VISITING FEMALE PRISONERS; NEWSPAPERS STILL PROHIBITED; RETALIATORY PROCEEDINGS; MORE RUMORS OF GEN. PRICE'S MOVEMENTS; REMOVAL OF ABSHIRE, FOR EXECUTION; REGULATIONS OF ROOM NO. 1; A PRISONER'S APPETITE; &C., &C.

OCTOBER 4, 1864.—Well here I am, and here I arrived with some forty others about eight o'clock last night, after a pleasant and somewhat adventurous trip on board the St. Louis and Keokuk packet. On our arrival, we were relieved of our jewelry, and our money also, and were searched from head to foot. I lost nothing from the ceremony except my money, and some private papers, which were returned this morning. After the search was over, we fell into line and were marched around to the old Penitentiary, where we were consigned, two together, to cells which served to remind me of an old Dutch bake oven. We rested there until morning when I sought out my ancient quarters, where I discovered a number of old friends, Col. and Capt. Winston, Capts. Muir, Muse, and others, whom it was truly refreshing to meet. Alton prison is very much improved since the time of my stopping here before. Everything is much cleaner; a large hospital has been built, lathed and plastered, and lit with gas, and the authorities, I am told, manifest a greater degree of humanity. So far it is decidedly preferable to Gratiot. The fare is much better and we are permitted to correspond with our friends, but newspapers are strictly prohibited—any prisoner caught with one will be locked up forty days. After eating a hearty breakfast of biscuit, beef steak and coffee, I was called out and my name placed on the *Citizen sentenced* list, where I will have to answer roll call night and morning unless I can get it changed, and placed where it was before, which I prefer.

The principal amusement at this fashionable place of resort, is breaking rock, making jewelry, card playing and walking about the yard. Preparations are now under headway, for sending off the sick and wounded on exchange.

OCT. 6.—Took a walk around through the yard yesterday—saw a great many persons engaged in making tooth picks, rings, breast pins, and such like, and many of them were executed with a great degree of skill; also saw at a window two of the female prisoners. One of them is a Miss Lundy, from Memphis, whose brother was killed when Forrest made his raid into that city. She is a very fine looking young lady, and, I should judge, possessed of considerable intelligence. This morning, Westerman, who was handcuffed to Bob Loudon, was called into the office and questioned in relation to the manner of his escape, but not giving satisfactory answers he was ordered to be taken into the yard, and *bucked* and *gagged*, which was performed in the following manner : he was made to sit on the ground with his legs drawn up, and a crow bar placed under his knees and over his arms, while his wrists were tied with strong cords in front ; then a stick, eight or ten inches in length, with a string at each end, placed in his mouth, and tied behind his head. Several of the sentenced prisoners have been busy all day long breaking rock inside the yard; sometimes a detail is made to go outside and work in a quarry near the prison. I often feel disposed to complain of my lot, but when I see others fare so much worse, I find, with all, I have much to be thankful for. There was nothing said about "labor" in my sentence, and if the influence of friends secured this esteemed favor in my behalf I am indeed very thankful.

OCT. 7.—The persons here in charge of the prison, are very sociable. Hardly an evening passes without some of them paying us a visit, and we have very lively times; some fine music, both vocal and instrumental. We have two violins, a guitar, a banjo and castinets. Among the songs sung this evening there was none received with more genuine favor than the following, composed by Capt. Joe Leddy, of Gratiot, and entitled

### THE PROCLAMATION.

Dars great commotion in dis town, in fact all thro' de nation,
Every one is upside down about de Proclamashun.
Abe, set us niggers free and sed, 'twas his expectashun,
To make a black man good as a white, by his grand Proclamashun.
 CHORUS:—Li-tu-rul-lu-li-tu-rul-lu,
  I'm down on Yankee doodle.

One day when I was shucking corn, on Massa's ole plantashun,
I heard a noise, it was de boys, crying out "Emancipashun."
A Yankee came to me and sed, you'r in too low a stashun,
So cum with me, I'll make you free, by Abram's Proclamashun.
 CHORUS:—Li-tu-rul-lu, &c.

So I packed up my duds dat day, and started for dis city,
I soon got here, 'twas bout New Year, but was'nt it a pity?
For when I cum, I wanted rum, and stole a coat to buy it,
Den I was took, and ten times shook, and den sent down to Gratiot.
 CHORUS:—Li-tu-rul lu, &c.

I soon got out, and looked about, for money I had none,
To hunt me up a job of work, I wanted some more rum,
So I went down to Sigels's camp, to get a situashun,
None could I get, nor have I yet—G—d d—n dat Proclamashun.
 CHORUS:—Li-tu-rul-lu, &c.

When I was at my massa's house, I never wanted bread,
But now I'm free, an' you all see, dat I'm about gone dead,
For three days and three nights, I've not had a ration,
It am a shame, myself I blame, and dat d—n Proclamashun.
 CHORUS:—Li-tu-rul-lu, &c.

If some white man in dis big town, will pay my passage home,
I'll go straight back to Arkansaw, and neber more will roam,
I'll pick de cotton, hoe de corn, and mind de whole plantashun,
But all de time, I'll cuss de man, dat wrote de Proclamashun.
 CHORUS:—Li-tu-rul-lu, &c.

We have the privilege here of purchasing such additional articles of comfort as we have the means of procuring, and one expense is thrown upon us which we did not have at Gratiot, and that is lights. Government does not defray the expense of our illumination. After Westerman was relieved of his gag yesterday evening, he was confined in one of the cells, where he will be kept until he tells how Bob Loudon made his escape. Saw a prisoner tied up by his thumbs to-day. His thumbs were tied firmly together and the end of the rope was then placed over a peg projecting from the wall and pulled sufficiently taught to allow his toes simply to touch the ground, then fastened; in which condition he would be left from a half an hour to an hour and a half at a time.

The privilege is occasionally granted to Confederate soldiers of visiting the quarters of the female prisoners; and an evening is never passed more pleasantly than in the enjoyment of their society. The lady prisoner who seems to preside over the feminine household, and matronize the younger members of the company, is said to be possessed of a great deal of quiet womanly dignity. I have not yet enjoyed the pleasure of a visit. A striking instance of the sociability of our Fed and Confed officers occurred to-day, when the Commanding officer invited a Confederate Captain to walk out with him and consult on the plans for fortifying the prison. Of course our Captain was in honor bound to give the best advice he could, even though it served to fasten himself more securely in his prison home.

OCT. 9.—On Friday night the musical members of our fraternity, styling themselves "the Band," visited the windows of our lady prisoners and entertained them for some time with a serenade; the fair ones seemed highly delighted with the music, and rewarded the minstrels with a couple of very handsome boquets. There are two married ladies—Mrs. Mitchel and Mrs. Hanie—and two Misses— Miss Florence Lundy and Miss Goggin. We are not permitted on any condition to see the papers, and all the news we get is merely such as we obtain from heresay rumors, and from that source we learn to-day that Jefferson City is in the hands of Confederate troops and that the excitement is still high in Missouri. Also that the Lieutenant who had charge of us from St. Louis has been cashiered on account of the escape of Robt. Loudon while on the way here. I am happy to learn that Westerman has been released from further punishment, as he was not a whit more guilty than several others. All the parties concerned are under special obligations for the firmness he manifested under the torture.

Preparations are now being made to have water forced from the river into a large tank, from which it will be carried through leaden pipes into the different quarters of the new hospital. I was told that while the workmen were engaged in digging the sink for the new building, they came to a large box containing the remains of five or six human beings, the flesh still hanging to some of the bones, and the hair in a good state of preservation; it is supposed they have been placed there since the breaking out of the war, having been foully dealt with, and secreted to avoid detection. I have no doubt but there has been many a horrible crime perpetrated within these prison walls, which will never come to light until the great day of general reckoning.

While our officers are gentlemanly and courteous, they are at the same time rigidly strict in the enforcement of the prison discipline. We answer to roll call twice a day, nothing but sickness taken as an excuse. Any failure in yielding to a prompt response is sure to be followed by extra duty. Of this no soldier will complain, who understands the first principles of military subordination. An officer or private is bound to obey the orders of his superior, and the manner in which he executes such order, rests all the difference between the ruffian and gentleman. About a hundred and twenty of the sentenced prisoners were out breaking rock, or working on the fortifications to-day, and another poor soul was "bucked and gagged." It was reported yesterday evening and to-day, that Rosecrans had ordered a number of men to be placed in close confinement and held as hostages for the men who were handed over to Reeves, to be dealt with as he saw proper, in retaliation for a number of his men who were murdered by the Federals some time last winter. There has been a good deal of surmising as to whom the unlucky ones would be—whether they would be selected from prisoners here or sent from St. Louis. Some said if it fell on them to die they would meet death bravely, while others said they "didn't care about having any shooting in theirs," as they were more than satisfied with what they had already received. Their minds however were set at rest about nine o'clock, when one of the sergeants came in and reported that six men had just arrived from St. Louis, who were ordered to be placed in close confinement, and that the order had been complied with, and they were said to be the hostages. There is one Major yet to be added before the number of the unfortunates is complete, but he is expected to be sent from some other prison. We have all kinds of startling rumors about the proceedings of the southern army in Missouri, such as, that Thornton had captured St. Joseph and Kansas city, while Gen. Price has released at Jefferson city, about thirteen hundred prisoners, mostly Federals. One young lady, Miss Anna Fickle, sentenced to ten years in the penitentiary, is said to have been set at liberty. Several boats were seen to enter the mouth of the Missouri river to-day, and the supposition is, that they were carrying troops to be used against the forces in that section.

OCT. 18.—Nearly ten days have elapsed since my last writing, but during the time nothing strange or startling has occurred. On the 10th, we saw sixteen steamboats puffing and snorting up the Missouri river, carrying reinforcements, we suppose, to join the pack that are already yelling in the scent of the lion hearted old Price. God grant he may turn at bay and trample them under his feet. If our little recruiting force could have only escaped capture until this time, we might have joined our noble old leader with a handsome body of troops; but while he has come into the State, and is making a last grand effort for her salvation, too many of her sons are pining in Northern prisons, or else fettered with "Iron Clad Oaths." As we lie here in prison and catch an occasional echo from the field of action, we experience a sensation similar to that imagine of a drowning man, who sees a plank floating past him but just beyond his reach.

On the 11th, seventeen more prisoners arrived from Gratiot, among whom was a Miss Hanie, whose mother has been for some time a prisoner at Alton. The men were taken from that imaculate body, the Paw-paw Militia, to fight against whom is so heavy a sin, that death accompanied with all imaginable ugly names, is scarce a vengeance sufficient to atone for it.

> "Take them up tenderly,
> Lift them with care."

Mr. Abshire was taken to St. Louis on the 12th, to be executed on the 14th. I do not know what the charges are, but most likely he was found in arms against the *Pets*. The 13th was a big day for me, had four letters, two from a sister at Cairo, one from my wife, and one from the Inspector at St. Louis, enclosing two dollars sent me by my wife over two months ago, but stolen by sergeant

Barnes, who is now in Myrtle street prison. The Inspector writes, "I enclose you two dollars abstracted from a letter written you by Mrs. Griffin Frost, mailed at Palmyra, Mo. The letter we will have to retain to use against the party who abstracted the money."

We have two negroes in prison here, one of whom claims to be a conscript, he is inclined to think that the course of freedom, like that of love, does not run very smooth, and he has a hankering after the "flesh pots of Egypt." Says he wishes he was back on "ole massa's plantation." The other is a sulky dog, does not say much. During his drafting operation, our belligerent old uncle, not unfrequently hauls out a fish from his brother's pond, and the unlucky individual can only escape by furnishing a substitute, which is a rather expensive business, the demand being so great as to run up the prices very high—not only Confederates, but non-combatants of the Union persuasion dealing extensively in the article. Capt C., one of the rivals of Gratiot, who was taken off by the celebrated *node* of Joe S., had the pleasure last Friday, of receiving a visit from his lady friend, Miss ——, of St. Louis. She reports Gratiot looking rather gloomy; several of our old friends in the lock-up—Joe Elliot and Joe Soward among the number, they are a gay couple, and if there is any sweetness even in a lock-up, they will extract it, and work it into honey.

On Saturday another letter from Mrs. F., states that she has written to Washington concerning my release, but the answer was about the same in substance, with the last communication which I received from official quarters. It was with great reluctance and many a painful misgiving in the region of my stomach, that I replied to a note from my sister Rebecca, inquiring if she could send me a box of the cake and wine from her wedding dinner, that it was positively forbidden by the rules of the prison. Sunday and Monday passed off with nothing worthy of note; to-day not much better. There is a rumor going the rounds of the yard that Mexico, Audrain county, Mo., is in the hands of the Confederates; captured by Clarke with a loss to the Federals of near two hundred. We never believe anything we hear, and yet we are eager to catch every report that is going, it has a stimulating effect if nothing more. It is just one year to-day, since I was taken prisoner in Ray county, Mo., and I may safely state it has been the longest year of my existence.

Oct. 26.—One week ago to-day, Maj. Rucker and Capt. Muse enjoyed the rare pleasure of a visit out in town in company with a sergeant. They were absent two hours; the sergeant was very agreeable and they reported the trip as exceedingly pleasant. The city is as full of rumors as the prison, and it seems impossible to get reliable information anywhere; the following are some of the items which they picked up while out, but no one puts any confidence in them:

"Steel's forces are occupying and fortifying Springfield, Mo., with Magruder close at hand." "Hood's army is within thirty miles of Chattanooga." "Sherman's communication is cut off." "Grant is going to withdraw his forces from around Richmond, and go into winter quarters on the coast," besides a whole host of lesser crumbs, scattered from the loaf of news as it is broken and handed round. Thursday about forty of our boarders were locked up in cells and feasted on bread and water—there is always a large number here in close confinement. Thursday night a poor ragged degraded woman was picked up somewhere and brought into the prison. I saw her next morning as she was being conducted to the office. She was barefooted, and so scantily clad that she evidently suffered with the cold—but then she was white. An envelope reached me on Friday, directed in my wife's hand, but marked "contraband," inside was a slip containing these words, "would be best to send our letters by way of Springfield." The Inspector wrote that her letter was all contraband, being filled with war news, and such matter as was not allowed to pass. One of the Federal prisoners got drunk on Saturday and was bucked and gagged to make him tell where he got the whisky. Sunday afternoon, Lieut. Dyhrenforth, the prison commander, escorted four ladies, Mrs. and Miss Wentz, Miss Bell Post, and Miss Gutzweller, also the same number of gentlemen, through all the different parts of the prison. They were a very pleasant and sociable party, and their visit was appreciated in all quarters; they were laughing and talking all the time, and on leaving, expressed themselves as very highly pleased. Yesterday we heard that Lieut. Dyhrenforth had been relieved, and a Major Morgan placed in command of Alton prison as his successor. We had quite a shipment from Gratiot last night; some twenty head of prisoners, and among them Capt.

Robt. Trimble, lately tried by a Military Commission, acquitted, and placed on the list of prisoners of war.

OCT. 27.—Having nothing else to write about to-day, I will present the rules and regulations by which the members of Room No. 1 are governed. They are as follows:

1st.—Col. Winston—Chief.

2nd.—Only cooks are allowed in the pantry.

3rd.—Cooks will have the exclusive right of the North and West sides of the stove.

4th.—No member of the mess will be allowed to wash his person after the usual supply of water has been obtained for the same.

5th.—No member will be admitted into the mess except by order of the commander of the prison, or by consent of two-thirds of the mess, with the consent of the commander of the prison.

6th.—Police duty of the room will be done by regular detail—the Chief and those on daily duty, only exempted.

7th.—It is the unanimous desire of the room, that visitors will not monopolize the windows.

8th.—Members of the room will keep their feet off the tables.

9th.—Inmates of the room will carry out their water immediately after washing.

10th.—Any member violating any of the above rules will do such extra duty as the Chief may dictate.

The following is a list of the members of Room No. 1:

Col. Winston—Chief; Calvert, Carter, Dawson, Gibbs, Frost, Lowrey, Muir, Muse, Peery, Ripley, Rucker, Scott, Smith, Wright; Brown, Boyd, Berry, and Turner.

OCT. 28.—The six men who were placed in close confinement on the 9th of this month, were handcuffed and taken to St. Louis this morning, where, it is said they will be shot some time to-day. They are to be executed in retaliation for a Maj. Wilson and six men, who were turned over to Reeves and by him shot, in retaliation for the murder of the same number of his men. When will this thing stop? This game of *lex talionis* makes sad havoc upon the lives of innocent men.

OCT. 30.—Learned yesterday that arrangements have been made, which permits all prisoners, North and South, to receive whatever clothing or provision their friends might see proper to send them. Also heard that Maj. Wilson's body was lying in state in the Court House at St. Louis. To-day the following note was handed me from Miss Sallie Linton, a cousin to Miss Bessie Bury; both these young ladies are well known to many of the inmates of Gratiot and Alton, and their numberless deeds of kindness will be remembered long after the war, which called them forth, shall have passed into history and song. Their lives of innocent usefulness are like

> "A sacred stream,
> In whose calm depth the beautiful and pure
> Alone are mirrored; which, though shapes of ill
> May hover round its surface, glides in light,
> And takes no shadow from them."

ALTON, Ills., Oct. 30, 1864.

CAPT. FROST—I have just come up from St. Louis, and was commissioned by your cousin Bessie Bury, to enquire if anything would be allowed you, the Commander informed me not unless by special order from Gen. Copeland. If you desire anything, or wish to send any message to Bessie, I am at your service. She I am sure, will apply to the General if you need anything. We are both now, allowed to write to our friends Joseph Elliot and Soward, who seem to miss you very much.

Your friend, SALLIE LINTON.

NOVEMBER 3. 1864.—I was told that last Monday a man made a bet that he could eat forty biscuit inside of an hour. The bet was accepted, the cakes counted out and the man fell to eating. At the close of the hour the biscuit had disappeared, and the voracious eater was informed that nine more had been added to the lot during the meal. The dimensions of his stomach must be somewhat on the Falstaffic order.

A female, dressed in male attire, and calling herself Mollie Hays, was brought in night before last—she is said to be a very hard case.

Saw a prisoner yesterday morning sitting on top of the wood shed, bucked and gagged—the weather being quite cool, his position was by no means an enviable one. All day we have had a cold drizzling rain, and our quarters have been very uncomfortable, nothing but a cooking stove to heat our room.

I had an amusing and interesting letter from my little friend Joe Elliot, of Gratiot; he says, "the inmates of room No. 1 are living on rats; not altogether from necessity, but as a luxury. They caught four last night and had them fried for dinner to-day.

The parson (Patterson) and Weaver are the most enamored of the game."

Nov. 4.—Miss Sallie Linton has paid another visit to Alton. She made an effort to see me, as she was the bearer of a hat for Col. Winston, and a letter from my lady friend Miss Bessie Bury, which reads as follows:

St. Louis, Nov. 2, 1864.

Capt. G. Frost—*Dear Friend:*—I was delighted when our friend Sallie told me she had a few lines from you. I have been most anxious to go to Alton to see you, but have been ill ever since you left the city. Do write to me, and let me know if you or any of your friends, need anything in the way of clothing. I send the hat you mentioned, for Col. Winston; I hope it will suit, if not I will change it as soon as I am able. I will go and see Gen. Copeland and beg permission to send you in some provision—I hear he is very kind. Please send me word if I can do anything for you. Capt. Keyser allowed me to see our little friend Joe Elliot, on Monday. He told me he had heard from you. He and Joe Soward send respects. Yours truly, Bessie Bury.

In a very short time after receiving the above, the following note was brought me from Miss Sallie Linton, written just before she left Alton:

Alton, Nov 4, 1864.

Dear Friend—This morning I applied for a pass to see you— the General was very agreeable, but said it was impossible unless you were in the hospital. Last Monday Capt. K. permitted Bessie to see Joe E., who told her you liked your present quarters better than old Gratiot; is that so? The boys are all well, and begged to be remembered in case I saw you, but as that is impossible you will have to accept of their assurances in writing. Excuse haste. With best wishes I remain your sincere friend, Sallie Linton.

Nov. 5th.—Thirty-eight more prisoners arrived last night from Gratiot, but I have not learned that any of our acquaintances were among the number.

There is a man here, Capt. Lineback, whom I met last spring in Gratiot, who has always appeared to be of a most melancholy disposition, caused by hearing of the death of his wife, shortly after he was captured on Island No. 10, several persons told him of her death, and one man, a fellow prisoner, assured him that he attended her funeral. The news made a deep impression on the Captain, who would sit for hours thinking of the dear companion he would meet no more, and wondering what had become of their little daughter. Imagine his joy, when a short time since, he received a letter from her own hand, telling him of her welfare, and that of their little child. The whole story was a mistake—must have been some one else. Capt. Lineback is a new man—acts like a different person altogether.

Nov. 15.—Sunday morning, Nov. 6th, I saw a Federal prisoner sitting on the top of the woodhouse, "bucked and gagged;" enquiring into the cause which promoted him to that "bad eminence," I was informed that he had been for some time engaged in stealing the hospital rations, especially the coffee and sugar, and selling them to his fellow prisoners. Complaints being made from the hospital, the matter was investigated and traced to this fellow King, who was then being punished for his crime. On the 8th we had a "grape vine" dispatch, announcing that Forrest had captured eight transports and three gun boats in the Tennessee river. The news arrived on the ninth, of the re-election of old Father Abraham to the Presidential chair. Suppose now he will be more "joky" than ever, and quite as full of proclamations.

The 10th brought me a letter from home, stating that our little daughter Annie had been severely injured by a dog, she was thrown down upon a rock and her arm broken. About this time our surgeons begin to bestir themselves with regard to our diet, they have procured such changes as are greatly conducive to health, and at the same time decidedly more pleasing to the palate. On the morning of the 11th, they condemned the beef which was furnished us and the butcher had to take it back and bring in better. Potatoes, onions and cabbage are now issued, with a marked effect in the improvement of the spirits of the prisoners. Last Saturday I saw the *female man* (Mollie Hays) for the first time, as she was on her way to dinner. She was still arrayed in masculine attire. Her features are coarse, face round and full, a turn up nose, hands and feet small. She has rather a masculine appearance, and is by no means a pleasing object to look upon.

Sunday* night eleven more prisoners came up from Gratiot, among them a lady named Douthett. Capt. Carter was the same night placed in a cell and kept there until morning. We were all greatly surprised when the sergeant came with the order, as Capt.

C. had been very sick for several days. Dr. Wright went around to Head Quarters and remonstrated, telling them that Carter was in no condition to go into a cell; but his pleading did no good; they were very angry at something he had written in a letter to his wife, and the order was peremptorily enforced.

Our lady prisoners lost their friend Mrs. Mitchell, who was released yesterday. Last night there were ninety more arrivals from St. Louis. One lady also with them; she is a Mrs. Martin, formerly a Miss Blanerhassett, they tell us that in St. Louis one of their female prisoners is wearing a ball and chain, "and still they come." The wonders of this progressive age still continue to announce to an astonished world, similar brave feats. We are in the full blaze of the nineteenth century. Women wearing balls and chains, as political offenders.

Nov. 24.—On the night of the 15th, between sixty and seventy prisoners captured at Pilot Knob, were brought in from Ironton; I made the acquaintance of several of the officers, particularly of Surgeon Gullet and Capt. McPike, who told me that the Federals treated the wounded at Ironton very badly, beating them over their heads with their revolvers, kicking them, slapping them in the face, calling them all sorts of names and threatening to shoot them if they made the least resistance. Forty or fifty of these wounded men were brought in here the same night, and they filled the hospital to overflowing. Next night one hundred and five more were brought from St. Louis. On the 17th Capt. Carter was paroled to the city, to enjoy the company of his wife, when he returned he brought in a large basket of provision. He thinks he will shortly be paroled from prison to remain east of the Mississippi and north of the Ohio. On the 18th we read the annual message of our own beloved President—the truly honorable Jefferson Davis—a statesman of whom any nation or people would be justly proud. On the 19th I received a letter from John Frost, at Fort Delaware, which states that all the sick and wounded prisoners have been sent off on exchange; it is rumored that a general exchange is about to take place. St. Louis shipped to Alton on the night of the 19th a hundred and thirty-five more prisoners, and among that lot I discovered a young man who used to belong to my old company, named Frank Hope. I had a good long talk last Sunday with Mrs. Martin, lately from St. Louis. Monday on going around among the prisoners, I found that many were suffering from the cold, their clothing being insufficient and having only one blanket—quite a number have been taken sick and had to be sent to the hospital. Tuesday we had another arrival from Gratiot and several hundred passed up on their way to Rock Island; prisoners are said to suffer very much there from the cold. Yesterday the water pipes were all frozen up, and we had great difficulty in getting sufficient water. The hospital is very much crowded, and there are a great many deaths and the number is increasing daily.

Fifty-seven more prisoners from Gratiot last night. Yesterday evening the sergeant sent us a special order stating that to-day—the 24th—was appointed as a day of Thanksgiving by the President of the U. S., and that there would be no work done on that day more than was actually necessary.

We have heard it said by those of olden time, that one claiming to be Lord of Lords, and King of Kings, did, from a certain mount amid thunder and lightning, and a thick cloud, and the voice of the trumpet exceeding loud, proclaim: "Remember the Sabbath day to keep it holy. Six days shalt thou labor and do all thy work; but the seventh day is the Sabbath of the Lord thy God: in it thou shalt not do any work, thou, nor thy son, nor thy daughter, nor thy man-servant, nor thy maid-servant, nor thy cattle, nor the stranger that is within thy gates; for in six days the Lord made the heaven and earth, the sea and all that in them is, and rested on the seventh day; wherefore the Lord blessed the Sabbath day and hallowed it." This reads like a special order, and no one pretends to question the high office or unlimited authority of the Potentate from whom it proceeds; even the celebrated joker at Washington, newly elected as he is, and firmly seated in power upon the necks of a blinded people, will bare his head if he ever seeks the presence of this Prince. And yet, during the twelve months in which I have sojourned as a "stranger within the gates" of his servants, I have never once, on the evening before this day set apart and appointed by God, as specified and directed in that august command, never once, been visited by a sergeant, and notified that "no more work would be done on that day than was actually necessary." Is the re-election of Abraham Lincoln the triumph of a party built upon the ruins of the state—the opening afresh of all the ports of the sea of blood, this hatching of the eggs of treason which has been in process of incubation since long before the Constitution was declared "a league with hell," and the "star-spangled banner" a "flaunting lie" is this, the occasion which calls for a day set apart and observed with a solemnity never once accorded to that day which was "blessed and hallowed" by the express command and awful proclamation of Him who "maketh the thick clouds his pavilion," "who boweth the heavens and cometh down," and "on whom no man may look and live."

*Thanksgiving!* if it was "prayer and supplication in sack cloth and ashes, I could bow myself down and worship with them, but I will never smile in the face of heaven, with a lie on my lips, crying "Peace, peace, when there is no peace."

Nov. 25.—Received an interesting letter yesterday evening, from my young friend Joe Soward at Gratiot. He writes that J. B. Jones, of "our mess" has been tried before the Military Commission, acquitted, declared to be a regular U. S. soldier, and ordered to the 7th Mo. Cavalry. Clinton Burbrage, he says, has been on trial for two weeks and expects it will end in his release. He and our little "feminine" favorite, Joe Elliot, are getting along about as usual, though the old quarters are not so lively as they have been. We had some excitement in our community last night; four prisoners, George Phillips, Rollins, Maupin, and Gallagher, tried to make their escape by bribing the guard and getting the countersign, they agreed to pay four hundred dollars, probably did pay it, and succeeded in getting past the first guard, but when they came to the passage leading from the prison, they were met by four or five sergeants, armed to the teeth, who informed them that they would have to go back. The guard it seems humored the proposition, pocketed the money, and reported them to the commander, who made preparations to receive them. They are now in cells, and will no doubt be kept there some time.

There is a great deal of sickness among the inmates of this prison, the hospital now contains over one hundred and eighty patients, and there are more than a hundred sick in their quarters, principally from cold and diarhea.

DECEMBER 1, 1864.—Last Saturday, a young lady, and young

gentleman—both sentenced to be hung, but whose sentences were commuted to imprisonment during the war, were brought up from Gratiot—the name of the young lady I have not heard—that of the gentleman is Vandiver. On that day the lady prisoners were permitted to visit the hospital, and for a short time minister to the sufferings of the patients; the sickness is on the increase and a great many are dying. There were more than one hundred and fifty new prisoners arrived on Sunday night from Little Rock, and several of them were dead, but they were thrown around, and handled as though they were dead hogs. Prisoners have been added very rapidly to this establishment, and the commissary arrangements have probably not been enlarged as freely as the demands require, at any rate a great many of them complain of not getting enough to eat. Whether they have just cause for such complaint I am not able to say—but I can say, and that safely, that some of them can be seen every day gathering up the potato and apple peelings, which have been thrown out among the rubbish. They gather up the coffee grounds which they boil over, and last Sunday I saw some of them picking pieces of bread and meat from the slop barrels, and gulping them down as though it was the last morsel they ever expected to see. One poor lean, lank looking fellow, was seen to pick up an old bread and milk poultice, and eat it, which he seemed to relish with infinite gusto. Nothing is lost here, everything is eaten; the men often bring their dry bread to us, and ask us to trade them biscuit for it, as they are considered a very great luxury. In some parts of the yard they are made for sale, and those who have money can buy them; they are sold, four very small ones for five cents—a pint of coffee may also be obtained for the same price. The steamer Joab Lawrence, on Tuesday, landed for "our house" one hundred and nine gentlemen from St. Louis, many of whom claim to have been conscripted by Gen. Price. Scarcely a day passes without a cargo of new recruits, and every day sickness is reported on the increase. Small-pox has showed itself in some eight or ten cases. Father Wilby of St. Louis, visited the prison Monday; many of the men were very glad to see him; he appears to be a kind hearted gentleman, and I have no doubt is a good christian.

John A. Bayse being in very bad health, and told by the doctor that he could live only a short time in prison, took the oath, gave a bond of a thousand dollars, and was this day released.

DEC. 4.—On Thursday evening, Capts. Muir, Lowrey, Muse. Dr. Wright and myself, had the pleasure of visiting the lady prisoners. We called at half-past six and remained till half-past nine. Five of the ladies were present, Mrs. and Miss Hanie, Mrs. Martin, Miss Lundy and Miss Goggin; Miss Douthett and Miss Smith did not make their appearance during the evening. I enjoyed a long and pleasant conversation with Mrs. Martin, who has had quite a hard time during her imprisonment—at times been treated very badly. The evening passed off so agreeably that for once, we all forgot we were in prison. Their rooms are good and comfortable, the floors nicely painted, and everything exhibited such perfect order that we were forcibly reminded of home. The fairy touch of woman's fingers had left its impress as far as her sphere extended. Mrs. Hanie acts as commissary and presiding matron, and they all seem to show her a great deal of respect. She and her daughter, it is thought, will be released in a short time.

Friday night one hundred and fifteen more prisoners of war arrived from Gratiot; among whom was Jarred Kelley, of Marion county, Mo., and formerly a member of Co. "A." Yesterday we received the pleasing intelligence that Gen. Copeland had given permission for us to send to our friends for boxes of provision for a Christmas dinner. We had several more prisoners brought in from St. Louis last night, and I think they are about the hardest looking cases I have yet seen, they claim to have been conscripted, and say "Old Price ought to be hung." They were sent to the citizen's quarters last night, and this morning, one of them was asked "if he was a conscript," and "if he wanted to take the oath," and "thought " Old Pap ought to be hung ?" to all which he answered in the affirmative, when some sentenced "rebel" stepped up and gave him an awful blow on the back of the head, remarking, "you think "Old Pap" ought to be hung, do you." The poor fellow bawled out, "somebody has broke my neck—I'm killed—I don't want to stay here."

Guess after this he will be a little particular how he says anything about "Old Price," as he called him, especially before Missourians, who have served under him in the Southern army. Preparations are now being made to send off a large number of prisoners. Some say it is a transfer to another prison, while others think it is on exchange, which is to take place at the mouth of Red River—none but privates are allowed to give in their names. Some change ought surely to be made, and that at an early date, as there are over two thousand prisoners here with a great deal of sickness among them.

DEC. 9.—Billy Bamburg's release was ordered on Saturday last, on oath and bond of five hundred dollars. He had filled the bond, taken the oath, and was getting his clothes ready to leave, when an order was received from St. Louis, countermanding everything, and he is now running around here with his "iron clad" in his stomach, and no prospect whatever of gaining his liberty. A letter from my little friend Joe Elliot, on Tuesday, tells me that Sam. Clifford is again in the lock-up, wearing a ball and chain. This time it seems he wrote a letter to one of the female prisoners which was intercepted. Poor Sam., he hardly gets out of one difficulty than he plunges into another.

A man named Thorp was released from his cell the other day—he was sentenced to be hung and has been in close confinement ever since he has been here; never once being near the fire until his release. He says he does not know whether his sentence has been commuted or not, but any way he enjoys with a decided relish the luxury of getting warm once more. Tuesday night, seventy four more prisoners of war came up from Gratiot. Col. Shanks and two or three other officers, whose names I have not learned, were among the number. However we sent the same morning, five hundred to Rock Island, so that our ranks are somewhat thinned even with that addition, though we doubt if the poor fellows who have gone North will fare better than to have remained crowded in here; as the climate there is colder, and we already hear of suffering from that quarter, and they are not by any means prepared for the rigors of a winter season. I have no doubt but they were exceedingly cold and disagreeable. A great many left under the impression that they were going off on exchange, but when they find they have only made a change of prisons, and that a change for the worse, I fear they will experience a sad disappointment.

Yesterday afternoon I had the pleasure of calling on the lady prisoners, and found at their quarters, that faithful friend of the unfortunate, Miss Sallie Linton, of St. Louis. She refreshed my drouthy ears with a great many spicy and interesting items of information—gave me the news from Gratiot, and also told me all about our circle of friends outside; like our grandmothers in the olden time, who carried sweet cakes and apples in their reticules to amuse the restless children that were taken to "meeting," her capacious pocket was filled with toys and trifles suited to us children of a larger growth; gutta percha, silver and pearl, to be worked up into our famous prison jewelry. She took charge of several articles I had prepared for my wife, promising to forward them to her address; among them a handkerchief, embroidered by our eccentric little "feminine" messmate, Joe Elliot, which Mrs. Frost will know how to fringe and appreciate. Miss Sallie was not aware that we were still without tools, our little kit having been taken from us at Gratiot, and not since returned. She says she will make an effort to have us supplied, so there will be no excuse for our idleness in the future, and we will dispose of our little trinkets when we can, for money, with which we can supply in some degree our many wants. Money is in great demand with us, our purses all having run down below zero. I had been without for over a month when I got a letter from my brother, W. P. Frost, of Mexico, Mo., enclosing two dollars. I regarded it a perfect "God send." I had a letter also, from my friend Ben. Dobyns, who is now enjoying his liberty in Dover, Ky. To-day (the 9th) it is bitter cold. We can scarcely keep from freezing; everybody and everything looks cold; the river is full of running ice, and our room is full of outsiders, who have run in to try to warm by our stoves. We give way to them for they suffer very much from the cold. A great many are dying in the hospitals connected with the prison and eleven new cases of small pox have broken out on the Island. There were three deaths last night; learned yesterday that my friend Billy Spires, the "lamp boy," is dead.

SUNDAY, DEC. 11, 1864.—There were thirteen deaths in the hospital Friday night, and in the Rock building, a prisoner was found in his bunk frozen to death. The weather continues very cold, the river is completely blocked with ice, and the hospital is so crowded it is impossible for a sick man to gain admittance; when one goes in, the doctor tells him to "take a seat, there is no room now, but some fellow will die in a few minutes, and you can take his place." Within the last fifteen days eight prisoners have escaped by putting on old clothes and going out with the Commissary detail and watching when the guard's backs were turned and slipping off. Lieut. Farh was the last to try the experiment, and I am happy to say that it resulted in a perfect success. It is always a matter of rejoicing, when one of our number obtains his freedom by the exercise of his wit or daring, we applaud the lucky adventurer, while we turn our attention to making the best of our own lot. To-day we were engrossed with discussing the merits of a dish which we style a desert, and call "Old Woman," Miss Lundy says we should say "antiquated lady." It is made with first a layer of wheat dough in the pan, then pork chopped fine, with spice, ginger, apples and sugar—then dough again, and so on, until the pan is full, a layer of dough being placed on top for a crust. We considered it a very fine treat, and at the close of the meal were willing to retract anything we might ever have been guilty of saying derogatory of the merits of any portion of that respectable population regarded as ancient, among persons of the feminine persuasion.

DEC. 13.—Twelve more deaths in the hospital during the last twenty-four hours—that is, twelve to my knowledge. Gen. Copeland a short time since gave permission to the prisoners here, to send home for a Christmas dinner—Major Ripley notified his mother of the order, and requested that he might be remembered and his share of the Christmas jollification forwarded to his address at Alton. His mother hastened to fill a box with all the good things she thought her son would relish, and shipped them at once, stating in her letter what she had sent. Yesterday the Major was informed that his box had arrived, and congratulating himself on being ahead of his comrades in his holiday arrangements he went down to receive and examine his present, but what was his disappointment when he discovered that a greater portion of his provision had been confiscated. It threw quite a damper over the big anticipations of the whole mess, if we are only to receive a few fragments from the contents of our boxes, we would prefer that our friends would not take the trouble of sending them.

Miss Sallie Linton in accordance with her promise, has it seems, sent up a nice selection of tools for my use, but I have not as yet been permitted to receive them, if it is against the rules for them to be admitted, they should have told Miss Sallie so when she spoke of buying them. I told Mrs. Martin of the female prison, that I was sorry Miss Linton had incurred the expense and taken the trouble of sending them, since I would not be allowed to use them. She says she thinks she can prevail on the officers to allow me to have them.

DEC. 17.—The eloquence of Mrs. Martin has prevailed, it appears in my behalf, as Miss Sallie's present, or at least what was left of it, was sent up to my room after I had gone to bed on Wednesday night; the things had lain scattered around until part of them were lost, however, I guess I can "open my shop" with what I received. The federal prisoners confined here are getting to be a very annoying nuisance; they robbed Capt. Calvert of his hat the other day, and while Capt. Dawson was down in the yard, five of them attacked him with their knives drawn, and ordered him to give up his checks, he told them he had none, when they threatened to kill him if he made any resistance, and proceeded to search his pockets and person, the only booty they secured was his knife, after taking possession of that, they let him go. I called on Major Morgan with regard to my missing tools, and was treated by him in a very courteous and gentlemanly manner. The prisoners are dying off at a fearful rate, eighty-three deaths have occurred since the first of this month. Every morning as we go to roll call we can see four or five dead bodies with nothing over them, lying in coffins under the hospital. It is almost impossible for the undertaker to furnish coffins as fast as they are needed. Old Mr. Boyce, a citizen, who lived near Helena, Ark., died very suddenly in his quarters Wednesday morning. There is great destitution of clothing among the men, and during the cold spell a few days ago there was a great deal of sickness contracted from exposure. This morning we held a meeting for the purpose of electing officers to act as agents in receiving and distributing clothing furnished by the Confederate Government for the use of Confederate prisoners at this prison. The house was called to order by Col. Winston, who made a motion that Dr. Wright be elected President, the motion being seconded, Dr. Wright offered the following amendment, "That Col. Winston be nominated as President; Col. Shenks, Vice President; and Capt. Muse, Sec'ry." The motion was seconded, vote taken and the ticket elected. The following candidates were then proposed for the agency: Major Rucker, Dr. Wright and Capt. Muse. The vote was taken by ballot, and when the polls were closed it was discovered that Major Rucker was elected—the vote standing thus: Rucker 25—Muse 12 and Wright 11.

A committee of four was then appointed to assist the Major in the performance of his duties, Capt. Cotter, Dr. Wright, Lieut. Allen and myself, received the appointment, after which the meeting adjourned.

SUNDAY, DEC. 18, 1864.—To-day we called the prisoners in line, for the purpose of ascertaining how much clothing was necessary for this place, when we made out the list as follows: coats 850, pants 900, shirts 1,250, drawers 1,250, blankets 850, hats 750, boots or shoes 850, socks 1,600.

DEC. 21.—On Monday there was some dissatisfaction manifested with regard to our late election, and a proposition was made to take it to the yard and receive the vote of the whole prison population, but there was no action taken in the premises, consequently the officers elected on Saturday are discharging the duties pertaining each to his official station. Yesterday I received an interesting letter from Joseph Elliot, of Gratiot, in which he tells me that Joseph Soward has been unconditionally released, and also states that Ab. Grimes is now at liberty, he was sentenced to the penitentiary at Jefferson City, to remain ten years, or during the war; while he was there they resorted to corporal punishment, and the poor fellow, just recovered of a wound which nearly cost his life, was flogged unmercifully. Joe writes that he is now the only representative of the old stock of last spring—says he never wanted to be out so badly in his life, and if crying would do any good, he could shed a little river of tears. Poor Joe, I know it is lonely for him, I wish he could be released, or else transferred over here to our mess. We had a nice time yesterday evening visiting the lady prisoners, went round at one, and remained till nine, had an introduction to Mrs. Martin's mother, Mrs. Blannerhassett, I met her sister Miss Blannerhassett, on a former visit, they are a very interesting family of ladies, and of course very patriotic Southerners. Mrs. B. brought me from Miss Linton a fine selection of jewelery tools, and in return I was able to send her a very pretty sample of my work.

DEC. 24.—Gen. Copeland has still further extended his kindness to some of the prisoners at Alton, by granting to the lady prisoners permission to invite their friends among their masculine fellow-captives, to partake with them of a Christmas dinner. Most of the officers of No. 1 have received invitations, and all parties are busy making preparations for the grand affair. All of us who receive our boxes from home in time, expect to contribute toward the feast. Monday is the day appointed for the dinner. I have a letter to-day from my old mess mate, Capt. G. W. Carter, who says he feels like a different person since he has gained his liberty.

DEC. 25.—Morning!—Christmas!—And a merry one it is, almost as much so as last. A number of us have been very much disappointed at not receiving our boxes of "good things," and to-day we have to make our Christmas dinner on bacon and cabbage. The only pleasure I expect is in writing to my friends, and talking to the lady prisoners from the window. Capt. Muse and our cook Boyd, received a box a piece yesterday evening, Muse's contained some nice large cakes, oysters and crackers, and a quantity of fine smoking tobacco; Boyd's was mostly filled with good warm winter clothing—a few dainties were added. A Mr. McCan of No. 2, had a large box sent him, but it was riddled of nearly every thing it contained, they left him a splendid fruit cake, several cans of oysters, some butter and sausage; he thinks some of the renegade rebels had a hand in robbing it. Evening: Well, I am happy to state, Col. Winston, Capts. Muse, Winston, Lowrey, and myself, were agreeably disappointed when we were sent for by our friend Capt. Muir to take dinner with him. We accepted the invitation with very little reluctance, and reported to his Headquarters immediately, when we were invited to seat ourselves at the table, where we found a fine roasted goose, nicely dressed, excellent biscuit and butter, and a dish the Captain calls "Old Woman," served with brandy sauce. We all enjoyed ourselves to the fullest extent, only regretting that we have not more Capt. Muir's among us while in prison.

MONDAY, Dec. 26.—Great preparations are now being made by the lady prisoners, to have a number of Confederate officers dine with them this afternoon. Our friend Capt. Muir, is assisting them in the cooking, and all who can are lending a helping hand. We are to go round at three o'clock and remain until eleven, as will be seen from the note given below:

MILITARY PRISON, Alton, Ill., }<br>
Dec. 26, 1864. }

COL. WINSTON AND OTHERS—*Gentlemen :*—The ladies wish your attendance at three o'clock this evening. You will be allowed to remain until eleven P. M.    JAS. M. MORGAN, I. A. M. P.

As they are now getting ready, I will have to close, and write about the dinner to-morrow.

DEC. 27.—Yesterday evening at a quarter past three, Col. Winston, Maj. Rucker, Capt's Muir, Muse, Lowrey, Gibbs, Corder, McPike, Peery, and myself, with Lieut. Ponder, started on our visit to the ladies, but before we reached their quarters we were joined by Surg's Wright, Brown and Gullet, Messrs. Davidson, Robinson, Preston, Parmel and Crow. On our arrival we were shown into the room occupied by Misses Lundy and Goggin, where the usual form of introduction was gone through with. Our fair hostesses all appeared to be enjoying excellent health except Miss Goggin, who has been quite sick for several days. The Misses Lundy, Douthett and Hanie were very entertaining, and expressed themselves highly pleased with the visit. Mrs. Martin kept every one she met with busily engaged in conversation—both she and Mrs Hanie, did all in their power to make the evening pass off pleasantly. Miss Smith, the lady, or rather child, that cut the telegraph, informed me that she was captured with the hatchet in her hand, and after her trial, they told her she was sentenced to be hung, but they would release her if she would tell who told her to cut the wire. She told them she would rather be hung than tell. While she was in prison at Rolla, they treated her very badly—gave her nothing to lie on for six weeks except the bare rock floor.

Dinner was announced at half past four, when the company repaired to the dining room, where we found a large table richly laden with everything the most epicurean taste could desire. Below I will give our bill of fare for dinner:

### BILL OF FARE.

|  |  | ROASTS. |  |  |
|---|---|---|---|---|
|  | Beef, |  | Turkey, |  |
| Goose, |  | Duck, |  | Chicken. |
|  |  | BOILED. |  |  |
|  | Bacon, |  | Cabbage, |  |
| Turnips, |  | Potatoes, |  | Tomatoes. |
|  |  | SIDE DISHES. |  |  |
|  | Light Bread, |  | Butter, |  |
| Crackers, |  | Cold Slaw. |  | Pickles. |
|  |  | DESERT. |  |  |
|  | Mince Pie, |  | Cranberry Tart. |  |

After we had finished eating, discussing and praising the dinner, and congratulating ourselves over the rare good fortune of partaking of it together, we returned to the room temporarily appropriated as a parlor, some to engage in talking, others in singing, but the majority amused themselves in promenading the hall and passing from one room to another. Mr. Davidson passed off his time in fanning the sick lady who looked as though she was very thankful for his attention. About 8 o'clock we received the announcement that supper was waiting, and were all of one mind on the instant, and proceeded with great alacrity to the dining room. The following was our bill of fare for supper:

### BILL OF FARE.

|  | Coffee. |  | Tea. |  |
|---|---|---|---|---|
| Fruit Cake. |  | Jelly Cake, |  | Pound Cake. |

After supper the enjoyment was about the same as before, and at 11 o'clock we bade our lady friends an affectionate good bye, and returned to our quarters very much delighted with our evening's entertainment. If all our boxes had arrived in season the ladies would have had a larger store from which to select their table comforts; but as it was, they were able to furnish a well filled board, even from their own resources, to say nothing of the contributions from such gentlemen as had heard from home.

So much for Gen. Copeland's kindness, and Maj. Morgan's courtesy, without which we would have been condemned to our lonely prison and the coarse fare which the government issues to her captive boarders.

DEC. 31.—Our lady friend, Miss Mollie Goggin, who was complaining on the evening of our pleasant reunion, was the next day taken quite ill and the doctors have entertained some fears with regard to her recovery—but her symptoms are at this date more encouraging, and with the kind attention of the excellent ladies with whom her lot is cast, we hope soon to see her gentle face with a smile; perhaps sadder and sweeter, giving us a friendly greeting from the window. I also have had an attack of neuralgia, result of a cold attended with a slight cough, which procured me the pleasure of receiving from Mrs Martin a bottle of cough medicine.

My box came on Thursday, it contained a large piece of baked pork, two rolls of butter, seven or eight mince pies, some sugar and coffee, a jar of jelly, three bags of sausage, a jar of tomatoes, one pòund and one sponge cake, and about a peck of very fine large apples; everything in tolerably good order, except the pies, which were mashed and broken to pieces. The box had been ten days on the way On Friday, our mess gave something of a dinner, gotten up in honor of our friend, Capt. Muir, whose hospitality we enjoyed on Christmas day. Our boxes furnished forth quite freely for the occasion. My brother William, at Mexico, instead of provision, sent me money and stamps. Sister Rebecca, at Cairo sent me five dollars and a receipt for a box, which is now at the Express office, and is said to contain a fine cake for a New Year's present. Gen. Copeland having been relieved, his successor, Gen. Stone, made a general inspection of the prison to-day. I had not the pleasure of seeing him but those who had were agreeably impressed by his manner and appearance.

TUESDAY, January 1, 1865.—Last Sunday being New Year's day, I "pulled off my coat and rolled up my sleeves" and went to work to celebrate the advent of the young stranger, "'65." If Joe Soward had been in No. 1, we should certainly have required of his pen the production of an "address" or "node," but since he is rejoicing in his liberty, and both the poetical Captains are free, the best that we could do, was to cook in honor of the new fledged year. I tried my hand on that original prison dish, the "Old Woman," or, as Miss Florence L. insists we shall call it, the "Antiquated Lady," and rejoice to say that the ancient dame was a complete success, as also some apple pies, besides our beef, potatoes, biscuit and butter. In the afternoon we were invited to dine with the ladies; but I was compelled to decline on account of fatigue and ill health, however, Capt. Muir and another gentleman went over, and when they returned, reported a very pleasant visit indeed. Miss Mollie Goggin is recovering rapidly from her late illness.

But after all, Maj. Ripley and Dr. Wright drew the grand prize of the day. They were paroled to the limits of the town—the Major to see his mother, and the doctor to see his wife—and allowed to remain out until 12 o'clock P. M. Learned yesterday that Joe Soward was in the city, stopping at the Alton House. He sent me his photograph and says he will remain several days. Capt. John Muse was paroled yesterday to see his wife, whom he has not met since his capture—some fifteen or twenty months ago. Paroles seeming to be granted so freely, and having something of an appetite for the fresh air, I sent in a polite application, and had the pleasure of being respectfully refused. I then turned for consolation to a long and interesting letter, received by the underground route, from my dear friend "Mary,"* which was filled with good advice, home news, and such words of gentle affection as none but "Mary" would write." In alluding to my long imprisonment, and her occasional despondency, she writes:

"I am wearied out with watching,
And the lamp light burneth low—
Fitfully it gleameth, catching
Phantasies that none may know—
Wondrous dreamings, yearnings, ever
For the perfect love of yore;
When a blest united family
We shall sever—never more."

There has been in the hospital, since the first of Dec. 1864, one hundred and seventy deaths.

JAN. 4.—We were not a little surprised this morning, at seeing our friend Joe Soward, introduced into No. 1. He was arrested this morning at the Alton House, on what charge, or, for what offence, he was at a loss to imagine—but he remembered hearing a lady friend remark in the presence of others, that he had been in

---
* Mrs. Frost.

the Southern army which it is supposed must have led to his arrest. He manifested considerable uneasiness, was not still a moment at a time, was restless as a "fish out of water." He wrote to me yesterday, sending a lot of chewing tobacco, and to-day he had a fair prospect of helping me use it. We enjoyed seeing him and having him with us, but of course were sorry to have him restrained of his liberty. Towards evening he became more reconciled, and had made up his mind to go quietly in to quarters, when he was agreeably disappointed at being invited into the office and honorably released. I did not see him after he left our quarters, but am of the opinion he will bid Alton a hasty farewell and sail for some other port. Mrs. M. from the female prison had permission to go out and see him, but his being arrested, deprived her of the opportunity. However she may have met with him this evening, after he was released. Capt. Muse brought his wife and baby to the prison this afternoon, and introduced her to us through the iron bars. It was a little more than the poor lady could stand, so after a glance or two she went into the office, with the tears running down her cheeks.

## CHAPTER XI.

ANOTHER ATTEMPT OF PRISONERS TO ESCAPE; "COOK'S PILL'S;" STEALING PRISONERS' PROVISION; THE OLD TRACT MAN; THE NAVY MESS; MORE RUMORS OF AN EXCHANGE; A SINGULAR MODE OF PUNISHMENT; ARRIVAL OF UNITED STATES "GUTTA PERCHA" SOLDIERS; NAILING DOWN THE WINDOWS IN THE LADIES' QUARTERS; ARRIVAL OF MORE FEMALE PRISONERS; DEPARTURE OF COL. WINSTON FOR ST. LOUIS; STRINGENT ORDERS WITH REGARD TO LETTER WRITING, &C., &C.

JAN. 5.—About thirty men were discovered yesterday morning, in the act of making their escape through a hole some forty feet in length, which they had dug from a cellar to the outside of the wall. Quite a number were in the hole at the time of the discovery, and others were preparing to enter, when the whole lot was captured and confined in cells. Capt. Muse's wife having left for home, he returned to his quarters last night. No. 1 offers fewer attractions capable of captivating his fancy now, than ever before.

Joe Soward was permitted to call on the lady prisoners after his release, and enjoyed a long conversation with Mrs. Martin. Miss Goggin has so far recovered as to be able to appear at the window. There is still a great deal of sickness; small pox seem to be on the increase, several new cases yesterday. The physicians here are possessed of a mania for "Cook's Pills." One would think Government had bought up a lot at auction; no matter what the disease or complaint, the universal remedy is "Cook's Pills," and it is impossible to get any other medicine.

This morning the box sent by my sister, was delivered to my hand; I found one fine large cake in it, with some oranges which were spoiled. The box was not full, but as it was opened before I saw it, I am not prepared to say whether it was sent in that condition, or had been robbed. There were a large number of expresses received by different prisoners—heard one box called for a poor fellow, who is in the hospital, too sick to enjoy the good things prepared and sent by his affectionate friends. Another was called for a prisoner who has been dead for several days—no doubt it was gotten up by a loving mother, wife or sister, who, while engaged in packing the different articles would imagine to themselves how much pleasure he would take in eating, and sharing with his fellow captives the many nice things they were sending him, but alas, sad will be their disappointment, when they hear of his untimely death. A great many of the boxes were robbed—butter, ham, chickens, apples, and pickles, being mostly taken. A prisoner's life is hard enough at best, without being deprived of the few luxuries which are contributed by the kindness of distant friends and relatives—but there seem to be people mean enough to steal the grey hairs from a dead man's head, because they resemble silver.

JAN 10.—On Saturday there were another large lot of express boxes received by the prisoners, but as usual they were rifled of half their contents. Sunday passed off in the long and lonesome manner, which is peculiar to prison life; there was preaching twice during the day, but very few from No. 1 availed themselves of the opportunity thus offered for joining in worship. Tracts and pamphlets are usually distributed every Sunday morning, but very few receive them with any encouraging interest, the man who carries them round is generally the subject of some joke, and he and his tracts are laughed at as soon as he is gone. They call him the old "paper man." Yesterday some sixteen prisoners, styled the "Navy Mess" were released from prison, they are said to be the refusal of over one hundred men who foreswore the Confederate Government for the purpose of entering the United States Navy, but after examination, having been discovered to be unfit for service, they were provided with quarters to themselves, where they have remained ever since, until their release. They have been distinguished from the other prisoners by the title given above—the

"Navy Mess." Twenty prisoners arrived last night from Gratiot, who represent themselves to be citizens; this morning about four o'clock, some thirty or forty more were brought up from Memphis. Three officers were with them, who remained here until evening, and were then shipped to Johnson's Island. For several days we have heard considerable talk about a general exchange. An arrangement is said to have been made between the two governments, but whether the cartel will include sentenced prisoners remains to be seen. It is thought now there will be an exchange beyond a doubt, and all the prisoners of war are very jubilant over the prospect. Our roll-sergeant, Richard Robinson, was released this evening on parole, to remain in the "loyal" States, and east of the Mississippi river, during the war.

JAN. 15.—A Federal soldier was killed last Wednesday while on guard. Two of them it seems got to fooling with their guns, "charging bayonets," &c., when one of the weapons accidentally went off, the ball entering his breast and killing him instantly. A young man named Estes, sentenced during the war, had rather a severe punishment inflicted on him the same day. He had committed some little offense, for which he was made to wear a barrel during the afternoon. It was put on him by having a hole cut in the top for his head, and one on each side for his arms. He presented a very rediculous appearance, and the weather being quite cold, he suffered a great deal during his unsightly promenade. The regulations here are more strict than they were at Gratiot, and the slightest offense is punished with great severity. But those who write the laws legibly in their memories, and are careful to observe and obey them, are treated decidedly better than the same class were in St. Louis. The guard and petty officers manifest no disposition to indulge in disgusting insolence; on the contrary they are respectful and gentlemanly in their deportment.

Capt. Gibbs, had a brother from Mexico, Mo., who came down for the purpose of effecting his release on oath and bond. The Captain was permitted to spend the day on Wednesday with his brother out in the city where they were busy making arrangements for his release. Friday was unusally dull, the weather being moderate, we were confined to close quarters on account of the mud, which was nearly shoe mouth deep on the yard. We heard a vague rumor concerning peace, but place no reliance in any thing of the kind. Yesterday we had some more prisoners from Vicksburg, rather a mixed assortment—three ladies and nine or ten colored individuals in the lot. The Sambo's were rigged out as United States soldiers, it is a pretty good burlesque on the uniform, to see the nigger naps sticking out of the upper end of a suit of the National blue.

The lady prisoners and our mess are accused of communicating political news through the medium of our window gossip, and consequently we are forbidden to talk any more, and the ladies' windows are nailed down, with the threat of boarding them up if any symptoms of insubordination should be observed. We consider it a stroke of most deplorable misfortune, and the ladies have been nowise backward in speaking of it as such, which has provoked the still further rigor or having a heavy padlock placed on the outside of their side door, and a guard beneath the windows. The first sentinel placed there, I am told, entered upon the duties of his office under the refreshing influence of a bath from one of the wash pans. Maj. Morgan told them it was not decent to be talking from the windows, when one of the spicy creatures replied; "she would admit the fact, if they were talking to Yankees, but conversing with Southern gentleman was altogether a different matter. The Major could not help being a little provoked; guess he finds it something like stirring up a "mare's nest" to undertake to discipline a lot of ladies. One of them suggested to sergeant "Killposey" the propriety of "puttying" their eyes so they could not see out of the windows.

I would not be a gentleman and compelled to guard and occasionally punish a lot of lady prisoners for all of Abraham's greenbacks. It is a barbarous thing to imprison them at all, and none but a savage is fitted for the office. Why don't it occur to them as we are mixed up in the offence, to visit us with a double portion of the well "nursed" governmental wrath, and let the untamable fair ones escape. Col. Winston, Capt's. Muir, Lowry and myself made application yesterday for permission to visit the infuriated feminines, and were told to "get ready," which we did immediately, and staid ready until nine o'clock, when the permit not arriving, we concluded we were sold and pocketed the disappointment as best we might.

JAN. 18.—About three o'clock yesterday morning, five hundred of the dirtiest, raggedest men I ever saw, arrived as prisoners from Mississippi. If they are a fair sample of the wretchedness and poverty to which the Southern people are reduced, their prospect is dark indeed.

> Oh how the Yankee's do gloat on the splendor
> That follows the wake of their banner's advance—
> What brotherly love all their teachings engender,
> Where burning, and pillage, and murder, do render—
> The music to which all their gay squadrons dance.

An abstract from a letter written by John Frost, who is still at Fort Delaware reads as follows: "What do you do there? Peck rock? If so, I judge you like it about as well as I do this famous watering place, where one is so much benefitted by the cool and refreshing sea breeze, which is wafted around us in a keen whistle these raw days in January." He also writes that the Philadelphia Enquirer of the 11th, states that the exchange will be resumed, and that "the boys are praying that it may prove true, for we are all more than anxious to get released from this terrible place." Last Saturday evening, several of us were sorely disappointed, and regarded ourselves as a very ill used company of gentlemen, but it seems there was not much blame attached to the affair after all— our discomfiture was caused by a new leaf being turned in the book of regulations, and it is provided that Wednesday shall be the day set apart for prison visiting, and the reception of visitors, and in accordance with this new arrangement, Col. Winston, Maj. Rucker, Maj. Ripley, Capt's. Muir, Muse, Peery, and myself, with Mr. Davidson and Dr. Wright, were informed that we could visit the ladies this afternoon, calling at half past twelve and staying until five o'clock. We of course availed ourselves of the opportunity, at the earliest practicable moment, and before one o'clock, were seated in the ladies department listening to the "tale of all their woes," and offering such consolation as our unavailing sympathy might afford. We found Mrs. Blannerhassett visiting her daughter, Mrs. Martin, and made the acquaintance of the three ladies brought up from Vicksburg; two of whom, Mrs. Reynolds and Miss Oliver, are from the state of Louisiana, Mrs. Russell is from Mobile; they are all sentenced to remain in prison one year. We found them very pleasant and entertaining; especially Mrs. Reynolds, and her niece

Miss Oliver. Our friends of an older date, expressed a charming delight at seeing us once more. The conversation was general, and some passages decidedly rich. There is a fountain of wit pent up in several of the feminine bodies, so carefully guarded here by bayonets. Miss Lundy and Miss Douthett, are young ladies of quick apprehension, bright fancy, and conversational powers of the highest order. The little telegraph girl, Miss Smith, is much admired for the heroic firmness, with which she bears her lot, and her invincible determination not to be coaxed or scared into turning traitor against her friends. The married ladies treat her with a great deal of motherly kindness. Mrs. Hanie is a perfect model in her way, she is looked up to and loved by all the ladies in the prison. Indeed I have never met in our most refined and select circles with greater delicacy and more eminent sense of feminine propriety, than is manifested within these strongly guarded prison walls. The married ladies extend a watchful, motherly care over the young creatures snatched from their indulgent homes, and incarcerated within the bounds of this loathsome military prison. Their fair young faces smiling unconsciously in this sink of moral corruption, are like "rich jewels in an Ethiop's ear."

"There was a little bird upon that pile;
It perched upon a ruined pinnacle,
And made sweet melody.
The song was soft, yet cheerful and most clear,
For other note none swell'd the air but his.
It seemed as if the little chorister,
Sole tenant of the melancholy pile,
Were a lone hermit, outcast from his kind,
Yet withal cheerful."

Maj. Rucker received from Mrs. Dr. Samples, and other ladies of Boonville, a barrel of provision, consisting of everything "good" a person could call for, with orders to distribute "the contents" among the Boonville prisoners. The boys from that section of Missouri are now disposed to "bet their bottom dollar" on the Boonville ladies. It would do them good to see the enthusiasm with which the poor fellows receive their munificent bounty. "Good things" among the privates, are not near so frequently discussed as in the officers' quarters.

Capt. Muse, of our mess, had a nice box from his friend Miss Johnnie S., which besides the "chicken fixens," contained some very useful articles of clothing; one garment however, puzzled the boys considerably, and I believe, the Captain himself—has no name for it.

(14)

JAN. 23.—Miss Mollie Goggin, through the influence, as Madam Rumor says, of a gentlemanly Federal Lieutenant, to whom she is engaged to be married was released on the morning of the 19th, by taking the prescribed oath. Their mutual compromise and concession, will no doubt result in a loving and a lasting peace. If our Confederacy must be married to the United States Government and lose its name and identity in the union, we trust the connection will be formed in the same liberal spirit and terminate as happily for all parties concerned.

The last few days have been exceedingly dull; last Thursday, we had a fresh cargo of prisoners arrive—twenty-seven of whom were Federal soldiers, two citizens, and five *gutta percha gemmen*. Mrs Martin spent that day out in town with her mother, who left in the evening on the David Tatum. Next day I had a letter from "cousin" Bessie, wanting to know if I could receive a box of edibles and a supply of cough medicine.

In the evening of that day the five hundred "forlorns" from Mississippi, were supplied with blankets, which took all the committee had on hand. Uncle Jeff. will have to ship us another lot, as the members of his family which come into our quarters, are generally in a rather destitute condition. Saturday I had a letter from home and wife writes that their last negro man is getting ready to leave; she seems rather low spirited, says her father is getting old, has worked hard, and raised a large family white and black, and to be left now seems hard. A negro woman who was raised up among the white children has expressed her determination to make no change, she says "what's de gobernment got to do wid me? I don't belong to de gobernment—Abe Lincum nebber raised me, an' did'nt pay no money for me. What right he got to take dis nigger from ole master, whose done gone and bro't me up? He'd better buy me fust, den set me free if he wants to. Bress de Lord, I'll praise de bridge what carries me safe ober, an' I'se nebber wanted for nothing in master's house." Good for Em. if she sticks to it, she knows which side of her bread is buttered.

Yesterday a Federal soldier was put in a barrel and promenaded round, for stealing some money from a little boy. To-day it is very cold indeed, and there is a great deal of suffering among the prisoners. Col. Winston, Capt. Calvert and Capt. Peery, have been out all day breaking rock, and they came very near freezing. It is downright shocking cruelty to force men out on such an errand in such weather as this.

JAN. 29.—Last Monday night, a prisoner named Roberts, quartered in the rock building, was robbed of all his clothing, and was compelled to lie in bed next morning until his friends went around and gathered up something for him to put on. On Wednesday several members of No. 1, repeated their visit to the ladies. The restrictions with regard to the windows have been removed, with this warning injunction, that if they talk to us too much, or permit us to talk to them beyond a very limited scope, the windows will be boarded up entirely for the future; and as Maj. Morgan is a man of his word, we know what he means, and shall strive to conduct ourselves accordingly. We stand back in the room and spell on our fingers once in awhile. In this way Mrs. Martin communicated to me the news of our little favorite, Joe Elliot's release, but I have not yet ascertained the terms on which he procured his liberty; however my heartiest congratulations, and warmest good wishes are with him wherever he may be. As a man he is a perfect gentleman, as a prisoner, he was eccentric, original and generous, almost to a fault; his versatile talent, ready wit, and queer conceit, were an inexaustible fund of amusement for old "mess No. 3."

Col. Winston left us yesterday for St. Louis, he had been notified the day before, but was not apprised of the reason which induced the change; some think he is to have a new trial, but others are of the opinion that he was only called as a witness. He is the Chief of our mess, and in parting with him, we felt as if we were losing a father or a brother; his uniform kindness has endeared him to every occupant of the room, and we trust that unless he is released he will be restored to the little family of which he is the acknowledged head.

We have this evening a number of prisoners brought up from St. Louis, who are gorgeously ornamented with showy and conspicuous jewelry worn upon the wrists and vulgularly called *hand cuffs*. The weather continuing intensely cold, our water pipes are frozen up, and we experience great difficulty in procuring a sufficient supply of water, but for all that we obtained enough to scrub up our quarters, and put on our prettiest looks, when we heard that some ladies were going to visit the prison, and make a special call at No. 1. We were quite elated at the prospect and put our house in order with a great deal of care and precision, and then set down and waited for the company, but the hours rolled by and they failed to make their appearance. We afterwards learned that Maj. Morgan refused to permit the visit.

JAN. 30.—Three of the sentenced prisoners were notified Saturday to be ready to start for Fortress Monroe to-day. Had a letter yesterday from our former messmate, Ben. Dobyns, who writes from Covington, Ky., but expects to leave in a few days for his home in Missouri. He tells me that he met with Joe Soward on the packet going to Dover.

Maj. Rucker was allowed to attend church out in the city, and says the peace question is raging to a great extent; the general impression seems to be that the difficulties pending between the North and South, will be doubtless amicably adjusted by the first of March.

Yesterday evening I saw Miss Florence Lundy standing near the window; I was glad to see her, but she shook her head to tell me not to attempt any conversation. Mrs. Martin also came to the window. She had just recovered from a spell of sickness, but was looking better than I expected to see her. Mrs. M. is a very kind and amiable lady, and our mess is indebted to her for a number of little favors, such as pearl and gutta percha for our jewelry works, and often suitable medicines, when we could procure nothing from the doctors except their everlasting "Cook's pills." Her mother has always been allowed to visit her, and through that medium she has access to the outer world, and is able to be a benefactress within the prison.

Our old "Tract man" is still faithful in his rounds, but I fear that most of his good seeds are scattered on stony ground. There is a suspicion in the minds of our people, with regard to everything which eminates from the Yankees; it is hard for them to believe that the same fountain can yield both bitter and sweet waters; they know that they are drinking the bitter cup, and that the very dregs are wrung out to them and they don't care to taste any further. Maj. Morgan has issued a more stringent order with regard to our letter writing; it has always been the rule to allow but one page, but it has never been strictly enforced until now, the letter Inspector is positively required in all cases, where more than one page is written, to cut off the address and signature, enclose them in an envelope, and send as directed on the back. The weather having somewhat moderated, the skaters are out in swarms; the ice extends from the prison to a considerable distance out into the river, and is covered with gay parties of ladies and gentlemen amusing themselves in the exciting and exhilerating pastime of darting like arrows over the surface of the frozen element. Some of the ladies move with such even, steady grace, that they look like tiny vessels wafted along by a gentle breeze, while others hobble and tumble and swagger along in the most awkward and rediculous manner; falling and bumping upon the ice, calling forth a great many vulgar remarks, and insinuations; it is a pity but such could have some private skating park where they could practice and be instructed, and in this way become proficient enough to make a respectable appearance among the public skaters.

FEBRUARY 1, 1865.—The following announcement was clipped by Miss Bessie Bury from the St. Louis Republican, and enclosed with the accompanying note to my address.

### DEATH OF A MISSOURIAN.

LOUISVILLE, Ky., January 24th, 1865.

*Editor Republican:*

DEAR SIR: Please publish the following account of the death of a Missourian, as his friends may not have received intelligence concerning it.

On Saturday the 21st, a scouting party of Union soldiers came upon a young man and attempted to arrest him, but he resisted and was shot. He lived but a few moments and did not speak. From some papers found upon his person, he is supposed to be a citizen of Missouri named Joseph A. Soward. He was about twenty-two years of age, five feet eight inches high, had light hair and blue eyes.  Yours, Respectfully,

JNO. R. CAMPBELL.

Capt. G. FROST:

*Dear Friend:*—I write to give you the most sad news of the death of our friend, Joseph A. Soward. I can write but a few lines, for my heart is too full of sorrow. I intend to write to the person who had his death published, to learn more about it.  Yours truly,

BESSIE BURY.

Several Confederate prisoners at letter call, yesterday evening, received the most gracious information, that they would not be "compelled to go on exchange against their will."

To-day being Wednesday, and of course "reception day," the usual company from our mess, with the exception of Col. Winston, who is still in St. Louis, called and paid our respects at feminine head-quarters. Mrs. Martin, Miss Douthett, Miss Maggie Oliver, and Mrs. and Miss Hanie, were the only ladies able to be present, the others being excused on account of illness. We had expected to meet Miss Sallie Linton, and Miss Alice Blannerhassett; and Mrs. Martin and myself were particularly disappointed at their non-appearance, and were talking the matter over—Mrs. M. proposing to write and ask them to bring some one along to introduce them, when Maj. Morgan came in and announced their arrival. They were greeted with a most cordial welcome, and plied with many questions as to why they had not come sooner; the failure of an omnibus was all the excuse they had to offer, they were all ready to come in the morning, but not being called for in time they had to wait for the afternoon train. Miss Sallie's "capacious pocket" was filled as usual with little articles for the amusement of her captive friends. A bottle of cough medicine was my especial favor. At five o'clock we were notified that it was time for us to return to quarters, when Mrs. Martin requested of Maj. Morgan that I might be permitted to remain and take tea with them; he willingly granted her request, which was regarded as a great favor, for the privilege of sitting around the same board with Southern ladies, is a boon not granted every day to prisoners. We enjoyed our meal with something like an old fashioned relish, seeing a lady sitting at the head of the table, and receiving our coffee from her hands was a strong reminder of those

"days of auld lang syne."
When ere this bloody war began,
Each prisoner was a happy man.
"But pleasures are like popies spread,
You seize the flower, its bloom is shed;
Or like the snow flake on the river,
A moment white—then melts forever."

Ere we were half prepared for the unwelcome moment, "the hour arrived" and we must go. We bade them a reluctant farewell, and turned our footsteps in the direction of our own gloomy quarters.

FEB. 4.—Gen. Dodge of St. Louis, and a Major from Washington City in company with Maj. Morgan, our present commander, visited and inspected the different quarters of the prison and expressed themselves as highly pleased with everything except our comforts. Gen. Dodge thinks we are having too good a time altogether, and has forbidden any more "expresses" being received; has prohibited all visiting among the prisoners, and ordered that the ladies shall do their own cooking, a man only being allowed to furnish them with wood and water. No permits are to be granted hereafter to any one to go out into the city. Gen. Dodge is a good man, a kind man, a brave man, the very quintessence of gallantry, chivalry and magnanimity to say nothing of the brilliant charge in which he repulsed and defeated all the joys and hopes of hundreds of languishing, helpless prisoners. Last month there were a hundred and twenty deaths in this prison, and on the third of the present month eleven had been counted. Yet for all that, we are having "too good a time" and our privileges "must be cut off—cut off, in the future." We love Gen. Dodge. The following notice was left in our room this morning.

(*Circular.*)

INMATES OF ROOM NO. 1., A. M. PRISON:

I am instructed to inform you that all visiting on the part of the prisoners is prohibited for the future. You will therefore make no application for such privilege.

A. O. INGALLS, Sergt. & Supt. A. M. P.

Had quite a row in the yard this evening, between a party of regular Confederate soldiers, and a lot of "galvanized rebels." Some fifteen or twenty were engaged, and I am told that the Confeds had the best of it.

FEB. 9.—It is at last a settled and decided fact, that an exchange of prisoners is to be made, but I am sorry to state that officers and sentenced prisoners, are not included. A large number of privates signed their paroles on Tuesday, and will be sent in a short time to Fortress Monroe. They are all in fine spirits, and full of rejoicing at the prospect of getting back to Dixie.

On Sunday and Monday the yard was full of rumors concerning peace. An armistice of sixty days is reported to have been agreed upon, with a good prospect of a permanent arrangement, but Tuesday we learned that the peace question was at an end, the Commissioners could not agree, and both parties agreed to fight it out. Yesterday (Wednesday) being the day on which we have usually made our calls on our lady friends, we realized more than ever before the length and breadth of our "deplorable misfortune." The day seemed to try how long it could lag on, and how lonesome it could be, and in the evening one of our number received the sad intelligence of the death of a son. To-day I heard that Joe Elliot received a letter from Beardstown, Kentucky, which tells him that Joe Soward is there and well. Some one suggests that the account of his death was published as a blind, to secure him from the annoyance of future arrests, as he probably slacked his thirst for prison life. Billy Bamburg and Henry Martin got into a difficulty this morning, with our roll caller, Mr. Dyer, and both of them struck the old fellow several times about the face, and are now paying for their folly by being bucked and gagged and sitting on top of the wood shed.

They are having a pretty hard time of it, as the day is very cold, and the wind has a fair sweep at them. I have not learned the cause of the difficulty, or whether they were in any degree excusable. The offence should have been very grave indeed to justify so severe a punishment.

FEB. 10.—Another one of the many sad scenes which occur in a prison, was witnessed here to day by a very large number of prisoners. A Mrs. Schull visited the hospital for the purpose of seeing her husband, who was very sick. She remained with him all night, and did all that lay in her power to relieve him, but she could not save him—he died early this morning. She had her little boy with her, and the poor child seemed to realize the nature of their terrible loss—his childish grief was truly pitable to look upon. When the husband and father had ceased to breathe, his remains were laid in a rough coffin and placed under the hospital. The bereaved and desolate wife obtained permission to remove from the beloved form, the garments worn and soiled during his illness, and to replace them with a shroud. She accordingly procured the necessary material, and seating herself beside her dead husband, proceeded stitch after stitch, to sew up the winding sheet which was to enwrap and hide from her eyes, the mortal remains of her dearest and best friend. All out in the cold, her orphan boy crying at her feet, her own heart breaking with its unutterable sorrow, that lone woman sat at her solitary post, watching and working for her dead. She had an outer box made in which the coffin was placed for preservation, until she can have his remains removed and taken home.

Fifty-nine more prisoners arrived from St. Louis this evening. Some are prisoners of war, and some claim to be conscripts, saying they were "forced into the service." Joseph Boyd's wife and two sisters came yesterday to see him, and he has been with them ever since their arrival. Joe is a No. 1 fellow.

FEB. 17.—A Federal prisoner, named Galvin, one of the most troublesome fellows, thay say, in the whole prison, got to fighting on Monday, and the officer commanding ordered him to be bucked and gagged every day, and when off that duty, to be kept in close confinement in a cell. Hearing of what was up, the pugnacious individual retreated into a hiding place, and succeeded in keeping himself concealed for the space of an hour or two, during which time a pretty lively search was conducted. He was finally unearthed and after a punishment duly administered, he was conducted to a private apartment set apart for his especial use. Every morning this week he has been seen "taking an airing" on the woodshed. On Monday night February 14th, the river "broke up," and the ice has continued to run ever since. Tuesday I had a letter from Fort Delaware. The boys are all in fine spirits over the exchange; they have signed their parole and expect to start at any moment.

Wednesday, seventeen negro prisoners were sent up from Vicksburg—they were charged with mutiny, tried by the Commission, and sent here to serve out the sentence passed upon them; one of them is a woman, and the lady prisoners have employed her as a waiting maid.

Yesterday the prisoners for exchange were called in line and notified to be ready to leave at a moment's warning. Last night, in company with sixteen others, all handcuffed, our old friend and fellow prisoner, Col. Winston, arrived from Gratiot. He represents that prison as being a much harder place than it was before we left, executions have become so frequent that they have erected a scaffold in the back yard. The prisoners sometimes witness preparations which tells them that death is in store for some one—and no one knows but he may be the unfortunate individual. A case of that kind was on hand when Col. Winston left. It has transpired that the intended victim on that occasion was a man named Thorpe, who was sentenced to be hung on the 16th of last July, but whose life was spared by Gen. Rosecrans, who ordered him sent to this prison, as was supposed by all, with his sentence commuted, but night before last, an officer came up with the intention of taking him to St. Louis, where he was to have been hung to-day, but a kind Providence had interposed in his behalf—he was too sick to be moved. The officer looked at him awhile, and then sent for the surgeon, who pronounced him too near death already, to be disturbed. Five hundred prisoners left to-day for exchange. They were heartily rejoiced at the idea of getting back to their Dixie homes once more. Some of them came out of the hospital and were scarcely able to walk—we begged them not to undertake to go—told them they would certainly die by the way. They said it was but death any how, as there was no hope for them here, and it would be some comfort even to die on the road going South. The poor fellows with their trembling legs, their hollow cheeks, and their unnaturally bright eyes, reminded me of the dying girl who sang, "Are we almost there." Some will be apt to die on the road—some will reach home to die—while others may be nursed back into health and strength, if once they reach their comfortable homes and can receive the kindly ministrations of their affectionate friends.

FEB. 23.—Maj. Rucker and Capt. Gibbs attended church out in the city last Sunday, and I suppose for the want of something to engage his attention, the Captain amused himself in counting the masculine heads, as he made the following report on their return: Number of males in the congregation, 49. Number dressed in uniform, 19. Nothing stated with regard to the text or sermon. If I had been one of the company, my report I think, would have had special reference to the ladies. I should have counted bonnets by all means.

We had quite a stir the other day, over an order which was received here, calling for all who had ever been in the "rebel" army to be forwarded with their charges immediately—our spirits were greatly revived, for it seemed as if there was hope for us too, but the General, fearing he might not understand the order correctly, telegraphed to the War Department, to know if "sentenced prisoners" were included, when he was informed they were not. We hope that a time may come when all Southern soldiers will have the opportunity of being exchanged, though I am sorry to find that not a few have refused to be thus sent back to the Confederate service. On Tuesday two hundred and seventy-five were forwarded for exchange. Yesterday we received a budget of "grape vine" intelligence, which contained the list of interesting items which we give below.

"Charleston is evacuated." "Columbia, S. C. in possession of the Federal forces." "The Confederacy recognized by France." "Rebel deserters coming inside the Federal lines by hundreds." Whether any of the above is true, is beyond our power to tell—time must determine. We have learned to put no confidence in anything we hear. The prisoners who were sentenced to labor are being worked very hard; a detail of twenty-five is made every day to be engaged in breaking rock; the whole number is to be divided into two squads, and required to perform severe labor every alternate day.

Yesterday there were ten releases granted—three to sentenced prisoners. One to Capt. McPike, who was a regular Confederate soldier, with no impediment to his exchange. Mrs. Martin's mother (Mrs. Blannerhassett) has paid her a visit and encourages her to hope for a speedy release. She (Mrs. M.) was permitted to spend the day out in town yesterday and found it very pleasant. Miss Maggie Oliver of the female prison, presented mess No. 1 with a most delicious peach pudding, which was received with abundance of thanks, and eaten with continued applause. They inform us that Mrs. Hanie and daughter are to be released to-morrow. I had a letter to-day from Benj. F. Dobyns, the whole story of Joe Soward's death is false. I also received one from a brother in Missouri, who writes that there will be a general exodus from that section in the spring. Nearly every one talks of leaving. They are striking out in every direction—for Oregon, California, Arizona, Central America, or anywhere to get rid of radical misrule and oppression. He and his family think of starting for Arizona some time in May.

JAN. 29.—Friday it was reported that all Missourians here were to be sent to Jefferson city; the penitentiary there having been converted into a military prison. On the same day some hundred names were handed in by persons wishing to take the oath; there were citizens, conscripts, galvanized rebels and regular prisoners of war; but no sentenced prisoners, the invitation not being extended to them. Saturday, Col. Winston was ordered to Head Quarters, where he had the rare felicity of meeting with a beloved daughter, and a new son-in-law. The happy couple were on their bridal tour, intending to visit the East. They brought a liberal supply from the wedding feast, which was highly appreciated by our mess after the Colonel's return. Champaigne, cakes, candies, peaches, berries, sardines, &c., were discussed, and we almost imagined ourselves at the wedding, as we partook of the generous donation of our beloved chief. Our friend Mrs. Martin has gone; her mother came up on Saturday and brought her word that she was to be banished, and yesterday both her mother and brother were up to see her. To-day Col. Winston, Capt's. Muir, Muse and Lowry, Dr. Wright and myself, had the pleasure of going round and bidding her a last farewell. We remained about three hours and spent the time very pleasantly. She was not to leave until to-morrow, but a new order was received this evening for her to be sent on her way at eight o'clock this evening. A detective came in at six, and told her to be ready by eight; she said it would be impossible, as her trunks were not packed, and she could not go before morning. He told her that his orders were imperative, and she would have to go, even if it became necessary to carry her. Her friends advised her to get ready the best she could and obey the order, for fear the authorities might get mad, and inflict some severer trial upon her than that contemplated in the decree for her banishment. After studying over it awhile she concluded to do so, and proceeded at once toward making her arrangements. At half past seven, a sergeant sent in word that it was time for us to go to our quarters, so after bidding her good bye we took our departure, not however before I had received as a parting gift, from this excellent lady and true friend, a beautiful photograph album, which I shall prize as a rare and valued memento of my prison friendships. I clip the following item from the St. Louis Republican of the 26th.

"RELEASED FROM PRISON AND SENT SOUTH."

Mrs. Anna B. Martin, who was sent South at her own request by the military authorities in April, 1863, not to return during the war, except by permission of the Secretary of War, and who returned in September last, without obtaining such permission, and in consequence of which was sentenced to imprisonment during the war at the Alton prison, was yesterday ordered by the commanding General to be released and to be again sent beyond the Federal lines, by way of Memphis, Tennessee."

TUESDAY, MARCH 7, 1865.—Last Friday, Miss Nannie Douthett received a letter from Mrs. Martin, from which she permits me to make the following extract:

GRATIOT PRISON, ST. LOUIS, }
Feb. 28th, 1865. }

MISS N. L. DOUTHETT.—*Dear Friend :*—As you see I am in my old quarters again, though not exactly my *old* quarters, for I am in the building you were. I have heard nothing yet as to my departure. Whether I am going alone or with company. There are five prisoners here and all from the interior of the State. I was almost frozen when I arrived last night—covered with mud and well tired too; and it was so late I had to take a room without fire, so I had to amuse myself shivering until morning. But at this time (two o'clock in the afternoon) I'm all right. You may imagine Mike was surprised to see me."

To-day I had a letter from Miss Sallie Linton, telling me of the departure of our friend. She says that Mrs. Martin left on the 3rd, with but an hour's notice in which to get ready; she had scarcely time to bid her mother good-bye, she was so hurried off. Miss Sallie Linton, just like herself, true to the instincts of her noble womanhood, and the cause to which she has devoted so great a portion of her time, is ever to be found among the sorrowing captives, who are suffering for their devotion to the principles which they hold dearer than life itself. Quite unostentatious and unpretending she goes about on her errands of mercy, dispensing her gifts with a grace and cheerfulness that seems like the sun to brighten and warm up the hearts of all those who come within the sphere of her influence. It is the same at Alton as at Gratiot—time or place makes no difference with her, and this noble devotion, this unchanging and untiring application of her earnest heart's promptings has justly won for her, at both these Bastiles, the title of the *Prisoner's Friend.*

On Tuesday, fourteen citizen prisoners were notified to be in readiness to leave for St. Louis the next day. One of them is a negro who claims to have been the body servant of Col. John Beall of the Confederate Army. It is presumed that they were sent for to undergo trial. Major Rucker was paroled to the city limits on Saturday, for the purpose of receiving and distributing clothing purchased by the Confederate Government in New York City, and sent to this place by Brig. Gen. Beall, of the C. S. A., for the use of her unfortunates. This clothing consists of pants, jackets, drawers, shirts, socks and shoes, of a good quality. The weather is so cold and many of the prisoners in so needy a condition, that these articles are very desirable indeed, and the kindness of our Confederate officials is kindly appreciated. Uncle Samuel, in the kindness of his heart, would see his poor, half starved captives continue on in their rags and semi-nakedness, ere he would donate them even some "old clothes."

On Sunday, eight deaths occurred in the hospital. The disease mostly prevailing is pneumonia fever.

## CHAPTER XII.

ARRIVAL OF MORE PRISONERS; BRUTALITY OF A SERGEANT; RETURN OF CAPT. DAWSON FROM THE HOSPITAL; VISIT OUT IN TOWN; FEDERAL PRISONERS BURNING THEIR BEDS; FIGHT BETWEEN A "GALVANIZED REB.," AND A FEDERAL SERGEANT; A NEGRO SHOT AND KILLED FOR CROSSING THE DEAD LINE; DEATH OF MRS. REYNOLDS; HER BURIAL BY THE CATHOLIC CHURCH; LETTER FROM MRS. MARTIN; MISS LUNDY RELEASED; LETTER FROM ANOTHER TRUE PRISONER'S FRIEND; &C., &C.

SUNDAY, MARCH 12, 1865.—Sixty-five prisoners arrived from St. Louis, on Friday night; they were as miserable a looking set as I ever wish to see; they had started for exchange, but stopped here on the way; their condition was such as to excite the pity, and call for assistance from every man whether friend or foe, who was possessed of a soul; and yet, wretched as these poor creatures were, a lot of Federal prisoners attacked a number of them, beat and bruised them unmercifully, and robbed all who had any money, and stripped half the clothes off of those who had not. It is surprising that the "human form divine" can hold such malice as inhabits the breasts of some monsters claiming to be men. Within the compass of these walls I believe that every grade and species of the genus homo can be found.

The sergeant who superintends our squad at roll call, made quite an exhibition of his temper this morning. A man named Cobbs left the ranks before the order was given, and went to his bunk and laid down; the sergeant saw and followed him, and taking him by the collar dragged him to the floor, where he stamped and pounded him over the face and head, cutting a deep gash under the right eye; he then took him to the head of the stairs and deliberately kicked him down the steps.

EVENING :—The men engaged in the "mugging" last night have been undergoing pretty severe punishment all the afternoon; four of them have been "bucked and gagged," and one of them hung up by the thumbs; it seems that robbing and thieving can only be stopped by resorting to the most extreme measures. Offenders of that class have no business being quartered with military or political prisoners; their crime is against the civil law and they ought to be off by themselves where they and their State can adjust and settle their difficulties. Soldiers and citizens are supposed to be gentlemen, and with us usually are, and it is extremely disgusting to have to come in contact with the rabble which are herded here. Even the poor negroes are jumbled into the mess; innocent inoffensive creatures, with all their ignorance, they have been too well bred on their masters' plantations to relish the coarse surroundings in this place. They get together in little black clouds and talk over matters according to their comprehension. One of them was heard to-day saying to his fellow darkies,—"dis does not look much like freedom; forcin' us into de fight, and den puttin' us in prison, an' dar starvin' us mos' to deff. Dis chile wud rather be on de ole plantashun, hoin' de cotton—sure." Some of their expressions sound very odd to persons unacquainted with their way of talking; but to Southerners, negro lingo is very natural. We were not surprised to hear one of them enquiring of another who mentioned his having been around to Head Quarters—"who give you *commission* to go roun' dar?"

Mrs. Russel and Miss Maggie Oliver were permitted to attend church to day.

Capt. Dawson returned on Wednesday from the hospital, where he has been laid up with a bone felon. He was attacked with erysipelas, which broke out on the felon, and from the effects of the two together, it is feared all the flesh will leave the bones of his hand. Yesterday I enjoyed the privilege of spending the afternoon out in town—went in company with sergeant Leigh, who proved to be very accommodating; took me wherever I desired to go. After visiting all the principal stores, I concluded to call on Maj. Rucker at the residence of Mrs. McGuire. The gentleman was not in, but I enjoyed a very pleasant hour's chat with his landlady; and then started out to perambulate the ups and downs of Alton; found it very rough and hilly, but withal a very pleasant looking place. The change and variety of scenery was decidedly refreshing, after a long confinement within the walls of our gloomy prison. Strolled around for about four hours: dropped into a gallery and ordered a dozen and a half photographs—began to feel a little tired and started "home."

This morning all the prisoners, whatever their creed, color or crime, were ordered to sun their blankets and turn their ticks over to Head Quarters—also all blankets, where there were more than two to the man. The ticks were all carried around with the straw still in them, and deposited in a huge pile; when some of the Federal prisoners, not relishing the idea of being deprived of their soft beds, declared that if they were not allowed to use them, they would be d—d if the United States Government should, and forthwith proceeded to fire the pile. The wind was blowing at the time and the flames spread with great rapidity, catching and destroying the wood shed, and had nearly reached the cook house when its progress was arrested. For a short time there was considerable excitement, and several fights took place; one in particular, between a sergeant and a "galvanized rebel." The former ordered the latter to assist in extinguishing the fire; which the "reb." flatly refused to do, adding that he did not care if the old prison burned up. Upon this, the sergeant "pitched into" him and gave him such a mauling as leaves his face this evening, looking most terribly out of fix, his nose leaning to one side. Over a hundred and eighty of these galvanized prisoners have enlisted in the United States Army, for frontier service, during the term of three years, or the continuance of the war.

One of the lady prisoners, Mrs. Reynolds, is very sick—has been insensible for three days; her friends, especially her cousin Miss Maggie Oliver, seems greatly distressed about her.

Col. Winston received the cheering intelligence to-day, that he and his brother Sam. had been demanded by the Confederate government. It has been stated to the Confederate authorities that they were wearing balls and chains, and required to work on the rock pile every day, which was not wholly correct. They have only worked on the rock pile about two days in the week, and the balls and chains they have not worn at all—at least not to my knowledge. They were both called to the office for the purpose of signing documents relative to their treatment. The river is rising so rapidly that if it continues a few days, it will be necessary to remove the patients from the small pox Island.

MARCH 19.—Yesterday morning one of the negro prisoners was shot and killed instantly for stepping beyond what is called the *dead line*. Poor nigger, there never was any "dead line" at home. They find freedom a pretty "hard road to travel" in the land of their friends.

About five o'clock in the evening, Capt. Gibbs came in and announced the death of Mrs. Reynolds, which had occurred some ten minutes previous. He was also the bearer of a request that Capt's. Muir, Lowry, Peery and myself should set up with the corpse, permission having been granted, we proceeded to the room where the dead lady was laid. We found there the Misses Lundy, Douthett, Oliver, and Mrs. Russell; and with them we all kept a sorrowful watch until seven o'clock in the morning, when Capt. Muir and myself repaired to our quarters, for the purpose of getting our breakfast and changing our clothes.

Mrs. Reynolds was a member of the Catholic church, and just before she died a candle was placed in her hand; not understanding the meaning or reason of the ceremony, I concluded it was to light her through the valley of death. Candles were also kept burning at her head and feet night and day. She was shrouded and laid out on a table, with nothing but a veil thrown over her face, and as she laid there cold and stiff in death, I thought she was beautiful. The intense suffering of two weeks illness, left not marks upon her calm sweet face in death. Yesterday evening the Bishop, Mrs. Wentz and Mrs. Wise came in, and before they left made several prayers, and gave special directions not to let the sacred candles go out, but to keep them burning continually. The

Bishop called again this morning and said she could not be buried before ten o'clock to morrow morning, on account of their not being able to get a coffin ready sooner. She will be put in a metallic case and kept in a vault in the Catholic burying ground until an opportunity offers to send her South for interment. The Catholics desire to bury her at their own expense: at first the officers objected to the arrangement, and said she ought to be buried with the rest of the rebels, but upon reflection that it would be a saving to the Government, they consented.

Mrs. Wentz and Mrs. Wise came again this evening, accompanied by Miss Gutzmiller and her brother; they manifest a kindly interest in the deceased, and express a deep sympathy for her bereaved relative. Miss Maggie grieves a great deal. She says it is hard for her poor cousin to have to die so far away from her friends, and in a Northern prison. Her only consolation seems to be the entire preparation which her cousin exhibited for the approach of the awful messenger. Death had no terrors for her; though the summons reached her through the guarded walls of a gloomy prison, she was found with her lamp trimmed and burning, and was ready to enter into the marriage supper of the Lamb.

Her husband, when last heard from, was in the Southern army—one of the immortal few, who offered themselves to do battle against the myriad hosts of Northern Vandals, who came down on their raids of destruction against the homes and lives of the bravest and most chivalrous people that ever were called upon to defend their lives, liberties and sacred honor, on their native soil, and under the very shade trees which their grandsires' hands had planted. He was far away upon the bloody war path, following the flag which his people had chosen. Sometimes it was floating aloft to the music of a splendid victory, and anon trailing along through the night watches of an almost hopeless defeat. Still the brave sons of Dixie's land stood fast by their colors, while the ruthless invaders had penetrated the sacred homes where the wives and children of the patriot warriors had hoped to enjoy a peaceful asylum. It was thus Mrs. Reynolds was arrested and dragged away from the sunny South, to meet and battle against the rigors of a Northern winter—rigors which were too severe for the tender frame of this sweet exotic from the tropical clime. She withered and chilled to death amid the rude blasts which assailed her in a Northern prison, and now she lies beautiful in death, smiling as though she had passed away amid a company of angels—awaiting the last sad office which humanity claims, and which must be rendered by the hands of strangers—while her husband is ignorant at this moment of her arrest or imprisonment, and fondly imagines she is waiting for the hour of his blest return. When I left at five o'clock Miss Maggie Oliver was nearly frantic—morphine had been administered, which instead of quieting her nerves, had only produced a greater degree of excitement; I have just been informed that she is sinking into a kind of stupor. Poor, desolate child; how dark and lonely her prison life will seem when she awakes and realizes again the sad, sad loss she has sustained.

After having a good night's rest, we who watched with the corpse on Saturday night, went around to the ladies' quarters and offered our services to render any assistance in our power. The coffin arrived about eight o'clock, when the body was lifted tenderly and reverently and placed in, and the lid placed on and closed forever. In the mean time one of the Sisters and Mrs. Morgan, the Major's mother, and another lady, came in. The lid which covers the glass over the face was removed, that all present might have an opportunity of taking a last look at the dead. Miss Maggie had expressed a desire that Confederates only should handle the body, and Maj. Morgan, with his characteristic kindness and courtesy, at once consented for Maj. Ripley, Capt's. Muse, Muir, Dr. Wright and myself, to attend the funeral and act as pall bearers. At ten o'clock we carried the corpse to the hearse, and accompanied it to the Catholic church; Miss Maggie, with Mrs. Russel, and the Misses Lundys' and Douthett were accommodated with a carriage. In the church, the coffin was sprinkled with holy water, and at the head were placed two dark colored candles—while two white ones were burning at the feet. The Bishop made a few very appropriate remarks, when the coffin was again placed in the hearse and we repaired to the burying ground.

There were a great many strangers present, and the funeral cortege was much longer than I expected. All seemed impressed with the peculiar sadness and solemnity of the occasion. Four of the pall bearers rode in the Bishop's carriage, the rest were furnished with seats elsewhere. We proceeded for about eight miles, when we arrived at the grave yard—a beautiful spot, selected with admirable taste, as the last resting place of the consecrated dead. A large cross is erected in the centre of the enclosure, to the foot of which each corpse is brought and laid, from thence it is taken to the grave. We carried Mrs. Reynolds about three hundred yards from this central cross, to where a grave was newly dug for her reception; it was decided that the remains would keep in a better state of preservation in a grave, than in a vault, hence she was laid away in the earth.

While the dirt was being thrown in, Miss Oliver screamed out frantically. "Oh, Maggie, Maggie, is it possible we have been brought away up here for this?" Again she wailed out—"You have found a Northern home." Then, while she clung to a lady friend, she said—"How I do hate to see that soil thrown upon her." When the grave was filled up Miss Maggie was placed in the carriage, her lady friends with her, and we all took our seats and rode back to town. When we reached the city I was permitted to remain out several hours. I called at the artists' where I had ordered my photographs, and was informed that they were not ready. I then went with Maj. Rucker to Mrs. McGuire's and took dinner—in the afternoon we called at Mrs. Drouns' to see my old lady friend, Mrs. Blannerhassett, but was informed she had left and would not return to Alton again for two weeks—from there I wended my way to my present quarters, where, as I sit and think of the events of the day, I am seized with a solemn melancholy, and realize how touchingly true it is, that

"Friend after friend, departs—
Who hath not lost a friend?
There is no union here of hearts,
That find not here an end."

MARCH, 25.—Tuesday, some three hundred of the "galvanized rebels" were sworn into the United States service, with the understanding that they are to go to the frontier and fight the Indians. Wednesday and yesterday, we were quite busy distributing clothing to the Confederate prisoners, and the boys look vastly improved in their new rig.

Capt. Morgan and Dr. Miller were added to our room yesterday, the former sentenced for life, the latter for fifteen years. Thursday night a man named Anderson, was brought in handcuffed; he was taken to a cell and confined all night, and next morning was heavily ironed and given in charge of a marshal, who took him to Jerseyville. This afternoon I was allowed the privilege of spending several hours out in town without a guard. Took tea with Mrs. McGuire, and had a long talk with Mrs. Wentz. Went down to the steamboat landing where I enjoyed the pleasant surprise of meeting with Mrs. Blannerhassett, and escorting her to her boarding house. After a long talk with her I returned to my "hotel." Received a letter from Mrs Martin, which I give below—it was written while she was at Pine Bluffs, waiting to go through the lines under a flag of truce.

PINE BLUFFS, ARK., March 9th, 1865.

*Capt. G. Frost:*—Here I am at last among the Arkansians, and to my own great amazement too. I'm inclined to think I'll be a travelled rebel, if I go through much more of this country. I left my quarters at Gratiot, the next Friday after leaving Alton, in company with two prisoners—like myself banished. We had quite a pleasant trip to Memphis. I had a parole there on Monday morning, and the same evening left for Little Rock on a Government transport. Last evening we landed here, and our escort found it to be the best place for us to remain; I am under parole, waiting to go out under flag of truce. There are two families going to Texas so we agreed to stay together. Take it altogether I have enjoyed the journey. Drs. Gullet and Brown, went from here not more than three weeks since. I was unfortunate enough to lose the breastpin you made for me, I would not have taken anything for it. When I received my trunk at Gratiot it was not inside, and I have not the most remote idea what has become of it. I will go to my sister the first good chance I have, so you see my journey is only just commencing.

I think of you all, so much, and wonder who is now talking from the window. See that Mr. and Mrs. C. take good care of my "Dixie." I wrote to Miss D. before I left—tell her I hope it will not be long before I see her in "Dixie." Write to mother and tell her you have heard from me—I am sending her a letter also, but she may not receive it. I intend going to see Gen. Price, but, love to all friends. Yours, Truly,
ANNIE B. MARTIN.

MARCH, 28.—Sunday I was permitted to spend the day again in town. Attended worship at the Catholic church; after the services were over, I accompanied Maj. Rucker to his home and dined with him. Made the acquaintance of several very interesting ladies and after dinner we visited the Sisters' hospital—the Sister Superior showed us all through the rooms, and was very pleasant and entertaining. We enjoyed an hour in her company quite as well as in a fashionable drawing room, with the ladies of the world. It is astonishing how cheerful and contented they appear to be. Their whole hearts are engaged in the work of mercy to which they have dedicated their lives. Yesterday Mrs Blannerhassett, Miss Gutzmiller and Miss Wier visited the lady prisoners, and we had the pleasure of a conversation with them from the windows. To-day I received a letter from my wife—which from its sad tone, I judge must have been written when she was suffering from the blues—at any rate it has a decided tendency to produce that state of feeling with me, and makes me more anxious than ever to be freed from this galling yoke of bondage which chains me here. She writes in this style:

"Sunday Eve., March 15, 1865.

This has been a lovely day—all nature seems lively with the thought of spring, and all happy, except this poor, sad, lone heart of mine—it feels as if it will burst with grief. I think I have not a friend in all this wide world. Were it not for our darling child and yourself, I would gladly lay me down to sleep where I hope my remains would rest in peace, and my spirit take its flight to a happier and better world. It has always been my earnest desire to live as long as my child, for what would she do in this cold and unfeeling world without her ma? You would not miss me so much—but enough of this—have already said too much, and I do not wish to make you feel as sad as I do."

March, 31.—Wednesday was a regular "blue" day—a miserable cold, rainy, sobby, dull day—it seemed as if night would never come, but when it did come, it brought fifty new recruits for the United States frontier service—men who had been enlisted at Gratiot. A man named Peter Mauley came up to our room yesterday and bade us all "good bye," saying he was going to have his liberty; leaving the impression that he meant he was going to die, and be free in the grave; but this morning it seems there was a double meaning in his "good bye," for he actually made good his escape during the night. All right for him, and success attend him. Capt. Gibbs' wife and three children have arrived from Mexico, Mo., and he has rented them a house. It is thought he will be granted a parole and be allowed to engage in some business to support them.

One of the rules of this prison is, that all the inmates shall retire to their beds at nine o'clock; and any one found up after that time, must pass the night in a cell. It so happened last night, that just after nine, the sergeant came to lock our door, and found Capt's. Muir, Lowry and Peery still out of bed. It was caused by Peery being sick, and they tried to make that explanation to the sergeant, but he only swore at them and ordered them off to the cell. They lay there all night on a bare stone floor, with nothing under or over them. Peery is looking very badly this morning. The river is rising very rapidly, and the prisoners have been busy to-day in removing the patients from the small pox hospital to one situated on a larger island, the small one having overflowed. There is a rumor in the yard that Lee, Beauregard, Grant and Sherman, are to have a meeting to arrange the preliminaries for negotiating peace. If there is any truth in it, my sincere prayer is, that they may arrive at a definite and amicable understanding, for I am truly sick of the part it has been my lot to be called upon to play in the *grand drama.*

SUNDAY, APRIL 2, 1865.—Was out in town yesterday, and had a splendid time considering I was a prisoner—bought the protographs of twenty-eight Confederate Generals at Hubbard's bookstore. To-day was out again to church—did not return to quarters until five o'clock, and after that had the pleasure of spending the evening with the lady prisoners. Miss Florence Lundy has just received her release; it was procured by her friends paying a fine which was imposed upon her. She had refused her consent to their paying the fine, preferring to let the Government vent the full force of its august and dignified anger on her own little person, rather than have her friends humor the greedy whim which demanded the money; but they, fearing her health should fail, have, it seems, without consulting her, satisfied the claim of the outwitted State, and her release has been formally granted.

Miss Mary Rayburn of St. Louis, has sent up a large lot of clothing, to be distributed among the Southern prisoners. She has taken a great interest in relieving the wants of the needy. She writes us as follows:

ST. LOUIS, March 30, 1865.

*Capt. G. Frost:*—Prisoners of war, Alton. I send you by Uni-

ted States Express, to-day, a box of clothing for the prisoners. Very little of it is new, but much of it is better than the new usually sent. Please acknowledge receipt of it; as soon as distributed send me the names of those to whom the good articles are given, as it enables me to get more; when those to whom it is given are known, it serves as a proof that care has been taken in its distribution. Give to those you think most in need. I wish you would send me, if in your power, some little mementoes of prison work, as I can do something more than this, if I had them. A mistake has been made in the address on the box. The name of Lieut. Moore, being substituted for Lieut. Cooper, but I presume it will go safe. Do not fail to advise me of the receipt of the box, and address your letter to
MISS MARY H. RAYBURN,
No. 112 Olive St., St. Louis.

This morning after getting in line for roll call, sergeant Jones demanded of us, who it was that was "cutting up" in the citizens' quarters last night. Of course no one could tell him, and he gave the command to "right about face" and "march to the cells." This did not suit me as I was in no mood to be punished for other people's offenses and I tried to tell Jones so, but he only answered with the surly order, "go on, go on," and go on I did, until I got to the foot of the stairs, and then I kept on to my own room. In about five minutes, he came, looked in, and enquired how many of us were there. I told him only Capt. Calvert and myself, at which he left, saying he would attend to us after awhile. We felt rather uneasy at first, for fear the bull-headed little Englishman would have us "bucked and gagged" or else suspended by the thumbs, but time wearing on and nothing transpiring, we came to the conclusion that if he had any such designs, they had been baulked by some higher authority. Maj. Morgan is very much of a gentleman, but some of the sergeants put on as many airs, and assume as much authority as commanding officers.

APRIL 5.—Monday was the gloomiest day we have spent in prison. Not that anything unusual had occurred among the prisoners—no sudden deaths, sad partings, or horrible punishments; on the contrary, all was calm and quiet, almost sullenly so. Scarcely a man lifted his head, and no one seemed disposed to talk. The day was bright as usual—outside there were busy feet going to and fro; cheerful greetings were exchanged, light laughter floated on the air, and music was heard from different quarters. Still the

(17)

prisoners at Alton were sad, for Federal flags were waving everywhere and the telegraph reported the fall of Richmond and Petersburg.

Tuesday, the news was confirmed. We know that the end has come. We try to engage our minds in other matters, and strive to banish all contemplation of the horrible fact that the worst has come to the worst, and our beloved land has fallen a prey to the wiles of wicked men—the future alone can reveal the extent to which they will abuse the power that has fallen into their hands, but judging their future course by their past history, there is nothing in truth, justice, the Constitution, nor the laws of God, that will check the carrying out of any design which their evil brains may conjure up. We can only hold our peace, and wait, and "see what we shall see." One hundred guns were fired here to day, in honor of the grand victories, and all business is suspended.

Yesterday a basket of fine apples was sent to me by a young lady whom I never saw, but who I am told called at Mrs. McGuire's on Sunday evening to see me, after I had returned to prison. We are told that our room will hereafter be used by the sergeants, while we will be lodged in one styled "No. 3." As Miss Florence Lundy leaves to-morrow for the South, several of us were allowed to spend the evening at the ladies' quarters. Miss Lundy, by her unvarying kindness, and lovely amiability of character, has endeared herself to every one who has formed her acquaintance. Her loss will be very sensibly felt by the inmates of the female prison, while our mess will realize every day that a kind friend is missing, and one of the chief attractions lost from the ladies' quarters. When we learned that she was to go, several of us set about preparing each a piece of jewelry for her as a parting gift, and token of our friendship. We presented them this evening—giving an inscription with each one, which Miss Florence says she will have engraved upon them as soon as she reaches a place where it can be done.

Dr. Wright's gift was a breastpin, with the inscription:—"Miss F. V. Lundy—the pride of all true patriots."

Capt. Muir gave an elegant cross, with the words, "Triumphant still."

My offering was a breastpin with the inscription, "Miss Florence Lundy—only to be known, to be loved by all true Southerners."

Sergeant Ingalls, alias, Killposey, left this evening for Chicago, to report for duty as 2d Lieutenant.

APRIL 8.—Miss Lundy left on the Alton and St. Louis packet on Thursday morning, and took a boat on the same day, at St. Louis, for Memphis. Yesterday evening we took tea with the ladies, around at Head Quarters, where we met with Mrs. Blannerhassett and Mrs. Droun, and read a letter from Mrs. Martin, who was five days out from Pine Bluffs, and expected on the sixth to be in the care of the Confederates. At "letter call," an order was read to the effect that "no prisoners are to visit town without permission from Head Quarters." A Confederate officer is said to have abused the privilege while at church a few evenings since, which it is supposed was the cause of the order last night. Another one of our lady prisoners is to be restored to her home and friends. On Thursday evening Miss Nannie Douthett was notified of her release, and banishment to Idaho Territory, but this evening, her uncle and cousin, Miss Belle Douthett, were up from St. Louis, and Mr. Douthett thinks he can obtain permission for her to remain in St. Louis. As Miss Nannie leaves in the morning, we desired to visit her this evening, but Col. Kuhn would not grant us permission, unless a Federal officer should accompany us. Lieut. Allen, very kindly accepted an invitation to call with us, and we all enjoyed a pleasant evening, and partook of a most excellent supper. The Lieutenant expressed himself as highly pleased with his visit, and said he would be happy to repeat the call.

APRIL 9.—A general search of all the prisoners, from head to foot, was conducted yesterday morning, in consequence of a fight having occurred among the Federal prisoners, in which one of them was wounded with a knife. All articles of that kind which could be found, were taken possession of by the authorities. The commander of this prison—Lieut. Cooper—has been promoted to the office of Captain. This morning, Maj. Rucker, C. S. A., came in and handed me the following.

HEAD QUARTERS, MILITARY STATION, Apr. 9th, 1865.

*Capt. Cooper :*—Permit Capt. Frost and Dr. Wright to stay with Maj. Rucker, until 3 o'clock, P. M., to-day.

JOHN H. KUHN, Col. Commanding.

So we got ready as soon as possible and went to the Catholic church, which was so crowded it was almost impossible for us to get a seat. It is what they call Palm Sunday, and a piece of cedar which has been blessed by the Bishop, was distributed to every member of the congregation. After the services were concluded, we went to Mrs McGuire's for dinner, and remained there until half past two, when we returned to prison. Capt. Trimble, Lieuts. Turner and Ponder, have been notified to get ready for exchange; they are the only officers who will leave this prison at present. Maj. Rucker has been to St. Louis for several days, attending to some private business, and only returned yesterday evening.

APRIL 10.—Passed the day out in town again, and as I was returning to the prison, was informed that my RELEASE HAD COME, and was now at Head Quarters. However, I will know more about it to-morrow.

APRIL 11.—Was informed this morning that my release had *certainly* come. Went round to the office and learned that I was released by order of President Lincoln.

APRIL 12.—Got on board the Steamer Warsaw about five o'clock yesterday evening—arrived at Hannibal this morning at eight—left there at ten o'clock, and reached Palmyra, Mo., at half past eleven. Met Mr. Bradley, who hitched up his horse and buggy and accompanied me out to my father-in-law's—Mr. James A. Johnson—living about six miles north west of Palmyra, where, after an absence of nearly four years, during which time I have suffered much, on the march and in prison, I found my wife and baby in the enjoyment of excellent health—the latter having almost grown out of my knowledge, the former about the same as when I left. My father and mother-in-law have changed a great deal; time has made its mark, leaving traces of care and trouble upon their brows, but, nevertheless, they seem cheerful and happy, patiently enduring the hardships of this wicked world, and traveling step by step, over its rough and rugged paths.

Time has also wrought many changes among the younger portion of the family—some having left the old homestead and gone to dwell in "stranger lands," while others still cling to the home that gave them birth. But one who was in the prime of life at the breaking out of the war, and who, had he lived, would have been with us, battling for the rights and liberties of our beloved South, had gone to dwell where sorrow and trouble are known no more. In keeping my journal from falling into the hands of my keepers, I have had considerable difficulty. I have filled four books (over 680 pages in all) and as soon as one was complete I would smuggle it out of prison through some friend, who would send it to my wife with instructions to take care of it until my return. One was taken out of the prison by a lady friend, in a small basket which she carried on her arm. My luggage was always searched, as I was taken from one prison to another, and each article was taken separately from my sachel and examined; but still I was fortunate enough to out-Yankee them with respect to my journals. And now, as I have reached my friends once more, I will close; but hope at some future day to lay it before the public, in order that the uninitiated may learn what we have undergone during the progress of the long and bloody war.

# APPENDIX.

## PARTICULARS OF NINE MONTHS' IMPRISONMENT AT CAMP MORTON, INDIANA.

QUINCY, ILL., AUGUST 21st, 1867.

Capt. G. FROST—*Dear Sir:*—In answer to your kind and courteous communication of the 13th inst., requesting a simple statement of the circumstances connected with my imprisonment at Camp Morton, Indiana, allow me to state briefly, that being a plain man, and but little accustomed to the use of the pen, I am fearful that my story will be told in a clownish, bungling style. Nevertheless feeling a deep interest in your undertaking, and a desire to accommodate a Southern man whenever an opportunity presents itself I shall begin, as they say in a novel, without farther preliminaries to narrate such events as came under my immediate observation while incarcerated in that infamous den of suffering and wretchedness. Yours respectfully,

G. M. BROSHEER.

There have doubtless many things escaped my memory, which might perhaps have proven interesting to the reader, but there are others which are indellibly impressed upon memory's tablets, as though written with a pen of fire, and shall only be forgotten, when this body shall have "shuffled off this mortal coil." Like Tasso :

"I have been patient; let me be so yet;
I had forgotten half I would forget,
But it revives—oh! would it were my lot
To be forgetful, as I am forgot!
Feel I not wrath with those, who made me dwell
In that vast lazar house of many woes;
Would I not pay them back the pangs again,
And teach them inward sorrows' stifled groans."

I once was quick in feeling—that is o'er—my scars are callous. After my release, I fain would have sought vengeance, but ever and anon a voice whispered in mine ear, "Vengeance is mine, and I will repay, saith the Lord." My first introduction to prison life was in St. Louis, Missouri, (Gratiot street) where I was sent after my capture at Vicksburg, Mississippi, on that memorable 4th of July, 1863, when the key to the Confederacy was given by Pemberton into the care and keeping of U. S. Grant.

I, with several hundred others were intended to grace the four walls of Alton prison, but our guard, upon our arrival, finding it already full to overflowing, started immediately with us back to St. Louis, where they found it but little better. However, they managed to store seven hundred of us away in a prison which at first contained a surplus of occupants; but there was scarcely room for us to stand, and as for sleep, that was quite out of the question; as there had been no understanding among us the first night, each found it impossible to woo the drowsy god. The next night we fared better, there having been an arrangement among us, that part should sleep at a time.

We could bear, with a moderate degree of patience, the maltreatment of prisoners of war, but when we saw political prisoners, men, whose only crime was, daring to exercise the reason which God had endowed them with, and refusing to acknowledge the sable African as the white man's equal, languishing day after day in a military prison, denied the luxuries, and even the necessaries of life, then it was our blood drew well nigh to fever heat. Many whose only crime was that Southern soil gave them birth. Oh, if there is any thing beneath the broad canopy of heaven that deserves desecration, it is persecution for opinion's sake. But this digression may perhaps be unpardonable by those who consider it their indisputable right to see the Union preserved. Well, they have *preserved* it, and the question now is, in its present condition, is it worth the sugar used in the cooking process.

After a visit of some two weeks duration at Gratiot street prison we concluded to go on an exploring expedition to Camp Chase, Indiana, in the hope that our delectable society would be better appreciated, and to see whether Uncle Samuel's employees would not at this point, put themselves to a little more trouble to entertain their distinguished guests. For certainly the fare set before us at Gratiot, was not such as we had been accustomed to while spending a few weeks at the house of a mutual friend. It had been the habit of our friends at home to set before guests the best the pantry would afford—but then you are aware that custom varies in different localities, and one just attributed it to the Yankee manner of doing up things, and tried to pass it by unobserved, as we had been taught that it was a breach of etiquette to seem to notice any deficiency in the arrangement of the table of our host, whose hospitality we were enjoying.

By our courteous demeanor, we certainly did not make an indellible impression upon the Yankees, for before our departure they made us sign a parole not to try to escape on our way to Indiana. "Thinks I to myself," they are preposessed in our favor most certainly, and I was revolving in my own mind as to whether it would be an unpardonable crime to violate that parole, when my cogitations were brought to a close, by the discovery that I was reasoning from false premises, that I was laboring under a false delusion. My inference drawn from the signing of the parole, was that we were to make the trip without a guard; but our dear old Uncle Sam's care, was more vigilant than this; he could not bear the idea that his unsophisticated boys should take a trip of that length without a suitable guard. After taking a tearful farewell of old Gratiot, we started en route for Camp Morton.

There was not much chance for escape or I fear that some of us would have become so lost to a proper sense of our obligation to Uncle Samuel as to have left his protecting care, and gone out like the prodigal son, into a foreign country and wasted all of our sustenance in riotous living, but unlike him, I fear we should never have presented ourselves to make the noble confession of "Father, I have sinned against heaven and in thy sight and am no more worthy to be called thy son, make me therefore, I pray you, as one of thy hired servants," for we did not particularly admire the conduct of his hired servants just at that time.

We saw nothing upon the route worthy of note, until we arrived at Terre Haute, Indiana, where the train stopped about an hour. There were quite a number of curiosity seekers about the depot, and ever once in a while you might hear some fair damsel of the Lincoln persuasion, exclaiming, "why they look just like other people !"—the very words precisely, relieved of the nasal drawl, with which they were uttered. I felt inclined to ask one of the dear ones how she imagined that we would look; if she thought we would have horns? But fearing she might deem my question an impertinent one, and not knowing how many big brothers she might have standing around, I wisely suppressed my curiosity and passed on repeating a couplet from a favorite author,

"How many soulless birds there are,
Of graceful mould and plumage fair."

There were assembled at the depot, a great many Union loving brethren, who (whatever might have been their honest convictions concerning a "Johnny Reb,") were quite willing to treat him with his due degree of courtesy as long as he had any money. And they seemed to deem it their especial privilege, to make as great a speculation while we remained, as the circumstances of the case would admit, or at least as the limited supply of our pockets would allow. To my great amusement, one of them was sold most beautifully. He was a long legged, gangling looking, "nigger" loving Vermonter, who had been disposing of articles at double prices to the Rebels, ever since the train stopped. One of our number, having bought a quarters worth of pies, presented a fifty dollar bill to be changed; which by the way was a grey-back, very much like a green-back in appearance; the man being in great haste, and anxious to dispose of as much as he could before the train started, handed him forty-nine dollars and seventy-five cents in change—all genuine green-backs. The result was, our party left Terre Haute in fine spirits, thinking that the Yanks had speculated a little that time to their detriment; at least we felt that they were heartily welcome to all the per cent. they gained from our party.

We arrived at the depot at Indianapolis about noon; then marched through the principal streets on our way to Camp Morton. We were halted on Illinois street, to change guard, and in justice to some of the fair sex at Indianapolis, I must say that they treated us with great kindness—bringing us water, and speaking to us kindly. But these were the exceptions, and by no means the rule; for by the majority we were laughed and sneered at, as though it had have been the especial duty of the guard to parade us around for the express purpose of exciting their risibles. It was after such demonstrations as this, of the hearts of the fair ladies of the North that I felt I had special reason to congratulate myself, that I had been born south of Mason and Dixon's line—where a lady never descends from her true dignity to laugh at poor suffering humanity, but without any outward display of heroineism, with a firm, determined resolution, befitting her exalted station she extends a willing helping hand to the distressed, showing by her conduct, that *selfishness* is not a universal despot. Such is my estimate of the general excellence of the gentle daughters of the Sunny South, considered either in relation to their natural goodness, or in reference to their susceptibility to sympathizing pity,

"And they will turn our wandering feet
And they will bless our way;
Till worlds shall fade and faith shall greet
The dawn of lasting day."

Having left the city of Indianapolis, we were marched for about a mile through a thick fog of dust, to the fair ground, and upon our arrival at the camp, we were almost famished for water; we found four or five wells of good water, almost as cold as ice. So great was our desire for the cooling draught, that one of our number drank so much that he was thrown into a fit. His friends thought to relieve him by throwing cold water in his face, but all in vain, he died almost instantly. I thought truly "in the midst of life we are in death."

Having undergone that most agreeable of all mortifications, to which prisoners are subjected, namely, that of being searched we were obliged to seek our quarters. Fortunately the prison was not crowded, and for once we had plenty of room. The prisoners that we found in the camp, were nearly all Morgan's men, and a more fun-loving set it has never been my good fortune to meet. They made the best of everything, and seemed to have adopted for their motto "an ill wind that blows no one any good." The Yankees seemed to be almost as much afraid of them as they were when they were armed and in the field. Their principal amusement was card playing, and they might be seen in groups sitting around the prison, each with his roll of Confederate money, for if any one was so fortunate as to be the possessor of a roll of green-backs, he soon discovered that it was not good policy to show them, as the Federals seemed to have an unconquerable weakness for them; I do not wish any one to infer that there was any selfish consideration in this, it was, I presume, merely a patriotic desire on their part to swell the coffers of Uncle Sam, who you know was engaged in a heavy speculation about that time, and most certainly stood greatly in need of all the surplus capital—"Only this and nothing more."

The camp guard consisted of the seventy-third and fifty-fourth Indiana regiments, and while in charge of these the prisoners fared as well as could have been expected. The officers were gentlemanly and polite, and every one seemed to feel for us. I had just begun to congratulate myself (that since I had to be a prisoner) on having fallen into good hands, and also on our very agreeable exchange—and was about arriving at the conclusion, that things might have been worse, when I had reason to realize "things we prize are first to vanish" for the seventy-third and fifty-fourth having been sent to the front in their place were sent, what they called the invalid corps—being called by us the condemned Yankees, which I am sure, was the true version. They were all men who had served their time in the hospital, commonly known as hospital rats, and now I am quite sure that every soldier will readily understand the term. With their reign we indeed found "Jordan a hard road to travel."

It is my private opinion, publicly expressed, that a premium had been offered to the man among them who killed the most rebels, and they lost no opportunity of mistreating and killing as many as they could. The prisoners were divided into divisions and each division placed under charge of a sergeant and corporal. It was made the duty of each sergeant to call the roll, and if any member was found delinquent, better for him had he never been born, or, "that a mill stone were tied to his neck, and he cast into the sea." Each division was placed in line, the roll called and there made to stand an hour each day, indifferent to the kind of weather. We were left in charge of the corporal while the sergeant went to Head Quarters to make his report, and a sorry time the corporal had of it, I assure you, for he could only watch one end at a time, and while he had his impudent peepers directed to one end of the line, the men from the other would break for the barracks. But he was prepared for all such emergencies, for no sooner would he discover the flight of one than he fired his pistol, for he never thought of presenting his ugly mug among us without one in his hand. It was his delight to get a shot at some "reb.," as he never ventured near enough to get a shot at one any where else. He could never think of returning home without thinning somewhat the ranks of Jefferson Davis. As for shooting them on the field of battle, that was out of the question, as the target might take occasion to return the compliment. But fortunately the rebels were too watchful for him as they had been before, where shot and shell flew thick and fast, and were not now to be intimidated by a pistol in the hands of one whose courage was confined to prison walls, and the consequence was he was generally left with about half a dozen men, who remained not through any veneration for his unworthy self, but kept through fear of the pistol. And judging from the number of pistol shots that were fired of a morning, other corporals were likewise tormented. Fortunately for us they lacked practice—they were not very good shots upon the wing. They had ample opportunity for practice but they failed to improve them.

The corporal of division No. 7 was more fortunate. He went on duty as a private—shot one man and was promoted to corporal—served in that capacity some time, where he shot two men and wounded several, when he was promoted to sergeant. He continued his heartless cruelties for some year or more, firing at the men for the least offence, when his career was suddenly brought to a close. He accompanied a lady to a concert, who it seems was the affiance of another man, who had left a big brother to look after his interest while he was in the service. He was assassinated on his return. Retribution overtook him, as it will, all tyrants, sooner or later. Not a tear was shed when the news reached the prison. None felt that the world was any the better for his having lived in it.

Upon our first initiation at Camp Morton, our fare was as good as it generally is in such places, but it was not long before there was a reduction in rations, and they gradually grew beautifully less. Our rations, at first, consisted of a loaf of baker's bread and a half pound of meat, and I recollect that upon one occasion I got three very small potatoes—the dose was never repeated. One tenth of a pound of sugar was allowed for three days. We had one spoonful of coffee and some corn, which was there recognized as hominy. Every once in a while, they would add a little vinegar in order to keep off the scurvy. In one months time we were put on half rations, and then the men took to eating them without cooking, they became so hungry from one day to another. Our rations were generally issued about noon, and when you divide a half loaf of bakers bread and six ounces of meat into three meals, each parcel will appear very small.

The men became so reduced in flesh that they could scarcely walk, and numbers of them died in their bunks without ever having been seen by a physician; but what signified this, they were nothing but rebels and had forfeited all claims even to a decent burial, and their bodies were even inaccessable to any good Samaritan that might have chanced that way. They were cut off from all hope of loyal clemency.

For the least offence the men were placed in close confinement in the guard house. This structure was only a temporary affair, used until a more solitary, dungeon looking place could be built. Shortly after the commencement of the new building, which was constructed with a dungeon underneath, a man by the name of Pace was placed in it for pretending to be drunk. It was the duty of the kind hearted physicians to furnish subjects for the dissecting room—and it was an easy task for them—there was no scarcity as long as I remained. There was an old house on the ground which was used some time for a dead house, but after a time they became ashamed of their inhumanity, and built a new one with a butcher house attached· and every subject placed in this building (the butcher house) was dissected for the amusement of the doctors, I suppose, I could see no other reason for it. I have gone into the room frequently after they had left it, and have seen the mutilated remains of three or four corses, which had undergone the kniveing operation. If there was any one in that room that had the least particle of humanity left in his composition, he was afraid to manifest it in defense of the injured ones. It was then I felt a contempt and loathing for all concerned. It is enough beneath the dignity of a true gentleman, to offer an insult to a defenceless prisoner, but he is a wretch indeed, who would thus abuse the dead. Who but an inhuman knave could ever gaze upon the face of the dead, and not feel a compunctuous throb that he ever warred with that handful of earth that lies mouldering before him.

There was a novel method of escape planned and carried out by one of the prisoners during my stay. One of the men detailed at the hospital grew very sick, and to appearances died, and was carried by a couple of men (whom he had taken into his confidence) to the dead house, and placed in one of the coffins used for carrying away the dead, where he remained during the night. The next morning the wagon came around as usual, and having a plenty to do, as there were about twenty deaths a week, he pitched them into the wagon in a hurry. Our make-believe friend was placed in with the rest, but being among the first put in, he found himself in the bottom of the wagon. The corses were taken to town about a mile distant, where they were placed in permanent coffins for burial. When the wagon had proceeded about a half mile, our would be dead friend concluded it was about time he was climbing towards the top, and with a tremendous effort, he threw off the coffins above him, frightening the whistleing teamster almost to death, who ran away, leaving the team, as he supposed, at the mercy of the resurrected "reb." After this, there was always a guard accompanying the dead wagon.

At first it was my good fortune to procure such little articles as I needed from the commissary. He was a true Yankee and loved money better than country, and would always find a way to slip in such things as we would pay him for. I ingratiated myself into his favor by making him a ring, for which he brought me a quart of whisky; after this I did not want for the article above mentioned. Another individual who succeeded in getting a quart of whisky, shared it with a friend, and both of them becoming rather loquacious, they called upon Col. Stevens, and expressed themselves very freely about his proceedings. The result was just what they might have expected; he ordered them to the guard house, and it was fully three months, before his royal highness felt that his anger had been sufficiently appeased to order their release.

My friend, the commissary, was suddenly relieved from duty, and my rations of "Ready Relief" were discontinued. I could but regret its absence, as did also several of my companions, and to add to our distress, the guard redoubled their vigilance, and we suffered in every way. There will be a day of reckoning, I fear, for those whose duty it was to administer the justice of their country. This world, is already for them, a den of wild beasts, strewed with the bleeding hearts and whitening bones, which they have trampled in the mire. A world which differs as much from the pure hearted, as light from darkness, or hell from heaven. When the secrets of all hearts shall be revealed, oh, what a blackened tangled revelation will theirs be, of crimes committed without provocation; then will they cry for the rocks and hills to fall on and hide them.

Whenever we were suspected of having any money we were ordered to cook our rations and get ready to leave at a certain time, which, for the first two or three times we obeyed with great alacrity I can assure you. We were then mustered by divisions, across a small stream running through the camp, which we called the Potomac, then they would place a guard around us and proceed to search us. Many were the expedients resorted to for the concealment of our money. Some would make a cavity in a piece of soap, and after inserting the money would place the piece back again. Others would rip the lining in their clothes and place it between the lining and the outside. Several were successful in concealing pistols, but these were generally more trouble than they were worth. There was quite an excitement in camp one evening by the suttler saying that he had been blown up with powder and it really looked like it, and the suttler said it felt more so. No one felt any sympathy for him, for it seemed he was in league with the government to swindle the poor prisoners out of their money. And if Col. Stevens was not a confederate, he must have taken great delight in seeing the men swindled out of their money. All money furnished us by our friends passed through Head Quarters—no, I am mistaken, it stopped there, and was given out in small quantities in suttler's checks—and there was a great deal we never saw at all. The letters in which it was enclosed were destroyed, and the money confiscated. I know that other things were. My kind friends at home sent me a box containing clothing, bed clothes and edibles. They sent me a part of the clothing, a roll of butter and a can of maple molasses—the rest of the things, I presume, were contraband. I had no knowledge of it at the time, and I am glad that I had not, for I should have been too angry to have enjoyed what I did receive. Among other things kept back was a nice warm winter coat, which I was needing very badly.

I spent one winter in Camp Morton, and I think it was the coldest that I ever experienced. It turned very cold on the 1st of January. I went out, it was so cold that I thought I should freeze, my clothing was insufficient for such inclement blasts, and I went back in the barracks, and went to bed, remaining there three days. Some of the men were actually frozen to death, others were frozen so badly that they were cripples for months. A great many of the prisoners were poorly provided with blankets, and therefore could not stand the excessive cold weather. I am sure that the authorities could have provided better for these poor fellows, if they would, and it is a burning shame that they allowed them to freeze to death, when succor might have been had even at the very threshold. "Oh, freedom, freedom, how many cruelties were committed in thy name?"

The guard would shoot a man for the most trifling offense. I knew one of the guard on the fence, to shoot a man for looking through a small window in the side of the house. Another (an old man) was shot without any provocation—he was standing between two of the buildings looking towards the fence, I suppose, very much as if he would like to get out, and for that reason the cowardly fiend shot him.

Each division selected one of their number to administer punishment to the guilty. Among us stealing a man's ration was a most heinous crime, and if the unlucky culprit was ever caught, he was roughly dealt with, and he was rarely ever known to repeat the offense. I once heard of a very amusing occurrence which took place in the prison, though I was not present at the time. A thief was found guilty of stealing some crackers—he was tried, found guilty, and the punishment awarded was—that the crackers should be covered with sugar, and the thief compelled to eat them, before the crowd collected to hear the trial. I learned that his cure was complete, he was never known to be guilty of a theft again.

The most lucrative employment in camp was ring making, and it was in that way I made most of my spending money. We did anything to pass away the long dull hours which passed in such tedious monotony. "We took no note of time," it was the same old thing day after day, no man truly appreciates his liberty until he has once been deprived of it. Freedom, blessed word:

"There is the moral of all human tales:
Tis but the same rehearsal of the past,
First Freedom, and then Glory."

Just before I left the prison, there took place one of the most dastardly murders on record. Two men were sent out with a wagon loaded with the sweepings from the camp. They were obliged to pass a guard on the outside, who had been wounded in some engagement, losing two fingers. He remarked that he intended to kill a rebel for each finger, and that that was as good a chance as any; accordingly, he commanded them to form a line, and fired at them. The ball passed clear through one of them, and nearly through the other. They were brought into camp, and placed in a hospital tent. I saw the men myself, and know it to be a cool, calculating, deliberate, uncalled for and unprovoked murder. The man passed through a mock trial, which was followed by promotion, as in most of other cases. The best recommendation for a candidate for promotion, among the condemned Yankees was, having been successful in shooting a Rebel prisoner, and immediately he was converted into a hero. It was their delight to sport with torture, and make martyrdom a farce to laugh at. They like to wring the mind in agony while they destroyed the body.

There has been a great hue and cry raised by Northern sensationists about the "dead line" at Andersonville, but they forget to mention the numberless, unknown, nameless graves made in Northern soil for those who have been made the victims of the law of the dead line established in Northern prisons. I can speak at least for Camp Morton. Let them first remove "the beam out of" their own eyes, and then shall they see clearly to take the motes from the eyes of the much hated Southerners. Camp Morton was surrounded by a fence ten feet high, on the top of which were placed guards thirty yards apart, and if a man by chance passed within ten feet of it his days on earth were numbered. It was our custom to amuse ourselves by playing base ball, and if by accident our ball passed within that fatal line, it was as much beyond our reach as if it had gone over the fence. They also placed large reflecting lamps, upon the fence at night, in order that the aim of the guard might be more fatal.

The unmitigated meanness of our sutler, must not be omitted. His conscience had many a long day before, grown seared, and his heart callous, so there was no compunctuous throb at the enormous extortionate prices, which he asked for everything, he was permitted to sell to the prisoners. And Col. Stevens being cognizant of this great wrong, and having it in his power, took no measures to amend it, was as culpable in the sight of the Great I am, as the arrant unscrupulous knave, who thus took advantage of those placed in his power. It took as much to live per week upon what could be bought from Roberts, the suttler, as it would have taken to have boarded at the Bates House in Indianapolis. Before the war he was a ten cent grocery merchant; after he received the appointment of suttlership, he accumulated money quite rapidly; but if he enjoys his ill gotten gain I am quite sure it is more than he deserves, for it was the "weighing of so many pieces of silver against as many ounces of blood." There is a just God, who presides over the destinies of nations, who will at last call every man to an account for the deeds done in the body, whether good or bad. The wicked may indeed prosper for awhile, and flourish like a green bay tree, but there will come a day of final reckoning, and of fearful retribution. Many will there be in that great and notable day of the lord, crying, "Lord, have we not prophesied in thy name, and in thy name done many wonderful works?" and will hear the blighting, withering mandate,—"Depart, ye accursed, into the everlasting fire prepared for the devil and his angels." The blood of these poor murdered prisoners will cry unto the Lord from the ground, like the blood of the righteous Abel; and he will avenge them speedily. Roll on ye wheels of time, and bring about a revolution of affairs.

Numbers of us had ample opportunities of learning mining during our sojourn at Camp Morton, and being almost starved from the constant reduction of rations, and in almost a nude state, we became desperate, and as "a drowning man will catch at a straw" we readily availed ourselves of anything that seemed to offer an opportunity for escape; anything to relieve us from that den of wickedness, and enable us once more to breathe the fresh, pure air of heaven. We knew the penalty if discovered, but we felt that it could be no worse for us. "Desperate diseases require desperate remedies." Mining became the favorite mode of escape because attended with the least danger. Having been engaged in several mines, I learned somewhat of the manner of proceeding. The barracks were not more than fifty yards from the fence on the west side, and not more than half that distance on the North. The manner of the operation, mystified the Feds no little, whenever they found that an opening had been made. The tunnel was commenced on the inside of the house, with the intention of coming out on the outside of the fence. There were never more than four or five at work at a time, for there were spies in our midst, and we were sometimes at a loss to distinguish friend from foe, so we were a little cautious whom we trusted.

In the first place the floor of the lower bunks was made movable, and the work only carried on at night. After a sufficient cavity had been made to admit two men, after digging down about four feet, the work could then progress more rapidly. After we reached a layer of sand and gravel, it was quite easy to dig. At first the dirt was quite troublesome to dispose of, and we were obliged to carry it away in haversacks, and throw it into the Potomac, which I have said before was a small stream running through the enclosure. It was a slow, tedious operation, and required months for completion; and I am very sorry to say that I never knew of but one entirely perfected, and that cost one noble fellow his life. The first night after its completion, seven men were enabled through its instrumentality to breathe the pure air as freemen. By the exceeding watchful kindness of some "wolf in sheep's clothing," the Feds were made acquainted of the fact, of which they said nothing—it being a fine opportunity in which to glut their vengeance upon the unsuspecting inmates of the prison. That night, after dark, they placed a guard around the opening. There was a Dutch Lieutenant (I wish I knew his name) you could by no means conceive of a meaner man, were you to give your imagination full vent (his Satanic majesty not even made an exception. If there was another there more bloodthirsty he failed to make it known by any outward demonstration. He was on hand promptly to take his part in the wholesale massacre. He, with his guard were on the inside of the fence, not over twenty paces from the barracks.

At ten o'clock P. M., the party whose aim was freedom, headed by a stalwart Missourian, slowly wended their way through the long dark tunnel that had cost them so many hours of labor; but no sooner had their leader placed his head above ground than he fell, his head having been pierced by a musket ball. As soon as the shot was fired from the outside, then the brave Lieutenant from the inside, commenced firing at the house. The weather boarding being only thin pine boards, the shot easily penetrated, and retained force enough to have killed any one they might have struck; but thanks to a kind Providence, each shot failed in its mission. This unfortunate circumstance prevented any more releases through this channel.

There were numbers of men confined among us, who, supposing they would obtain favor by reporting to the authorities what transpired in the prison, made it their especial duty to point out every effort made for escape, of which they could gain any knowledge. But one of them certainly had reason to rue it. The first cowardly villain was sent back to his quarters; it is presumed that the officers deemed him safe. The next morning he was found suspended from a beam by the neck, where he had hung until he was dead, dead, dead—three times dead; and as Mrs. Parthington would say, "that is more deaths than the scripture tells on." No one could tell how it was done; for how could any one suppose that a poor harrassed, half-starved prisoner, could have any resentment left in his composition. It was suggested that he died like Judas, for conscience' sake. I am inclined to think he had help. After this, all reporters were kept at Head Quarters, the place for them, as "birds of a feather will flock together," "like loves like," &c. There was another attempt made to dig out, and had almost succeeded, after six weeks of hard labor, when we were again discovered by one of those Argus eyed watchers, and again doomed to disappointment; but not despair, for we allowed nothing to cause us to despond, for our motto was in schoolboy phrase,

"If at first you do'nt succeed,
Try, try again."

When the Yanks found out that we were mining so extensively, they determined to countermine, or make us do it, by digging a ditch clear around the enclosure, so deep that we could not dig under it. Every morning there was a squad detailed to work on it. It was my fixed determination, as well as that of severel of my friends not to strike a lick on it. Being detailed several times I succeeded in getting off without much trouble, but some of my messmates were not quite so fortunate. A brave courageous fellow who refused to work, was threatened with the dungeon. He told them that they could put him in the lock up, but that they could not make him work upon that ditch.

He was thrust into the dungeon, in order (the officer said) to bring him round, but if that was the case they most signally failed, for he remained there until the work was completed. Had the keeper of these brave fellows, had hearts of flesh and blood instead of flint, such heroic endurance, and patient suffering, for the sake of the "land they loved," would have called forth the highest mead of praise, and excited their wondering approbation; and whilst they would have regretted the stringent rules of war, which demanded their imprisonment, they would have ameliorated the sentence by strictly regarding the courtesy due from a captor to a captive—and would not by any means have sought to add insult to injury upon men, the "latchet of whose shoes they were unworthy to unloose." But, alas, let a man but once infringe upon his *quantum sufficiet* of native leniency and he will feel at once that of his own accord, that an irreparable damage has been done. A true soldier will not launch out into reckless schemes, heedless of what disasters his actions will work to others. He will take no undue advantage of the misfortunes of others. He will admire true bravery, and nobleness of soul, though found in a captive. In short he will be governed by a rule which will bend to no chicanery—to no slipperyness—to no equivocal devices, so readily sanctioned by those narrow contracted minds, those mammon-worshipping office-seeking wretches now threatening to engulph the land.

I am inclined to say that if any of the officers at Camp Morton, are ever permitted to enter the gates of the New Jerusalem, and walk the golden paved streets, they may exclaim truly, "Christ Jesus came into the world to save sinners, of whom I am chief." But let us not attempt a further analyzation of actions so base, but throw over them the mantle of charity, and forget such heinous crimes have been perpetrated in this enlightened age—this nineteenth century.

Upon one occasion a doctor (rebel) came to me and requested me to get a hammer and nail puncher and accompany him to the dead house; this I did, wondering much what new feature was now about to be developed; but I was not long left in doubt, for as soon as he reached the desired point, he told me his plans, which were as follows: We were to take up one of the planks in the floor and then dig out. The house was about twenty yards from the fence, a much shorter route than we had tried yet, or indeed much shorter than could be had elsewhere. The plank was soon removed and the work commenced. I was under the impression that there was not room enough to stow away the dirt, but my friends contended that there was and I continued to work. It was thought by all concerned that I was the proper person for the work, because I was one of the men detailed at the hospital, and had worked in the dead house, and could therefore pass in and out, without exciting suspicion, whereas the rest could only work at night. The first night's work proved conclusively to me that the undertaking was a failure. I reported it so the next morning and it was reluctantly given up. It was better so, than to have worked some two or three months, and then been compelled to abandon the scheme. If any have toiled month after month for the accomplishment of some much desired purpose, and when you begin to feel that the goal is about reached, that you are rapidly nearing the culminating point, the grand acme of your ambition, the climax of your hopes, and then suddenly find that your efforts have proved futile—your labor was in vain; such, and such only can fully realize our disappointment.

A man whose name was Rease, and myself, were detailed as carpenters to the hospital, where we had the floor of the main hospital to raise. "Thinks I to myself" there will be a fine opportunity to lay a foundation for escape at some convenient season in the future, and acted accordingly, raising the floor high enough to admit a man between the ground and the joist. At the rear end of the building was our shop and sleeping room, the floor of which was about there feet from the ground, and this proved a splended place for commencing operations. After finishing the floor, we commenced our tunnel. It was by far the most formidable undertaking ever set on foot in camp, and the safest, for the simple reason, that the officers did not dream that we would go to work so close to them. We worked under the chief surgeon's office nearly all the time; we were obliged to work slowly and carefully—the distance to be bored was about one hundred and fifty yards—it looked large, but we were becoming desperate. It was our purpose first, to cut a hole in the floor, and then fit the plank back so neatly, that it could not be discovered; it was a perfect success. We then cut a ditch from the front to the rear of the building, so that we could pass from one end to the other of the building with but little trouble. Our next duty was to construct a wagon to carry the dirt away. The work was carried on systematically: No. 1 did the digging, which had to be done with a butcher knife, No. 2 loaded the wagon with the dirt, and wheeled it back after it was emptied, No. 3 hauled the wagon out and disposed of the dirt by scattering it to the right and left. The work had been carried on in this manner about six weeks, when I succeeded in securing my liberty, in another and much easier way. Previous to this I had tried numerous ways to make my escape, but all had proved futile. I had obtained at one time the countersign but failed to make use of it on account of a comrade, who afterwards treated me very badly, for as soon as he obtained his liberty, he seemed to entirely ignore the existence of rebel prisoners. He seemed to keep a careful look out for No. 1. How proud I was to walk the earth once more a freeman. War at best is horrible, but I would rather spend a life time in the field, than six months in one of those gloomy, loathsome dens of the North designated prisons, by those who considered it their indispensible and patriotic duty, to see men languishing in prison, day after day, when they had it in their power to grant an exchange and have sent the prisoner on his way rejoicing back to his native element—to his own bright sunny clime. Could this have been so, how many a sad heart would have beat with gladness, how many a dull eye would have become animated, and have beamed forth its gratitude from its round full orb. A reckoning for these heinous crimes must needs come sooner or later. When will these things undergo an investigation? echo answers—when. God hasten the day when the pure hearted, yet left in our land, may raise their voices to the powers that be, and loudly and explicitly demand an investigation of these wanton, cruel, heartless, uncalled for and unprovoked murders, "demand them in such a manner that if they do not reach the Government, will at least reach the Heavens, and plead their cause before the God that fitteth them." A few more words and I leave this matter to those orators and statesmen, whose eloquence of diction will enable them to handle the subject rightly, and whose experience in prison life, has been longer, more enduring and their sufferings more intense. I wish to see them hurl back upon the enemy these taunts about Libby, Andersonville, Belle Isle, &c.,—silence them forever :

> "Explain about it, and explain till all men know it;
> And talk about it, and about it, and about it."

And let not those who survive this struggle, forget those brave ones who languished, suffered and died, in those loathsome dens of many woes—they are indeed deserving of marty's crowns. On tablets of immortal minds, let us write inscriptions of them, that can never be effaced. The future may be indistinct, dimly seen ; but it shall be to us one of glorious reward.

> "How sleep the brave who sink to rest,
> By all their country's wishes blest!
> When spring with dewy fingers cold,
> Return to deck their hallowed mold,
> She there shall dress a sweeter sod
> Than fancy's feet have ever trod."

# THE HORRORS OF CAMP DOUGLAS AS RELATED BY A PRISONER.

PALMYRA, MARION CO., MO., August 22, 1867.

MR. G. FROST—*Dear Sir :*—In answer to your letter requesting a statement of such facts as came under my observation, while imprisoned in Camp Douglas, allow me to give a brief statement of my capture and subsequent imprisonment before I reached that place. After which I shall take a retrospective view of my imprisonmeut in that hellish den of iniquity, which makes my blood boil even now, at the bare memory. Fiends incarnate in the shape of men, had charge of that prison during my stay of two years, and each vied with the other in devising some mode of punishment more fiendishly inhuman than any which had preceded. But here I need say no more, all that is needed to convince the world of the truth of what I say, is to simply narrate facts, the truth of which thousands now living can testify, and many, many of them will still live to bless you that such barbarism has been heralded to the world. They deserve notoriety; and in meanness, littleness of soul, and in short in the very quintessence of wickedness, if the officers who presided over the above named prison have any supreiors, if indeed any equals, I pray God that it may never be my unhappy lot to be thrown among them; I would shun contact with their vile polluted person as I would the bite of the deadly coya— and feel that their presence would be more blitheing and destructive in its nature, than the blasts of the simoon. In comparison with either of these the vileness of their nature seems intensified, and from the malevolence of their dispositions they fail to excite any commiseration. And even now, doubtless every breath they draw, is laden with execrations, against those who they allowed to escape from their hands, with life even remaining in their poor emaciated bodies. The *modus operandi* now is to disfranchi:e them and elevate in their stead, the flat nosed, woolly headed, greasy heeled "demon de Afrique"—not content with having abused, reviled and spit upon while in their power, as unarmed helpless prisoners, they would carry their malicious hatred still farther, and tell them that they are a helpless, subjugated foe, the malled, beaten, condemned objects of their betters. God speed the day, when a little retributive justice will be poured upon the heads of these self-constituted righteous ones—and when there shall be a glorious outpouring of wrath upon those who like Hamaan, have pronounced their own doom. It was in the hearts of those intrusted with the prisoners to kill them with every available means of cruelties, and in many cases the shaft told but too well. I know of these things, they are no hearsay, for I witnessed them with my own eyes, and there is yet approaching a day when these things shall be dragged from their hiding places, to the everlasting detriment of those engaged in these fiendish and unwonted cruelties, and the whole civilized world shall know to what source to trace the honor of these disgraceful proceedings. The Federal authorities shrink, and well they may, from an investigation, for well they know what horrid butcheries it would reveal to their *eternal dishonor*—(excuse me, that is a misapplication) disgrace, for I do not think that the men, who took a part in these horrible murders, ever could lay any claim to the word honor—it was erased from their vocabulary, and the import of the word had entirely escaped their memory. And the leaders of the party of which they are members, do not conceive the necessity of attending to such small matters. After again thanking you for your commendable undertaking I shall close. Very respectfully, yours,

M. J. BRADLEY.

I was a private in Company "G." 10th Kentucky Infantry, Col. Caudill, commanding, and was captured near Pound Gap, Va., on the 7th of July 1863, where our regiment was then doing duty; and after marching as prisoners of war until our feet were sore, we were then put on board of a flat boat at the mouth of Beaver, and floated down Big Sandy to the Ohio river, where we were placed on board of a steamer and conveyed to Cincinnati, and placed in Kemper Barracks, in which place we were treated, during our short stay, like so many dogs; and like *mean* dogs at that, for I know that were any of the good canine species called upon for a statement of his treatment from his keeper, he could be enabled from the facts in the premises to draw a much more satisfactory conclusion than I am able to do with regard to *our* keeper's and their behavior to those in their power.

From thence we were hurried off to Camp Chase, where our treatment, was by no means good, but at the same time could be tolerated much better than at the former place. From there we were taken to Camp Douglas, near Chicago, Illinois, where our persecutions commenced on the 25th day of August of the same year. Sheds roughly constructed of pine lumber constituted our barracks, and we were constantly exposed to the rigor of that severe Northern climate, on account of the inefficiency of those sheds to protect us—here again was our treatment worse than that of the brute creation—for had we been a lot of horses under their care and keeping, we would have been provided for, by having good warm stables, to ward off the inclemency of the blast, and with plenty of good substantial food to satisfy the cravings of our appetites, but, being rebel prisoners we were denied either of these essentials.

Though our rations for the first two or three months were not to be complained of, the friends of the prisoners were allowed to furnish them with clothing and such things as they needed for some time after our arrival there. But after a time our prison became crowded, and communication with friends more restricted—our rations were reduced to a small piece of tough beef or pickled pork and bread, with occasionally some beans and a little vinegar, and our condition was subsequently rendered intolerable. You who sit down to your nicely fried or broiled steaks, your delicious warm rolls and fresh butter, your cups of piping hot coffee, morning after morning, can form some idea of what it would cost you to be shut up in a close prison and deprived of all these luxuries, and not only of the delicacies, but the necessaries of life.

And many of those who agreed with me politically, had an opportunity of trying the foregoing of these luxuries, without entering the service—they suffered for mere opinion's sake. In the prison they allowed us neither sugar, coffee, bacon, potatoes, or vegetables of any kind, and were told by those in authority, that this was in retaliation for what their prisoners were suffering in Southern prisons—at Andersonville, Libby, Belle Isle, &c. Most noble revenge! Strange that this should excite their human natures to such deeds of heartless cruelties. But some excuse is better than none, even if it does limp a little. His Satanic Majesty is swift in excuses, and is always prompt in furnishing them to his followers, when called upon.

We were compelled to muster and stand in line every morning' whether cold or hot, and there to remain in the scorching sun, the pelting rain or the driving snow, sometimes for hours. And it would have moved any hearts, save those of stone, to see with what meek patience some of the brave heroic prisoners endured such treatment. Although their noble souls chafed under such brutality yet not a moan or groan, or any outward demonstration showed what their noble natures were undergoing. They were always cheerful, light-hearted and happy; extracting fun from whatever presented itself that they could, and enduring that which they could not, with a fortitude worthy of the noble cause, in which they had staked their lives and their sacred honors.

At sundown the bugle was sounded and all the prisoners were obliged to go to their bunks, which consisted of pine planks, minus a matress, or any kind of ticks to prevent their hardness. One blanket to two men was allowed, and some poor fellows were even left without blankets; not a word was allowed to be spoken by us from the time the bugle sounded at sundown until its sounding at sunrise next morning. Sentinels were near us on duty, and spies and informers called "patrol men" were all around watching and constantly annoying us. Those brave men (spies) who were engaged in such laudable undertakings, will doubtless feel proud when they read this, will rejoice that they were thus enabled to do something so magnanimous for their country, and their hearts will swell in triumph that they have contributed their feeble might in bringing about the present state of affairs in their native land. They have a right to.

Owing to our short allowance, and our exposure to the severity of a Northern winter, which continued up to the day of my release on the 27th of March 1865, a period not very far short of two years, I may safely say that thousands of my fellow prisoners died of privations—or, in other words—*starved to death!* Murdered by slow torture, being denied month after month even the common necessaries of life—while their fat fed, well-clothed sentinels mocked our sufferings and laughed at our miseries. Oh, it was all human nature could endure to see these brave men thus dying of starvation day after day, at the hands of those vile, detestable, unfeeling villains, who were rolling in affluence, stolen from the letters of these poor prisoners whose friends had sent them aid, which they poor deluded mortals, thought the federal authorities would allow them to receive. They might have bettered their condition, as far as physical suffering is concerned, by turning traitor to their beloved South, and swallowing the oath that was poked at them every time they turned round—and then swelling the federal ranks against their brethren ; but this, the majority scorned to do—choosing rather to suffer present ills than fly for succor to those vicious, bigoted, depraved, accursed keepers, who had sought to make them, by such inhuman treatment, prove recreant to their trust. They remained true to their country, and firmly resolved to mantain their position of loyalty to their beloved land, and save themselves from partaking in the acts of that party, the guilt of which it will take rivers of blood to wash away.

For a time the cooks allowed us to eat such of the meat bones as would cook soft enough to be masticated by our teeth, and those which were too hard and tough for that operation were placed before the fire to extract the grease, which was eagerly sopped up as a dainty. After a time however, the Yankee authorities began to repent their leniency, and to think this kind of treatment entirely too humane for Southern soldiers, and accordingly they issued orders to stop such extravigancies These bones were then put into a slop barrel, which after being filled with scraps was hauled out and thrown away, and orders were also issued forbidding the touching of these bones after they were thrown into the slop barrels, and he who took anything from them, to satisfy the cravings of his appetite, did it at the peril of being shot by the guard, or punished by the authorities, should he be so fortunate as to escape the shot from the guard. But the constant knawings of hunger sometimes induced the poor, half-starved prisoners to take a bone from the barrels at the risk of being fired at by the guard on duty. And many a poor fellow has been shot at for merely attempting to approach these barrels, and looking wistfully at the bones therein. This I have witnessed a number of times. The indignities and wrongs thus heaped upon those superior, by the laws of God and nature, to the vile wretches who perpetrated them, were of common occurrence, by those inferior, ignorant and debased mortals.

If a lucky fellow was caught with one of the bones from the slop tubs in his possession, trying to knaw a little substance out of it to appease hunger and protract life, he was punished for it, by having the bone fastened between his teeth, across his mouth, and then tied like a gag; and then the poor fellow was made to fall down and crawl around on his hands and knees like a dog, a laughing stock for Federal soldiers, spies and camp followers. There is more inventive meanness in the Yankee composition, than any other nation upon God's green earth could conceive of during thousands of years.

Numerous descriptions and modes of punishment were practiced upon the prisoners on the slightest pretext. And it seemed to gratify every desire of their nature when they could find the smallest pretext for inflicting some innocent prisoner with some mode of torture, of which they were the inventor. I sometimes wondered that the ground did not open and swallow them up, while practicing some unmitigating meanness. One would think that humanity and self interest both would have prompted better treatment at their hands, but there were few pitying eyes that gazed upon the prisoners—few that showed any of the kind promptings of a pure heart, that wore the pale blue uniform furnished them by the Federal government—and to this day, that color is suggestive to my mind of every species of wanton cruelty, and upon meeting with one dressed in it, I am tempted to put my hands into my pockets and get as far beyond their reach as the case will admit of.

A piece of timber four feet long had four legs nailed to it, and made very much to resemble a carpenter's tressel ten or twelve feet high, was made into what they called, by way of taunt and ridicule, "the wooden horse," or "Morgan's mule." For the most trivial and almost unavoidable violation of any of the rules and regulations, we were made to climb up as best we could, and set astride of this narrow piece of wood for hours at a time—day or night, hot or cold, rain or snow, exposed to all the inclemency of the weather.

Another mode of punishment was, to make a man stoop forward, keeping his legs stiff, and, touching his hands to the ground, remain in that position with the blood rushing to the head, and every vein in his body swelling until the protruding eyeballs became bloodshot, and almost bursting from their sockets with pain. And if any have any doubts upon the subject of this being a cruel mode of punishment, let him place himself in that position and remain a few minutes, and he will soon have occasion to change his mind. The ball and chain—the thumb screw, and various other modes of torture were daily and hourly practiced—including the dungeon (a dark, filthy, lousy cell, eight feet long, four feet wide, and six feet high—without anything to lie on but the bare floor.) Here prisoners were shut up from the light of day, and were not allowed to converse with any one for weeks at a time.

From the manner of our treatment, and the inhumanity practiced upon us; our nervous system was so taxed that it became a general feeling of indignation among the prisoners against the officers presiding at the prison, and also a feeling of contempt for the sentinels and guards, who thus allowed themselves to be tools in the hands of petty officers to gratify the malicious propensities of their depraved grovelling natures, and we agreed among ourselves, in a fit of desperation to rush upon our oppressors, unarmed and defenceless as we were, and wrenching their arms from them, use them in making our escape.

The plot was all ripe, and the prisoners would have undoubtedly gone to work, and carried out their ideas of mutiny, had the whole scheme not been discovered by some one and made known to the officers. How this came about we never knew, but if the vile wretch who revealed it should ever chance to see this sketch, allow me to whisper in his ear, that it is well for his lordship that he was never discovered, and if it will afford him any comfort, or he can draw any consolation from the knowledge now of this fact, he is welcome. In his latter days, if he will only reveal, he shall have a marble monument erected to his memory, and his noble deed inscribed upon it, so that future generations may know what a vile, execrable wretch once stalked this earth of ours. And I presume his last few moments will be sweetened by the fact, that he did what he could, and that he will now go to his reward—and that every prisoner is willing that he shall reap it.

After this discovery the discipline was somewhat relaxed, and we were allowed some few privileges, but this only lasted some few days. Frequently outbreaks occurred, by squads attempting to escape, for which offense terrible tortures were inflicted, and it would seem on such occasions that their fiendish propensities would never be satiated. On one occasion there was an attempt made to dig out, and to this end a long trench, three feet deep and two feet wide was made with knives and spoons, the whole length of one of the buildings—which, I suppose, was a distance of some ninety feet. From this a tunnel was excavated of sufficient depth and width to admit a man, from the inside of the barracks, extending clear through underground, beyond the high enclosure upon which the sentinels were placed. The dirt taken from this tunnel was carried and placed in the trench before mentioned to conceal it from those watching around the prison. We had everything ready for escape and by some means, to this day unknown to me, our plan of escape was revealed, to our great mortification and disappointment. But few persons were familiar with this plot, and had it not have been detected and made known as soon as it was, the whole garrison would have had a chance to escape. How detestable seemed our prison life after this. It was ten times as hard to endure it after having liberty so near within our grasp. Indeed it seemed as if we would never become reconciled to it again. But still time rolled on, and seemed as monotinous in our prison as ever.

After the discovery of this tunnel, the men in the barracks from which it commenced were searched, and the inmates all taken, and drawn up in line and surrounded by an armed guard, and then ordered to stand exposed to the weather, until every man connected with the plot should be designated. Exhausted by hunger and disease the prisoners grew faint and weary, and several through exhaustion sank to the ground, whereupon they were fired upon by the guard, and several fell mortally wounded. Could the imagination conceive of torture more severe, for offense so trivial? Because a few half fed, wretched prisoners, dared to make use of their wits to devise a plan of escape, in order that their oppression might cease, they must be tortured and racked to death by those having them in their custody. I should like to have the pleasure of being guard to some of our heartless sentinels, for a little time, that I might show them by mild and humane treatment that power should not be abused, and also teach them what is due from a keeper to his prisoners. By my kindness I would heap, as it were, coals of fire upon their heads. But I might be mistaken in my reckoning, for they who allow themselves to show brutality to a prisoner, would have no sense of gratitude in their composition, but would presume upon my kindness, and instead of being thankful, would censure me for not doing more—this is the kind of feeling which animates their bosoms. The brave fellow who devised the arrangements for escape was one of Morgan's men, and seeing that the innocent were suffering equally with the guilty, nobly stepped forward and acknowledged himself the originator of the scheme. The punishment was however continued until several more were discovered, and then all were hurried off to the dungeon, to be heard of no more by us for several months.

The circumstance of the tunnel was at the time published in the Federal journals as "an attempt to revolt among the prisoners," which served as a pretext to justify the wholesale slaughter, and cowardly treatment of unarmed defenceless, half-starved and unoffending prisoners of war. And as a reading public could only hear one side of the story, they were under the impression that prisoners were treated as well as they deserved. And the keepers of the prisons managed, by giving out false versions of what took place there to keep up such false views. And I presume for our friends it was well it was so, for they knew enough at best, to make their hearts sick at the thought of dear friends who were thus exposed to the cruelty of "Lincoln hirelings." In their case, "ignorance was bliss."

The "dead line" was drawn around our prisons on the inside of the fence enclosing the barracks. Several men were shot by the guards upon this line, without any provocation whatever. I remember one circumstance in particular, which I do not think I can ever forget; a man who had just come into the prison, being very thirsty, and the water having been shut off from us, as had frequently been the case, seeing some snow lying near the fence, on the ground, attempted to pick up some and eat it, when he was shot by the guard without any warning whatever, and he fell near that infernal "dead line,"

There was held every Sabbath morning what was called "inspection." Each prisoner was required to bring everything he had (at the sounding of the bugle) and lay it down on a line. Blankets, wearing apparel, cooking utensils, and all camp furniture was thrown into a heterogeneous mass. Then commenced the examination; and there were hours devoted to this business, as may be supposed would be the case where the goods and chattels belonging to ten thousand men had to go through an examination. If an extra shirt, coat hat or blanket were found in the possession of a lucky prisoner, it was immediately appropriated by some of the examining committee, who I supposed used them for his own benefit.

This was the way these puritanical followers of "Uncle Abe" observed Sunday—it was the regular Sunday work. I sometimes wondered that they were not immediately destroyed by some unforeseen catastrophe, for such vile desecrations of the day concerning which the Great Jehovah had said, "Remember the Sabbath day and keep it holy; six days shalt thou labor and do all thy work, but the seventh is the Sabbath of the Lord, thy God; in it, thou shalt not do any work, thou nor thy son, nor thy daughter, nor thy man-servant, nor thy maid-setvant, nor the stranger within thy gates."

These proceedings often took place during the coldest weather, and its consequences were very serious to us, for while standing in the cold, hundreds were frost bitten, and those who escaped, contracted some disease, from the effect of which, very many were carried to that bourne from whence no traveler returns. We were often called out before breakfast and made to stand until the officers chose to come from Head Quarters and perform the delectable undertaking. Clad in their rich livery, and looking as comfortable in their warm clothing as possible, in order (I presume) to give the opportunity to the prisoners of seeing how a man looked when he was, as the ladies say, "dressed up." The least dereliction on the part of the prisoners, on such occasions was severely punished by a ride on the wooden horse—or some other mode of torture equally severe. No prisoner was allowed to have more than fifty cents in money, and on the pretence of detecting violations of this rule we were often unexpectedly ordered out, put into line and our persons thoroughly searched; no notice would be given of the time and place or manner of making the search; suddenly and unexpectedly we were ordered out, and everything must be dropped immediately, and the call obeyed. Every prisoner was carefully watched as he was hurried into line to see that he did not conceal any money. Prisoners coming in would often manage to conceal large sums in their clothing; this would get scattered among us in small quantities, by dint of trading which was carried on, on a small scale.

The Yankee officers in making this search would frequently deprive us of the last cent we had, telling us it would be returned some day. I once had only five cents between me and poverty, and this they took. Thousands were served in the same way, and none of this money was returned so far as I was able to learn. I know mine never was.

And now Mr. Yank, allow me to say to you yet, that I have often been told that it is "never too late to do good," and if you are done with it, I would gladly receive it yet with the interest, and whenever you find it becoming burdensome, just forward it to my address at Palmyra, Mo., and I will send you a receipt for the same, and pay the postage on it in the bargain. Come now, old fellow, "shell out," you have had the use of that money long enough.

Every petty annoyance that Yankee imagination could conceive of was practiced upon us. If at any time a prisoner was found with a knife, whittling a stick, his knife was immediately taken from him, and a word of complaint would subject him to some punishment. It seemed to afford them infinite satisfaction to get to offer us indignities and insults, and inflict punishments upon us. But I presume that they were never in the company of gentlemen before, and they wished to show their contempt for them as much as possible. If it had been a lot of wooly headed negroes they would have known better how to have behaved.

Now and then a gentleman would stray into their midst, and he would exhibit some humanity to the prisoners, but such were soon relieved from duty, and sent to some other post. Owing to our being denied suitable and sufficient clothing, bedding and food many became diseased and died through sheer neglect. From the constant and never failing watch upon us, to prevent the freedom of social intercourse, and the denial to us of newspapers, save the lying Yankee sheets, the spirits of many of the prisoners sank, and their tired forms gave way. Such as were able to bear up, tried to cheer up their companions, and each and all used every available means to keep off the sick list. Above all we dreaded the hospital, for comparatively few ever returned from that house of death, to resume his tortures in the ranks of the survivors. But, poor fellows, I presume very few of them laid down life reluctantly, for it had indeed become a burden, and oftimes, methinks, the stealthy steps of the fell destroyer was listened for with eagerness, and the harrassed worn spirit took its flight with joy from a world of matter to a world of mind What a joy to think that they were forever to be rid of spies upon their actions, and yet many a poor fellow died invoking blessings upon the heads of his persecutors. But it softened not their flinty hearts.

All these petty annoyances and ten thousand others did we endure and that too (be it remembered) within sound of the church bells, in the christian city of Chicago. As if to add insult to injury an observatory was erected just outside the gate of our prison, and spectators were permitted, for the sum of ten cents, to ascend to an elevated platform, where, with the aid of spy or field glasses, furnished them by the proprietors, they could look down upon, and inspect us as objects of curiosity, as they would wild beasts in a menagerie. And I suppose it was well, for *some* of the visitors who crowded that platform, had never in all their lives seen a gentleman, and the sight of one was well worth the money. In this saddened, sorrowful condition, we were told by our tormentors, that if we would forswear our Southern feelings, take that detestable oath of allegiance to the United States, and join the Federal army, that we would be pardoned, released, and organized into companies and regiments, and be allowed plenty of food and clothes, and be sent out on the plains to garrison the forts and guard the frontier. Exhausted by starvation and other agencies, enough of our men to constitute a regiment of a thousand, out of ten thousand, yielded to the temptation. They were dressed up and paraded before our eyes, and then sent out upon their mission. Poor fellows! instead of exciting envy in our bosoms, as their officers had thought to do, our hearts were moved with pity.

Officers came around urging us to enlist under them as Captains, who were authorized by the United States Government to tender these promises and rewards to us. Hundreds were dying daily, others were hourly growing weaker and weaker from their sufferings. But out of ten thousand, only one thousand could be seduced. The remainder determined to die of their sufferings rather than sacrifice their honor and their country. Whether these tortures were designed to convert us into Federal soldiers, or whether they were in "retaliation" for the way Federal soldiers were treated in the South, as was stated to us, is a question, the justice of which must be adjudicated and determined by future generations. That the reader may form some idea of the many and petty indignities, too small of themselves to be remembered or narrated, but still calculated to insult and wrong us, I will give the following: Several of us happened to be at the barracks where Benj. Dobyns, of this county, an old acquaintance and friend of mine, was quartered, sitting there conversing quietly and orderly, when a guard came along, and in an insulting and overbearing manner ordered me to "get a broom and go to sweeping." Not belonging there, I knew the fellow had no jurisdiction over me, but remembering my utter defenselessness, I got a broom and went to work, aided by another man, and swept out all the barracks. He then ordered the other four or five (who like myself had gone there to see how Mr. Dobyns' wound was doing) to rise up and dance before him—they did so. After he had displayed his authority and consequence, he ordered all, in an insolent and domineering manner, to "clear out, and keep ourselves away from there." I only mention this among thousands of various occurrences of the same kind, in Camp Douglas. Indeed tongue cannot tell, neither can the imagination conceive what countless horrors that we experienced while in the prison during the winters of 1863-4.

The Federals said it was too cold for them to go out, even with their thick warm clothes, and haul wood to keep rebels from freezing in their miserable and exposed sheds. Nor would they do it. The consequence was we were obliged to carry coal in our bare hands through the cold to keep ourselves from suffering. The hands, feet and ears of many of the prisoners were frozen, and many of them perished from exposure.

It seemed to me then that, if I had been warmly clad, and could have procured thick warm gloves, as they could, that I would have procured wood for the worst enemy I ever had, much more would

I have done so for those who had never wronged me in any manner, save they chose to differ with me politically. But this difference can be accounted for easily—the *one* was born upon Southern soil, where the heart grows large and warm, while the *other* was cradled in the icy regions of the North, where the heart is dwarfed ere it has attained its full perfection. It was the fault of their education.

In December, 1864, my wife and Mrs. Ayres, the sister of a fellow prisoner, whose name was Larkin, came to see us, bringing us some clothes, and a few dainties for our Christmas dinner. They were denied the pleasure of seeing us, although they had come several hundred miles to do so, and my wife was accompanied by her only child, a sweet little girl of only six summers, whom I had not seen for a period of three years. After going in vain from one office to another, seeking an interview with either of us, they finally succeeded in enlisting the sympathies of a kind hearted clerk, in one of the departments, who interceded for them. After much patient perseverence they succeeded in obtaining permission (after being sworn) to converse with us, in the presence of the guards and officers, twenty minutes.

The following memorandum is attached to the oath demanded of my wife:—"The above named Mollie J. Bradley, has blue eyes, auburn hair, is 26 years old, and is five feet four inches high." Here again my feelings were wrought to the highest pitch of excitement. Two helpless women coming on errands of mercy, to visit loved ones, whom they supposed were really suffering for the necessaries of life—traveling hundreds of miles alone, under circumstances the most inauspicious—only to be tantalized with a conversation of some twenty minutes with those dear ones whom they had not seen for years.

The Christmas presents they brought to us were otherwise appropriated. The cruelties practiced upon the prisoners inside of the garrison were horrifying in the extreme, but when the intelligence of the indignities offerred to our wives and female relatives, who ventured to ask the privilege of seeing us and providing us clothes, reached us, our feelings often rose to a pitch not far removed from madness.

A field officer, accompanied by several individuals unknown to us, was passing our barracks one day, when we all cried out "Bread! Bread!! Bread!!! in the hope of attracting his attention, and that it might lead to inquiry and relief; but, oh, we were "reckoning without our host," for we were ordered into line, and were not allowed to eat anything until the next day. It seemed to be the study of those who had charge of us to invent accusations and inflict punishments. Each vied with the other in adding to our mortification and disappointment. We were taxed to our utmost capacity of endurance. Thousands sank under it, and were made "to sleep the sleep that knows no waking." Daily did we witness the death of our brave comrades, who had endured the privations and dangers of active service in the field, overcome by their prison sufferings, and borne away to their rude burials, amid strangers in a strange land.

Thousands of pure, patriotic and brave men as ever saw the light of day, were butchered by the slow and grinding tortures that wasted and consumed them at Camp Douglas, whilst all around outside of the limits of the prison might be heard the sounds of mirth, revelry and sport, while we were pinched by cold, hunger, and thirst, and rendered as miserable as the fiendish malice of our persecutors could make us. Even the meanest of God's creation who hovered around to pick up fragments, and gather offal from the camp, were banqueting in plenty and reveling in the luxuries of vice.

We have been among Federal soldiers in Southern prisons, and although food was often scarce with the people of the South, yet the rebel soldier would share his last biscuit with a starving prisoner. And if the Federal soldiers ever suffered for food and clothes it was because the people had it not to furnish to them; but in our case it was not so. Hundreds and thousands of cattle, sheep and hogs, daily crowded the Chicago market; their stores were glutted with goods of every description and variety, and the Federal authorities were plethoric in their abundance, and yet they kept poor suffering rebel soldiers, languishing within their loathsome dens, without even the means of sustaining life—only dragging out a miserable existence.

And now many of these authorities visit the church of Christ, and with a sanctimonious air, send up long prayers, that sinners may be brought to see the error of their ways—when they, like the Pharasees and Saducees of olden time—only have made "clean the outside of the platter," or like the Pharisee, who stood up and prayed, "oh God, I thank thee, that I am not as other men." And I too have reason to congratulate myself that all men are not as they are, for what a miserable, depraved, wicked, abandoned world would we have.

Thank God, there are enough pure, whole-souled christians remaining in the world to keep the churches in existence. This subject is so revolting and its recollections so sickening that I can pursue it no farther—others must contribute their mite as I have done to the memory of the nineteen months of torment endured by myself and others at Camp Douglas. It brings such a crowd of horrors to my mind, that I can scarcely realize its truthfulness, although I personally witnessed all, and more than I have stated. Oh, horror of horrors! sooner than undergo their repetition, gladly would I rush upon the bayonet, or force my way to the cannon's mouth. Yea, I would welcome death as a relief. All this too from the hands of my countrymen, whom I would have called brethren aforetime. But all this is past, and may a gracious Heaven forgive those at whose doors these great sins may lie.

> "Man's inhumanity to man,
> Makes countless thousands mourn."

# THE McNEIL MASSACRE OF TEN REBEL PRISONERS AT PALMYRA, MO., IN THE FALL OF 1862.

In the fall of 1862, about the 1st of September, it was reported that a large body of Rebels under command of Col. Joe Porter, were marching in the direction of Palmyra, for the purpose, it was thought, of attacking the place. About eighty of the most influential citizens were arrested and placed in the court house, under guard, thinking thereby it might have some effect in keeping Col. Porter from entering. They were kept there three nights, but in the day time were paroled with instructions to report at five o'clock in the evening, or at the firing of the cannon; all of which was done with a view to save themselves from attack.

One Munson, a hanger on at the Commissary Department, proposed to the soldiers one night during the excitement, to get up a scare, in order that they might have an excuse for firing on the citizens then in confinement. However, for some cause Porter did not come, but shortly after sent in a flag of truce, requesting the surrender of the place, but his main object was to release the Confederate prisoners, then confined in the county jail. Word was sent back that they would not surrender, that if he wanted the place, he would have to come and take it. Col. Porter, with his men, then marched into town, and the Federals fled to the court house, jail, and Louthan's building for protection. In the mean time, however, the citizen prisoners had been released. Porter dispatched his men to different parts of the city and the fight commenced. Some of the rebel soldiers, under Col. Porter, and formerly citizens of Palmyra, who had before the war been very much annoyed and harrassed, and we may say almost driven into the rebel army, by certain would be "loyal" individuals, took the opportunity of arresting those of their persecutors, whom they could find—especially one Andrew Allsman, who was about the meanest man in Marion county. During the fight there was one rebel soldier killed in the alley near the Methodist church, and was afterwards carried by some of the citizens and laid in the church. One citizen named Laborious, was also killed, while standing in his store door, directly opposite the Court house. Another, (an assistant recruiting officer) was wounded while making his way to the court house, where a portion of the other Federal soldiers were stationed. After he fell, he threw up his hands as a sign of surrender, after which he was allowed to remain undisturbed, until some rebel sympathizers went to his assistance, and carried him to a place where he was well cared for, and we are told, succeeded in getting well.

After the rebels had left town, a recruiting officer, Lieut. Baird, of the 11th Mo. Cav., under Col. Moore, who had secreted himself in an office, to keep from falling into the hands of the rebels, to show his bravery after the danger was over, proceeded to the Methodist church, (South) caught the dead rebel by the heels or hair of the head, and dragged him around through the church, cursing and swearing all the time, venting his spleen on the body of a dead rebel, knowing at the same time, that if he was alive and standing before him, he would be the last person under the heavens to attempt such a thing, but would have sneaked off like a cowardly cur as he was. Not satisfied with what he had already done by disgracing his country's flag, in dragging the dead man around the church, he went to the pulpit, took the sacred Bible and tore it up leaf by leaf, saying: "the d—d Methodist and Baptist churches were the cause of the war." He also destroyed the lamps and committed other outrageous acts too numerous to mention. How much better it would have been had he have shouldered his gun and gone into the ranks, and showed his manhood by fighting for his flag, instead of disgracing it in the manner he did. But no, he preferred keeping out of danger, until the war was over, and then in places he was not known would no doubt talk and brag over his brave exploits; that he did so and so, but never once telling how he dragged a poor dead rebel by the hair of the head over the floor of the House of God, in Palmyra, Marion county Missouri.

After the rebels had taken possession of the jail and released the prisoners, they took the Militia that were guarding it, and marched them to their camp west of town, on Berkley Summer's farm. There they were required to take the oath not to take up arms again against the Confederacy, until regularly exchanged, and we were informed that a great many rejoiced at the opportunity. As far as the man Allsman was concerned, he was informed that he would have to keep them company, with the assurance that he would not be hurt, that they would take good care of him and treat him kindly, which no doubt they did. About nine o'clock in the morning of the same day, they took up the line of march in a north west direction, camping same night near the farm of Mr. Clemens, on the South Fabius river.

Next morning they resumed their march in the direction of Newark, and camped that night near Whaley's mill, where on the morning after they were attacked by McNeil's force. During the fight this Allsman was killed. After McNeil returned to Palmyra, he issued a proclamation, that if Allsman was not forthcoming inside of ten days, he would shoot ten men instead. For several days it was talked of between the particularly "loyal" men, as to whether it would not be best to take citizens, and among those who were so lively in agitating the matter, was an editor of an abolition sheet then published at that place, and who employed at the beginning of the war, a Mr. John M. Grier, who by the way was a true Southern man, to write articles for his paper, advocating the steps the South was then taking; and the same editor—so rumor says—succeeded in eluding the rebels, by secreting himself in his wife's bed room, and his own brother and partner, sought refuge in a rebel house, the owner of which took compassion on him, and told him not to be frightened for he would protect him. However, it was finally agreed between (Gen.) McNeil, Stachan, (the Provost Marshal) and the "loyal" ones above alluded to, to take ten prisoners from the jail, who were captured as prisoners of war. When the ballot was cast the ten unfortunate ones whose lot it fell to to be shot, were told to prepare for the terrible doom that awaited them—to be shot with muskets until dead! dead!! dead!!!

The wife of one Humphrey, who was at first among the sentenced ones, but afterwards released, on hearing of the doom which awaited her husband, proceeded at once to Palmyra, to see if she could not do something for him. After her arrival she went to Stachan, accompanied by a little daughter, leaving a babe and four others at home, and implored him to spare her husband on account of her children, begging as only a mother and wife knew how to beg for the life of a husband and father.

The fiend of hell in human shape, seeing that he had the poor heart broken woman in his power, told her that if she would accede to his wishes, and pay him five hundred dollars, he would release him and shoot another in his place. She, in order to save her husband from such a cruel fate as was then hanging over him, consented, when the cowardly villain committed the hellish deed of violating her person, and while he was thus engaged, the little child was seen on the outside of the door crying, which led to his detection—the Federal soldiers having suspected that something not altogether right was going on, and in a short time found him committing the act above mentioned; afterwards the brute (for a fiend like him cannot certainly be classed among the human species) released her husband, and took one Humstead, who had been brought in that morning, aged about sixteen.

The villain no doubt is now receiving his just dues, for afterwards he was often heard to say that his conscience troubled him so that he could not rest in peace. After the war he remained a short time in North Missouri, and then went to New Orleans where he took some disease, from which he died. We leave our readers to judge for themselves as to the journey he took after his death.

On the morning of October 18th, after the ten condemned men were notified to get ready, the mournful procession started from the county jail on Olive street, composed of the prisoners seated upon their coffins in wagons furnished for the occasion, closely guarded by Federal soldiers and Militia, and surrounded by a large number of heart broken relatives, weeping and sympathizing friends, idle and curious spectators, and bloodthirsty enemies—the latter seeming to rejoice over the bloody massacre which was about to take place. After marching east to Main street it turned south, wending its way up Main street, for the distance of some four or five blocks, when it again turned east in the direction of the Fair Ground, the place selected for the execution. As it passed up Main street the pulse of the crowd on either side, throbbed with different emotions. The great heart of the little city moved in sympathy with the condemned prisoners; bursting forth in lamentations and wailings, as ten innocent men were hurried on, professedly to avenge the death of one man, for which they were in no way responsible, but really to gratify the fiendish passions of the dominant party. Before proceeding farther we will say that on the night before the execution, one of the most prominent citizens of Palmyra, went to (Gen.) McNeil, and asked him if he could not and would not stop the execution—that he was about to take the lives of ten innocent men for one, who was of no earthly account, whatever, and that there was no telling at that time where said Allsman was—whether dead or alive. McNeil's answer was, that "Allman was a good Union man, and they would have to die between the hours of ten and one o'clock to-morrow." The kind and sympathizing citizen, seeing he could have no influence with the hardened wretch, left him. A petition was also gotten up for the purpose of having the execution postponed ten days, thinking that by seeing Gen. Schofield, who was then in command of the Department of the Missouri, he might be prevailed upon to stay the execution altogether. Several prominent Union men, some of whom afterwards held important county offices, were asked to sign the petition, but all to no purpose—the men ought to die, and die they should.

One man was told, when asked to sign it, that the men were innocent, and that he ought to sign it; but he refused, saying that if they were innocent, it would be a lesson to rebels; and this from a man who professed to be a christian. Great God! is that christianity? If so deliver us from all such.

We will now proceed. Without an order, or previous design all business ceased, and all offices closed. Gloom, horror, and anguish were depicted upon almost every countenance. A few heartless souls were indifferent, manifesting no sympathy or pity for the condemned, and no interest in the proceedings. A few others were jubilant and merry, as though they were going to some great fandango or wedding feast. Ten "rebels" were to be shot! and this to them was joy enough for one day. They were drunk with excitement, and rejoiced that they were to have the pleasure of seeing ten of their fellow men sent into eternity within the next half hour. As the procession passed the residence of Mr. Joseph McPheters, (one of the condemned prisoners being his nephew) the atmosphere was made to resound with the heart rending shrieks of relatives gathered there. The procession moved on to the fatal spot. As it neared the place, a little boy of some twelve summers—motherless—was seen to spring from one of the coffins and pass out through the file of soldiers unobstructed. He had heard in the morning that his father was condemned to be shot on that day, and had hurried to the city for the purpose of gazing on his loved face and form once more, and receiving from him his dying blessing. He reached the jail as the prisoners were being brought forth, and strange to say, was permitted by Federal clemency (?) to accompany his father to his execution. But ere he reached the designated spot his heart failed him. He could not witness the death throes of his innocent father, or see himself made an orphan in a cold, cruel world, under a tyranical government and in an unfeeling age. With a heart crushed he returned to the city, there to await the mortal remains of his last earthly protector.

The Fair grounds were reached; the prisoners were ordered to dismount—guards were placed over them—the coffins were transferred to the wing of the amphitheatre, and placed in a semi-circle. The prisoners were then marched between a double file of soldiers and seated each upon the head of his coffin. A file of sixty soldiers, ten to each man, took their station in front some ten paces distant. The Provost Marshal, Wm. Strachan, accompanied by a clergyman, entered the space between the prisoners and file of soldiers, and ordered the prisoners to approach his immediate presence. He read to them the sentence of condemnation, and his order of execution, both of which were signed by Brig. Gen. John McNeil. He then shook hands with the prisoners, severally asking forgivness for the part he took in their execution, claiming to be acting under the orders of his superior. Only two of them spoke during the ceremony of reading and parting, on the part of the Provost. One attempted to show that he was innocont of violating his parole, (of which he was charged) but one of his comrades stopped him, saying, "Boys, it is too late—let's be off." The clergyman then offered a few words of religious instruction, pointing them to God as their only hope, and to Christ as their only savior; reminding those of them who were professed christians of the promises of God to be with them in the valley and the shadow of death, and offering in the name of Christ, salvation to the rest upon repentence toward God and faith in Jesus Christ, witnessing the persistent thief upon the cross, having obtained pardon in the hour of death. Then, with the prisoners kneeling around him he offered to God a simple prayer in their behalf, that he would be with them in the death struggle and that, through the merits of a crucified Redeemer they might find an entrance into everlasting rest.

Arising from their knees, he bade them adieu with a faltering voice; expressing the hope to meet them in a better world. During these ceremonies they manifested no feeling of fear. They were calm in the very presence of death, and some expressed joy in the prospect of deliverence from the ills of the present life. None of them expressed any fear of death. The clergyman having passed out, they were ordered back to their coffins, upon which they took their seats facing the file of soldiers. Blinds were offered them, but all refused, wishing to meet death with their eyes open and uncovered. The officer in command of the soldiers who were to do the work of execution, advanced and reminded the prisoners, first, of the rebellion and its results upon them personally; and then the soldiers of their duty and its reward. Silence reigned one long minute—then the command—"make ready!" Not a prisoner moved, nor was there in all that vast throng a sound heard. Again the command—"take aim!" Not a muscle quivered in the countenances of the prisoners, but sympathizing hearts beat loud and quick. Again the command—"fire!" There was a confused report of firearms, but above it was heard the screams of heart agony, and ten men lay weltering in their own blood. Two were killed, the others mortally wounded. Of the two killed, one was Capt. Sidner—only one ball had struck him, passing directly through his heart. As Capt. Sidner was sitting upon his coffin he presented a most striking picture for an artist's pencil. He was neatly dressed in black cloth with white linen and vest, his hair of a jet black, was smoothly combed and hanging down upon his shoulders. He had requested the soldiers to aim at his heart, and as the command was given to "take aim," he raised his hand and placed it gently upon his breast, and then gracefully removed it to a recumbent position. The wounded were speedily relieved of their sufferings by means of side arms. The bodies were then coffined, placed in the wagons and returned to the city, where they were delivered up to their friends, who bore them to their respective homes for interment. On the way back the warm blood could be seen dripping from the rough pine boxes and wagons, as they passed through the streets toward the court house, where they were unloaded like so many dead brutes, and placed on the steps—after which they were taken away by their friends, as above stated.

Their names were, Capt. T. A. Sidner, F. M. Lear, E. Lake, J. Y. McPheters, Thos. Humstead, Willis Baker, H. Smith, H. Hendron, J. M. Wade, and M. Bixler. Mr. Baker, was quite an old gray haired man, supposed to have been well on to sixty years of age; so it will be seen that his murderers cheated him out of but few years, as his gray locks and tottering form, were assurances enough that he had but a short time longer to remain on earth, however, it was hard, very hard, that an aged man like him should be deprived of life in the manner he was. And one of his murderers is still living, a curse to the community in which he resides. However he is fast appoaching his end, when he will without doubt receive his just dues, for the Almighty, in his infinite goodness will deal justly with him.

Concerning the man Allsman, for whom the prisoners were professedly executed, Mr. R. G. Horton, in his "Youth's History of the Great Civil War," makes quite a historical blunder. He says, on page 249, in giving an account of the execution: "Afterwards, the man Allsman turned up alive and well. He had been absent of his own will and motive." There are two errors here. First, the man Allsman was not absent of his own will and motive. He was captured and taken from the city by troops under the command of Col. Joe Porter. Secondly, he has not turned up alive and well, at least in *these* parts. Let us be true to history.

## ARREST, IMPRISONMENT AND TREATMENT OF COL. JEFF. JONES, OF CALLAWAY COUNTY, MO., AS RELATED BY HIMSELF.

CALLAWAY Co., Mo., Aug. 1, 1867.

GRIFFIN FROST, Esq.—*Dear Sir:*—I have just been informed that you are about to publish a work, bearing the title of "Frost's Camp and Prison Journal," and that you want to speak of me, and my trials therein, and that you wish me to forward to you the facts of my imprisonment. Thanking you for this token of respect, and wishing you success in your new enterprise, which I highly commend, I send you the following: Yours respectfully,

J. F. JONES.

In the early part of September, 1861, I was at the head of a pretty large organization in Callaway county, the object of which was to prevent the invasion of said county by the Federals under command of Gen. John B. Henderson, then hovering upon its western border. After drilling my men for some ten days, and keeping a heavy picket near the enemy, I moved my main force near his Head Quarters. I then sent the General a note under a flag of truce, declaring it our purpose to suffer no invasion of our county, or its occupancy by Federal troops; that in passing through, when occasion required, they should molest none of our citizens, and pay full value for all they received, and that henceforward every guarantee to person and property in the Constitution and under the law should be religiously kept and observed toward all the inhabitants of said county, and also toward every man in my command from any other county. Told him if these terms were accepted, and he would pledge the faith of the government to their observance, I would disband my forces, go home and remain quiet, otherwise the strength of our forces should decide the issue, and the consequences would rest with him. He accepted the terms and I disbanded. Some of the papers denounced Henderson therefor in very severe terms. He sought relief in various exparte publications, and finding it not, he dispatched a messenger to me, under a flag of truce, requesting a personal interview on the 8th of October. I met him. He said he wanted the terms of our compromise so changed as to *relieve* him. I told him I had no power then to make any changes and declined doing so. This exasperated him, and the tearing up of the track of the North Missouri railroad in December following, afforded him the desired pretext for my arrest and his revenge. Immediately after this event, about one hundred of his cavalry came to my house, arrested me, searched my premises, took my arms and ammunition, an extra carriage and span of horses, and everything else they wanted, and since which time I have never been able to find a line touching our compromise, except one letter. I was taken to Mexico, Audrain county—his then Head Quarters—put into a dirty, cold prison, and for three days and nights was almost entirely without food, fire and bedding. During which time no interview was allowed me, and only once did I get to see his "Royal Highness," and their only to be told, *that he never had made any compromise with me at all.*

While this was going on, three regiments of cavalry—one of them "Dutch," and another, the 8th Ohio, were dispatched to quarter upon my family, eat up our provision and provender, and to carry off what they could not eat, and well did they do their work. After staying in mid winter a couple of days, they left, taking three or four wagons and teams (one a four horse) and all my riding horses and brood mares, and every piece of plow gear on the place, saddles, bridles, &c. In March following I was taken to Danville in Montgomery county, tried by a Military Commission, and a short time after the trial was over, I was boxed up in a stock car and taken to St. Charles, and turned over to old Krekel and his Dutch, where I remained for several months, before the finding of the Court was made known to me. It acquitted me from having violated the terms of the compromise. Halleck then ordered that I should be released on giving bond and taking the oath, which I refused to do upon the grounds: first, upon principle, and second, that they had no right or power to add or append any other condition to the compromise. Here the matter hung until they finally agreed to take my individual bond for ten thousand dollars, conditioned only, that I should not leave the counties of Callaway and Audrain, without a written permit from the commander of the nearest post, and that I should report when required to do so, in writing, by the commanding General. By the terms of this bond and a certificate given, I was thenceforth to be protected in person and property, and exempted from arrest. I gave this, came home, and found devastation, and from that day it seemed as if I was to be the sport of every upstart and vandal who could muster a force (whether a brigade or squad, was immaterial) and every one swore I had violated my bond, and forfeited my property, and the work of searching my premises and carrying away, or stealing, as you choose to term it, began.

All wanted the honor to *see*, to search, to seize, to insult, and to force me to feed, clothe and furnish transportation for the Federal army in North Missouri. Every spring I would be allowed to come home and fit up for farming, but just before, or about the time I would get my crop in some "necessity" would arise for my arrest, and all my stock, harness, &c., confiscated.

In May, 1864, without charges, or a moment's notice, my entire family and self were seized, under an order of banishment South, and without money, clothing, bedding, or any thing else, or an opportunity allowed to secure such, we were forced off to St. Louis, where my wife, nine children, and a governess, were taken to one prison, and myself and eldest son to another. Here we were kept until Gen. Schofield, through the interference of friends, who followed us in the course of a few weeks, released my wife, children and teacher, and allowed them to return home, to share in part with the vandals in possession, who had everything advertised for sale.

About the close of the year, after having been tantalized again and again with notices to get ready for banishment on a particular day, I was paroled to go home for a short time, and, as usual, just as I was about through planting, very soon in May 1864, I was seized and after being exhibited around for awhile, was taken to St. Louis, and there, as you know, kept in confinement until about the last of July 1865, without trial, without charges, or a sight even, of the authorities, and after losing in weight 152 pounds from a frame of 265, I was released, on depositing with the authorities one thousand dollars, and giving bond in the sum of five thousand, and to report when called for. J. J.

The above, comes to us from a well known, highly esteemed, old citizen of Missouri, whose character for truth and veracity is unimpeachable, and whose acquaintance we made within the walls of Gratiot street prison in the summer of 1864. His is one case out of tens of thousands in Missouri, where personal liberty, property, health, and even life became subservient to petty jealousies, political differences, personal spite, or to gratify that "brief authority" which was characteristic of the "loyal" stay-at-home soldiery of that State, and who proved so often a disgrace to the uniform they sometimes wore.

## HORRIBLE ATROCITIES—EMBRACING THE MURDER OF MAJ. OWEN, OF MARION COUNTY, GABRIEL CLOSE AND BLACK TRIPLETT, OF PLATTE COUNTY, AND ALSO LASLEY, PRICE AND RIDGEWAY, OF MONROE COUNTY, MO.,

About the 1st of September, 1861, John L. Owen, Captain of a Company of six months men, (sworn into the Missouri State service about the middle of June,) started on his way to join Gen. Price. Having been promoted to Major, he returned home on the 6th of December. After which time he had no company, nor part of a company—nor was he in any way connected with a company. He was opposed to bushwhacking, and always tried to avoid trouble by keeping out of the way of Federals, and for months he never left his mother's house, either by night or day. However, they had their spies, who watched him with an assiduity which was worthy of a better cause, and discovered by some means or other, he never left the house, and these same spies were two men, whom he had especially befriended. Then the soldiers went in search of him, but failed in their efforts to find him. After the first searching—which took place several weeks before they succeeded in capturing him—he never slept in his own house, but laid out on his own and his mother's premises. He had his own provision which his wife cooked and carried to him, when he could not go for it himself, and in this manner he lived some four or five weeks, sleeping in such places as were deemed the safest from his pursuers, and receiving his meals at such times as he deemed it most prudent to obtain them.

And now comes the capture and the cruel sequel. On the 8th day of June, before the family had risen in the morning, the house was surrounded by Militia soldiers, and the family were aroused by their knocking for admittance. His mother, her two sons, Asbury and William, and his wife and child, were the only inmates of the house at the time. The soldiers entered, took both Asbury and William prisoners, and after searching the house, carried their prisoners away, still keeping a guard around the house. Persons who saw them estimated their number at about three hundred. They were accompanied by their guides, rushed through the fields, and dashed over the meadow, where the Major had slept the night before, and in a little cluster of bushes, not more than two or three hundred yards from the house, they found the poor man alone, unarmed and defenseless—which the cowardly fiends knew before they ventured there, for they never showed cruelty to any, save those who were defenseless—in the presence of those who were prepared to defend themselves, they were as submissive and yielding as possible. They added another leaf to their wreath of victories, by capturing this poor man alone, who quietly gave himself up, without offering any resistance, relying upon their magnanimity as soldiers, to treat him as a prisoner under their protection. Oh, if it were possible, with pen, to tell the deafening yells they uttered when they discovered him. They took him to the house. His wife was greatly troubled when she saw him in their custody, but she like her husband, relied too much upon their leniency to a prisoner under their protection, to think that they would murder him in the cruel and fiendish manner they afterwards did. They all halted at the fence and obtained a drink of water, while they questioned the Major as to who stayed with him. They asked him several questions, and among others where his company was? He told them in a polite manner that he had no company—they replied, he was a liar, that they knew he *did* have a company. His mother and wife then corroborated his statement by declaring that he had no company. They made no distinction—no respect for females—but called them liars, and insisted that he did have a company, for they had been told so, and he had to tell where it was. The wife and mother again told them that he had no company. They then said, "take him away from these women, and he does not tell where his company is concealed we will hang him." He told them as they started that if they would treat him as a prisoner of war he should have no fears.

His poor wife, fearing that they might harm him followed them for about a quarter of a mile, imploring them in piteous accents, to spare her husband—that they should not take an innocent man's life. They assured her that they would not kill him, and told her to go back home, and come to Palmyra next day, and she could see him. That seemed to satisfy her, and she went home. They did not proceed a half mile further, until they killed him. From the best information obtained upon the subject of the murder it was conducted as follows: They made him sit down upon a log which was lying close to a fence; they then tied his arms across his breast, and his elbows back to the fence, so that he could not move; tied him with hickory bark—and then proceeded to take the life of one, they were well assured, was an innocent man to gratify their fiendish propensities to see human blood flow. They left him there, shot down, like a wild beast of prey, and proceeding to one of the neighbors, told them what a hellish deed they had perpetrated, and if he had any friends they had better go dig a hole, and throw him in. They sent his wife word, that they had shot her husband, and where she might find him. The poor fellow was found bound in the manner described, and his remains so mutilated that his features were not recognizable.

One ball entered his face just at the left side of the nose, and passed through his head; one through his collar bone; two through his breast, not more than two inches apart, passing entirely through his body, and lodging in the fence behind him. His left arm was shattered from the elbow down. The murderers stood so near him that his clothes were scorched by the powder. The unfeeling wretches sent his wife a cartridge, with a message, that they had put eight balls like it, through him. His body had also been pierced by a bayonet. Can any conscientious, christian person, of whatever political persuasion they may be, read of an atrocity like the above, and not feel their hearts throb with compunctuous regret, that such hellish fiends were ever allowed to stalk the earth, perpetrating such fiendish deeds, wearing the uniform of soldiers. Can they listen to the wails of woe, called forth by the "agonies of bereaved fondness" and not utter a wish, that these consummate scoundrels may yet reap their reward?

Here is also another furnished us by Mr. A. V. Combs, a nephew to one of the murdered men, which we give in his own words:

"On Sunday, July the 20th, 1862, I started to visit my aunt, who lived near Huntsville, Marion county, Mo. I arrived at my destination, a few minutes after the family had started to church, accompanied by two young ladies, and the same number of gentlemen from the neighborhood. I had only been there a short time when a squad of Missouri State Militia, (11th regiment) who were camped at the bridge, over Salt river, about a mile distant, came down to the house and demanded their dinner. At that time myself and two children, were the only white persons on the place. I was placed immediately under guard, and while dinner was in the course of preparation, the brave soldiers amused themselves by sticking their bayonets into the walls, breaking the clock, and committing other soldier like deeds.

While they were eating dinner, Mr. and Mrs. Lasley, Mr. James Ridgeway, Messrs. James and Thaddeus Price, together with three young ladies arrived. The boys were allowed to come in the house and get a drink, but Mr. Lasley was kept back. They were all taken about one hundred yards from the house, but Mr. T. Price who in the meantime was released. The others were shot and bayoneted several times. The soldiers then left for camp, and we then proceeded to take care of the bodies. Mr. Lasley lived about forty minutes, Mr. Ridgeway lived an hour, but Price was dead when we got to him.

These three persons were of good standing and left many friends to mourn their cruel butchery. After we took Mr. Lasley to the house, I pulled a piece of his shirt about two inches long out of one of the bayonet wounds. Mr. L. left a wife and two children. Mr. Price, a widowed mother, two sisters and two brothers. Mr. Ridgeway was the only surviving one of twelve children, his father and mother yet living. Already had mother earth taken into its embrace eleven beloved forms, and yet their hearts had not been sufficiently lacerated, but the only darling spared to them, must be wantonly, fiendishly murdered, and the wounds of their hearts, scarcely healed over, be torn open, and made to bleed afresh. But life is at best, nothing but a chain of many sorrows and deaths. Could any of my readers have been with me at that scene of horror and have seen those three innocent men, weltering in their blood, I am sure their hearts must have sickened and they would have turned (as I did) away, shuddering at the thought, of living in a country, where the perpetrators of such atrocities were allowed to go unpunished."

Here is still another tale of horror, the particulars of which we glean from the Platte county (Mo.) Reveille.

"Two citizens of Platte county, Gabriel Close and Black Triplett, were arrested in the early part of the war, by a squad of Col. Morgan's men who were stationed at Weston. They were arrested at Mrs. Kuykendalls, and were charged with being bushwhackers. Whether the charge was true or false, we know not. Securely bound and gagged the prisoners were started for Weston. At Bee creek bridge, the squad halted and determined to murder the two men. The fiends in human shape, who disgraced the uniform they wore, told the prisoners the result of their deliberations, and proceeded to carry their hellish design into effect. The bound and helpless victims were told to run for their lives. Triplett refused and was shot, the muzzles of the guns and pistols being so close that his hair, beard and flesh were so horribly burned as to render him scarcely recognizable. Close attempted to run, but mired in the treacherous bed of the creek, when the brutal soldiers deliberately fired charge after charge into his body, after which they thrust bayonets through his head. Not content with this monstrous barbarism, they dabbled their hands in the blood of the murdered men and wrote in great uncouth letters on each side of the bridge, "U. S." The horrible letters are still there. Kind hands, often attempted to obliterate this sign of blood and murder, but to day it is as plain as when it was made, by those brutal wretches. Time and the elements refuse to destroy the letters. The name of Morgan, the commander of the regiment, is faithfully preserved by the people of this county.

He burned the town and laid the court house in ashes. In the corner stone of the new one which has lately been erected, has been placed a parchment recording this fact. Wherever he goes God's wrath will follow him, and future generations will speak of James G. Morgan with a shudder."

# CONCLUSION.

A few more words to our readers, who have followed us thus far in our attempt to show forth the treatment of Southern prisoners, and we have done. For a long time after the capitulation between Gens. Lee and Grant, the Confederates had the horrors of Andersonville and of Salisbury, so clamorously dinned into their ears, that they found they could not, and at the peril of their lives they dared not offer anything by way of palliation or defense. The sense of *justice* was swallowed up in the loud clamor for *vengeance*. The poor, subjugated, down-trodden people of the South, were forbidden to utter anything to show that there were two sides to that momentous question.

There was a committee appointed after a passage of a series of resolutions in the House of Representatives "to investigate the treatment of prisoners, held by the Confederate authorities during the late rebellion." That committee consists of the following named gentlemen who are earnestly soliciting communications from every one who can show any mistreatment on the part of the Confederate authorities :—John C. Shanks, Wm. A. Pile, Abner C. Harding, A. F. Stenins, and Wm. Mungen.

An effort was attempted by one of the minority in Congress, to make the testimony complete by extending the investigation to the Northern prisons, and inquiring into the treatment of Southern prisoners confined therein. But this was negatived by the majority, for well they knew that they *dared* not allow an investigation—that it would drag to light such scenes of horror—so cruel, dark and thrilling in their nature, that it would stamp disgrace upon the perpetrators, so black, deep and lasting, that it never will be erased. But a revolution will take place, and now we are beginning to hear of deeds of cruelty from Elmira, Point Lookout, Alton, Johnson's Island, and many other places too numerous to mention.

We clip the following from the La Crosse Democrat, written by a gentleman in Louisiana, a member of company "C," 1st regiment Missouri Infantry. The facts in the case are given by Mr. Pomeroy in his bold masterly style, with a communication from the St. Louis Times.

On the 9th day of April, 1865, he was captured at Fort Blakeley, Ala., with others, sent to Ship Island, and landed upon that desolate strip of Gulf-washed territory, where the sand was knee deep at every step. For six weeks our informant was a prisoner, at the end of which time he was released on parole, at Vicksburg. The prisoners were unprovided with tents or shelter from the storms of rain and wind, seven of which occurred during the six weeks referred to, one of them lasting forty-eight hours, during which time 3,000 prisoners were compelled to stand without food or shelter, suffering terribly from cold and hunger. False alarms were frequently given by the guards, at night, and indiscriminate and reckless shooting would follow, keeping the helpless Confederates in continual alarm. At sunset the men were compelled to lie down, and no matter how urgent might be the cause, were not allowed to raise their hands until morning except at the risk of being shot. The rations provided were three ounces of pickled pork and a hard tack per day, sometimes a little mush was added, which the poor fellows were compelled to receive in their hat crowns, if they were so fortunate as to be the possessors of such an article. Notwithstanding they were served with such horrible and scanty fare, they were compelled to carry wood on their shoulders a distance of some six miles to add to the comfort of the niggers in blue guarding them. Sick or well the unfortunate captives were compelled to "tote" the wood, and if from weakness or exhaustion, they lagged in their pace, the bayonets of the negroes spurred them on, or a merciful bullet ended their sufferings.

During the first part of the stay of our informant, news was received of the killing of A. Lincoln, Esq. The officers in charge informed the helpless prisoners that if they gave any signs of joy, were found laughing, smiling, or in any apparent sport or mirth the offender should be immediately shot. We should have thought it would have been impossible in such a hell to have raised a laugh even at such tidings! Talk of Andersonville! The sufferings endured by the unhappy "rebel" captives of the Federal government, have no parallel outside the regions of the damned!

A Confederate officer gives the St. Louis Times some facts relative to the prisons at Nashville and Louisville. He was captured in Middle Tennessee, in August, 1863, and sent with twenty-three others, after being stripped of all valuables, to Nashville, in charge of a Capt. World, of Federal General Morgan's division. The officer gives us some particulars of the treatment endured by him and his fellow captives, as follows:

"While we were in his keeping all the indignities that a petty tyrant, elevated to the office of jailer, could devise, were heaped upon us. Locked up at night, eighteen men in a cell so small that we could not all lie down. This was in August and probably you can imagine the purity and sweetness of the night air when you learn that the night buckets holding the excrements of the prisoners were removed but every other day.

"The wing in the penitentiary in which we were placed was overrun with vermin of all description, from rats to body-lice; chinches and bugs swarmed in the walls in lumps—every little hole in the plastering was full, and the cracks in the floor were alive with the same plagues. Nor was it the prisoner's fault, as it usually is, as there were no facilities for personal cleanliness—no washing places for bathing the person or boiling the clothes, which alone will kill the body-lice and its eggs.

"Let us view the prison at night after taps. In the halls and rooms, lying so thick on the bare floor that the sore and weary sleeper cannot rest his aching bones, are packed hundreds of soldiers. Fortunate are those who have secured a plank near the window. How anxiously they wish for the morning, when they may exchange the close foul air of the cell for the pure air of the prison yard. One small hydrant supplies the water, around which crowd the sleep-worn prisoners to perform their scanty ablutions. Take a long draught of its water, for you must wait until half past nine o'clock before you can sit down to Uncle Samuel's table.

"The signal is given. At last it is our turn to crowd into the small room, where on tables covered with the slops of those just gone out, is placed a row of tin cups, in them a vile decoction made by pouring luke warm water over the dregs of what has probably been called coffee by prison books. By the side of the tin cup, thrown to you as a farmer throws corn to his hogs, you find a piece of bread from three fourths to an inch thick cut across a common loaf of bread. This alone constitutes your breakfast; eat and be grateful, if you can, to the best government, &c., that feeds its prisoners so luxuriantly.

"The long, weary day drags along. An inward monitor tells

you that dinner-time has come and passed, but no dinner for you. At five o'clock, the order is given to "fall in for supper." Promptly the prisoners obey, and in two files approach a table in the yard, where are piled pieces of bread and chunks of meat, of not more than three ounces in weight. As a special favor you may, perhaps, dip your bread in the pot in which the meat was cooked.

The Louisville Prison, as far as quarters were concerned, was a little better than Nashville. There was something wrong in the commissary department, as it was so common an occurrence as to become the rule, that prisoners went from twelve to twenty-four hours without anything to eat. I was there twenty-four hours before my piece of bread of Nashville dimensions, with a piece of meat of similar size was thrown to me by a filthy, greasy negro. If the prisoner had anything to hold it, he was served, as he passed from one door out by the other, with half a pint of some dark decoction called coffee. If he was so unfortunate as to have lost his cup, he washed his stale bread and rancid bacon down with water from the cistern."

The horrors of the prison-ships and sugar-houses, the dreadful cages where British malignity and cruelty were wreaked on American rebels who followed Washington in '76, sink into insignificance beside the cruelties perpetrated by the minions of Lincoln on the American rebels who bravely followed the glorious leadership of grand old Robert E. Lee, and immortal "Stonewall" Jackson, in 1861. Our Radical friends propose to investigate those hideous pages of rank injustice, culpable negligence, and shameless tyranny which should have been a sealed book at the close of the damnable war, but forgot, however, in their ferocity, that there was two sides to each page of the volume, and that both would be read, Loyalty to the contrary notwithstanding."

They still howl for more victims to appease their thirst for human slaughter. And it seems they are determined to do their worst in defiance of the opinions and remonstrances of the all great and good men everywhere. Mortuary statistics have brought to light the astonishing fact that the per centage of deaths among the Confederate captives, in the rich, well-fed, and teeming prisons of the North, was absolutely greater than that of the Federal prisoners in the blockaded, exhausted, suffering and starving South.

The New York Tribune disclaiming any intention of endorsing the charges against Federal authorities calls for enquiry and investigation. And from a report furnished by that organ, made by a committee of the Confederate Congress, during the last winter of the war, furnishes good evidence of the cruelties practiced at Point

Lookout, Fort McHenry, Fort Delaware, Johnson's Island, Camp Chase, Camp Morton, Camp Douglas, Elmira, Alton, and the prisons of St. Louis, together with the Ohio Penitentiary, at Columbus. Of the 3,500 prisoners sent from the North to Savannah, only 3,028 were delivered, the other 372 having died on the passage. Just in a single train of cars between Elmira and Baltimore, 67 deaths occurred. The details of the condition of these poor prisoners, on their arrival at Savannah are too revolting to be credited, were they not fully authenticated. In some cases the authorities of the Federal prisons treated the prisoners kindly and humanely, but the long and fearful list to the contrary leads to the inference that these were the exceptions and not the rule.

The same paper quotes the evidence, given under oath, of Capt. William H. Sebring, in regard to his treatment in the St. Louis prisons, of which the following is an extract:

"Two of us, A. C. Grimes and myself, were carried out into the open air in the prison yard, on the 25th of December, 1863, and handcuffed to a post. Here we were kept all night in sleet, snow, and cold. We were relieved in the day time, but again brought to the post and handcuffed to it in the evening—and thus we were kept all night until the 2d of January, 1864. I was badly frost-bitten and my health was much impaired."

The question next arises, after this array of testimony—the validity of which no one can doubt—who were the cause of all these prison murders? these shocking barbarities? Who starved the prisoners at Johnson's Island, Ship Island, Fort Delaware, &c? Or, if there were any starvations at Andersonville, Libby, Salisbury, &c., upon whom rests *all* the fearful responsibility? We answer emphatically, Lincoln, Stanton and that radical clique, who had it in their power to end all these sufferings and outrages by means of the cartel established for the exchange of prisoners. Instead of improving these facilities—instead of accepting the magnanimous offer of the Confederate authorities to this object, their stubborn, malignant refusal, continued the suffering of these men. Let the radical Congress commence the investigation of this matter if they dare, and they will be met at the very beginning by the frightful forms of these victims, whose frightful cries for vengeance will rend the very heavens.

Our task, now nearly done, would be but half finished, should we close without paying a tribute to the brave Confederate heroes, who perished in the conflict, covered with glory, or, those who died martyrs (in the loathsome prisons) to the glorious cause they had espoused. They have all won for themselves unfading laurels. Each forms a star in the galaxy of their country's glory. Like Horace, they have reared for themselves "monuments more enduring than brass , and loftier than the regal structure of the pyramids, which neither the raging storm, nor the fury of the impotent north wind can overthrow; nor the countless series of years, nor the flight of ages—*non omnis morair.*" The heroes among the Confederate dead stand together in solid phalanx, and with a halo of glory clustering around their immortal brows, a banner waves over them bearing the "strange device, *Excelsior!*" Sleep on brave ones, we would not pluck a single laurel from your glittering coronals, which were won by your animated appeals and defying bravery. May proud and existing monuments be upreared to thee.

"Let the mighty oaken lever,
Lift the blocks and plant them well;
Last they will till earth dissever,
Till the trump of Gabriel."

# DR. J. W. GRAIG,
## Eye and Ear Surgeon,
### QUINCY, ILLINOIS

Dr. Craig, having had the advantage of the New York Colleges and Hospitals, also Office Practice with some of the best Eye and Ear Surgeons in the world, is now treating with great success all curable diseases of the Eye and Ear, as thousands he has cured, can testify. In the treatment of Granulated Lids and all external diseases of the eye, he positively has no superior in the West.

**Cross Eyes made straight, and Artificial Eyes inserted, &c.**

☞ Office No. 39, Fifth street, near South East corner of Public Square, Quincy, Illinois.

---

## HUGHES'
# MISSOURI HAND CORN PLANTER.
### A SOUTHERN INVENTION.

This Machine so well known through Missouri, Illinois and Iowa, was Invented and Patented in 1855 and 1857, in Palmyra, Missouri, and Manufactured by its Inventor, up to the time the War broke out, in August, 1861. After his home was invaded by the enemy, he took the Southern field, since which time his Machine and Rights have been an article of public plunder. The demand being so great that many parties have been making them without the right to do so.

But peace again prevails and the Inventor is again in the Agricultural field, and will take pleasure in supplying all his old friends and others with his celebrated CORN PLANTER. together with any other Implements that they may want, from a Pitchfork to a Reaper, as he has opened a

### General Agricultural Agency House,

In Quincy, Illinois. His Planters will also in future be made in Quincy, and sold for the Spring of 1868, at the following prices

| | |
|---|---|
| Retail (single machine) | $5 00 |
| Wholesale, per doz., 20 per cent off | 48 00 |
| do 50 do 25 do | 187 50 |
| do 100 do 40 do | 300 00 |
| do 500 do 45 do | 1,375 00 |

The attention of Dealers and Traveling Agents and particularly called to the above price list—no business pays so well. Send for Circulars to

QUINCY, ILL.]     D. W. HUGHES, Inventor.

---

## D. S. CHERRY,
### 48 Hampshire St., Opposite Market House,
### QUINCY, ILLINOIS,
### Dealer in
# DRUGS, MEDICINES & CHEMICALS
**Fancy and Toilet Articles, Sponges, Brushes, Perfumery, &c.**
### CARBON OIL AND LAMPS,

Physicians' Prescriptions carefully compounded, and orders answered with care and Dispatch. Farmers and Physicians from the country, will find my stock of Medicines complete, and of the best quality.

## W. McINTIRE & BRO.,
## Wholesale and Retail Grocers,
### NO. 67, HAMPSHIRE STREET,
### Quincy, - - - - Illinois.

Country merchants and others wishing anything in the Grocery line, will find it greatly to their advantage to give them a call before purchasing elsewhere. They always keep on hand a complete and extensive assortment of Groceries, Provision, and **LIQUORS,** of the best quality. Highest price paid for country produce.

---

## FRANKE'S
# CLOTHING HOUSE

### WHOLESALE AND RETAIL,

### 63 HAMPSHIRE STREET, 63

(ABOVE THIRD.)

### QUINCY,           ILLINOIS.

---

### C. GOLL,
# Dyer & Scourer,
**West side of Third street, between Maine & Hampshire streets, Quincy, Ill.**

Gents' Coats, Vests and Pants dyed and cleaned with neatness and dispatch. Ladies' Silk and Woolen Dresses and Shawls dyed and cleaned in a superior manner. All work warranted.

# INDEX.

Abbeville, MS 14
Abshire, John F. 189
Adams, —— 53
Allen, —— 57
Allen, Dr. —— 98
Allen, Lt. —— (CS) 205
Allen, Lt. —— (US) 243
Allen, Capt. R. C. 175, 177
Allsman, Andrew 282, 283, 288
Alton Prison vii, 34, 35, 38, 40, 76, 78, 81, 84, 87, 88, 106, 108–118, 121, 122, 126, 127, 128, 130, 142, 143, 149, 150, 154, 159, 160, 176, 179, 181, 182, 183, 184–245, 299, 302
Anderson, —— 237–238
Anderson, "Bloody Bill" 180–181
Anderson, Samuel 92
Anderson, Maj. W. J. 69
Andersonville Prison (GA) vii, 11, 117, 257, 264, 267, 298, 299, 302
Andrew County (MO) 135
Arkadelphia, AR 68
Arkansas County (AR) 18
Arkansas Post, AR 18
Arkansas River 17, 18, 64
Arkansas Troops 1st Cav (USA) 23
Armstrong, —— 147
Asay, Kate 154
Athens, MO, Battle of 2
Atkins, —— 147
Audrain County (MO) 148, 150, 165, 178, 190, 290, 291
Augusta, GA 47
Austin, AR 54, 57
Ayres, Mrs. —— 278

Bacon, —— 126
Baird, Lt. —— 282
Baker, Dr. —— 174
Baker, Willis 288
Baltimore, MD 302
Bamburg, Billy 201, 224
Banks, Thomas 2
Barnes, Sgt. —— 189–190
Barr, Capt. Samuel 36, 38, 45, 48
Barry County (MO) 2
Bates, Moses 38

Batesville, AR 40, 57, 61, 120
Bayse, John A. 182, 199–200
Beall, Col. John 230
Beauregard, Gen. P. G. T. 240
Belcher, —— 19, 20
Bell, Dr. —— 53
Belle Isle Prison (VA) vii, 117, 264, 267
Beltzhoover, Capt. —— 104
Bently, —— 39–40
Bernard, —— 116
Berry, —— 192
Bixler, Morgan 288
Black, Col. —— 74
Blair, Maj. Gen. Francis P. 39
Blannerhassett, Alice 206, 222
Blannerhassett, Mrs. —— 205–206, 216, 227, 237, 238, 239, 243
Blogden, Maj. G. 173
Boebush, —— 156
Bogue Filia Creek (MS) 16
Boone County (MO) 142
Boonville, MO 217
Boonville, MS 11
"Bottle Neck" the mail boy 81, 82
Boulware, Walter 3
Bowen, Capt. Charles 176
Bower's Mill, MO 72
Boyce, William 204
Boyd, Joseph 192, 206, 225
Boyd, Dr. —— 142, 179
Bradley, M. J. 266
Bradley, Mollie J. 278
Bradley, R. P. 117, 118, 119, 121, 244
Bragg, General Braxton 38–39, 72, 87, 88
Brandon, MS 48
Bransford, M. B. 81
Brasher, Maj. E. M. 84, 86, 87, 89, 90, 93
Brosheer, G. M. 246
Brown, —— (Arkansas) 67, 68
Brown, Lt. —— (Gratiot) 96
Brown, Surg. —— (Alton) 192, 207, 238
Brown, John 62
Bryant, Sue 172
Burbridge, Clinton 104, 106, 174, 198
Burns, Capt. —— (Capt. Charles C. Byrne) 42, 84, 88, 93–94, 119
Burr, —— 182

## INDEX.

Burrowville, AR 21, 22
Bury, Bessie 151, 153, 155, 178, 193, 194, 218, 221
Byggart, —— 177
Byrne, Sallie 175

C——, Capt. —— 48, 52, 54, 56
Caddo's Gap, AR 70
Cairo, IL 89
Caldwell, Capt. —— 96
Calhoun, Mrs. —— 39-40
Call, Mary 172
Callaway County (MO) 135, 289, 291
Calvert, Capt. —— 192, 204, 218, 241
Camp Chase (OH) 38, 77, 97, 107, 267, 302
Camp Douglas (IL) vii, 265-280, 302
Camp Morton (IN) vii, 77, 81, 84, 246-264, 302
Campbell, Mrs. —— 41
Campbell, John R. 221
Canton, MO 88, 89, 123
Canton, MS 15, 50
Cantrel, —— 122
Cape Girardeau, MO 86
Caples, Rev. William G. 2
Carlin, Col. John C. 82, 101, 119, 140, 174-175
Carney, —— 158
Carroll County (AR) 23
Carson, Lt. James A. 130, 132, 142
Carter, Capt. G. W. 150, 192, 195-196, 206
Cash River (AR) 53
Cassell, Miss —— 165
Cassville, MO 2, 3
Caudill, Col. David J. 266
Chancellorsville, VA, Battle of 45
Charleston, SC 40, 41, 227
Chillicothe, MO 74, 75, 77
Christian Brothers College 121
Cincinnati, OH 266
City Point, VA 39, 41, 43, 44
Clarendon, AR 20, 56
Cleavland, Rev. —— 124
Clemens, —— 283
Clifford, Samuel 79, 80, 82, 101, 127, 160, 161, 163, 201
Clifford, Mrs. —— 77
Clinton, AR 60, 62, 63
Clinton, Lt. Thomas G. 84
Close, Gabriel 293, 297
Cobbs, —— 232
Collier, —— 67

Colclazier, James A. 140
Columbia, SC 227
Columbus, OH 302
Coale, Lt. —— 102
Combs, —— 93
Combs, A. V. 296
Conklin, William 156, 158, 159, 160
Cooper, Capt. —— 243
Cooper County (MO) 172
Copeland, Brig. Gen. Joseph T. 193, 194, 200, 203, 206, 209
Copperheads 85
Corder, —— 207
Corinth, MS, Siege of 8-11
Cotter, Capt. —— 205
Couch, —— 24-25
Cox, Parson —— 53
Crane Creek (MO) 5
Creary, —— 21
Cross Hollows, AR 5, 22
Crow, —— 207
Crowly, Martha 74
Curtis, Maj. Gen. Samuel R. 14, 38
Cypress Creek (AR) 17

Dade County (MO) 3, 71
Danville, MO 290
Darr, Col. Joseph, Jr. 182
"David Tatum" (steamer) 113, 218
Davidson, —— 207, 208, 216
Davis, —— 178
Davis, Dr. —— 93
Davis, Jefferson 32, 196
Davis, Adj. William 1
Dawson, Capt. —— 126, 192, 204, 232
Dawson, Col. —— 102, 105
Demopolis, AL 47, 48, 50
Des Arc, AR 8, 20, 21, 53, 54
Desha County (AR) 17
Dobyns, Benjamin 149, 150, 153, 157, 166, 172, 174, 178, 182, 202, 220, 227, 277
Dodge, Maj. Gen. Grenville M. 223
Douglas, William M. 140
Douthett, Mr. —— 243
Douthett, Belle 243
Douthett, Nannie L. 195, 200, 207, 216, 222, 229, 234, 236
Droun, Mrs. —— 237, 243
Dryden, Judge John D. S. 125
Dudley, Dr. George W. 96, 154

# INDEX.

Duff, Maj. —— 56
Durdy, —— 174
Duvall's Bluff, AR 56
Dyer, —— 224
Dyhrenfurth, Lt. Robert St. G. 191

Eddyville, MS 13
Edmonds, Lt. —— 29
Edwards, Mrs. J. R. 69
Elder, Laura 80, 81, 116–117, 124, 152
Elliot, Joseph (AKA "Feminine Joe") 131, 132, 134, 141, 145, 146, 148, 153, 159, 178, 190, 193, 198, 201, 202, 205, 219, 224
Elm Spring, AR 7
Elmira Prison (NY) 299, 302
Emerson, MO 1
Evans, —— 21
Evans, Augusta J. 170

Fabius River (MO) 2
Farh, Lt. —— 203
Farmington, MS 8, 9
Farmington, MS, Engagement at 8
Fayette Springs, MS 13
Fayetteville, AR 5, 6, 7
"Feminine Joe" 137, 145–146, 149, 161, 178, 190
Fickle, Anna 189
Fink, Elder —— 2
Finney, —— 36
Flanigan, William 158
Flore, Dr. —— 138, 149
Florida, MO 2
Fornchell, —— 92–93, 127
Forrest, Lt. Gen. Nathan B. 185, 195
Fort Blakely, AL 299
Fort Delaware Prison 43, 44, 75, 109, 122, 125, 135, 147, 148, 158, 196, 216, 225, 302
Fort McHenry, MD 302
Fort Smith, AR 7, 64, 68
Fort Sumter, SC 80
Fortress Monroe, VA 44, 220, 223
Foster, Maj. Gen. John G. 41
Frankfort, MO 93
Freeman, Sallie 15, 50, 79
Fremont, Maj. Gen. John C. 165
French, David 165
Frost, Annie (daughter) 19, 102, 119, 123, 125, 126, 195, 239, 244
Frost, Col. Daniel (brother) 33, 85, 121, 153, 155–156, 158, 168

Frost, Brig. Gen. Daniel M. 79
Frost, Elizabeth (wife) 19–20, 30–31, 35, 39, 42, 50, 82, 88, 99, 119, 123, 133, 189–190, 191, 202, 210, 218, 239, 244
Frost, John (brother) 15, 50, 52, 76, 78, 81–82, 84, 88, 101, 108, 122, 125, 135, 143, 147, 158, 166, 196, 216
Frost, William P. (brother) 136, 150, 156, 202, 209, 227

Gadfly, MO 2
Gallagher, —— 198
Galvin, —— 225
Gasconade County (MO) 97
Gentry, —— 77, 84–85
Gibbs, Capt. —— 192, 207, 214, 226, 234, 239
Giles, —— 173
Glasgow, MO 2
Glasscock, Lucy 124
Glenn, Sgt. —— 31
Godfrey, Mrs. —— 51
Goggin, Mollie 187, 200, 207, 209, 210, 212, 218
Goode, Col. —— 56, 57, 58, 60, 65
Goode, Maj. —— 58, 60
Gowing, Lt. —— 96
Graham, Robert 165, 177
Grant, Lt. Gen. U. S. 87, 88, 191, 240, 247, 298
Gratiot Street Prison vii, 27–41, 75, 76–107, 110, 118–183, 247
"Graybeards" 32, 80, 166
Green, Charles 159, 160
Green, Joseph H. 134, 147, 173
Green, Brig. Gen. Martin E. 1, 7, 134
Greenfield, MO 3
Grenada, MS 14, 15, 16, 50
Grider, —— 174
Grier, John M. 283
Grimes, Absalom 119, 124, 135, 138–139, 140, 141, 152–153, 170, 173, 175, 205, 302
Guitar, Col. Odon 75
Gullet, Surg. —— 196, 207, 238
Gutzmiller, Miss —— 191, 235, 239

Halleck, Maj. Gen. Henry W. 91, 290
Hancock, Jane 170
Hanie, Miss —— 189, 200, 207, 222, 227
Hanie, Mrs. —— 187, 189, 200, 207, 217, 222, 227
Hannibal, MO 102, 124, 244

# INDEX.

Harding, Abner C. 298
Hardinge, Dr. James (George?) 130, 132, 136, 142, 147-148, 150, 153, 173
Harlow, Mary A. 172
Harris, —— 178
Harris, Brig. Gen. Thomas A. 2, 3
Harrison, —— (Mississippi) 51
Harrison, Judge —— (St. Louis) 140-141
Harrison, Cornelia 152, 171
Harrison, Dora 81, 152
Harvey, Capt. James M. 138, 158
Hawkins, Col. Ben 34
Hays, Mollie 193, 195
Helena, AR 14, 51, 52, 204
Helena, Attack on 52, 76, 140, 143
Henderson, Brig. Gen. John B. 289, 290
Henly, George 95
Henry County (MO) 172
Hermann, MO 97
Hicks, Lt. John 1, 5
Highly, —— 130
Hill, Capt. Jasper C. 77, 78, 86, 140, 141, 147, 172
Hindman, Maj. Gen. Thomas C. 14
Hobbs, Capt. —— 119
Holmes, Mrs. —— 74
Holmes, Newland 159, 163, 176
Holmes, Lt. Gen. Theophilus H. 63
Hood, Gen. John B. 191
Hooker, Maj. Gen. Joseph 45
Hope, Frank 196
Horton, R. G. 288
Hudson, Hiram (given as Hendron) 288
Humphrey, William T. 284
Humston, Thomas 284, 288
Hunt, Charles 132, 133, 136, 139, 149
Huntsville, MO 296

Indiana Troops
    54th Inf 251
    73rd Inf 251
Indianapolis, IN 42, 249
Ingalls, Sgt. A. O. (AKA "Killposey") 215, 223, 243
Iowa 133
Iowa Troops
    7th Inf 31, 32, 166
Ironton, MO 196
Island No. 10 194
Iuka, MS, Battle of 38

Ivans, —— 53
Izard County, AR 57

Jackson, MS 46, 49, 50
Jackson, Gen. Thomas J. "Stonewall" 12, 169, 301
Jayhawkers 5, 62
Jefferson City, MO 93, 136, 149, 182, 187, 189, 205, 227
Jeffries, William 5
"Joab Lawrence" (steamer) 199
Johnson, Capt. J. W. 36
Johnson, James 133
Johnson, James A. (father-in-law) 218, 244
Johnson County (MO) 172
Johnson's Island Prison (OH) 51, 102, 105, 122, 214, 299, 302
Johnston, Gen. Joseph E. 49, 50
Jones, —— 98
Jones, Sgt. —— 241
Jones, Haith 93
Jones, J. B. 174, 198
Jones, Col. Jeff 135, 142, 161, 165, 173, 175, 289-292
Jourdan, Dr. Victor S. 132

Kansas Troops
    10th Inf 157, 166
Keelan, James 176, 178
Kelly, Jarred 21, 22, 200
Kennard, Lt. —— 40
Kerrick, Stephen 106
Keyser, Capt. —— 194
Keytsville, MO 72
Kincaid, Col. George W. 31, 32, 34
King, —— 195
Kirksville, MO 93
Kneisley, Capt. James W. 7
Kneisley's "Black Battery" 7
Knights of the Golden Circle 135, 143, 152
Krekel, Maj. Arnold 290
Kuhn, Col. John H. 234
Kuykendall, Mrs. —— 297
Kyser, Sgt. —— 31, 32, 37

Lafayette County (MO) 172
Lair, Marion 288
Laird, Lt. Benjamin (given as Baird) 282
Lake, Eleazer 288
Lake Bolivar (MS) 16

# INDEX. 311

Lake Lenick (AR) 18
Lake Massachupo (AR) 18
Lanier, Joseph 135
Larkin, —— 278
Lasley, Jim 77, 93, 293, 296
Lavalle, Lt. Robert 94–95, 126
Leddy, Capt. Joe 120, 135, 186
Lee, Gen. Robert E. 240, 298, 301
Leigh, Sgt. —— 233
Lewis County (MO) 21
Lewisburg, AR 64
Lexington, MO, Siege of 2, 72, 157
Libby Prison (VA) vii, 117, 264, 267, 302
Liborius, J. B. 282
Lincoln, Abraham 115, 124, 195, 197, 244, 299
Lineback, Capt. —— 194–195
Linton, Sallie 152, 193, 194, 202, 204, 206, 222, 229
Little, Fannie 172
Little Red River (AR) 22
Little Rock, AR 17, 20, 53, 55, 56, 61, 62, 63, 64, 66, 96, 238
Livingston, Capt. W. J. 154, 155, 159, 160, 161, 164–165
Lloyd, Dick 157, 162
Logan, —— 26
Logic, —— 22
Loudon, Robert 121, 126, 127, 155, 183, 185, 187
Louisiana, MO 106, 159
Louisville, KY 300–301
Lowry, Capt. —— 192, 200, 206, 207, 215, 228, 234, 240
"Lucy Bertram" (steamer) 117
Lundy, Florence V. 185, 187, 200, 203, 207, 210, 217, 220, 234, 236, 240, 242, 243
Lunonburg, AR 58
Lydick, Andrew W. 35
Lyon, Brig. Gen. Nathaniel 4
Lyons, Frank 48

Macon, MO 75
Magee, James 21
Magruder, Maj. Gen. John B. 191
"Major Reybold" (steamer) 43
Mallory, Jesse 158–159
Marion County (AR) 25
Marion County (MO) 1, 2, 3, 5, 7, 15, 34, 35, 41, 61, 103, 123, 146, 158, 160, 165, 200, 282, 293, 296

Markham, Lt. Henry C. 32, 166–167
Marks, Luther 18
Marmaduke, Brig. Gen. John S. 52
Marshall's Mill, MO 2
Martin, Lt. —— 95
Martin, Anna B. 196, 200, 204, 205, 207, 209, 211, 212, 216, 218, 219, 220, 222, 227, 228–229, 238, 243
Martin, Henry 224
Mason, C. Y. 168
Mason, S. W. 19, 20
Masterson, Capt. W. J. 31, 35, 36, 80, 89, 94, 95, 96, 101, 104, 107, 110, 111, 114, 119, 127, 178
Matthews, John E. 6–7
Mauley, Peter 239
Maupin, —— 198
May, —— 142
Mayfield, Miss C. J. 173
McAfee, John 3
McBride, —— 22
McBounds, Rev. —— 29
McCan, —— 206
McClellan, Maj. Gen. George B. 178
McClure, Capt. G. W. 158, 164, 170, 175, 177
McCulloch, Brig. Gen. Benjamin 7
McCullough, Frisby 77
McDonald County (MO) 3
McDonald, Capt. —— 133
McDonald, Emmett 133
McDonald, Robert 136
McDowell, Dr. Joseph 100–101
McDowell College (Gratiot Street Prison) 32, 76
McGinnis, —— 122, 136
McGuire, Mrs. —— 233, 237, 238, 242, 244
McIntosh, Brig. Gen. James M. 7
M'Keevers, Squire 20
McKim, Rev. Philip 167
McKinnon, —— 142–143
McLoud, Daniel 123
McLure, Mrs. Margaret A. E. 40, 178
McNeal, Col. John 93, 281, 283, 285, 286
McPheeters, John Y. 288
McPheeters, Joseph 286
McPike, Capt. —— 196, 207, 227
Memphis, TN 8, 14, 21, 41, 55, 69, 238, 243
Meredith, Mrs. —— 32, 35–36, 77, 82, 88, 152
Meridian, MS 48, 50
Merwin, Dr. —— 37

# INDEX.

Mexico, MO 149, 150, 181, 182, 190, 209, 214, 239, 290
Miller, Dr. —— 237
Miller, John 28, 57, 60, 65, 68, 69
Mississippi County (MO) 170
Missouri River 2, 3, 73
Missouri State Guards 1, 149
Missouri Troops (US)
  11th MSM 296
  11th Inf 282
  41st Inf 175
Mitchel, Mrs. —— 187
Mitchell, Gen. —— 19
Mitchell, Mrs. —— 115
Monroe, John 138
Monroe County (MO) 2
Montgomery, AL 46
Montgomery County (AR) 66
Montgomery County (MO) 290, 293
Moore, Col. —— (CS) 19
Moore, Col. —— (US) 282
Moore, William 174, 175
Morgan, Capt. —— 237
Morgan, Mrs. —— 236
Morgan, Brig. Gen. James D. 300
Morgan, Col. James G. 297
Morgan, Maj. James M. 191, 204, 207, 209, 215, 219, 220, 222, 235, 241
Morgan, Brig. Gen. John H. 78, 88, 250, 273
"Morgan's Mule" 270
Mower, Col. Joseph A. (given as Moore) 282
Muir, Capt. Edward 184, 192, 200, 206–207, 209, 210, 215, 216, 228, 234, 236, 240, 242
Mulligan, Col. James A. 2
Mungen, William 298
Munson, —— 281
Murphy, —— 127
Muse, Capt. John 184, 191, 192, 200, 205, 206, 207, 210, 211, 212, 216, 217, 228, 236
Myers, Felix 157, 159, 160, 163, 165, 166
Myrtle Street Prison (St. Louis) 94, 120, 123, 154, 167, 170, 172, 173, 190

Napoleon, AR 18
Nashville, TN 300–301
"The Navy Mess" 213–214
Negroes 75, 102–103, 115, 150, 156, 190, 215, 225, 232, 299
Neosho, MO 2
New Madrid, MO 179

Newark, MO 283
Newburg, AR 6
Newman, Lt. H. C. 5
Newton County (MO) 2
Newtonia, MO 2
Nichols, —— 76, 77
Noel, Frank 100, 127
Norman, Sgt. Jack 176, 182

Ohio Troops
  8th Inf 290
Oliver, Maggie 216, 222, 227, 232, 233, 234, 235, 236, 237
O'Neal, —— 97, 99, 103
Order of American Knights 174
Oregon, MO 3
Osage River (MO) 73
Osceola, MO 3
Owen, Asbury 294
Owen, Maj. John L. 77, 293–295
Owen, William 294
Owsley, W. 95
Oxford, MS 14

Pace, —— 253
Page, Lt. —— 74
Page, Mattie 75
Palmyra, MO 3, 62, 85, 92, 190, 244, 295
Palmyra Massacre 93, 281–288
Panola, MS 51
Parker, W. 106
Parmel, —— 207
Parsons, Brig. Gen. Mosby M. 10, 14, 16, 20, 21, 22, 52, 56, 57, 91
Pass, —— 23
"Patrol men" 268
Patterson, Parson W. M. 175, 194
Paw-Paw Militia 189
Payne, Capt. William 62
Peery, Capt. William 192, 207, 216, 218, 234, 240
Pemberton, Lt. Gen. John C. 247
Petersburg, VA 45, 46, 47, 242
Philadelphia, PA 42–43, 84
Phillips, Capt. —— 127
Phillips, George 95, 198
Pile, William A. 298
Pilot Knob, AR 23
Pilot Knob, MO 180, 196
Pike, Brig. Gen. Albert 6

INDEX. 313

Pike County (MO) 93
Pine Bluffs, AR 238, 243
Pineville, MO 3
Pittsburgh, PA 42
Platte County (MO) 120, 293, 297
Point Lookout Prison (MD) 299, 301–302
Pomeroy, —— 299
Ponder, Lt. Amos F. 138, 207, 244
Pontotoc, MS 13
Pope, Maj. Gen. John 8
Port Hudson, LA 53
Porter, Col. Joseph C. 1, 281, 288
Post, Miss Bell 191
Potosi, MO 147
Pound Gap, VA 266
Preston, —— 207
Price, Judge —— 63
Price, James 93, 293, 296
Price, Maj. Gen. Sterling 6, 7, 8, 12, 28, 54, 55, 56, 62, 63, 66, 68, 69, 70, 72, 96, 179, 180, 182, 189, 199, 200, 238, 293
Price, Thaddeus 296
Priest, Col. John W. 1, 3, 5, 8, 9, 56, 57, 58, 65, 66, 69, 73, 74, 85, 87, 96, 108, 114, 115, 117, 129
Priest, Mat 58, 66, 69
Primrose, Parson —— 56–57

Raglan, Sgt. —— 165
Ragsdale, —— 64
Rains, Brig. Gen. James 3
Ralls County (MO) 124, 160
Ravenswood, VA 128
Ray, —— 139
Ray County (MO) 73, 190
Rayburn, Mary 80, 87, 240–241
Rease, —— 262
Red Fork Bayou (AR) 17
Reves, Col. Timothy 188, 192
Reynolds, Capt. —— 48
Reynolds, Col. —— 71
Reynolds, Mrs. W. T. 216, 233, 234–237
Richmond, MO 73
Richmond, VA 242
Ridgeway, James 93, 293, 296
Ripley, Maj. Thad 135, 142, 192, 203, 210, 216, 236
Roberts, T. 103
Robertson, R. G. 86, 109
Robinson, —— 51

Robinson, Richard 207, 214
Robinson, Welthy 172
Rock Island Prison 105, 124, 201
Rocky Bayou (AR) 58
Roe, Elder —— 2
Roe, Sgt. —— 79–80
Rolla, MO 27, 80, 207
Rollins, —— (Alton) 198
Rollins, —— (Gratiot) 165
Rosecrans, Maj. Gen. William S. 39, 72, 118, 121, 124, 153, 156–157, 174, 175, 188, 226
Rucker, Maj. —— 37 (escaped from Gratiot)
Rucker, Maj. —— 165, 191, 192, 205, 207, 216, 217, 220, 226, 230, 233, 237, 238, 243, 244
Rucker, Harvey 37
Russell, Mrs. —— 216, 232, 234, 236
Rutherford, —— 112
Ryan, Father —— 29

St. Charles, MO 290
St. Francis River (AR) 51
St. Joseph, MO 120, 189
St. Louis, MO 26, 27, 31, 33, 74, 75, 113, 118
Salisbury Prison (NC) 298, 302
Sanderson, Col. J. P. 121, 173
Sarcoxie, MO 3
Savannah, GA 302
Savannah, MO 135
Schofield, Maj. Gen. John M. 285, 291
Schull, Mrs. —— 224
Schultz, Robert 85
Scott, Lt. —— 150, 192
Searcy, AR 21
Searcy County (AR) 22
Sebring, Lt. William H. 77, 78, 101, 119, 122, 132, 140, 147, 172, 302
Selma, AL 47
Semmes, Raphael 45
Sevier County (AR) 68
Shanks, Col. —— 201, 205
Shanks, John C. 298
Shelbina, MO 29
Shelby, Brig. Gen. Joseph O. 73, 79, 96, 167, 168, 179
Shelby County (MO) 3, 77, 85
Shelbyville, MO 28
Sherin, W. 148, 160, 176

Sherman, Maj. Gen. William T. 191, 240
Ship Island, MS 299, 302
Shore, Dr. —— 173
Short, —— 51
Shoteau, Mrs. —— 80, 87
Shultz, Lewis Y. 135, 140
Sidenor, Capt. Thomas 287, 288
Simpson, —— 130, 132
"Sioux City" (steamer) 2
Sisters of Charity 28, 34, 84
Smith, —— (Alton) 192
Smith, Miss —— (Alton) 200, 207, 217
Smith, Mrs. —— (Gratiot) 83
Smith, Maj. Gen. Andrew J. 180
Smith, Gen. Edmund Kirby 63
Smith, Hiram 288
Smith, Stephen R. 174, 175
"Sovereign" (steamer) 8
Soward, Judge —— 88, 89, 123
Soward, Joseph A. 123, 132, 134, 135, 141, 147, 157, 166, 178, 190,193, 194, 198, 209, 210, 212, 220, 221, 224, 227
Spencer, Eliza 172
Spencer, Harriet 172
Spencer, Mary 172
Spires, Billy 202
Springfield, IL 85
Springfield, MO 3-5, 92; military prison at 23-26, 28, 115
Standish, Col. E. M. 52
Stanton, Edwin M. 122
"State of Maine" (steamer) 44, 75
Steele, Maj. Gen. Frederick 191
Stemmons, Capt. —— 37
Stenins, A. F. 298
Stevens, Col. Ambrose A. 254, 255, 258
Stewart, —— 21
Stewart, Lt. —— 95
Stith, Jesse 68
Stone, Bvt. Brig. Gen. Roy 209
Strachan, William R. 283, 284, 286
Sullivan, Capt. —— 121, 122
Summer, Berkley 283
Sunflower River (MS) 16
"Sunshine" (steamer) 2
Swain, —— 157-158

Taylor, —— 136
Terra Haute, IN 248-249
Thaxton, Lt. —— 96

Thompson, Mrs. Jeff 39-40
Thornton, Col. John C. C. 149, 189
Thorp, —— 201, 226
Thrailkill, Capt. John 139, 149
Tombigbee River (AL) 47
Torbot, Mrs. —— 49, 50
Trimble, Capt. Robert 131, 138, 168, 179, 192, 244
Triplett, Black 293, 297
Tucker, Joseph 3
Tullahoma, MS 39
Tupelo, MS 12, 13, 14
Turner, Lt. —— 138, 192, 244

Van Buren, AR 7-8
Van Buren County (AR) 21
Vandiver, —— 199
Vicksburg, MS 13, 14, 35, 53, 80, 143, 154, 215, 216, 225, 247
"Virginia" (steamer) 47

Wade, John M. 288
Waitman, Sarah T. 173
Walters, —— (widow) 20
Wamsley, Kate 74
Ward, Jane 172
"Warsaw" (steamer) 244
Washington, George 301
Washington, AR 96
Washington, DC 147
Washington, NC 41
Washita River (AR) 66
Waterson, Lt. —— 24
Watkins, Capt. W. G. 95, 166
Waukley, —— 77
Weatherby, —— 52
Weaver, —— 194
Weaver, Emma 157, 178, 182
Weer, Col. William 114, 118, 166
Welsh, Sgt. Mike 140, 167, 172
Wentz, Miss —— 191
Wentz, Mrs. —— 191, 234, 235, 238
Westerman, Preston 185, 186, 187
Weston, MO 297
Whaley's Mill, MO 283
Wheeler, Maj. Gen. Joseph 41
Wheeling, WV 128, 154-155, 156
White, Maj. —— 42
White River (AR) 8, 19, 20, 22, 53, 56, 59, 60
Whitfield, Gaius 47, 48, 50

# INDEX.

Wier, Miss —— 239
Wilby, Father —— 179, 199
Willis, Lt. David 5
Wilson, —— 103
Wilson, Maj. James 192, 193
Wilson's Creek, MO, Battle of 4–5
Winston, Col. John H. 21, 57, 58, 69, 120–121, 122, 128, 129, 184, 192, 194, 204–205, 206, 207, 215, 216, 218, 219, 228, 225–226, 234
Winston, Capt. Samuel L. 57, 58, 63, 69, 72, 120, 131, 132, 147, 150, 159, 160, 184, 206, 234
Wise, Mrs. —— 234, 235
Wood, Col. Robert C. 62, 63

Woodrough County, AR 52
World, Capt. —— 300
Wousley, Maj. —— 70
Wright, Dr. William S. 125, 127, 192, 196, 200, 204–205, 207, 210, 216, 228, 236, 242, 243

Yalobusha River (MS) 15
Yates, —— 140, 147
Yazoo Pass, MS 40
Yellville, AR 21, 22
Youngblood, Dr. James M. 154
Youngblood, Capt. Theodore B. 23

Zarvona, Col. Richard Thomas 44–45

www.ingramcontent.com/pod-product-compliance
Lightning Source LLC
Chambersburg PA
CBHW031612160426
43196CB00006B/111